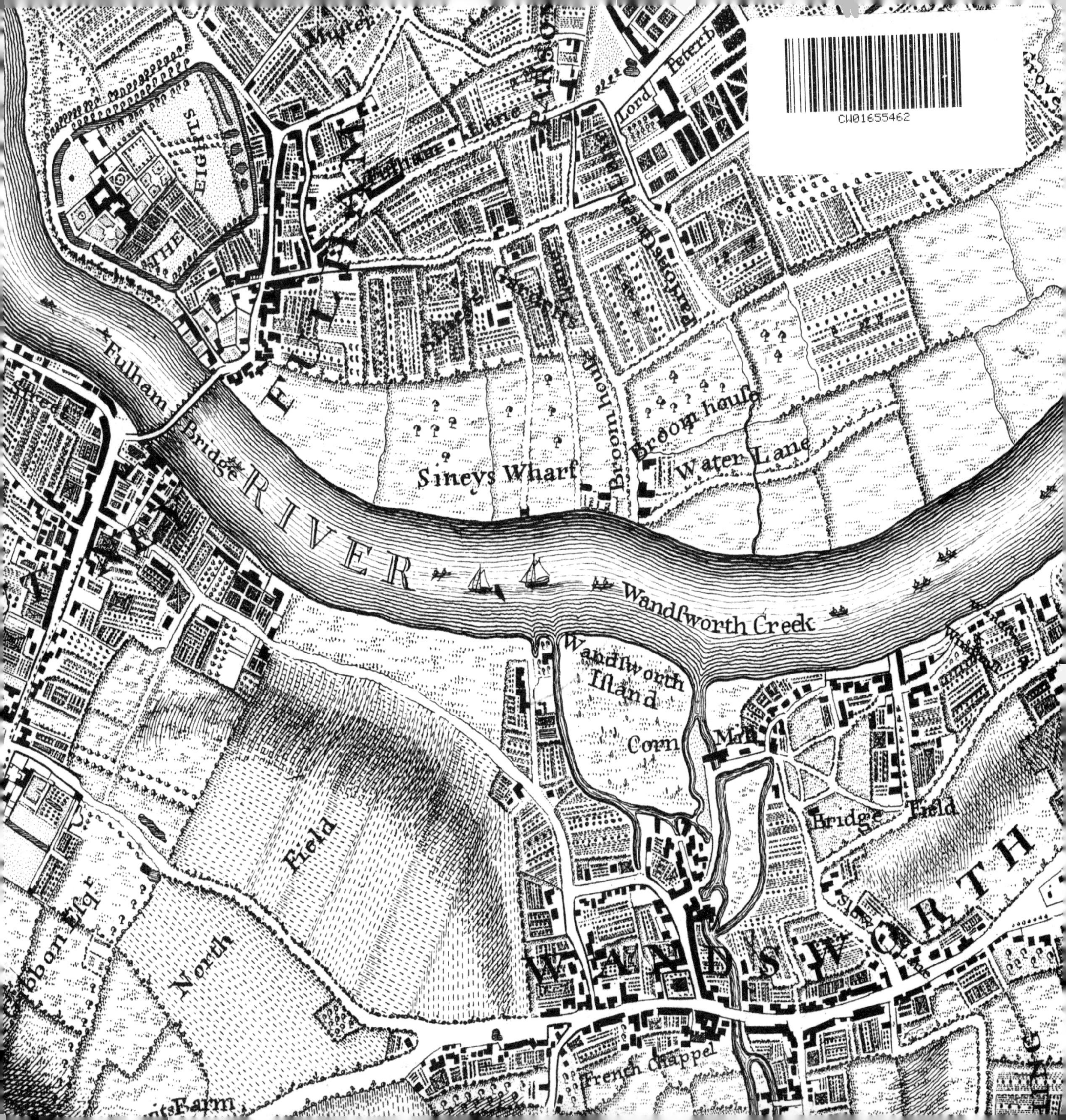
THE EIGHTS
Fulham Bridge
RIVER
Sineys Wharf
Broom house
Water Lane
Wandſworth Creek
Wandſworth Iſland
Corn Mill
Bridge Field
Field
North
WANDSWORTH
French Chappel
Lord Peterb

WILD ABOUT Putney

THE TOWN ON THE THAMES

By Andrew Wilson

Sponsored by

WARREN

The Putney Estate Agent

I would like to dedicate this book to the memory of my in-laws, Pam and Gerry, who had a hand in helping to shape the original edition of this book back in 2012 including some invaluable proofing and who sadly died in 2014.

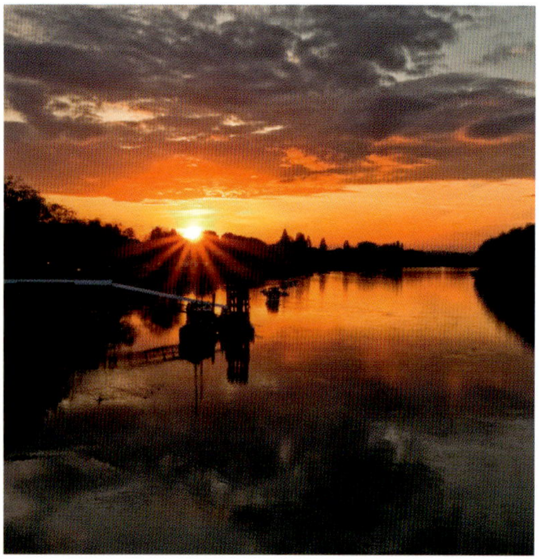

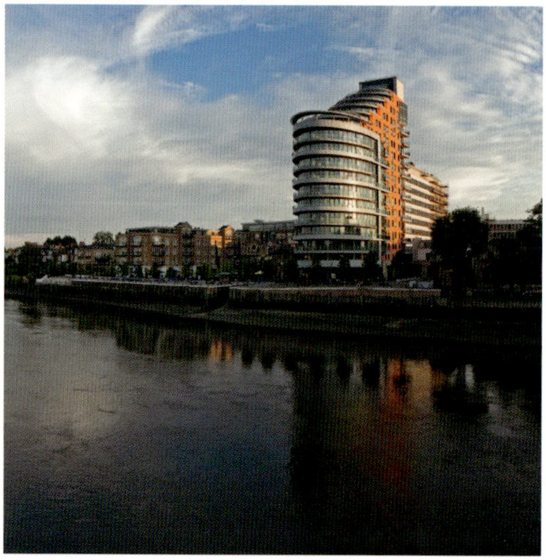

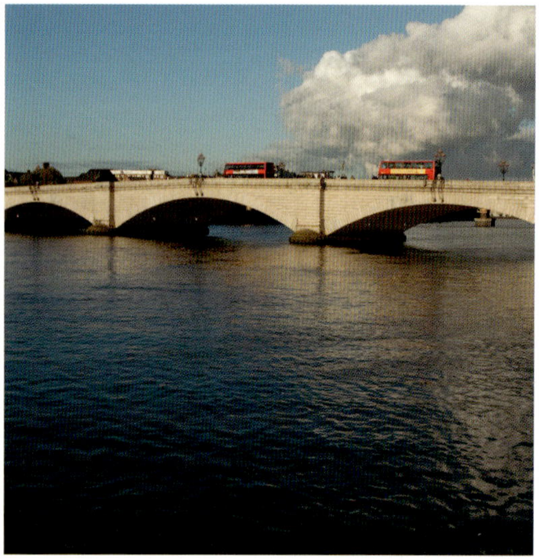

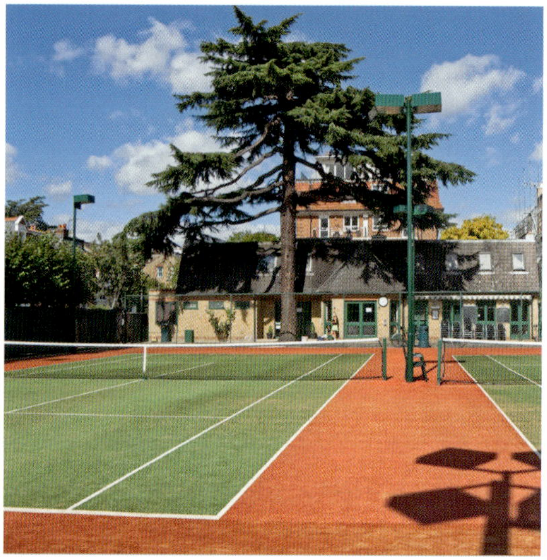

Clockwise from Top Left: Putney Embankment at sunset, Putney Wharf,
The Putney Lawn Tennis Club, Balmuir Gardens off Howard's Lane and Putney Bridge.
The map on the end papers is taken from John Rocque's famous *London Map of 1746*.

Contents

Welcome to Wild About Putney

Welcome to the new edition of my best-selling book on Putney. Since I first published it in 2012, over 2,000 copies have been sold, which makes this along with my book on Barnes two of my most popular books. As a Putney resident of some 25 years standing I feel I have got to know the place and it's with a sense of pride that I am able to share with you some of my favourite haunts. Much has changed since 2012, so in certain places through the book I have either updated an image or made an editorial correction to let readers know. Some things never change though, for instance, I never tire of places like Wandsworth Park or the Heath, where I regularly walk my Springer Spaniel. I love taking pictures and besides all the familiar places, a project such as this gave me the perfect excuse to visit some of the less familiar places, such as some of the schools, which was great fun.

I spent the best part of a year working on this book and although I might be the one behind the lens, it takes a lot more than that to produce a book such as this and I would like to thank the following for their help, which has been invaluable. Firstly, Tim Warren and Mike Crowther from Warren's, our local estate agents, who kindly agreed to sponsor my book. They know this area as well as anyone, so if you are looking to buy, sell or rent please be sure to make them your first call. Then there is my writer, Philip Evison. Philip has lived in Putney for over 30 years, is keenly interested in our local history and has written many books on the subject. He was also the editor of the Putney Society's monthly newsletter from 2009 to 2011. So there was no better person to help me when it came to the words. I would also like to thank Sally Burrough, who has kindly provided the map on page 9. Sally's a local artist, from just across the common in Wimbledon and specialises in pets, people and places, either in pencil or watercolour.

Further thanks should go to Simon and Tim from Ball Design, who kindly worked on the first edition and have helped me with the update of this one and what a fine job they have done. Paul Sherfield, my colour expert, who helps me get the very best results from my printing. My friend Amanda, who I'm glad to say never tires of championing what I do. Then there are the numerous people who have allowed me access to various places to take pictures, for which there are many, thank you and to Wandsworth Council, who either own or manage a good chunk of it. My wife and family for putting up with the long walks and late nights. With such a large book, there are many people I have met and far too many to mention in person, so my apologies if I have missed anyone. Wherever possible, I have tried to thank people within the relevant text. That also goes for some of the places I missed; it's just not possible to fit every school, pub or church in. Ultimately, I wanted to produce a community book, covering as much of Putney life as possible. I feel that I have achieved that and I hope that you enjoy the journey; it was certainly great fun compiling it.

Andrew Wilson
March 2016

To keep up-to-date with the latest Putney news, follow Sandi and her team by subscribing to the Putney SW15 weekly newsletter at *www.putneysw15.com*

Josie, my constant companion, up on Putney Heath

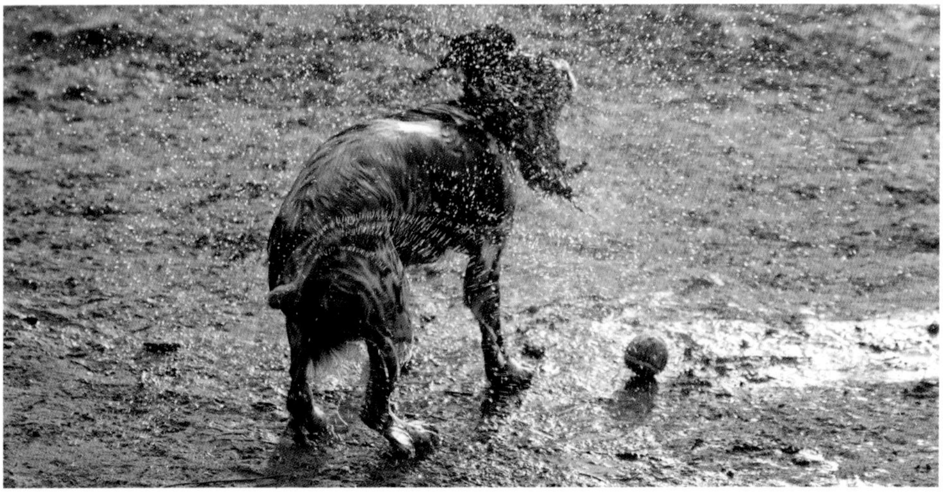

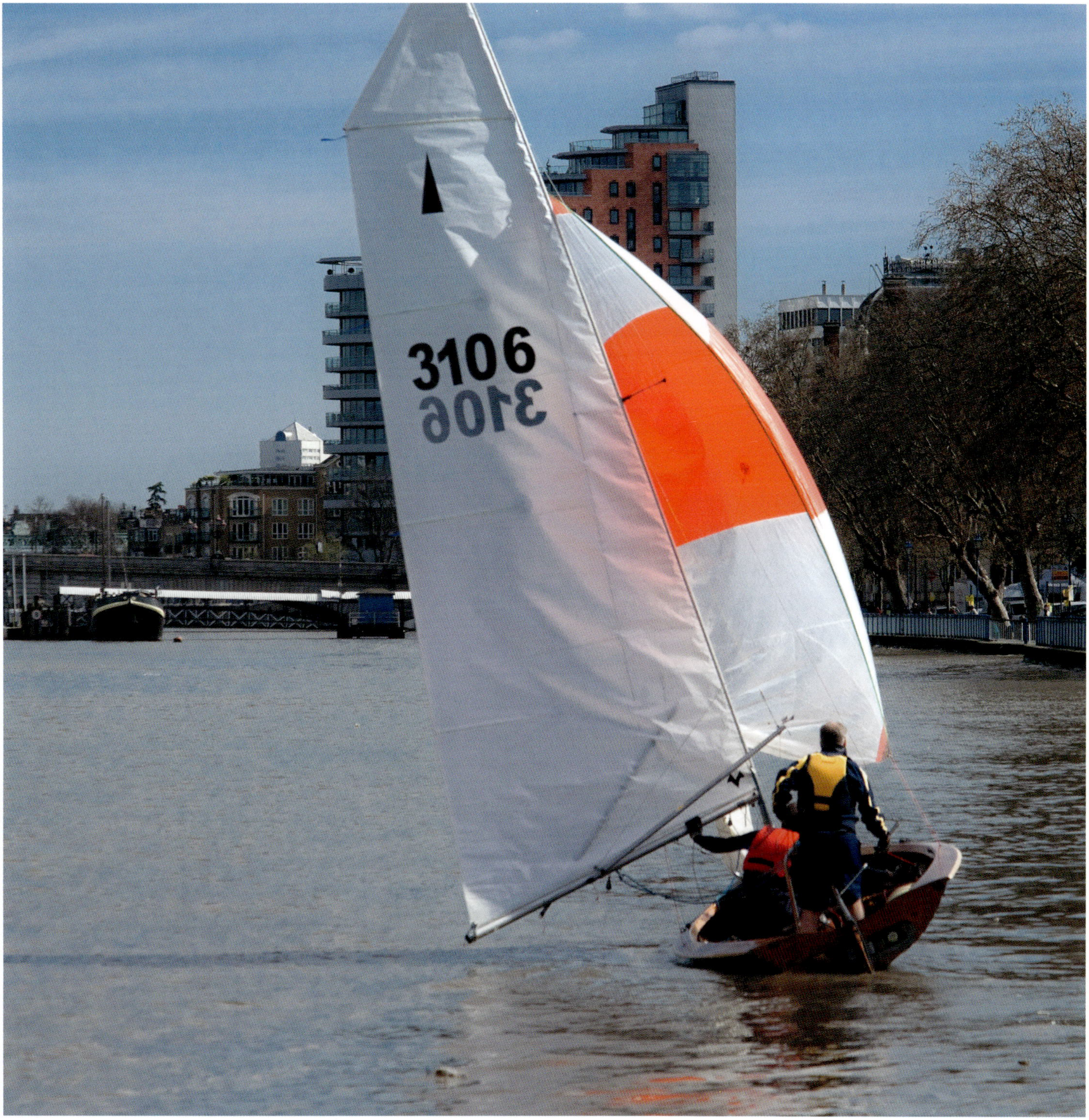
3106
3106

Putney

A SHORT HISTORY OF THE AREA
by Philip Evison

In the episode of *Hancock's Half Hour* in which our hero receives death threats, he asks Sid James how long it would take for his nemesis to get to East Cheam. *"93 from Putney,"* replies Mr J *"he can be here in half an hour."* One of countless references in popular culture to Putney, which I was thus aware of long before I lived here. Little did I know then how involved with, and fond of, the place I would later become.

What is the origin of the name? Its first recorded appearance is as Putelei (in the Domesday Book of 1086) and its next, in 1276, as Puttenheth – possibly the 'landing place' (heth/hithe) of Putta, an Anglo-Saxon name, though no-one knows who Putta was. The orthography changed over the years but from the 16th century onwards, Putney became the usual spelling – though Nicholas Lane's 1636 map offers Puttney, Puttny, Puttnye and Puttnie! The area was, however, settled much earlier and there have been finds (e.g. flint axes) from the late paleolithic, with evidence of more or less continuous occupation since then, though relatively few Bronze Age artefacts have been discovered.

The population was small in earlier centuries, and the first list of inhabitants (a 1332 tax list, probably incomplete) shows just 32 names. By the turn of the 15th/16th centuries, it had grown to about 300, and by the end of the 17th century to around 2,000. The 19th century saw more rapid growth, due in part to the arrival of the South Western Railway in 1846, and the population levelled off around 50 years ago to the present figure (depending on how you define Putney) of 80–90,000.

The fact that the 'heth' of Puttenheth suggests 'landing place' is no coincidence, since Putney has always, in a sense, been dominated – defined even – by the river, and the mediæval village grew up around the ferry landing at what is now the northern end of the High Street. It served boats coming up the river from London, or across it from Fulham, and there were, in the 17th century, half a dozen inns in close proximity, serving travellers transferring from ferry to coach and vice-versa, en route to and from destinations such as Richmond and Portsmouth. Agriculture was naturally important, but the river, and fishing, dominated, with some 40% of male householders being watermen – reflected in the names of Waterman Street, and the Watermen's (charity) School in Putney Bridge Road, opened in 1718.

Although the Parliamentarians built a temporary pontoon bridge between Fulham and Putney in 1642, during the English Civil War, pressure to build a proper bridge grew later that century, though it took until 1726 to get the Act of Parliament passed and

The new bridge, designed by Joseph Bazalgette, opened in 1886 by Edward, Prince of Wales.

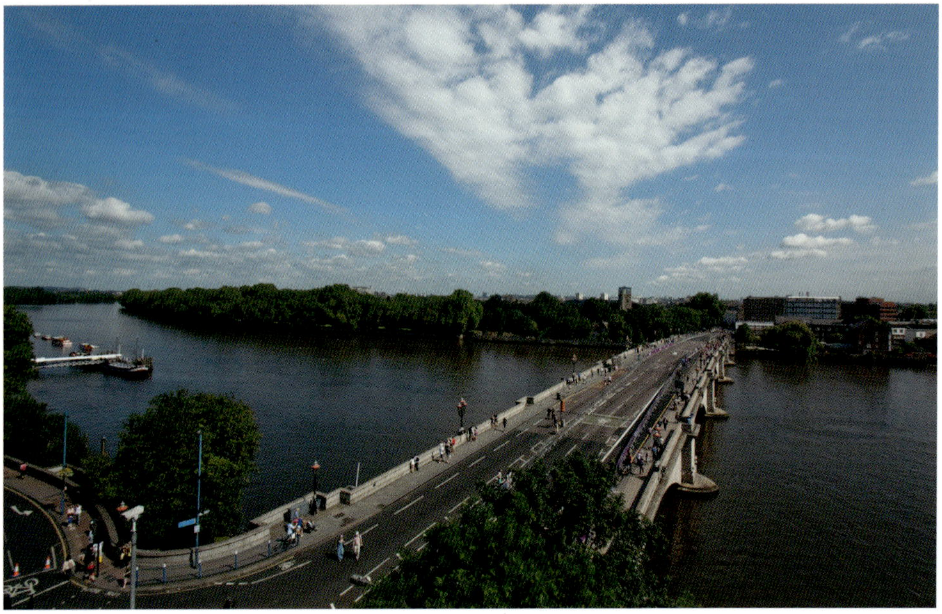

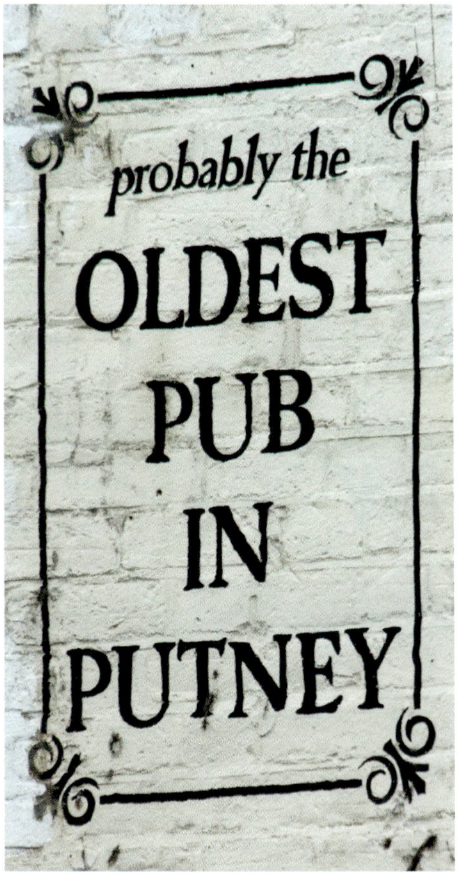

Probably not! The sign that used to be on the side of The Arab Boy pub on the Upper Richmond Road. The oldest pub is more likely to be The Green Man.

the bridge was opened three years later – a strange, sinuous, wooden affair, "humped in unexpected places like a dromedary", with toll booths at either end. It was, at the time, the only Thames bridge between London and Kingston and, a century and a half later, was proving inadequate to handle the increased traffic. The ending of tolls in 1880 was cause for a major celebration, attended by the Prince of Wales (the future King Edward VII) and Princess Alexandra and four years later, they were back to lay the foundation stone of a new bridge, designed by Joseph Bazalgette and opened in 1886. It was widened to four lanes in 1933 – and is now sometimes *claimed* to be London's busiest bridge!

Putney is rich in historical links. Thomas Cromwell, sometime chief minister to Henry VIII, until he fell out of favour, was born c. 1485, probably in or around Brewhouse Lane, where his irascible and roguish father Walter ran a brewery and tavern, amongst other activities – his story now chronicled by Hilary Mantel. A century and a half later, his great-great-great-nephew Oliver (whose family name ought strictly speaking to have been Williams!) would come to Putney during the Civil War – the Putney Debates being conducted in St Mary's Church in 1647.

Historian Edward Gibbon (*Decline & Fall of the Roman Empire*) was born in 1737 at Lime Grove, a large estate in the SE angle of Putney Hill & Upper Richmond Road; poet Algernon Swinburne lived at The Pines, 11 Putney Hill; Capt. Laurence Oates, who nobly sacrificed himself in 1912, during Scott's ill-fated Antarctic expedition, lived in Upper Richmond Road; J R Ackerley – author, literary editor and friend of E M Forster – lived in Star & Garter Mansions; the creator of Mr Benn, David McKee, lived in Festing Road (*Festive Road* in the books); and Arnold Bennett's reclusive artist Priam Farll, in the 1908 novel *Buried Alive*, hid from public gaze in Werter Road. Putney has been, and still is, home to celebrities too numerous to mention, to the point of being referred to, during Jilly Cooper's *Common Years*, as Media Gulch!

In 1938, at the official opening of Zeeta House, at the junction of Putney High Street and Upper Richmond Road, Trevor Bowen (Vice-Chairman of Barkers of Kensington and a Putney resident) spoke of: "*...a new departure in the wonderful old village of Putney*", and the late historian Tony Judt who, as a child, lived

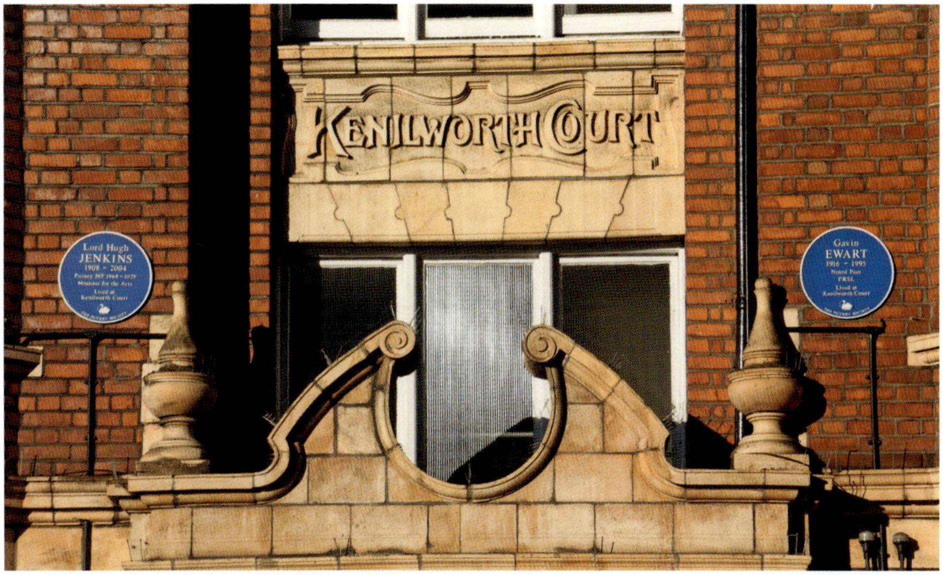

Some other famous residents of Putney have been recognised by the Putney Society on these blue plaques on Kenilworth Court. The Society was founded in 1959 and is concerned with aspects of the community which contribute to the quality of local life. These include the built environment and open spaces, transport and community services. The Society has played a key role in the enhancement and protection of these vital facilities in Putney and Roehampton since its inception. For more information visit *www.putneysociety.org.uk*

in Putney High Street in the mid-1950s, would write, in his memoir *The Memory Chalet*, published posthumously in 2010: *"From the perspective of Jones Mews, Putney was still a village."*

The perception of Putney as a village (which of course it once was) does seem to have persisted into the 20th century. Judt wrote fondly of the variety of shops to be found in and off the High Street, though the 'chains' were already in place – Sainsburys, Tesco, M&S, BHS, Home & Colonial, Woolworths, Lilley & Skinner etc. Is Putney still a village? Not really, and its High Street has sadly acquired the bland, anonymous character familiar from cities and suburbs across the country. As recently as 50 years ago, it boasted some 160 businesses of 55 different kinds; today, there are about 120, of 35 different kinds. There was more choice and more individuality 50 years ago, but that is the price of 'progress' and there is little we can do about it.

This historic corner of SW London nevertheless retains excellent restaurants, cafés, pubs and specialist shops, has a character all its own and is a sought-after suburb. The 'great houses' (Fairfax, Essex, Gordon, The Lawn, The Cedars etc) may have gone, but there are still noble streets and fine buildings, and the River Thames remains a major asset. Even to those who don't know it, the name of Putney is indelibly linked to the start of the annual Oxford & Cambridge Boat Race, which brings thousands of spectators to the Embankment.

Putney is also blessed with open spaces, such as Wandsworth Park, Putney Common, Putney Heath (scene of many a duel and the odd highwayman!) and a bit of Wimbledon Common, the last three under the assiduous stewardship of the Commons Conservators. Areas which have their fair share of wildlife.

Those of us who live here are 'wild about Putney'!

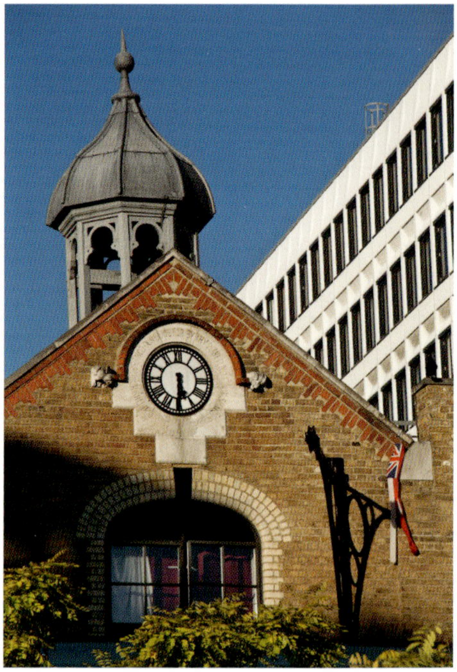

The pleasantly proportioned building behind the Boathouse pub on Putney Wharf dates from the turn of the 19th century and is the only remnant of the industrial history of the site. There is a long-standing legend that the stone surround of the clock, bearing the words *'Lord for this hour, Be thou our guide, For by thy power, No foot shall slide'* came from the old Newgate Prison, which has never been proved. It is persuasive, however, that the words are intended to be sung to the tune of the Westminster Chimes. Try it!

Grade I listed Parkstead House was designed for the 2nd Earl of Bessborough in the 1760s by Sir William Chambers – who was also the architect for Somerset House and the Pagoda at Kew Gardens. Since 2001 it has been a part of Roehampton University.

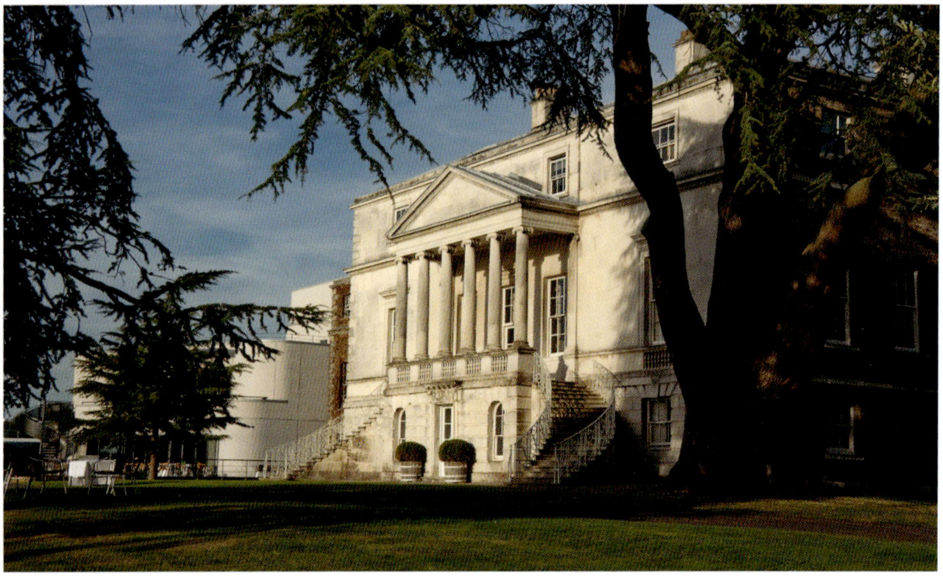

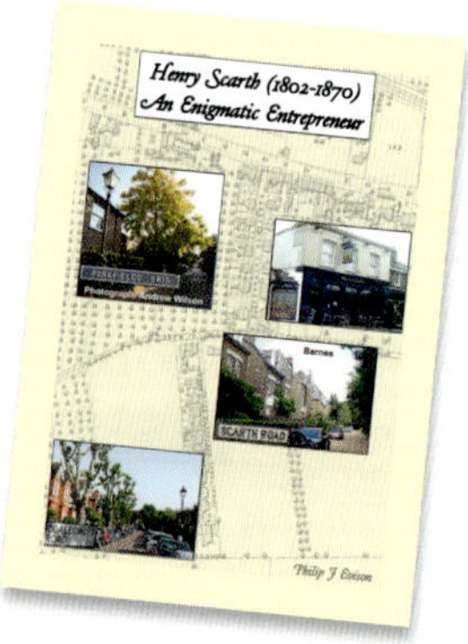

Philip Evison has published numerous books and articles about the history of Putney, one of his most recent being *Henry Scarth (1802–1870), An Enigmatic Entrepreneur.*
philipevison@btinternet.com

Putney

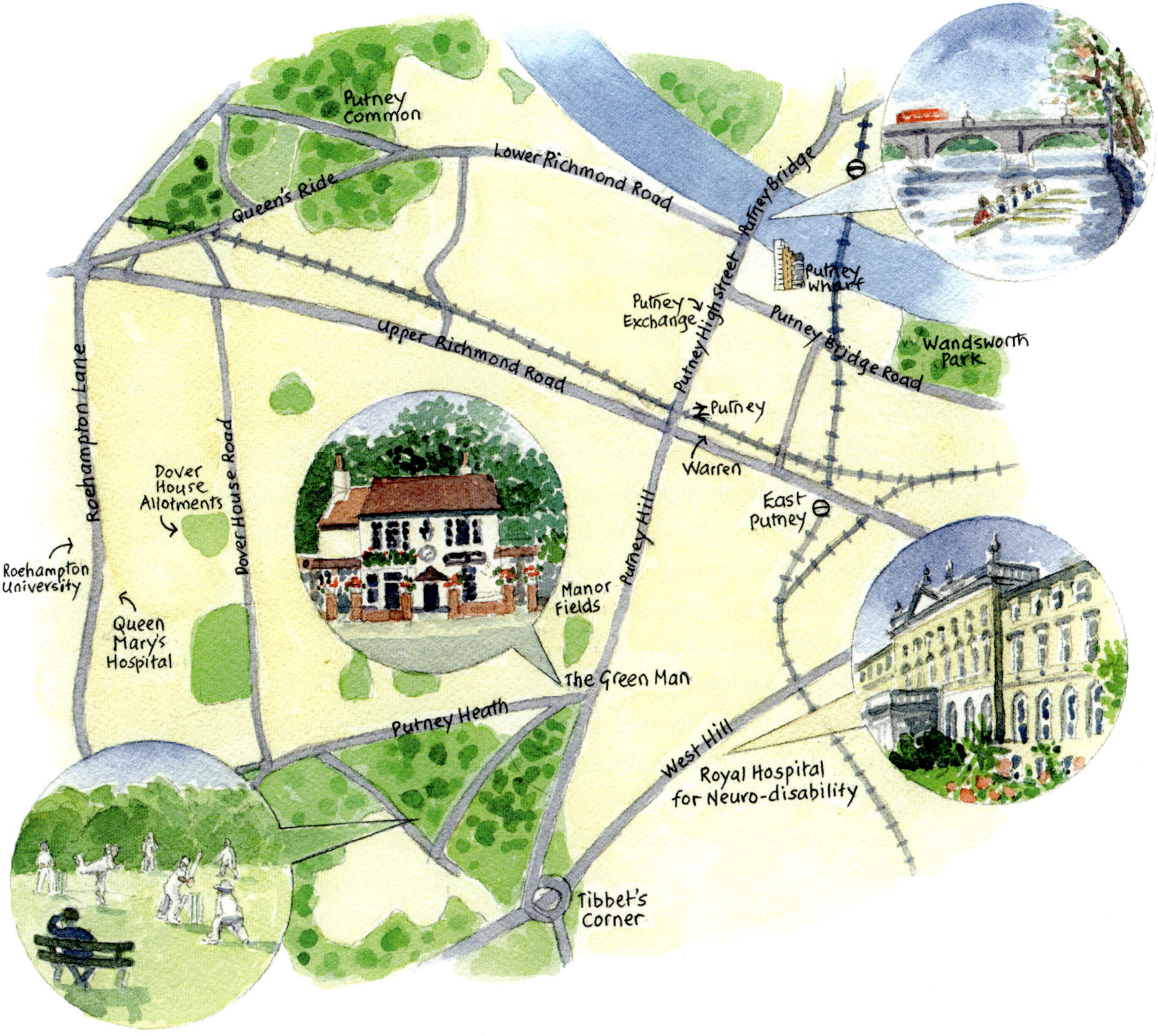

This map has kindly been provided by Sally Burrough, a local artist, and is not meant to be absolutely to scale but to give the reader a fun introduction to the area and some of the places covered in this book. Sally is a local resident and works mainly in watercolours and would love to paint your favourite pet, person or place – please contact Sally at *www.sallyburrough.co.uk*

The River

The River Thames has always been of great importance to Putney, which cannot be imagined without it. A short downstream boat trip would start opposite Fulham football ground, at Barn Elms playing fields, the site of the home of Sir Francis Walsingham, Queen Elizabeth I's spymaster. It is also here where Beverley Brook, which rises in Worcester Park, flows into the Thames. Across the small footbridge you join the embankment proper where you find Leader's Gardens, and a long line of rowing and sailing clubs, testifying to the still intimate links between Putney and the river. Just before the bridge are two of Putney's venerable riverside pubs, The Duke's Head and The Star & Garter. A third, The Eight Bells, was sacrificed in the early 1880s to make way for the approach to the new bridge, opened in 1886. Passing beneath it, we come to St Mary's Church and Putney Wharf – in the past, the site of a timber yard, a bus garage and a variety of industrial and commercial activities (not to mention Thomas Cromwell's probable birthplace!) but now home to up-market flats, restaurants, pubs and the imposing Putney Wharf tower. Our excursion ends at the District Line bridge and the wonderful line of plane trees that you find in Wandsworth Park. The bridge was opened in 1889 to link Putney Bridge and East Putney stations and connect to the London & South Western Railway's new line to Wimbledon.

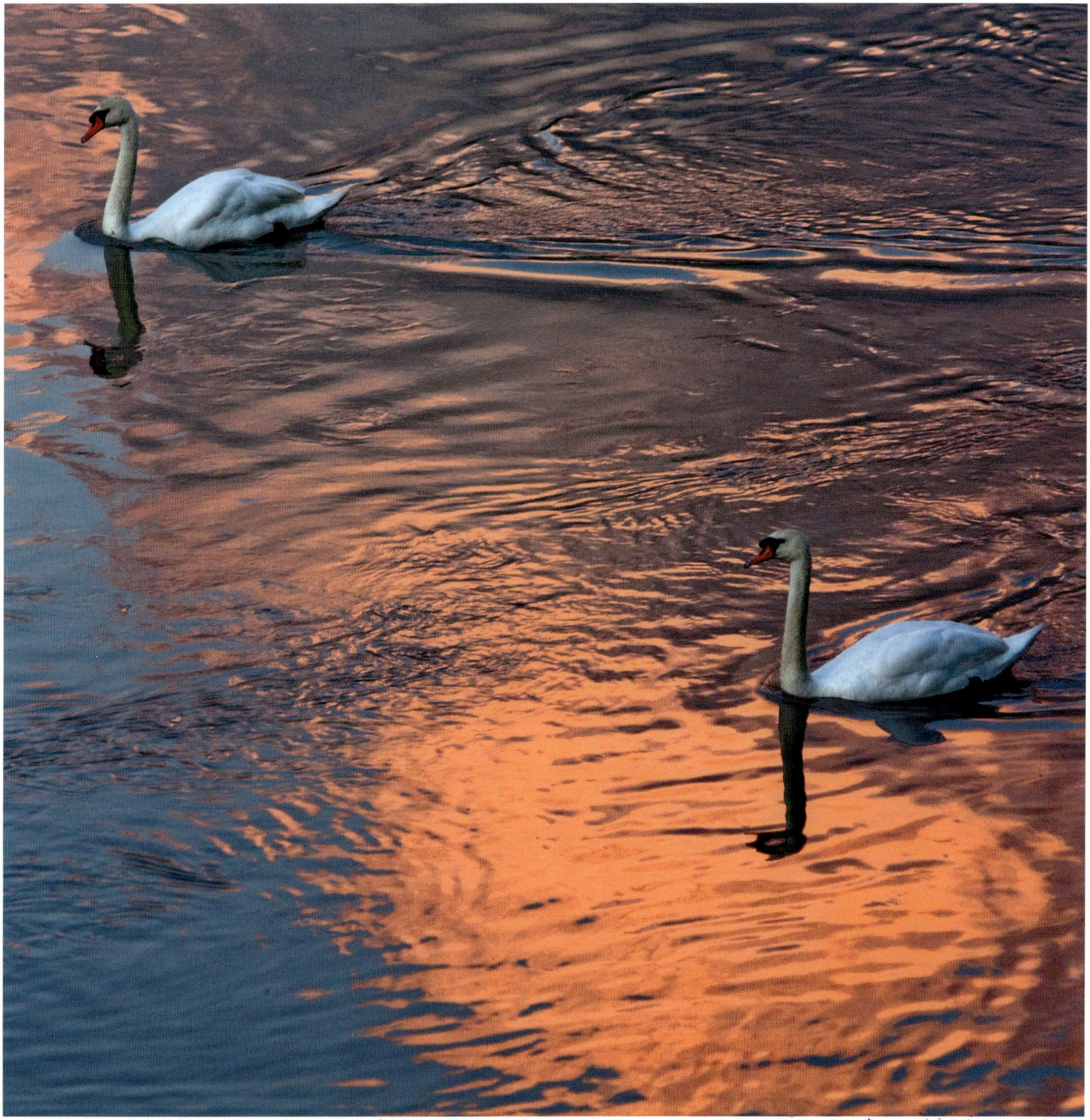

Putney Bridge

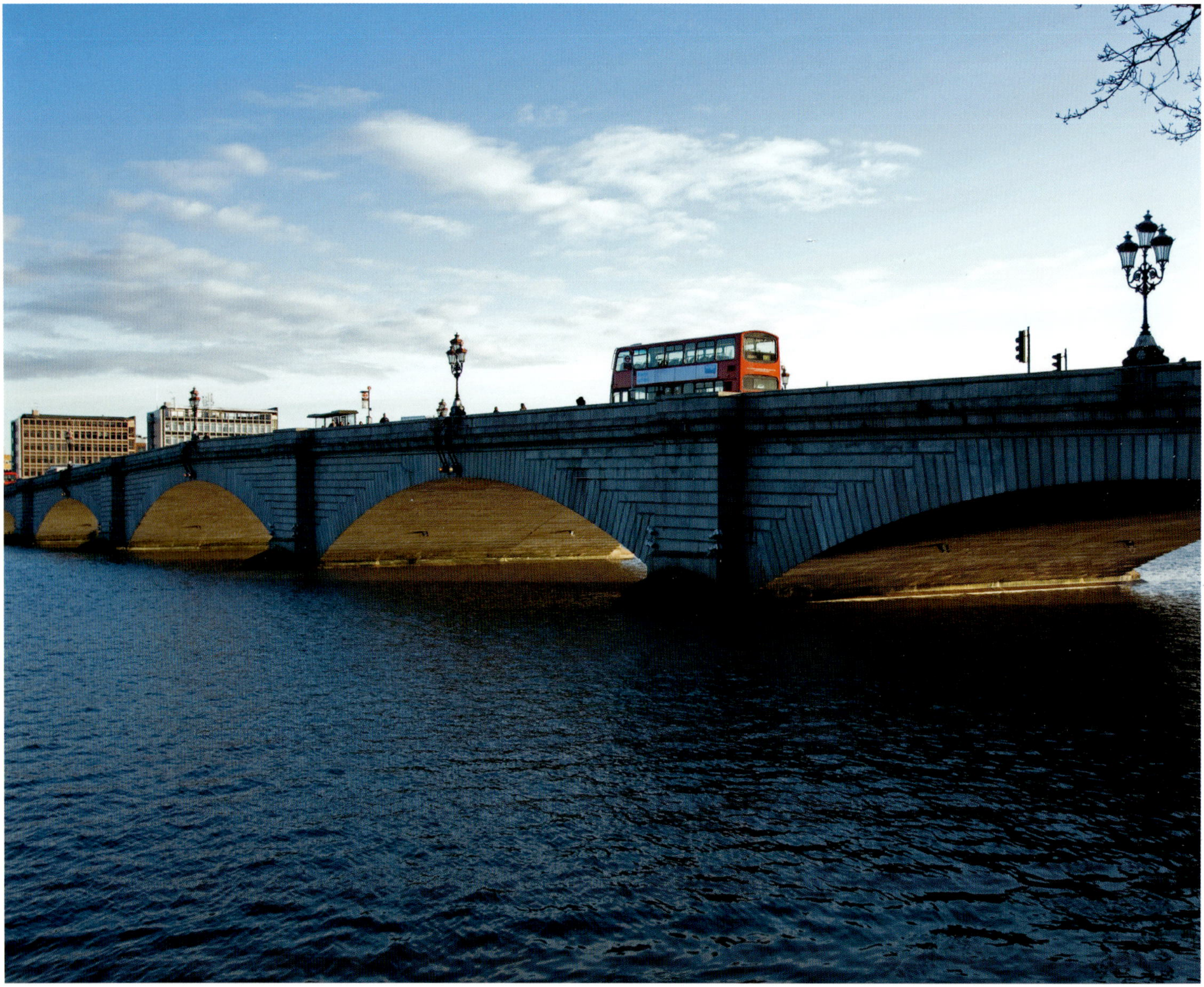

The current Bridge dating from 1886 is the second to be constructed here and replaced the rather inferior wooden affair that had stood since 1729. Designed by Sir Joseph Bazalgette, who was also responsible for London's sewage system, Putney Bridge is the only bridge in Britain to have a church at either end.

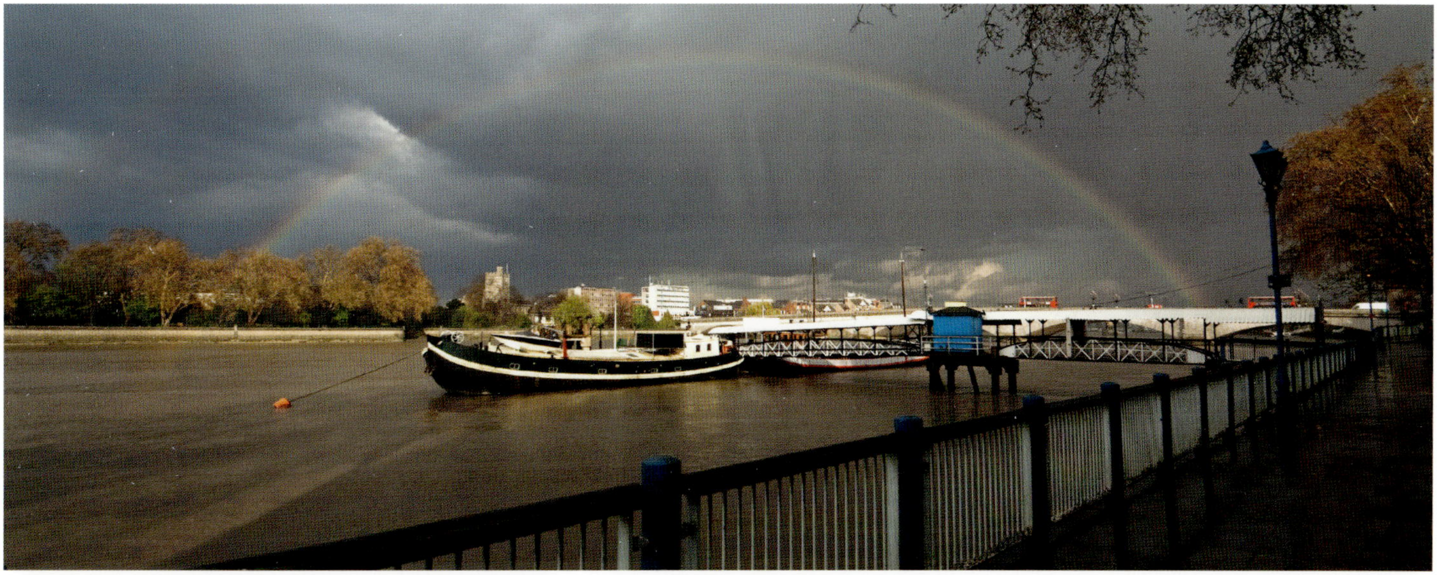

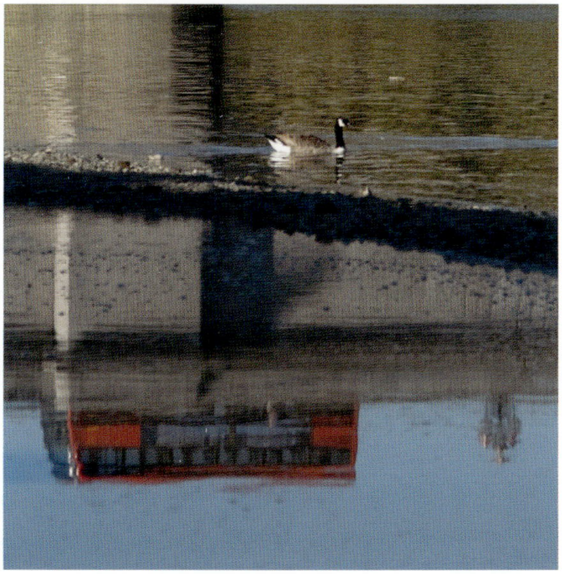

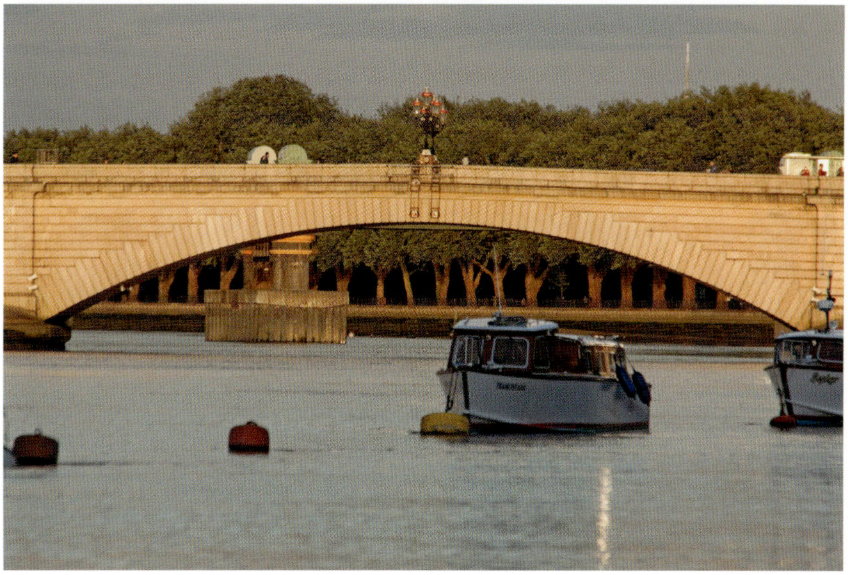

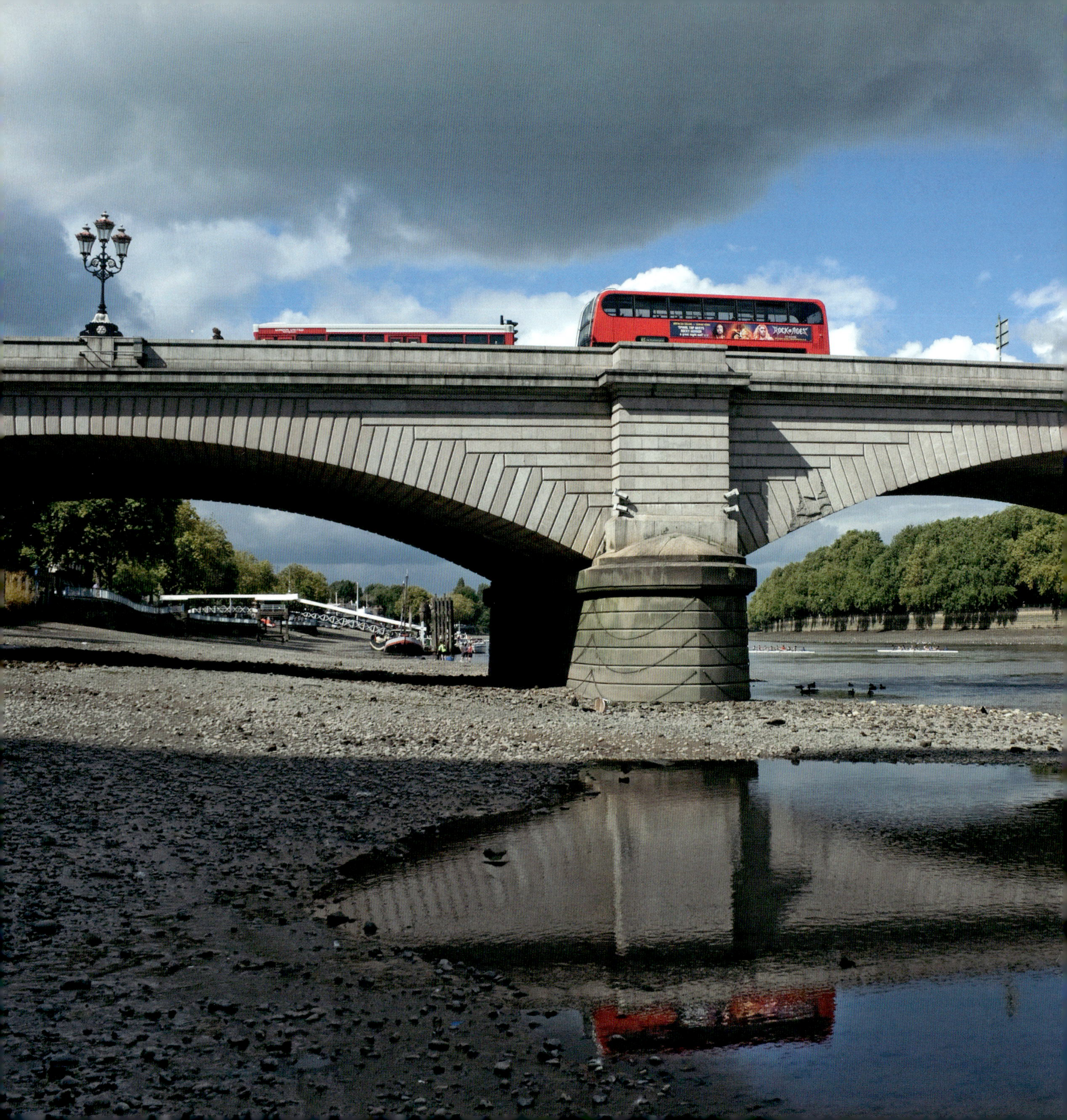
ROCK of AGES

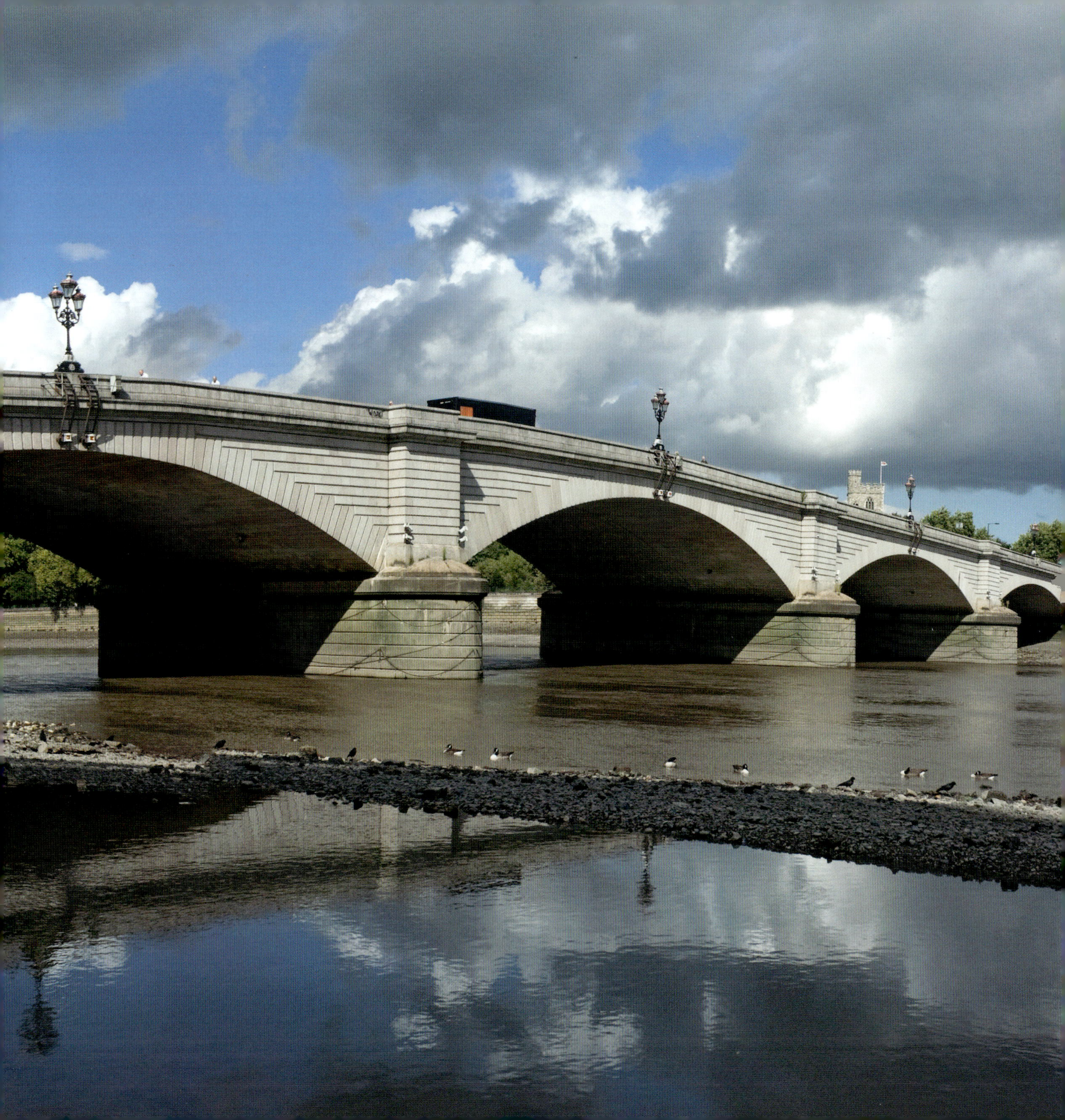

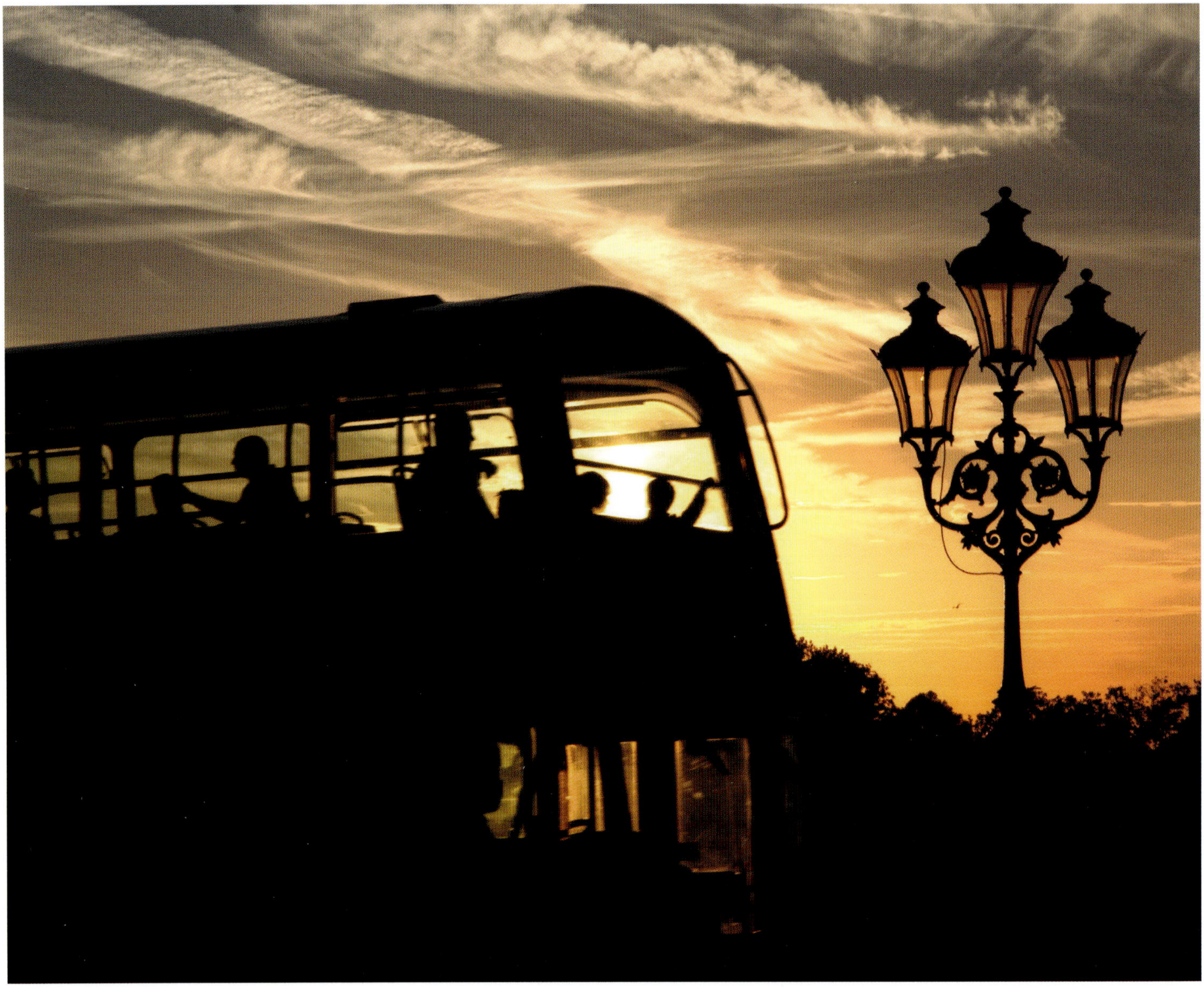

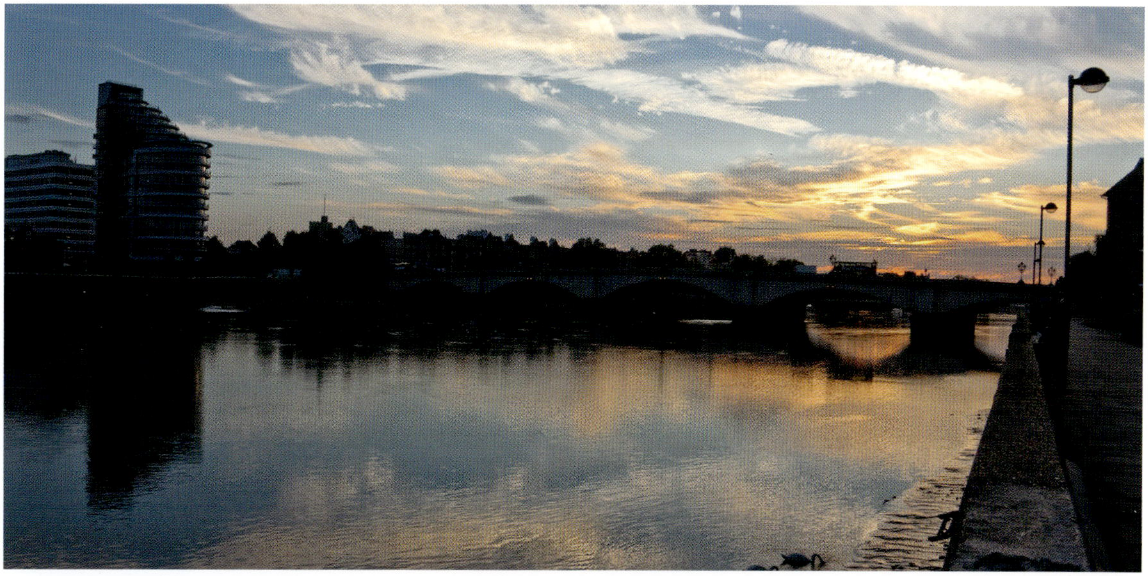

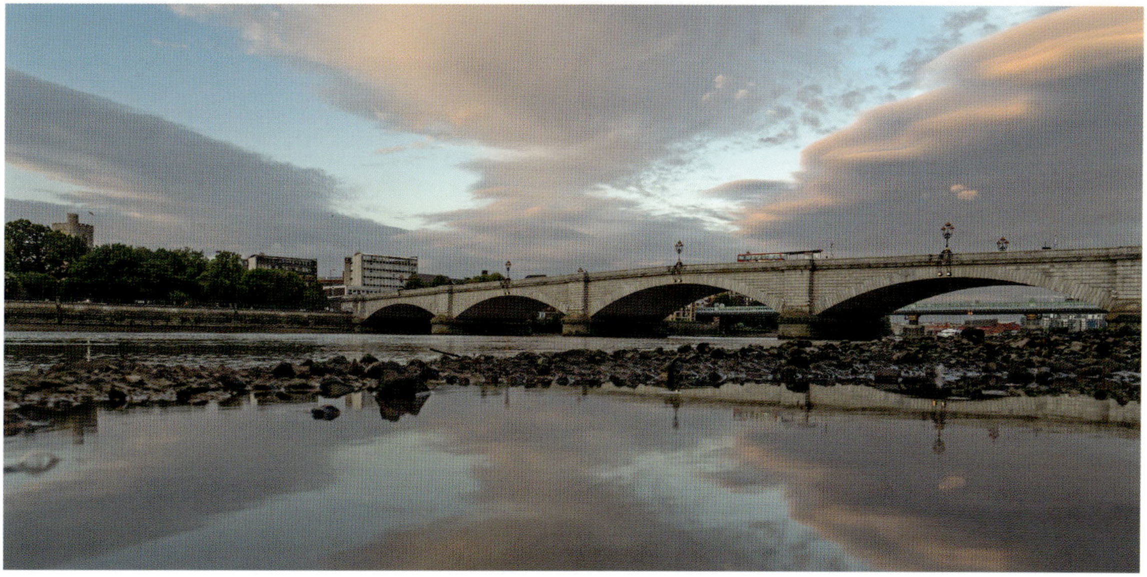

"Putney is a great place to live. We have the River Thames, Putney Common and Wandsworth Park on our doorstep, as well as good shops and plenty of places to unwind with a glass of wine or coffee with friends. Most importantly it's all within 30 minutes on the District Line into central London."

RT HON JUSTINE GREENING, LOCAL RESIDENT AND MP FOR PUTNEY

The view of the Bridge and the start of The Lower Richmond Road from the top of St Mary's church, taken on the first day of the London Olympics, when the cycle race came through Putney, hence the most unusual sight of no cars on the bridge.

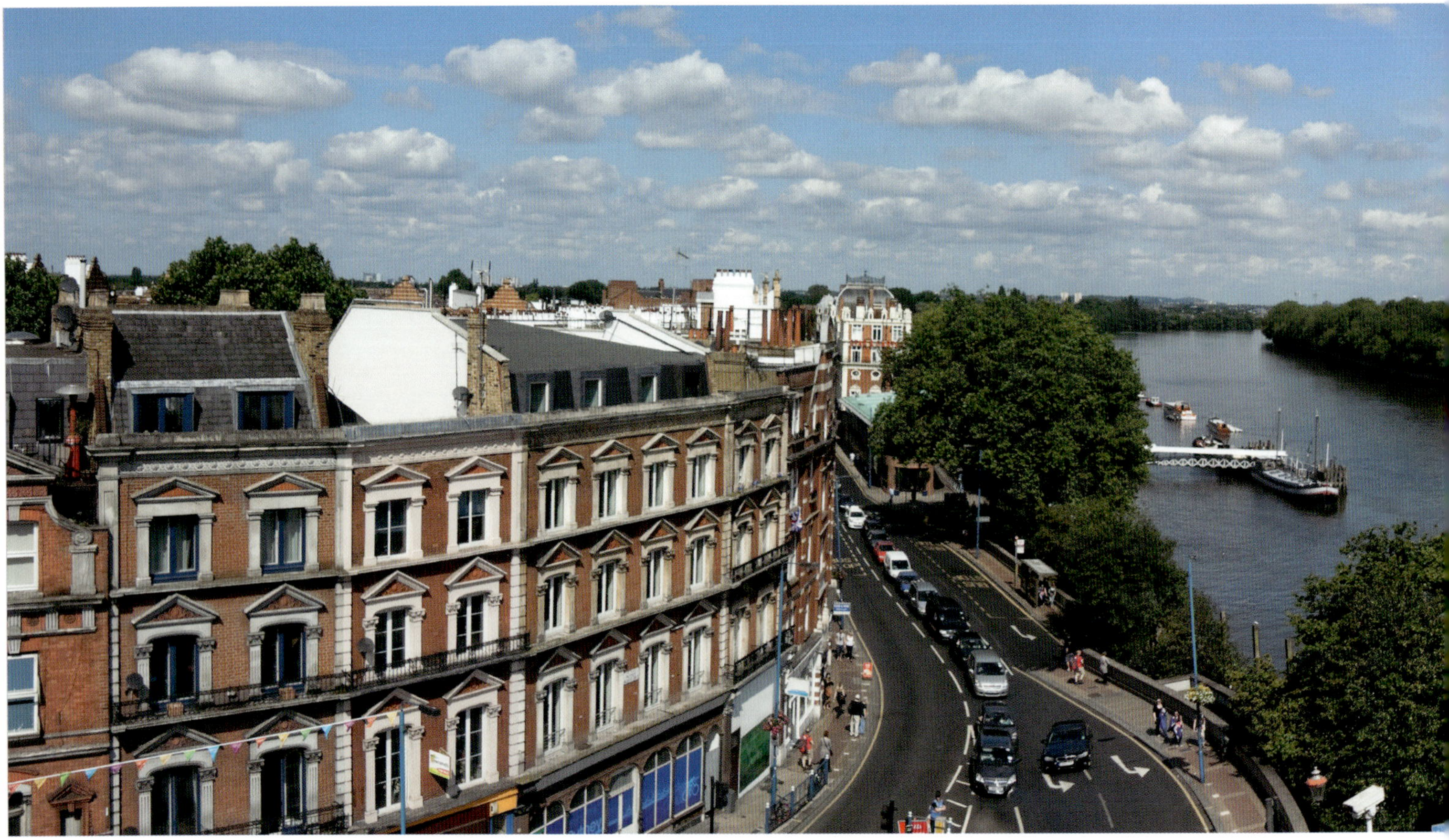

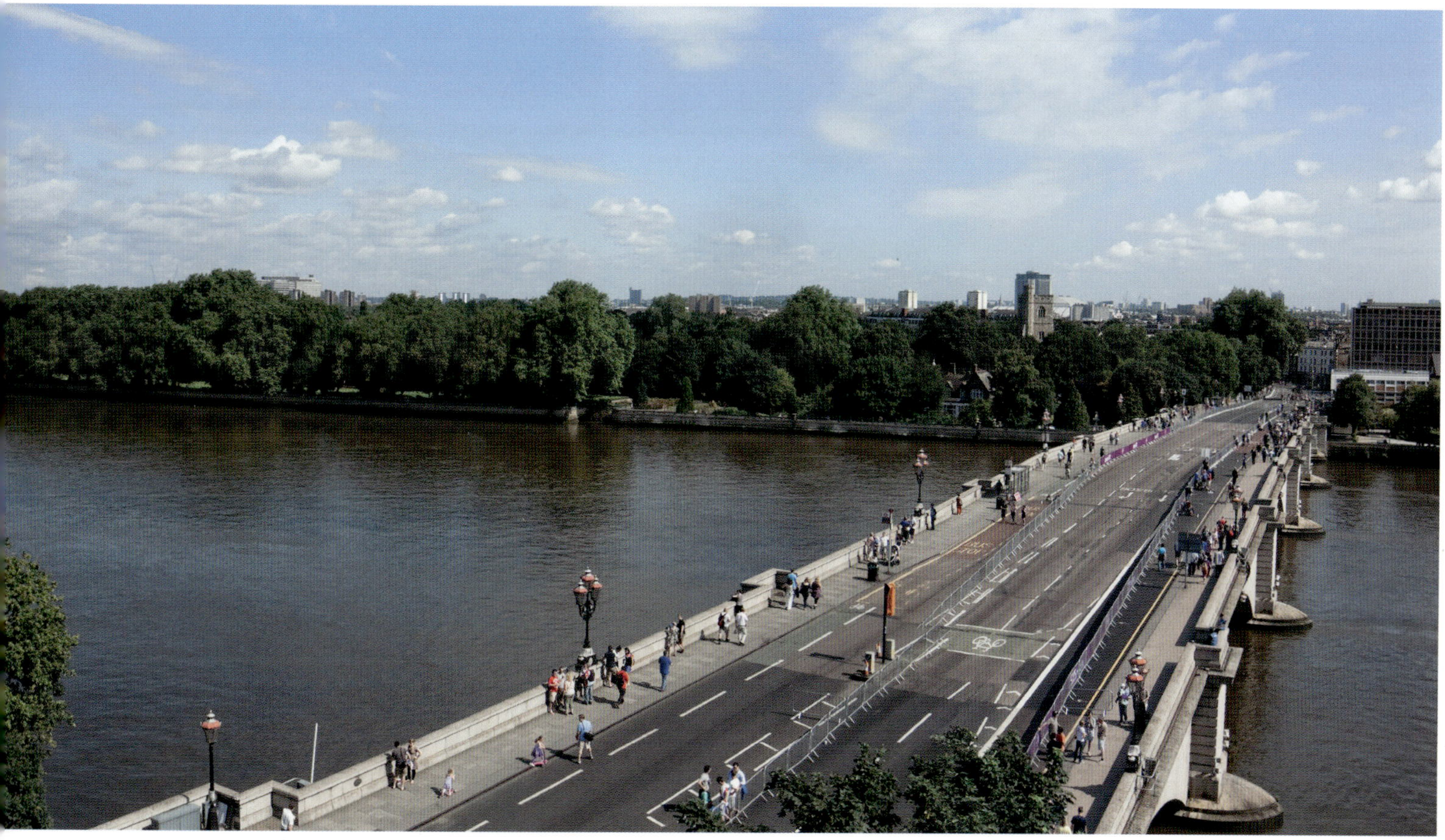

Bottom Left: fans crossing Putney Bridge having enjoyed an evening's Polo at Hurlingham Park.

Opposite: The bridge is adorned with some rather spectacular lights.

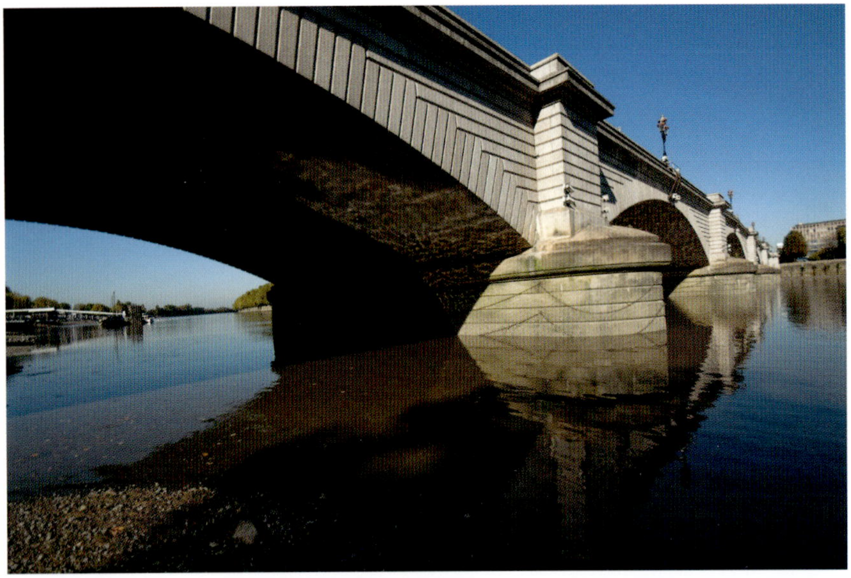

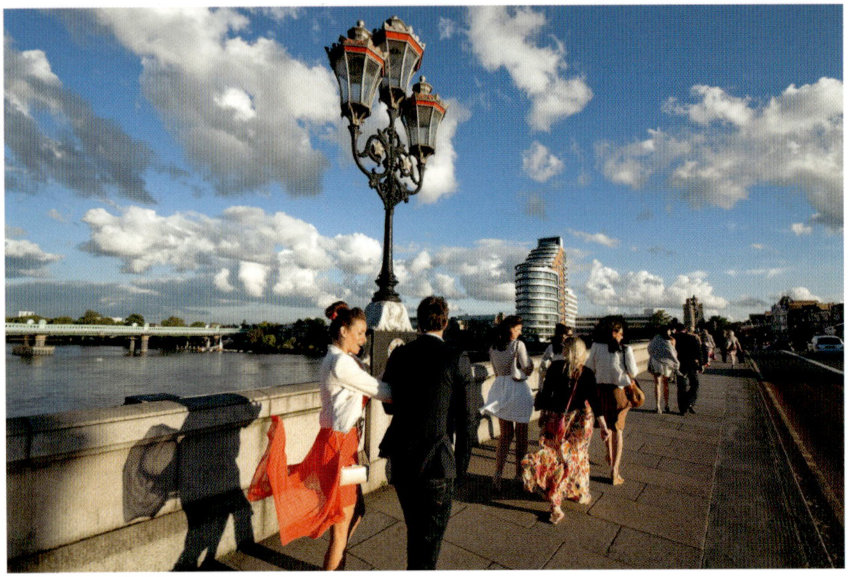

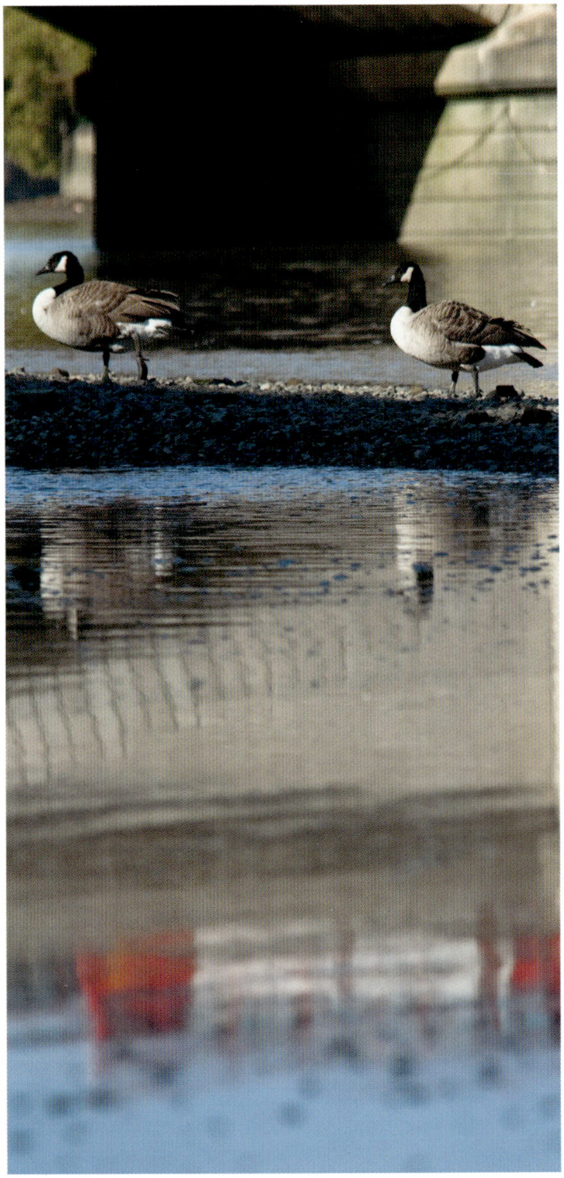

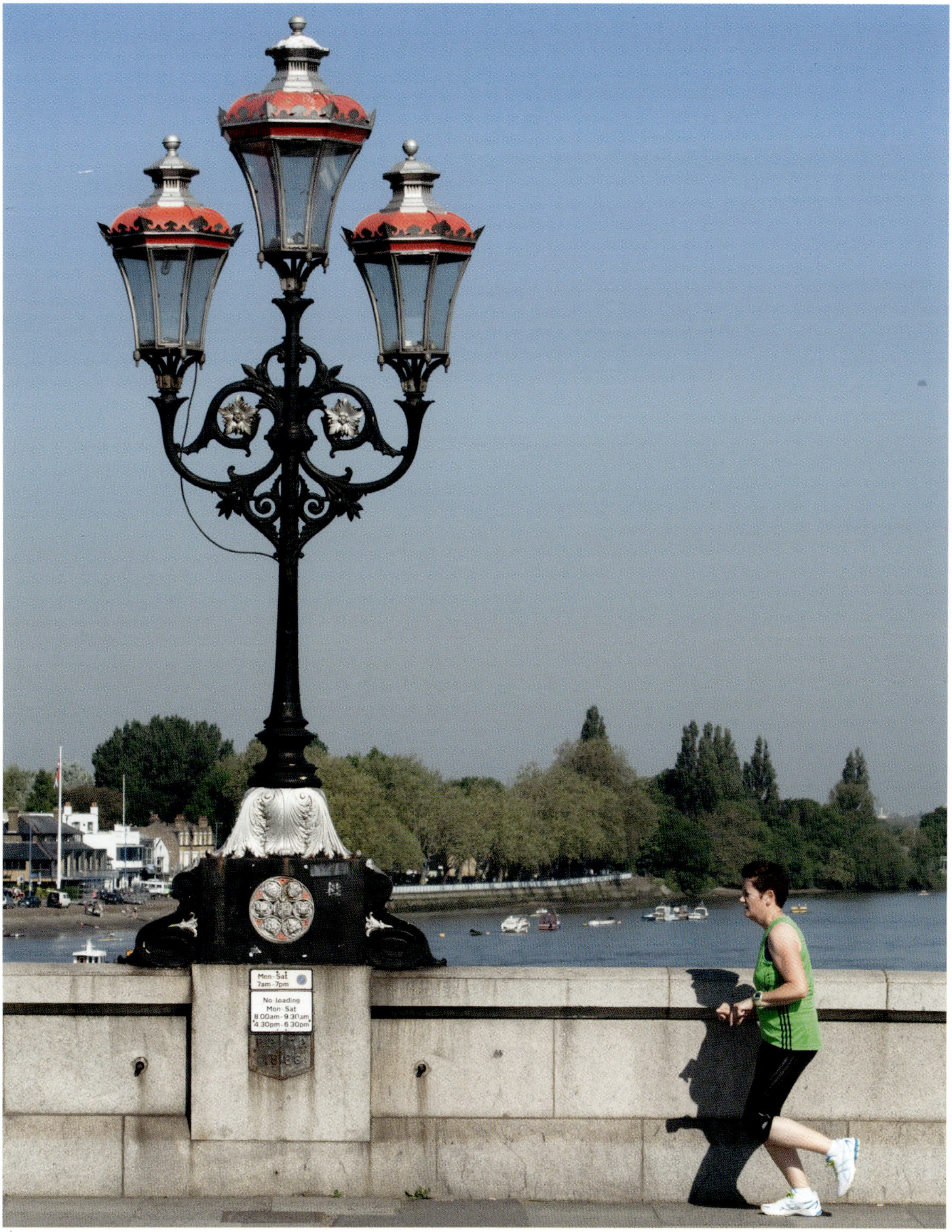
Mon-Sat
7am-7pm
No loading
Mon-Sat
8.00am-9.30am
4.30pm-6.30pm

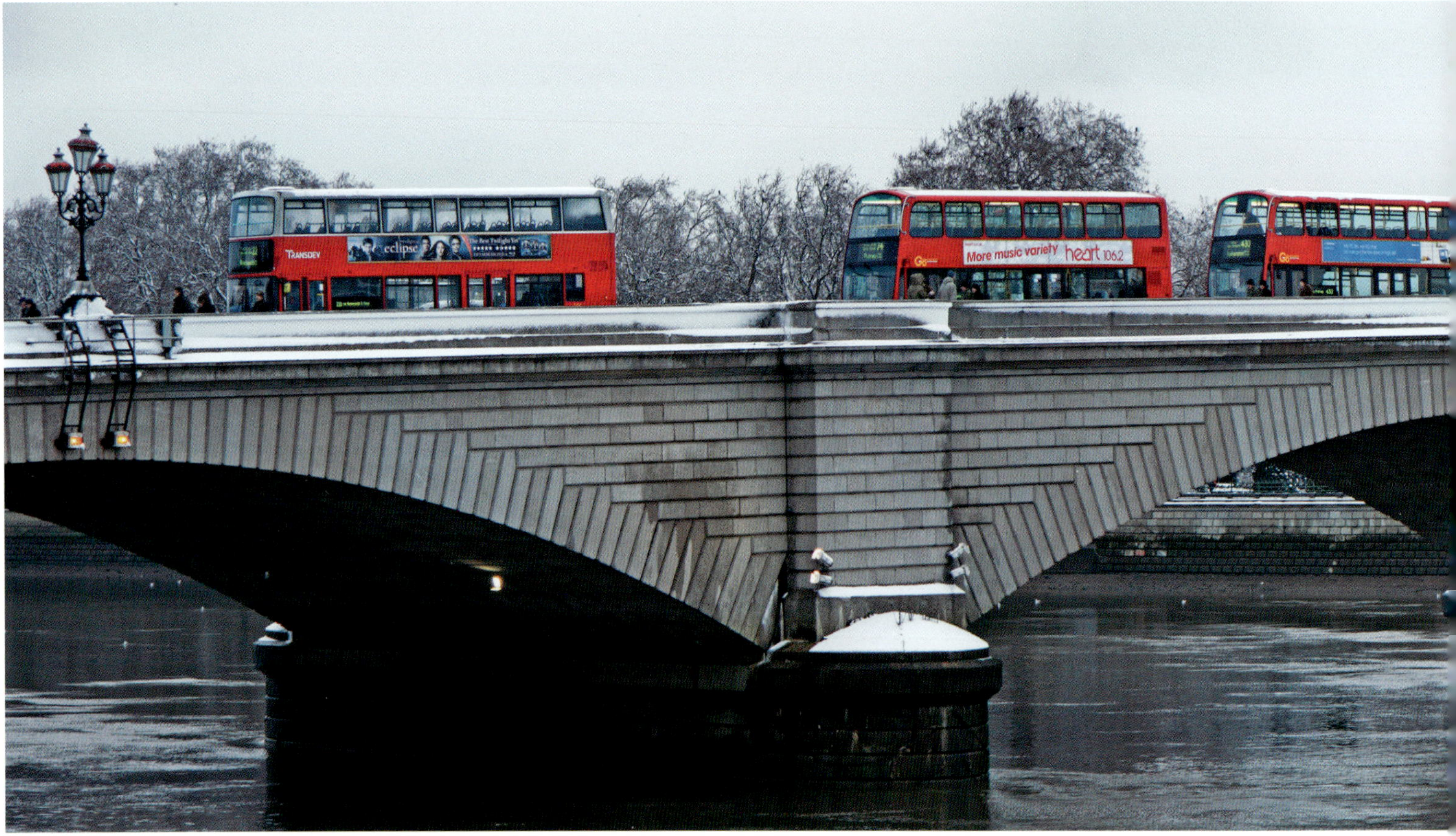

The traffic can sometimes be very slow up Putney High Street, which frequently means that the cars and buses back up onto the bridge and you can sometimes witness this kind of scene, taken at Christmas 2011.

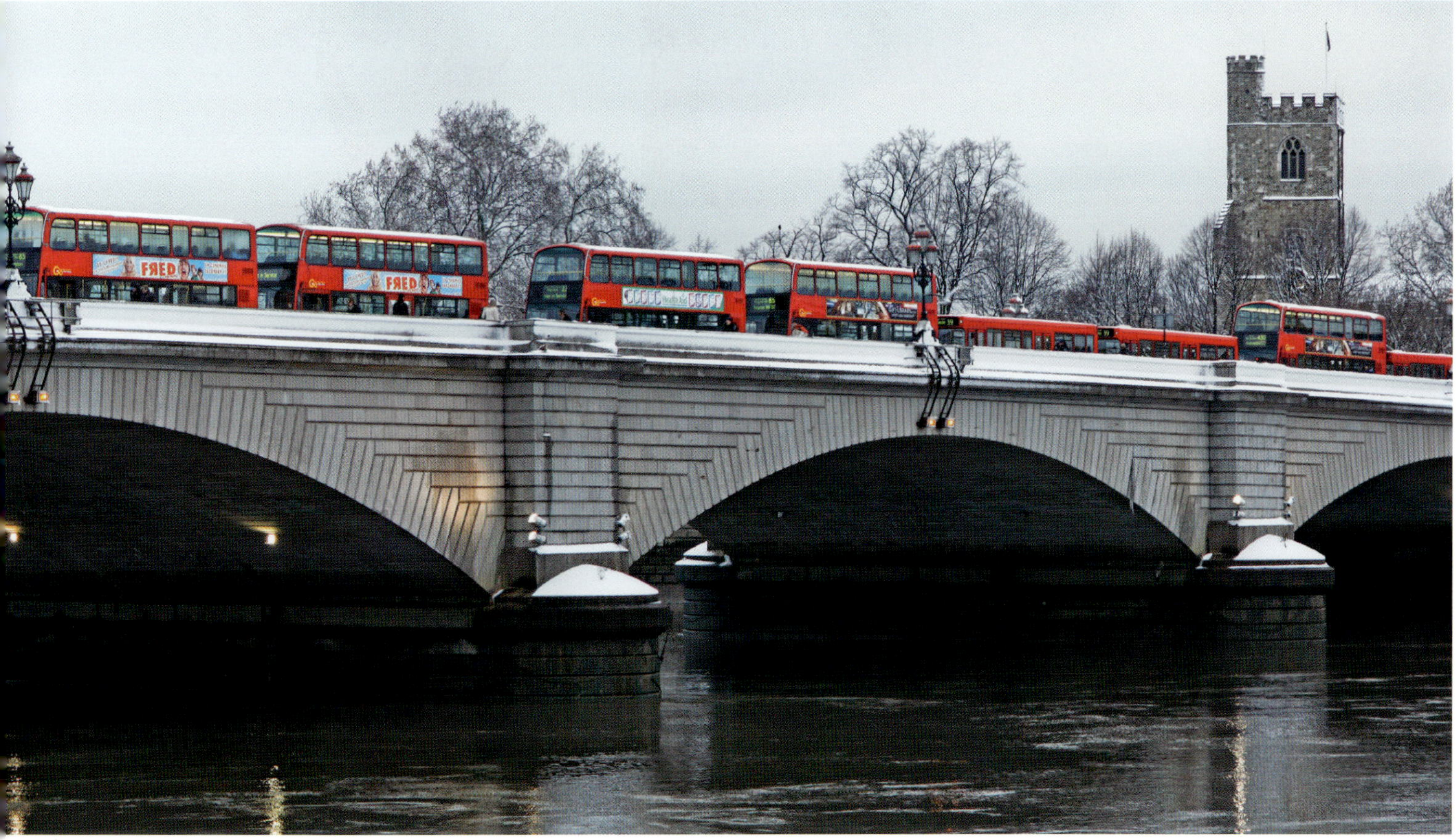

"Putney's historic riverside is not just famous for the University Boat Race – it is also a hugely popular destination in its own right. In recent years, much of the area's hidden river frontage has been opened up and now boasts attractive homes, shops and restaurants. Yet it also offers quiet and tranquil areas like Wandsworth Park and Leader's Gardens where people can escape the hustle and bustle of the city. Our over-riding aim has been to support changes that are sympathetic to its unique historic character that Putney residents can be proud of for generations to come."

COUNCILLOR RAVI GOVINDIA, LEADER OF WANDSWORTH COUNCIL

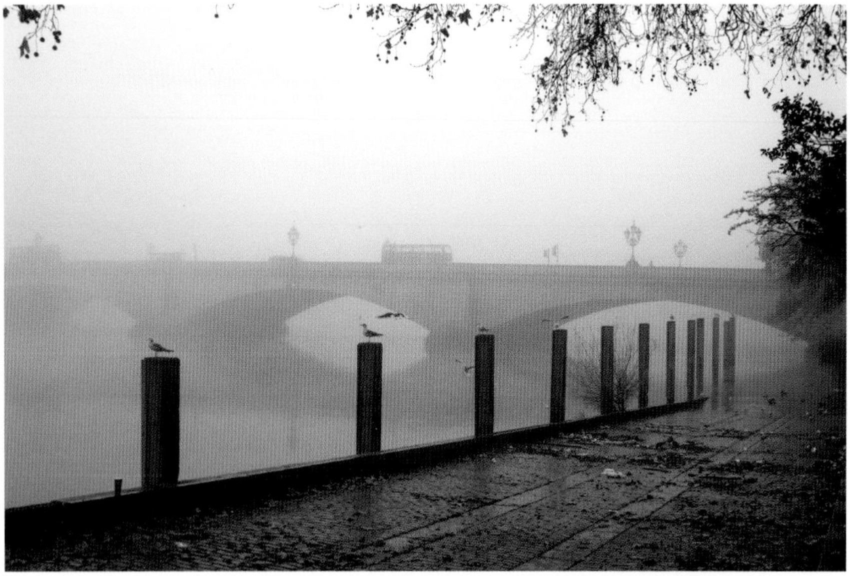

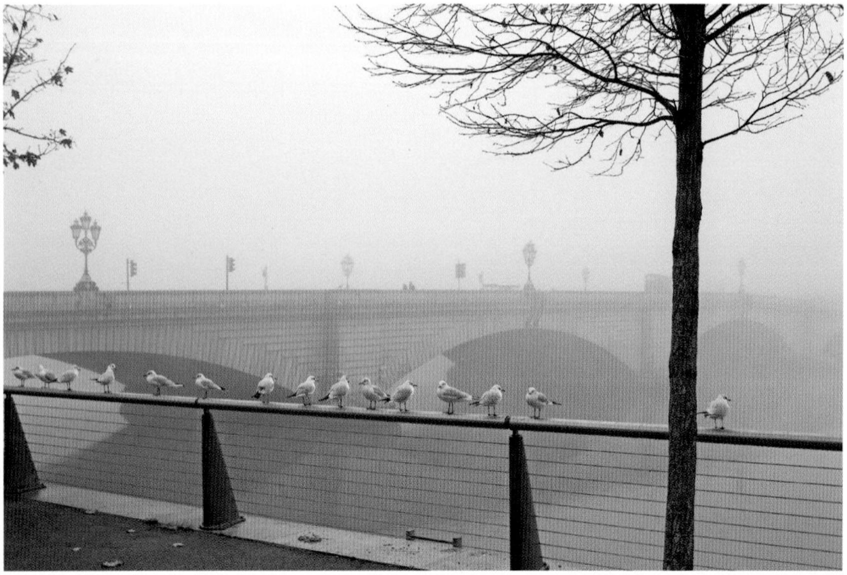

Putney Bridge in the November fog.

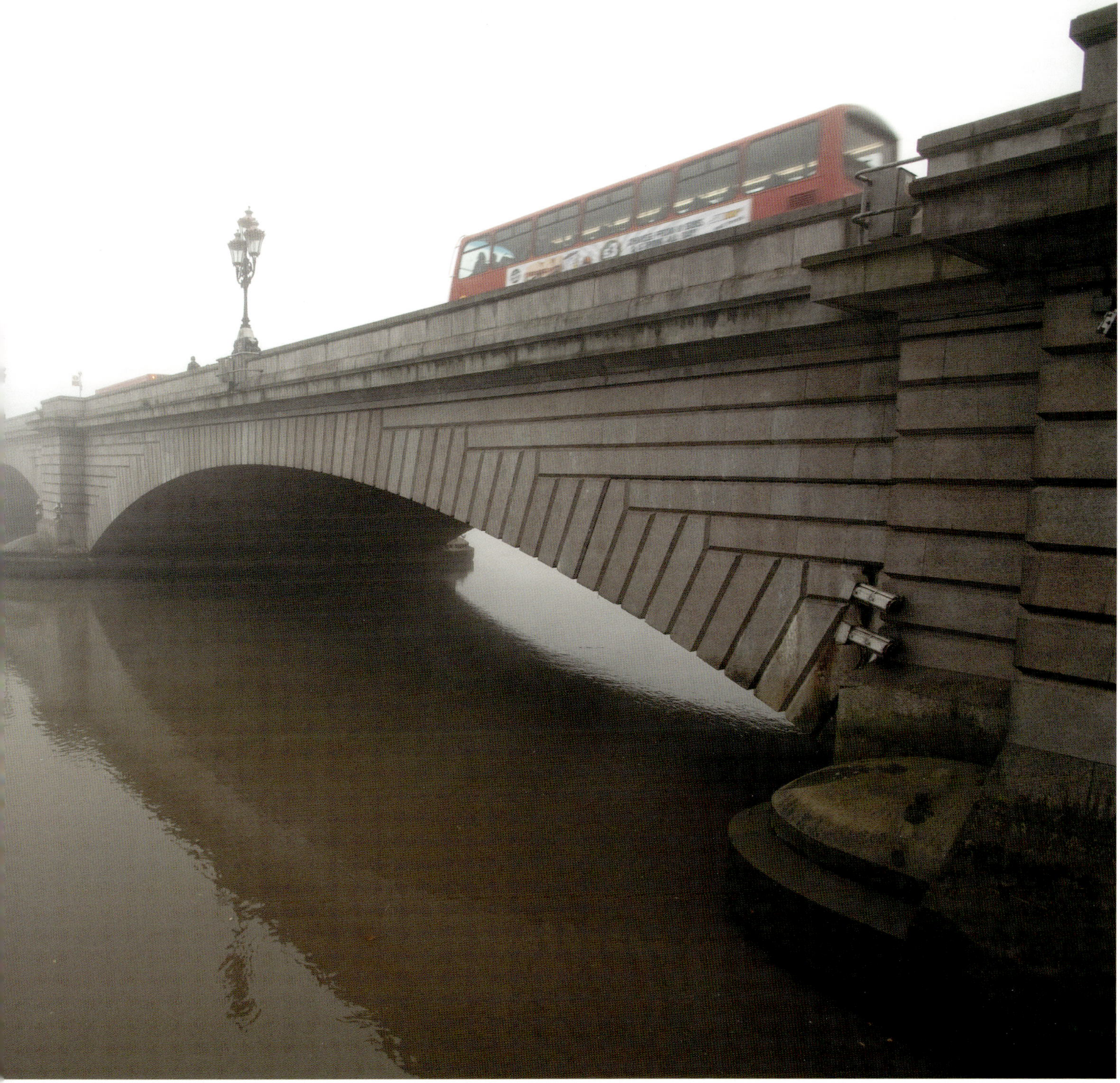

The Embankment

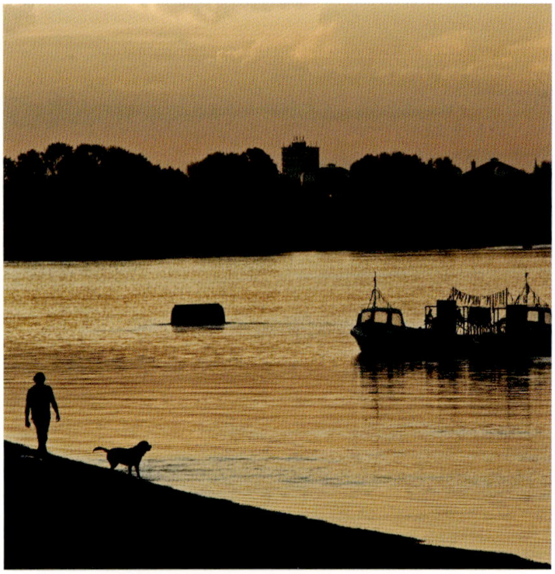

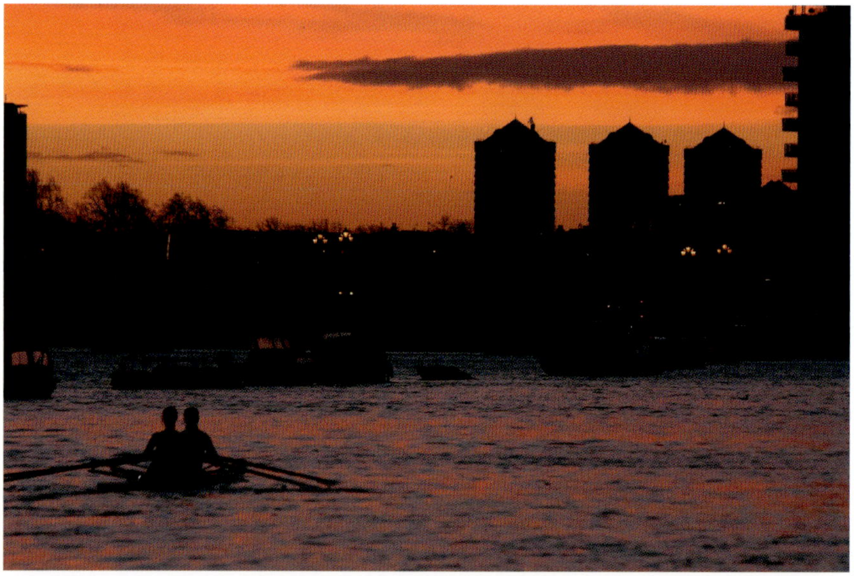

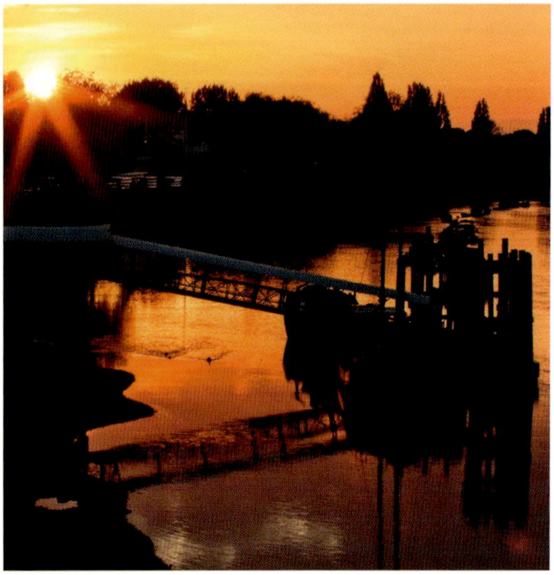

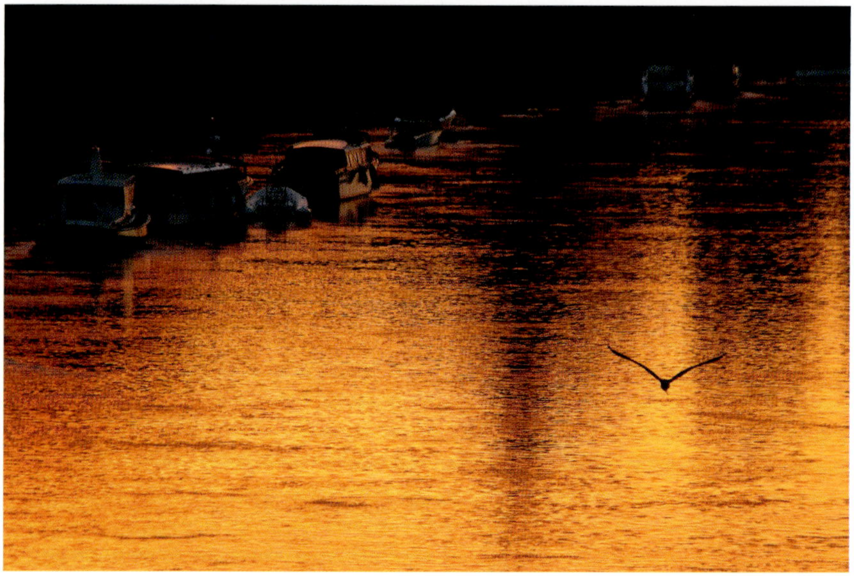

This Spread: Sunrise and sunset over Putney.

Overleaf: The wonderful row of boathouses as viewed from Bishop's Park in Fulham.

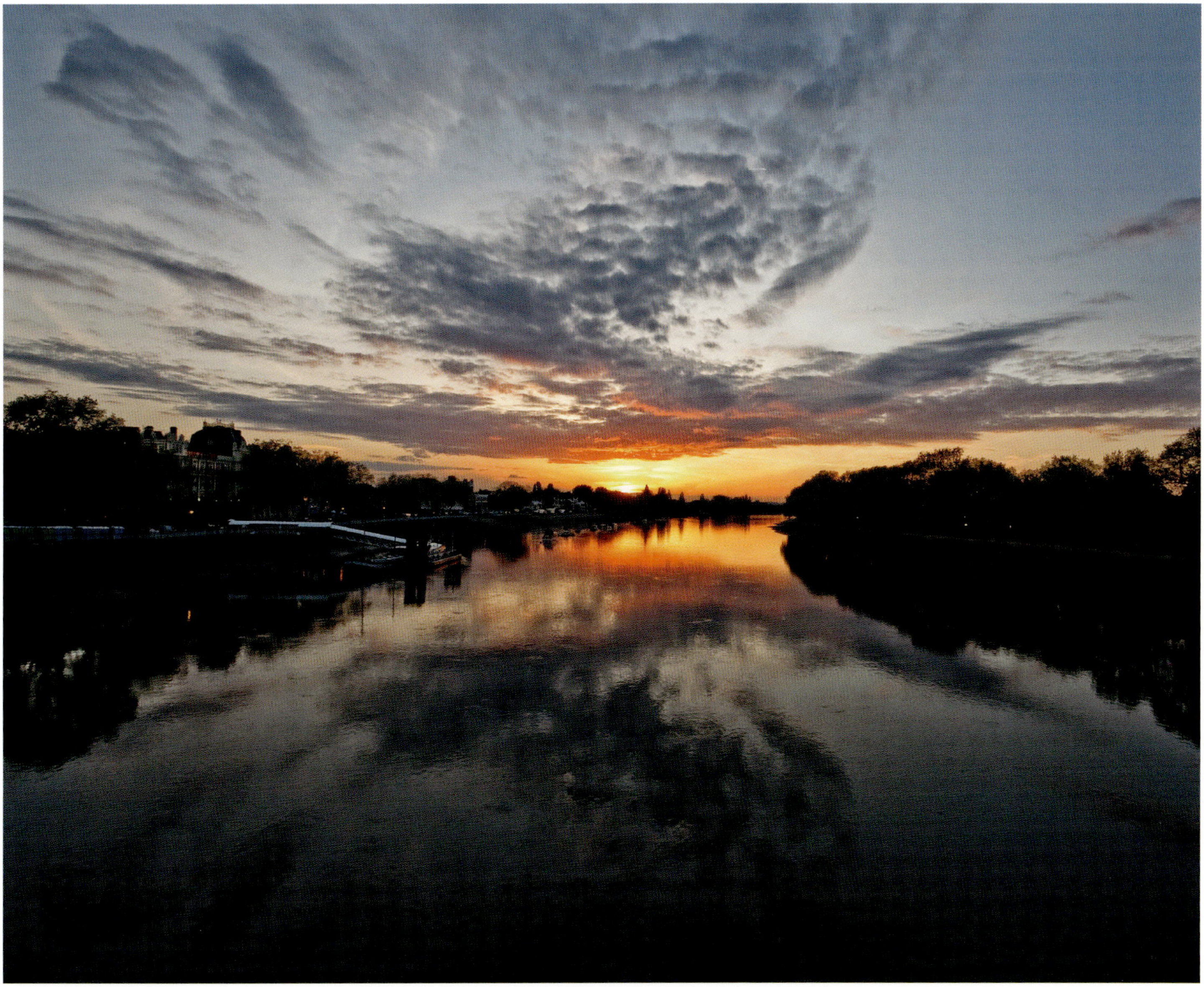

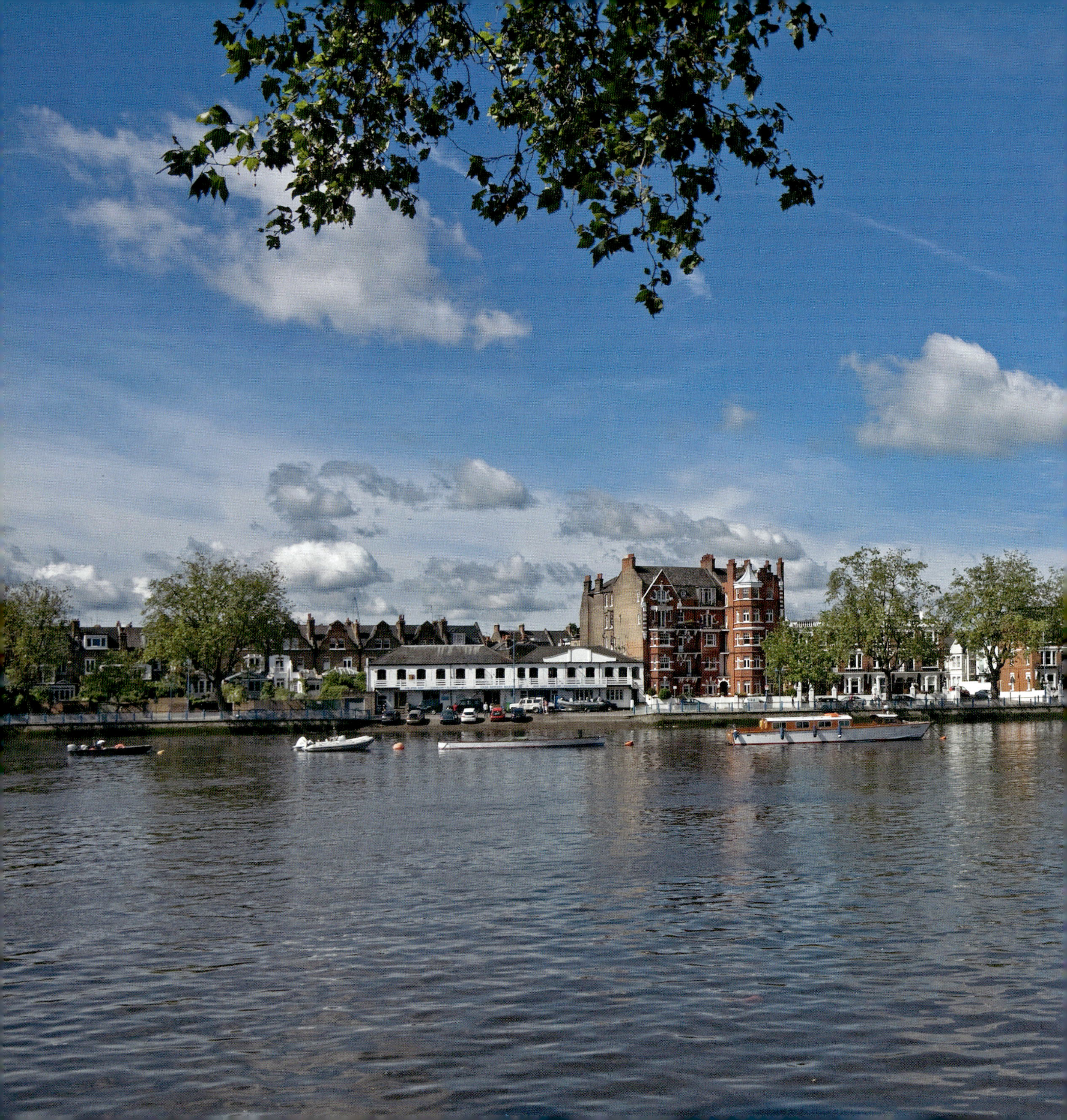

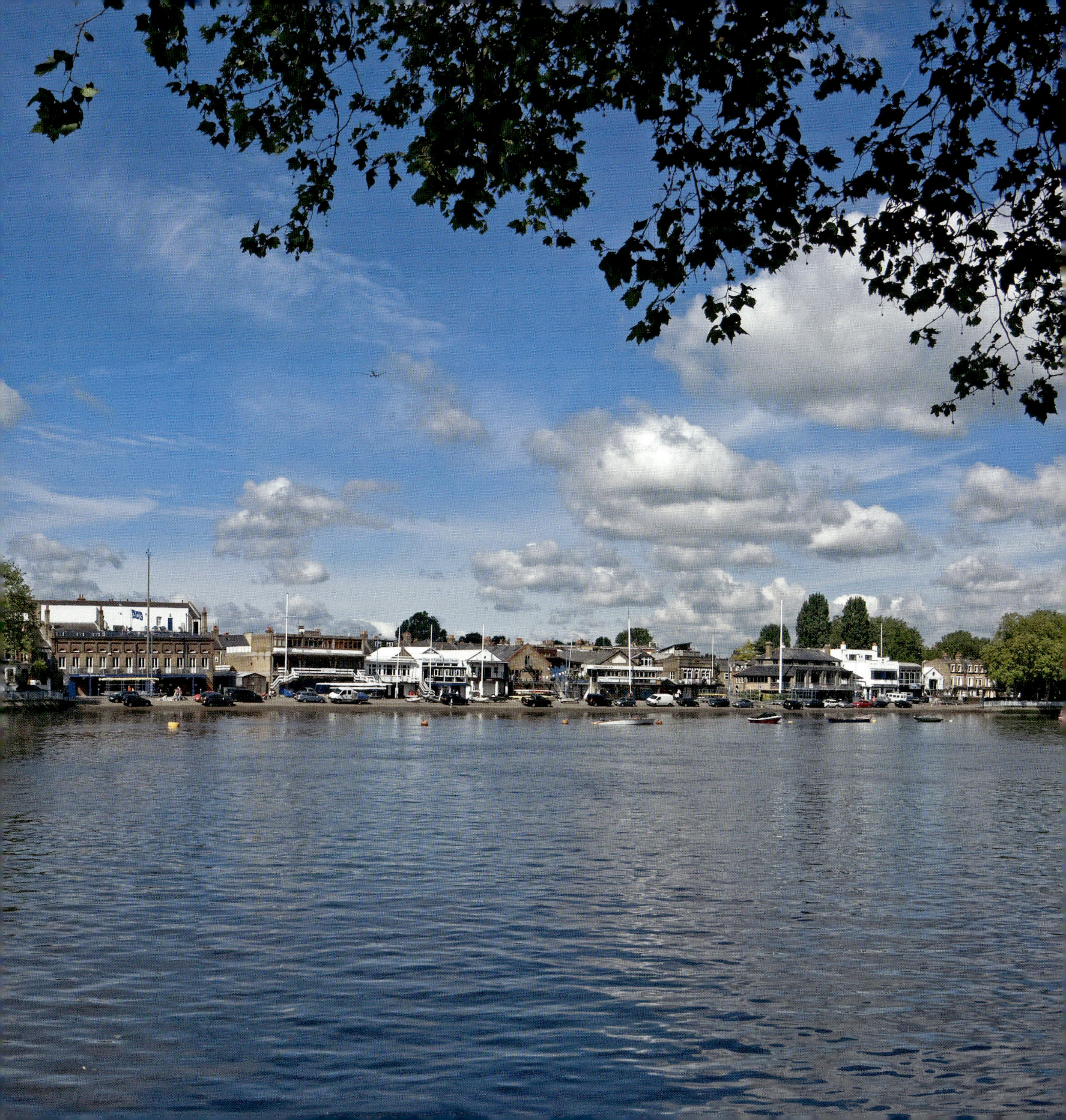

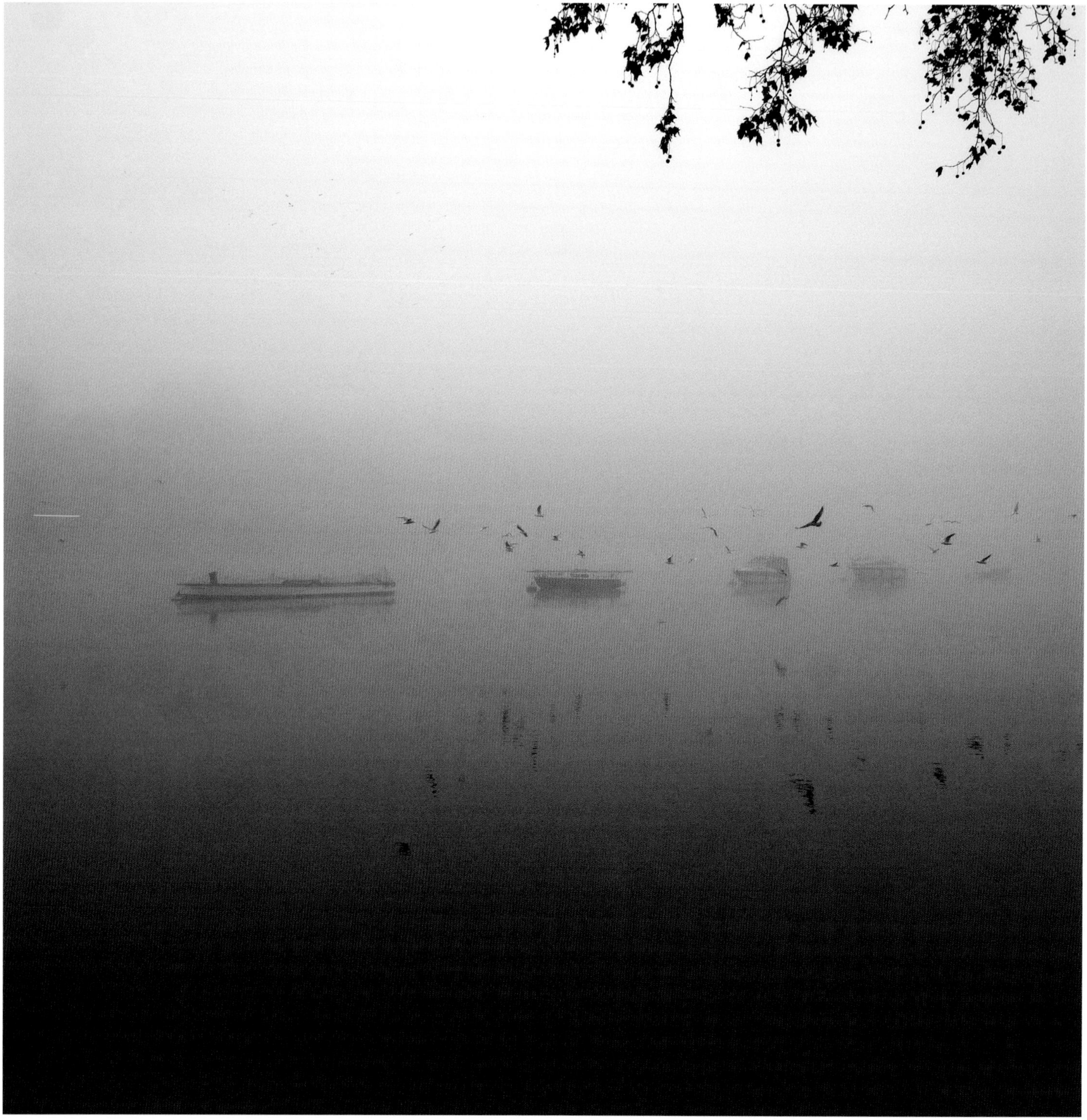

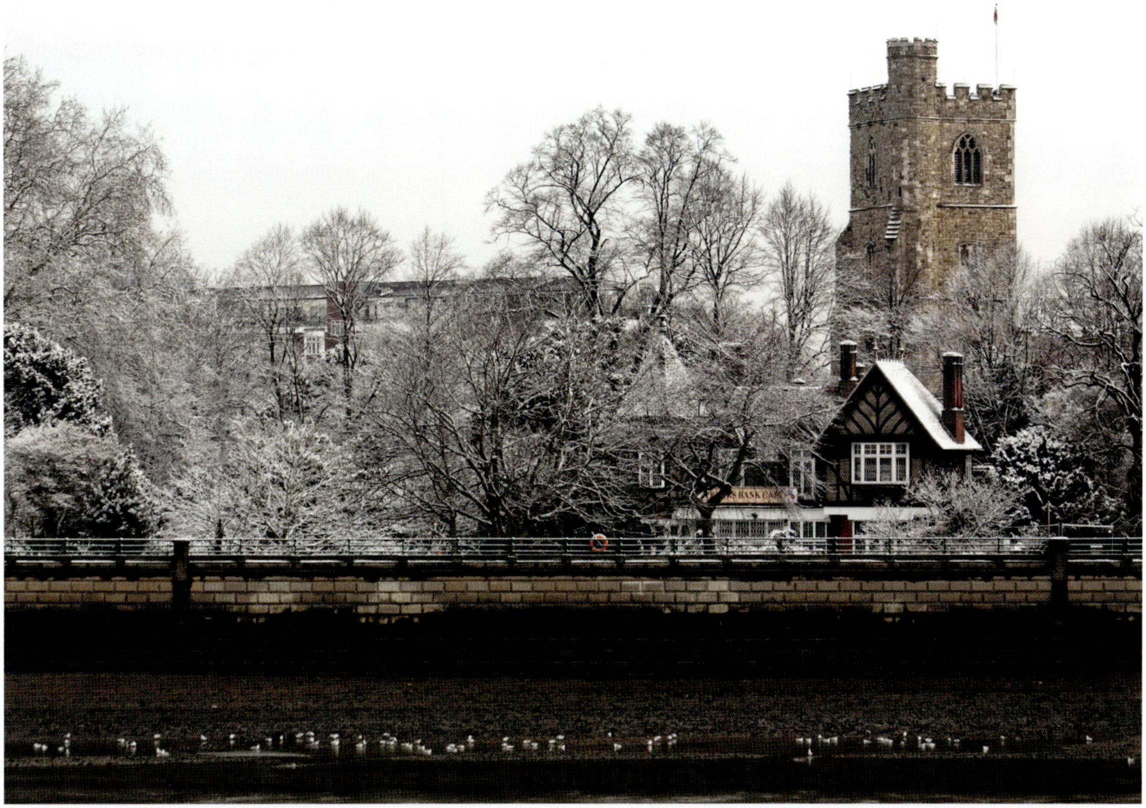

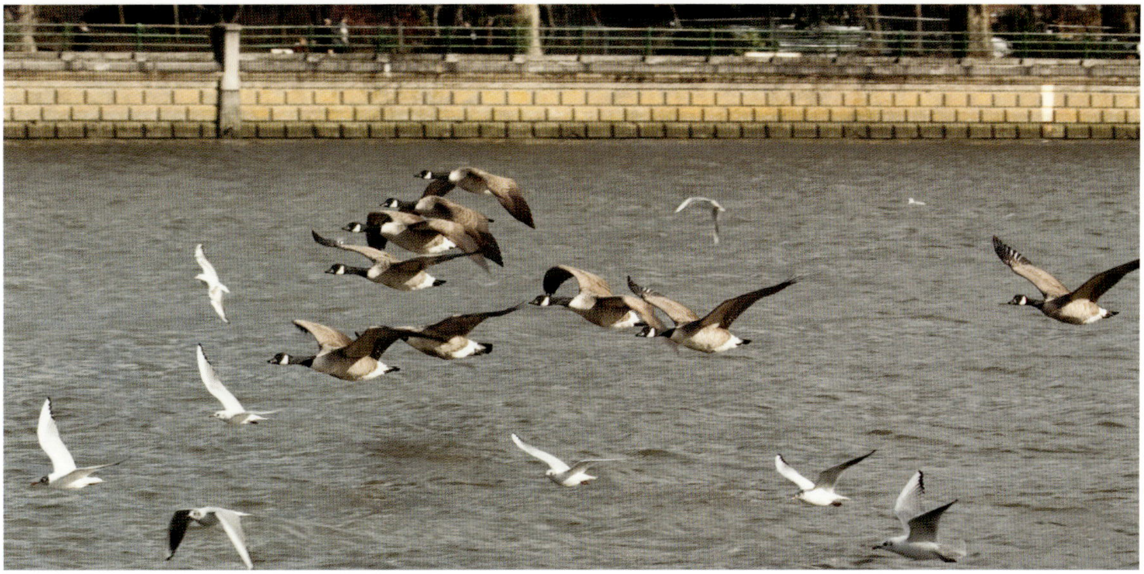

Top: All Saints Church, Fulham.

Bottom: A flock of Canada Geese flying upstream.

Opposite: the row of boats upstream of the Bridge.

This page and opposite:
The spectacular line of plane trees in Bishop's Park, Fulham, as viewed from Putney Embankment.

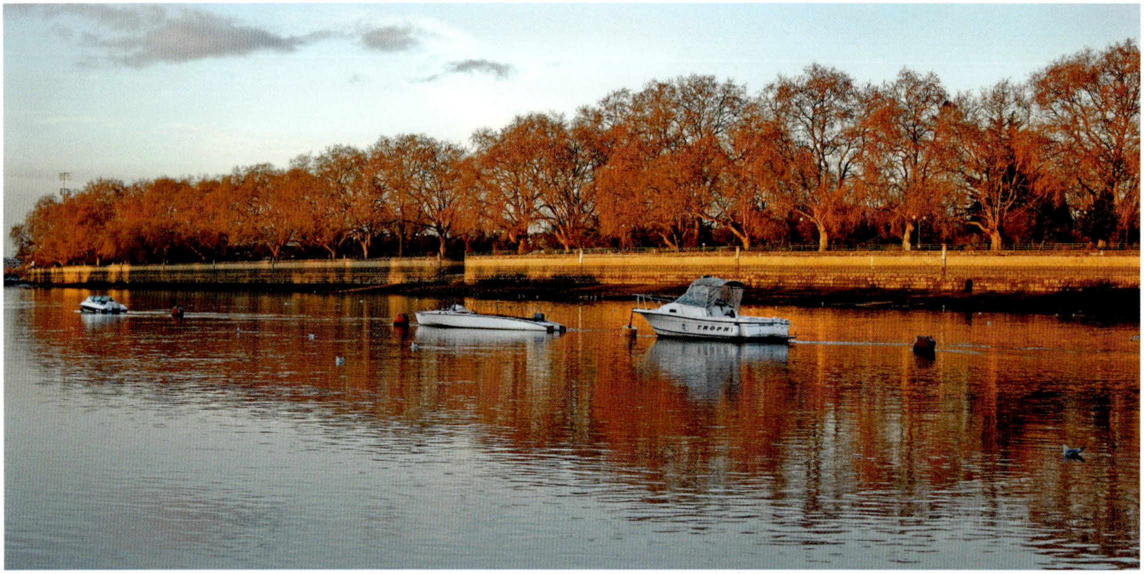

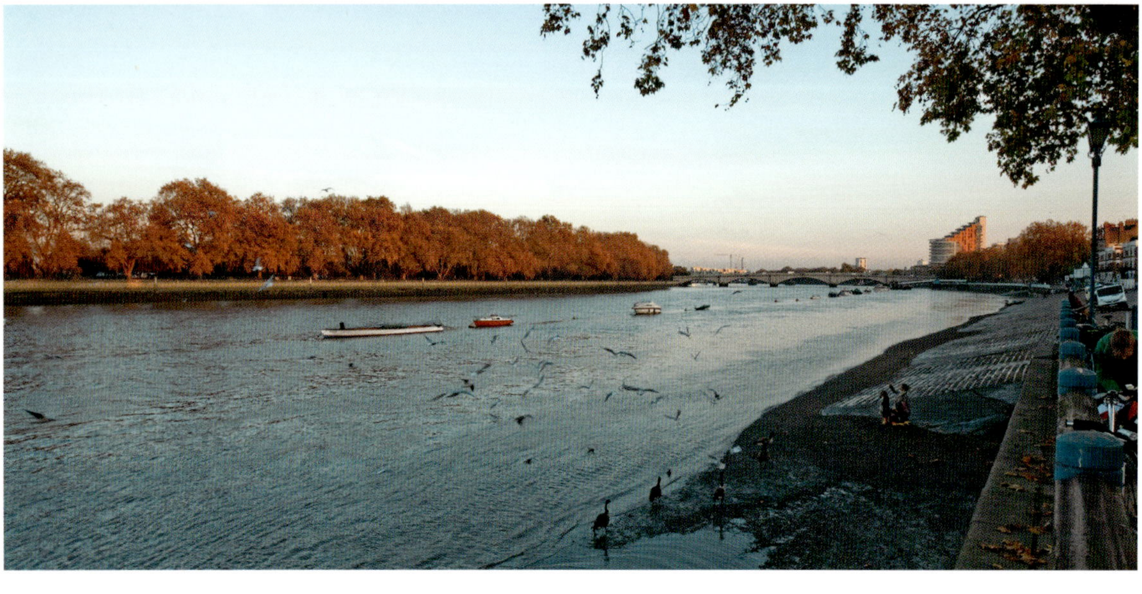

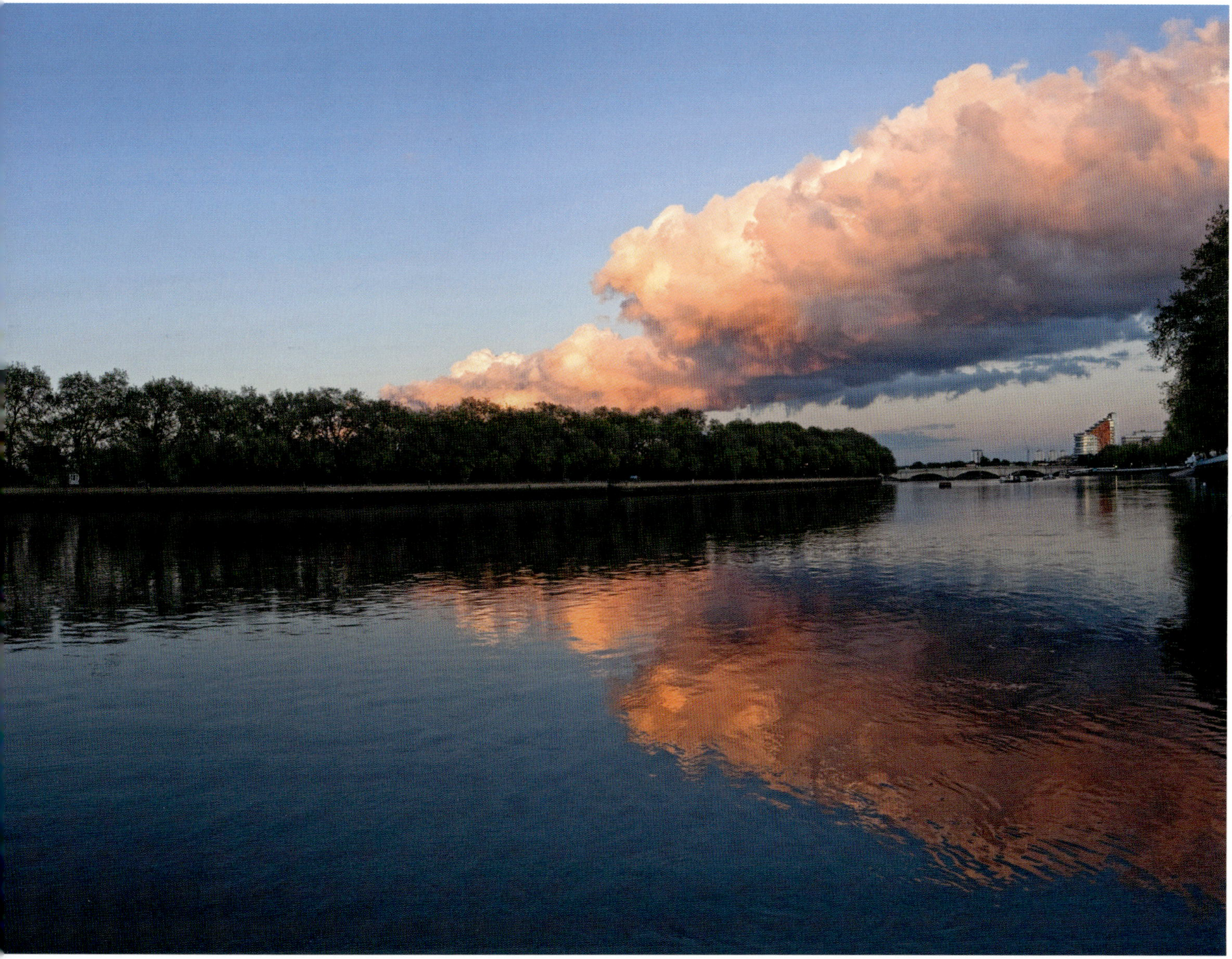

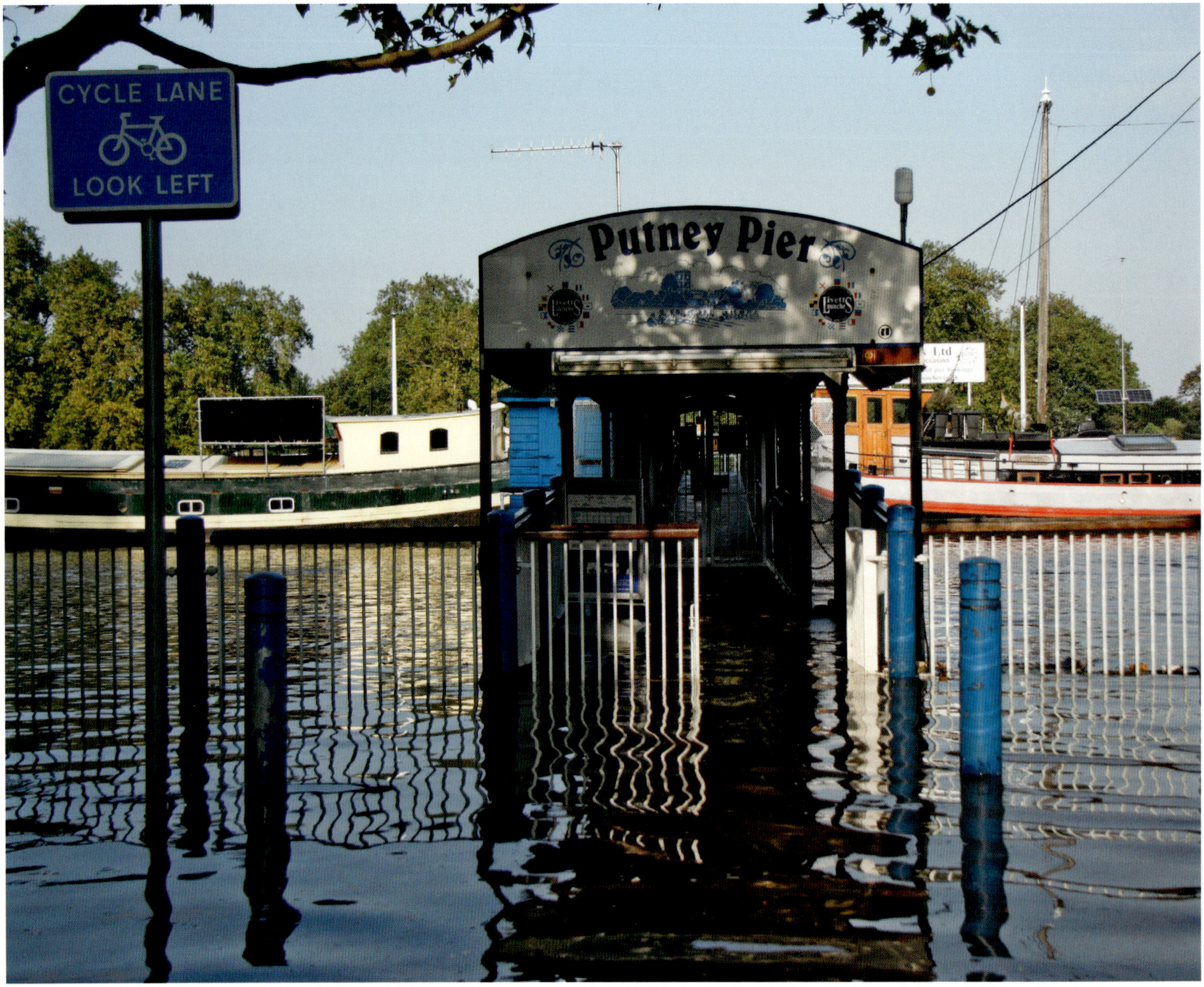
CYCLE LANE
LOOK LEFT
Putney Pier

Opposite: At high tides, the Embankment can become flooded.

Top Left: Feeding the birds in winter, notice in the background the unusual site of a Routemaster bus on the Embankment. These traditional London Buses went out of service some years ago but are still used by private companies for parties, weddings and so on.

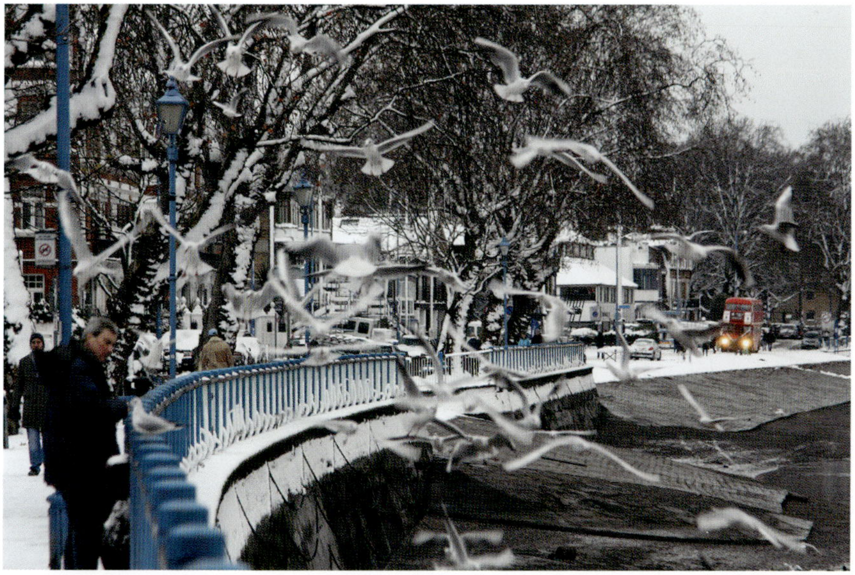

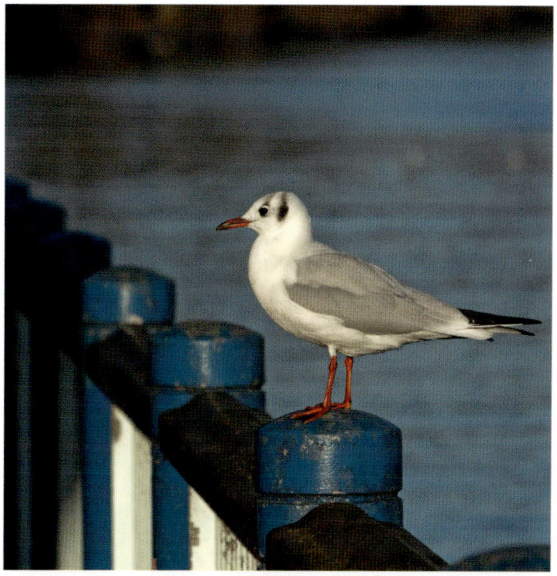

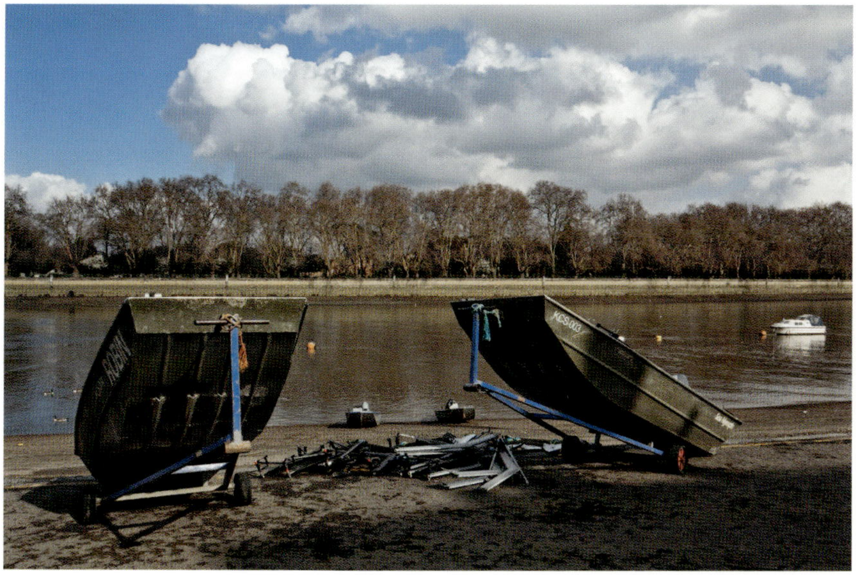

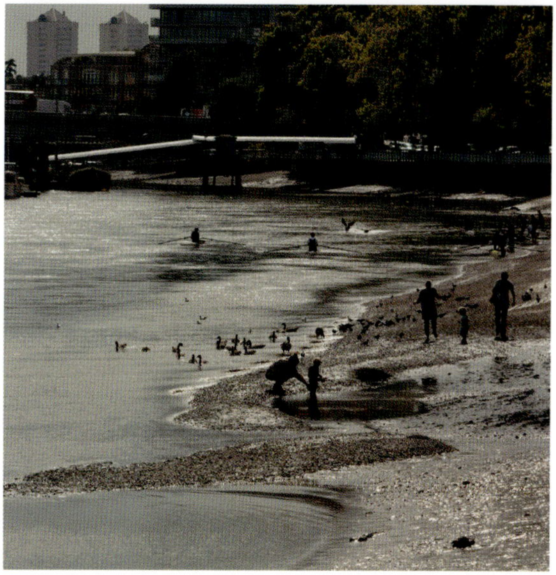

Rowing

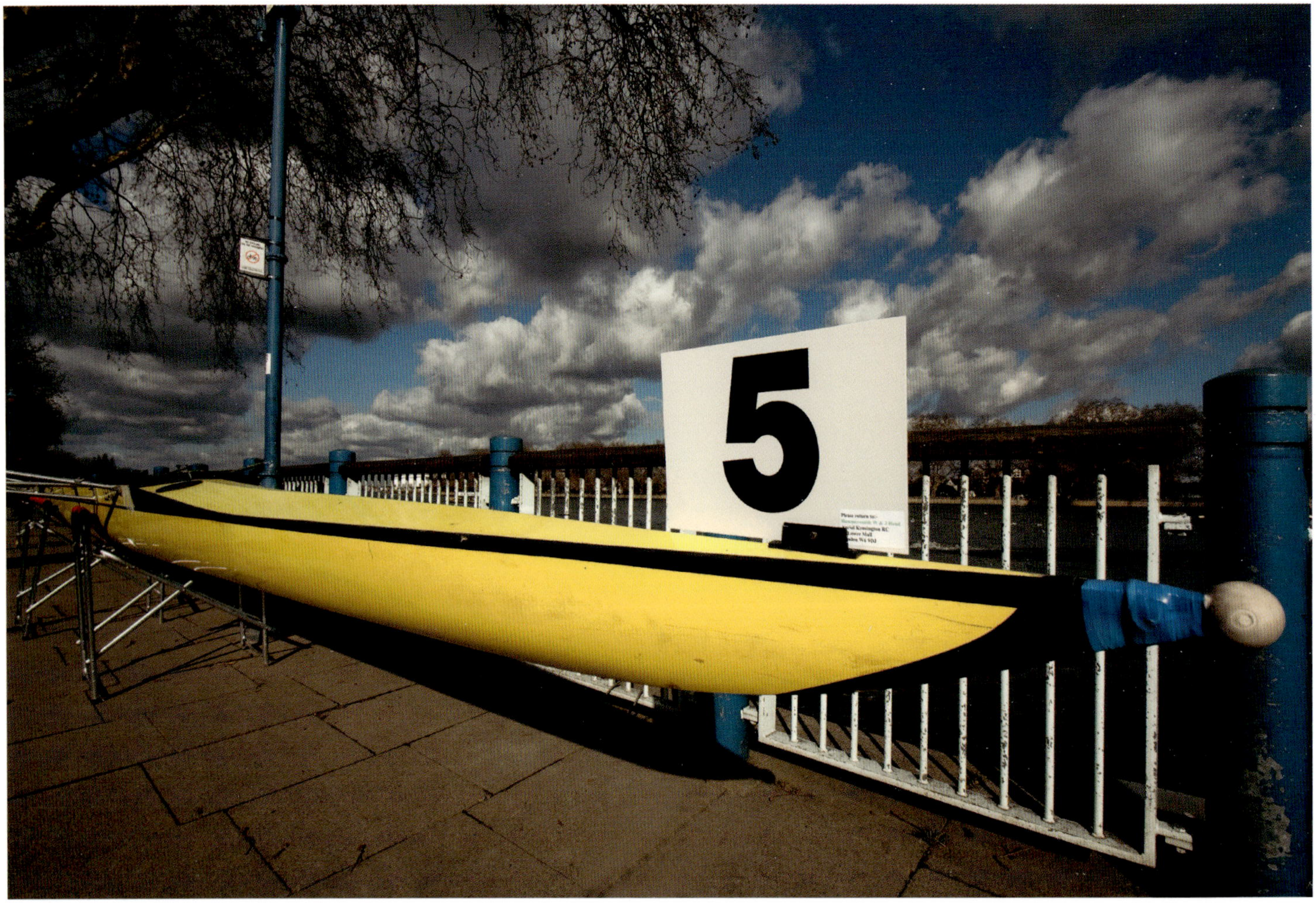

Putney has a long and distinguished tradition of rowing, and it is worth noting that, in the annual Doggett's Coat & Badge race (from which the Lacy Road pub took its name, see page 121), held since 1715 from London Bridge to Chelsea, more winners have come from Putney than from any other part of the river!

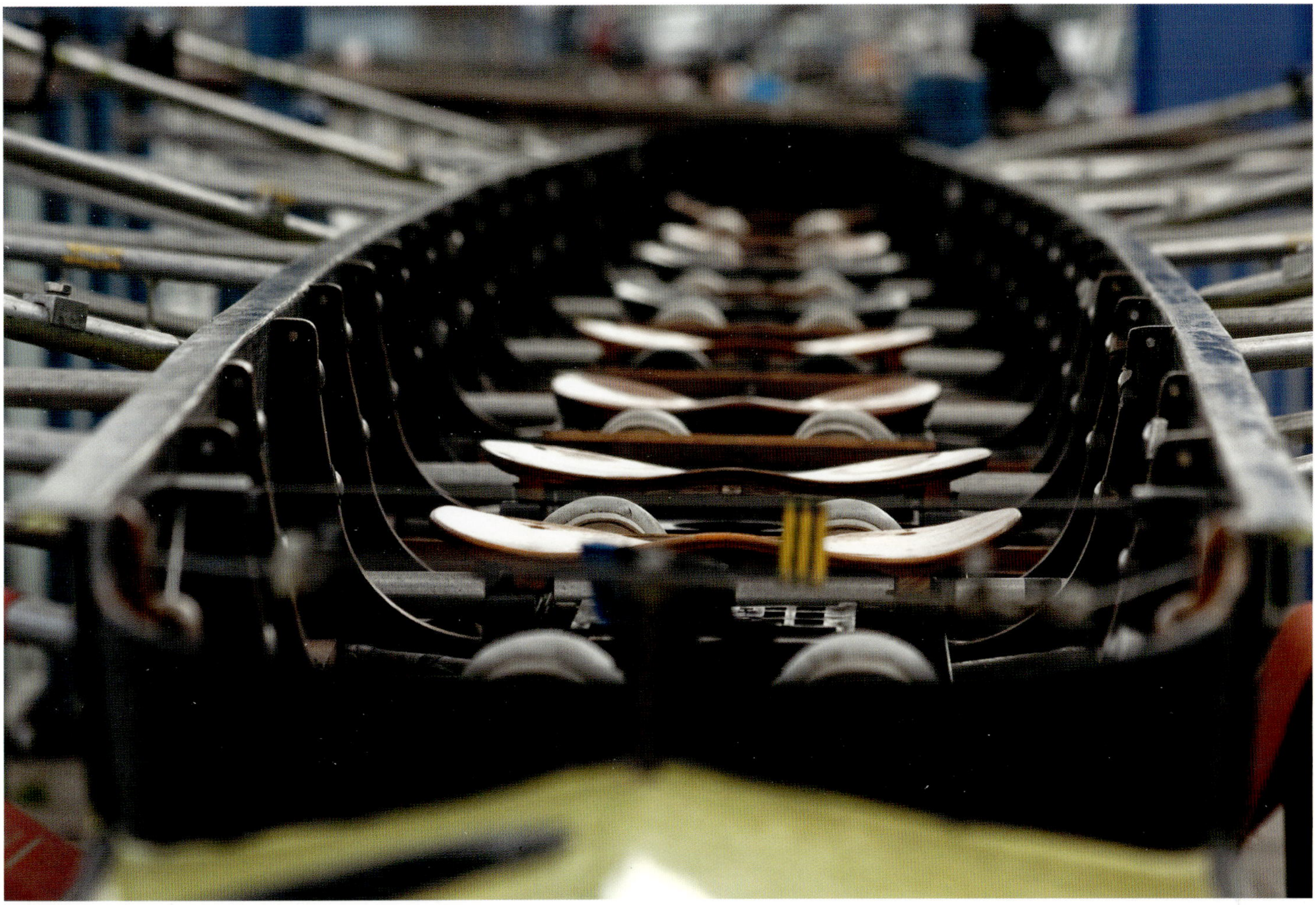

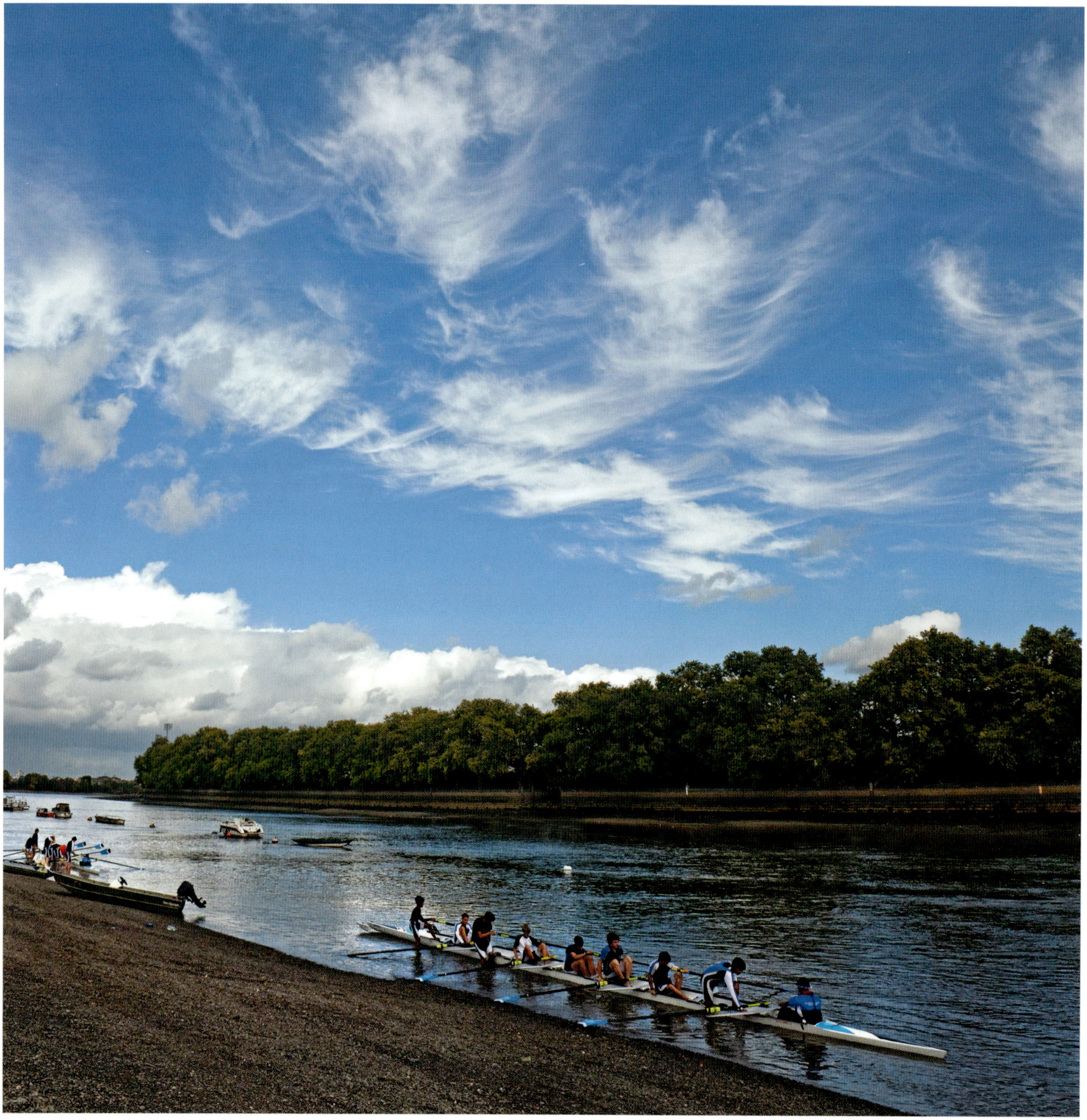

Numerous events and regattas take place throughout the year, with the embankment regularly being taken over by large amounts of boats and crew, especially in the spring and early summer. One such event is the Great River Race in September each year (below top), which features over 450 boats that travel from Greenwich to Ham. This is some distance if all you have is a small rowing boat. Everyone seems to enjoy it though.

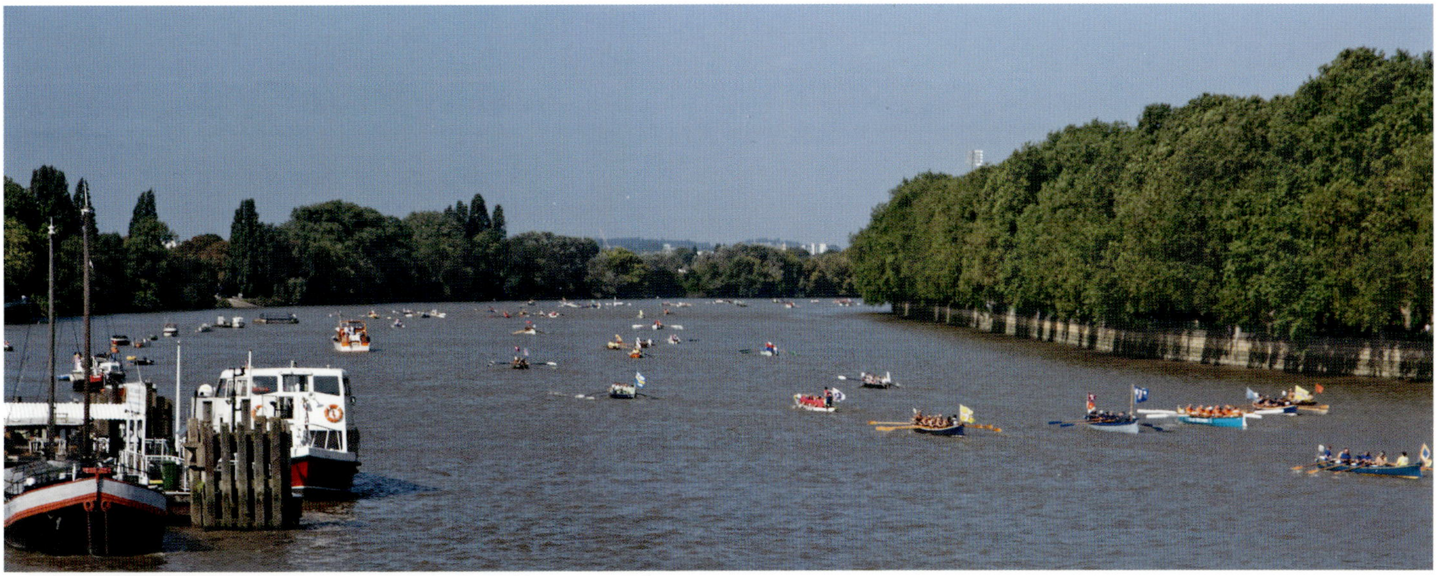

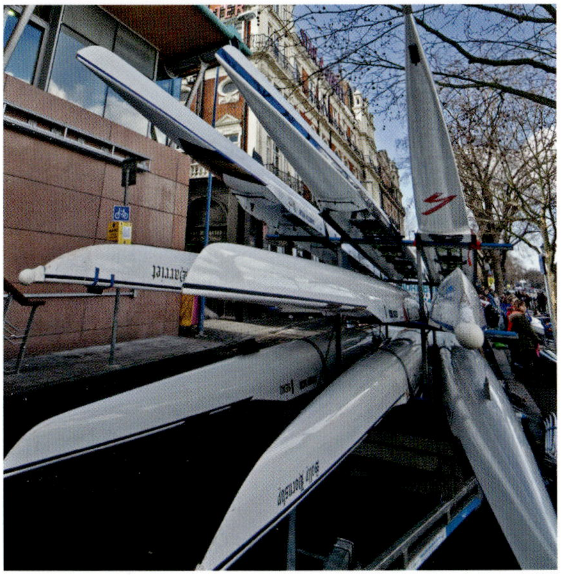

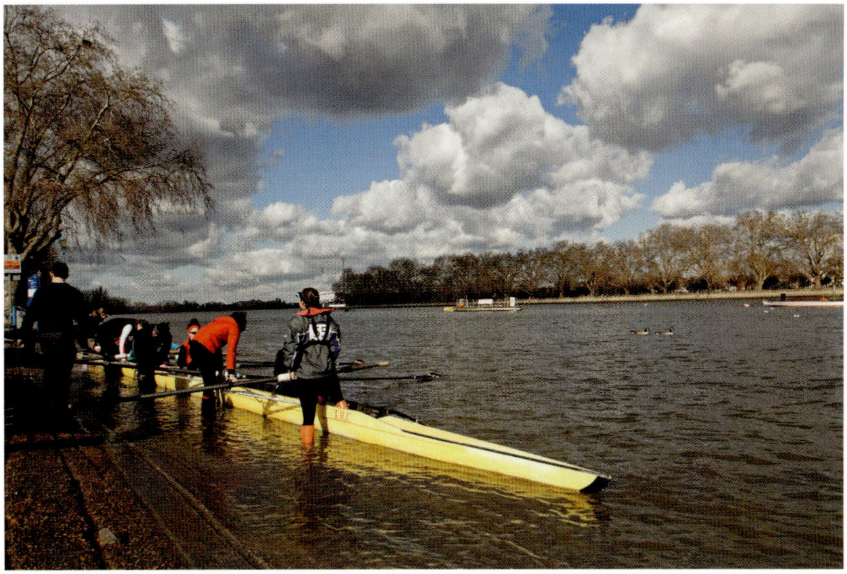

The Boat Race 2012

The Oxford & Cambridge Boat Race, which starts at Putney Bridge, draws thousands of animated spectators every year. It was held sporadically from 1829, becoming an annual event in 1856. The first was at Henley-on-Thames, the next, in 1836, from Westminster to Putney, and the 4.2 mile Putney–Mortlake course was established in 1845, though the race was run in the opposite direction four times between 1846 and 1863. As at 2015 Cambridge have the edge 81–79.

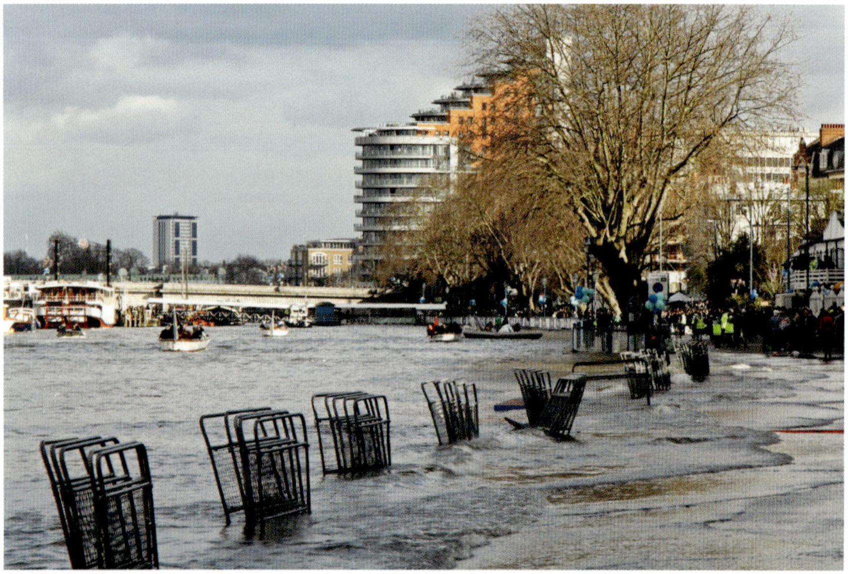

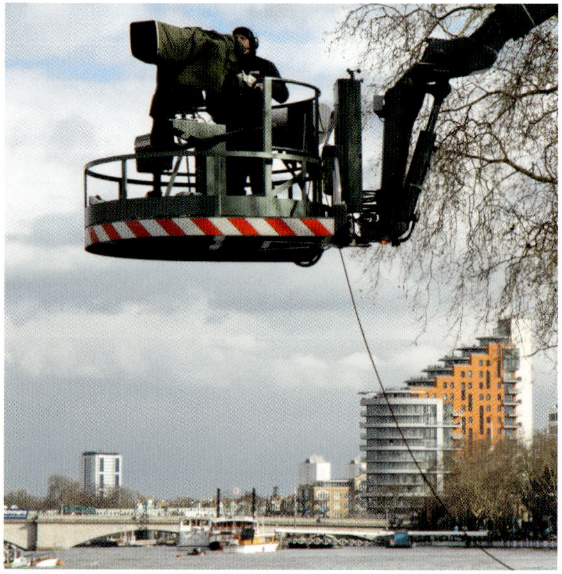

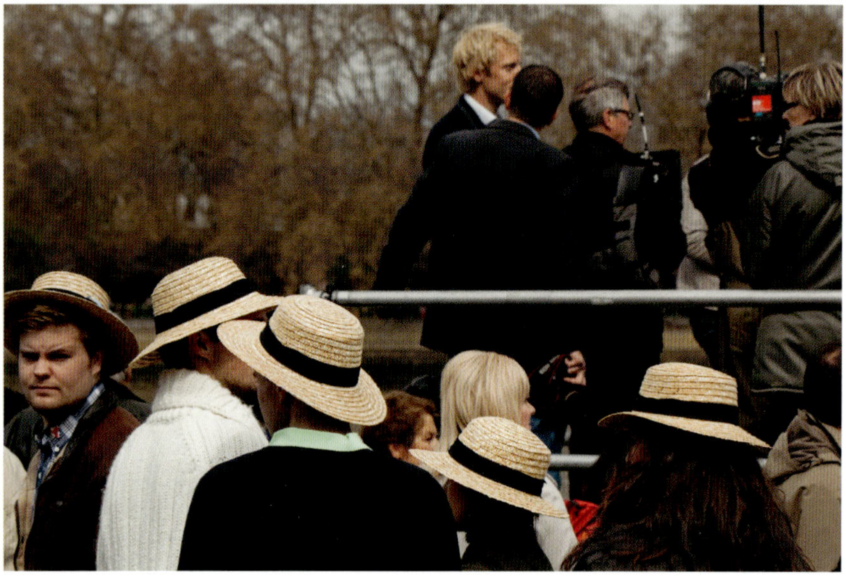

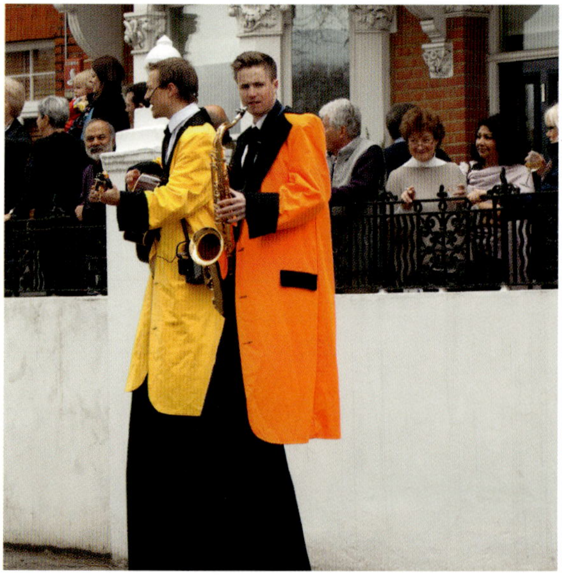

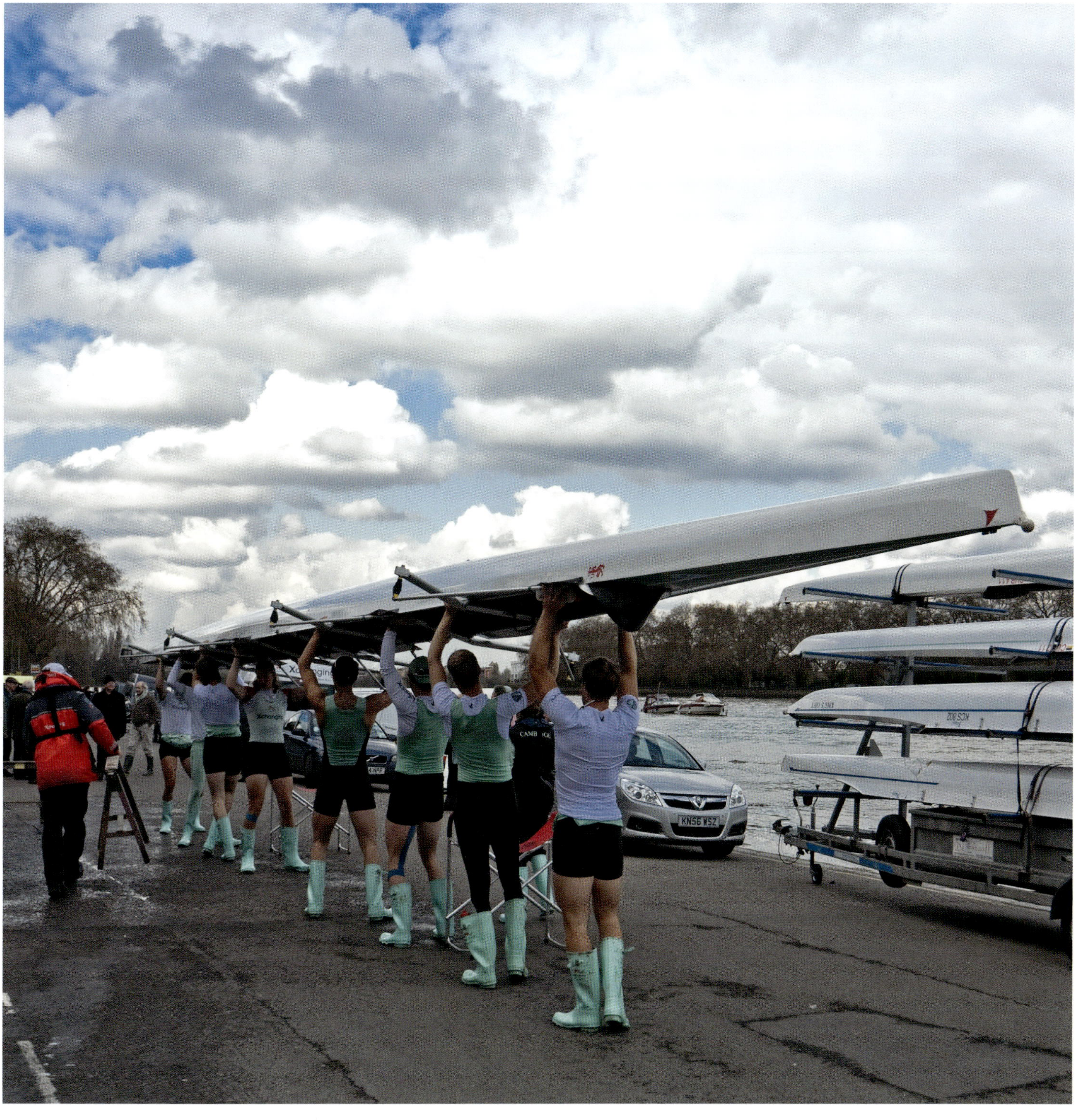
KN56 WSZ

Hurlingham Yacht Club

Hurlingham Yacht Club is unusual in that it could be said to be on the wrong side of the river, as Hurlingham is on the other side in Fulham. Based off Deodar Road, the club played a major role in the Queen's Diamond Jubilee River Pageant, with many of its members taking part (see overleaf for more on the Pageant, as it passed through Putney). Besides the use of a dry dock, as pictured below left, the club also plays its part in the local community, hosting numerous events and raising money for a variety of charities.

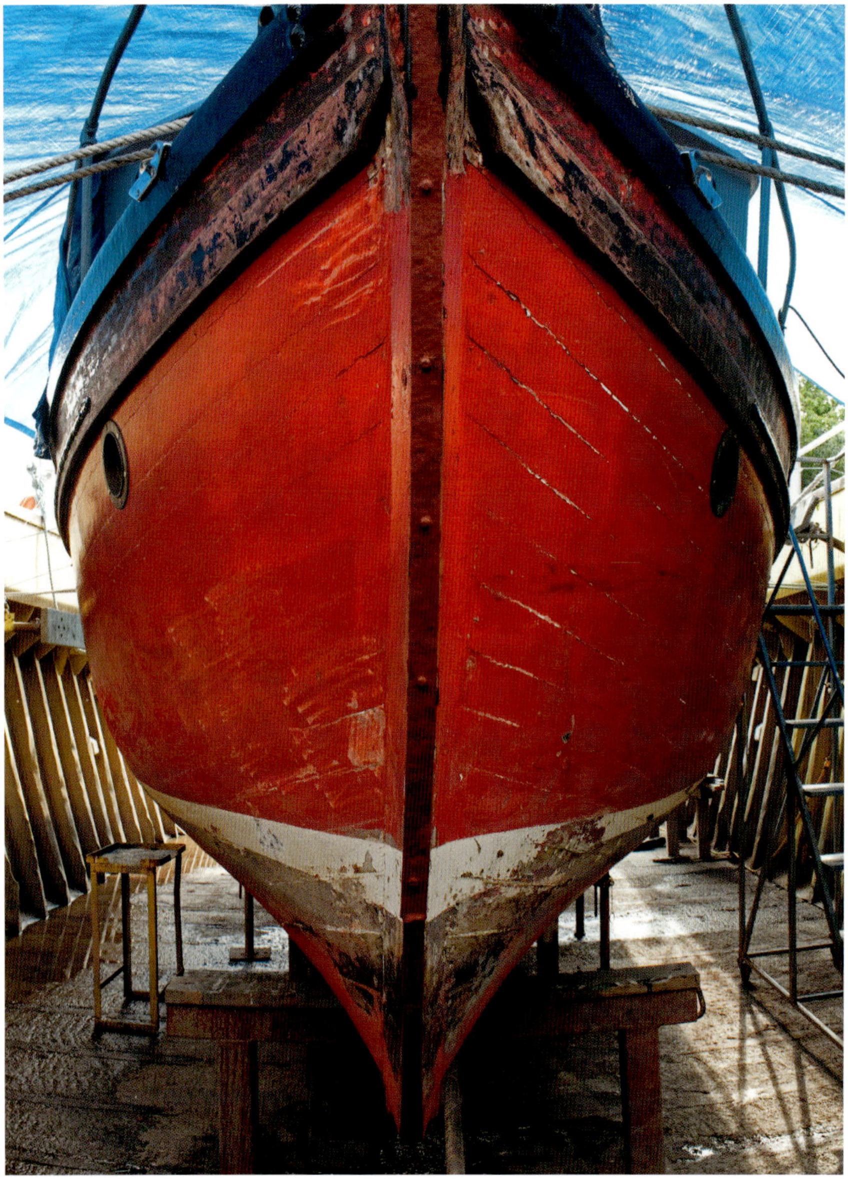

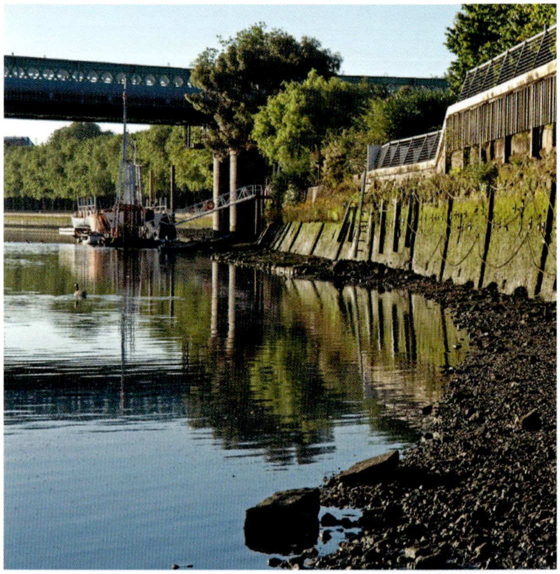

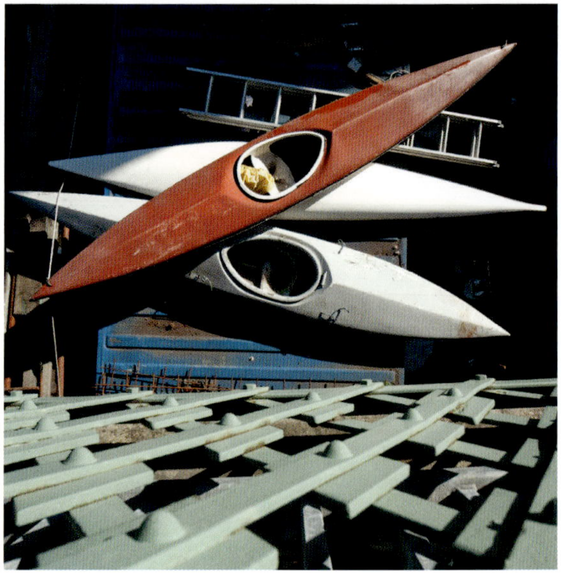

Fulham Football Club

Fulham Football Club has been a major fixture on the river since the club moved to its riverside location in 1896.

Bottom Right: Paddle Surfing is a fairly recent phenomenon on the river and is probably harder to master than first appears.

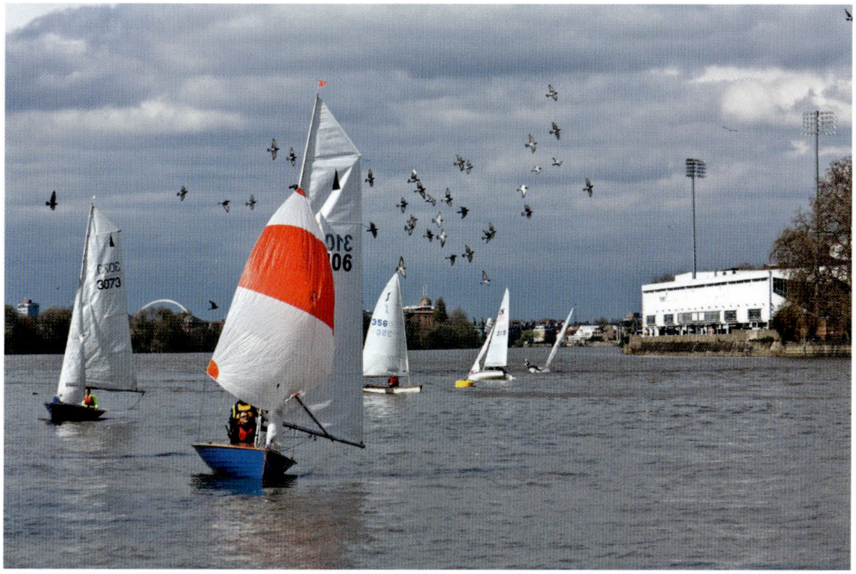

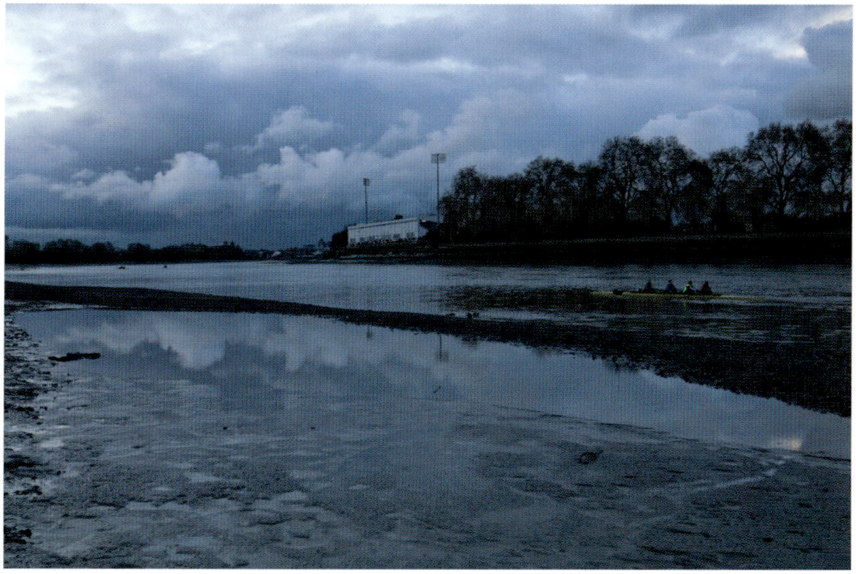

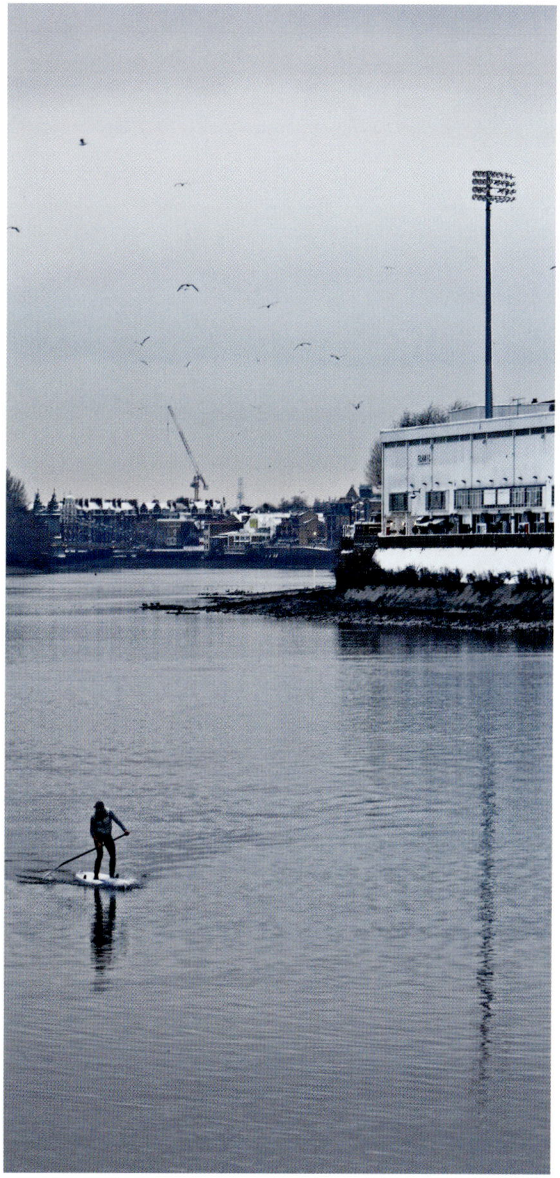

The Diamond Jubilee River Pageant

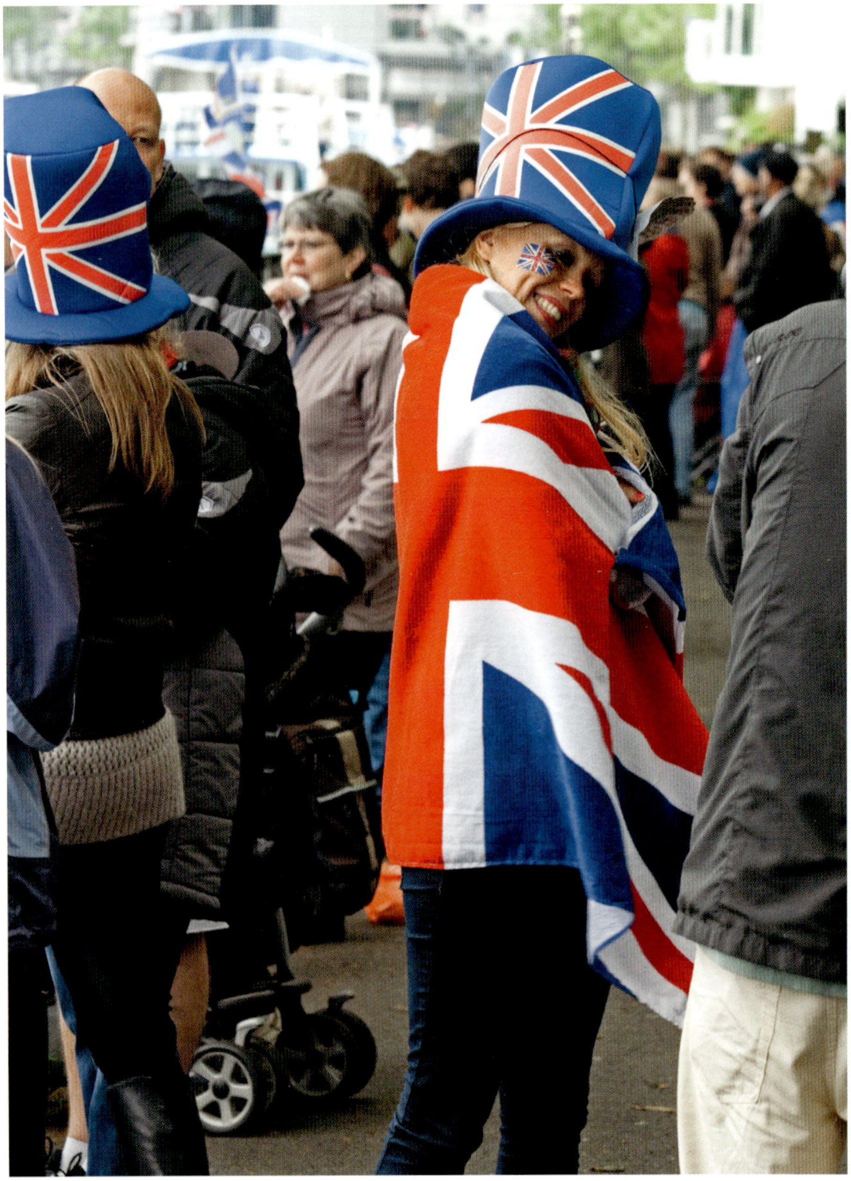

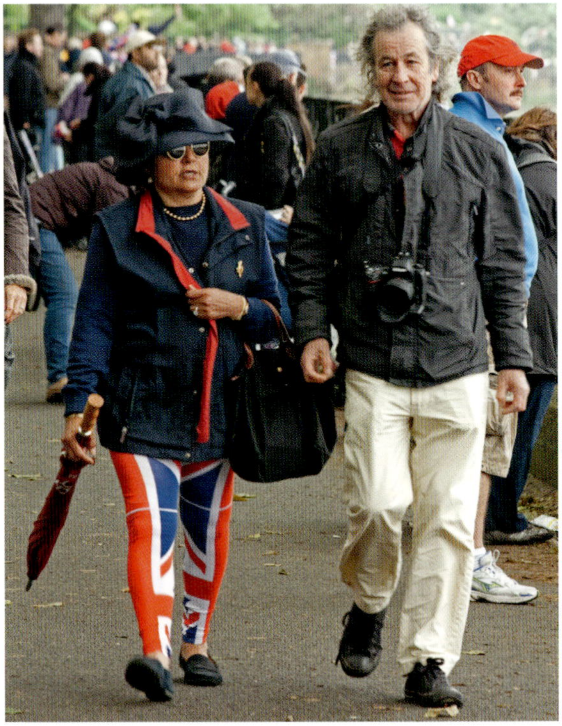

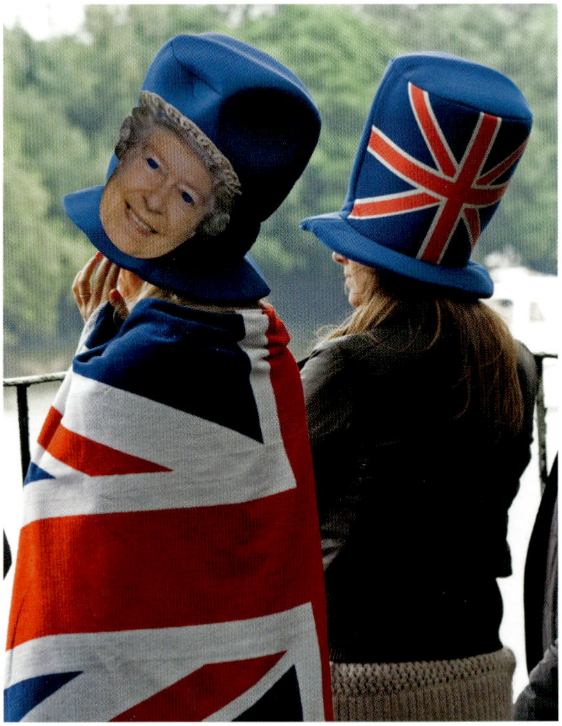

The Jubilee River Pageant was a major event back in June 2012, with a flotilla of over 1,000 boats taking part, many of which passed through Putney. Put on to celebrate the Queen's Diamond Jubilee, the event was a huge success, with thousands of people lining the route, many in fashionable Union Jack colours. The only shame was that we didn't have the weather to match. It was simply awful for the beginning of June. A particular highlight for local people in Putney, was the site of hundreds of small boats moored up along the river upstream of Putney Bridge (see picture overleaf).

Right and Bottom Right: Another striking feature of the day was all the Sea Cadets in their bright blue outfits, who set off from Putney Bridge. Each carried the flag of a Commonwealth nation on their boat, in honour of the Queen and her role as Head of the Commonwealth.

Below: The flagstone laid to commemorate the event near the river end of Festing Road.

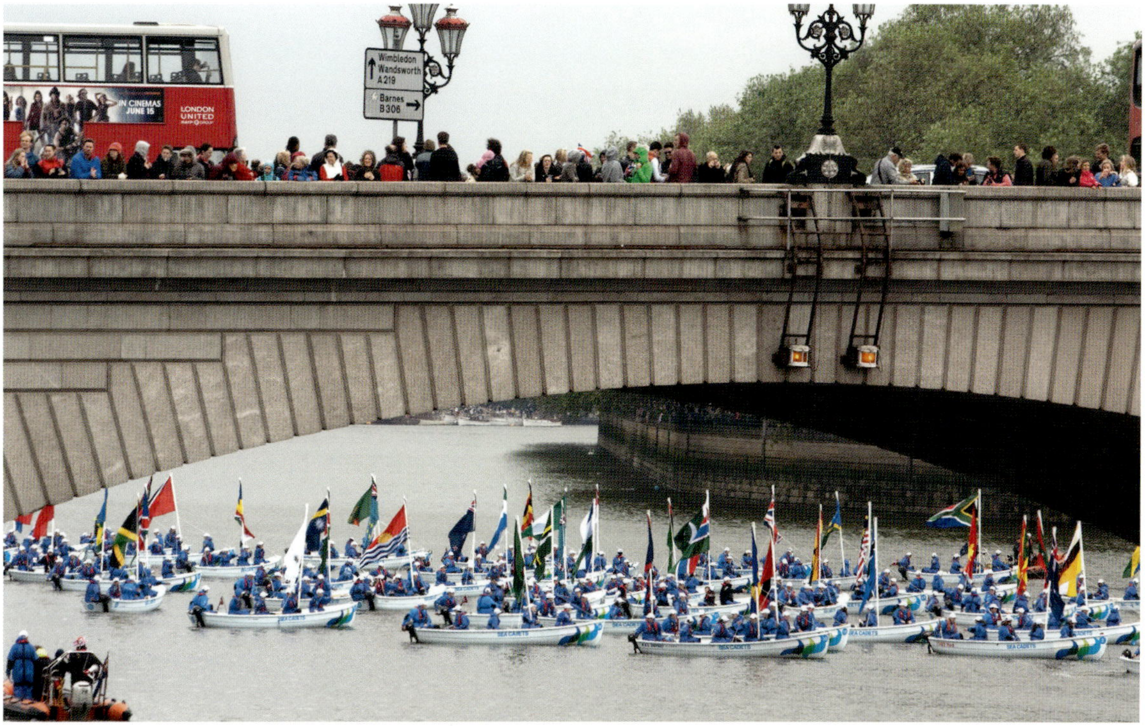

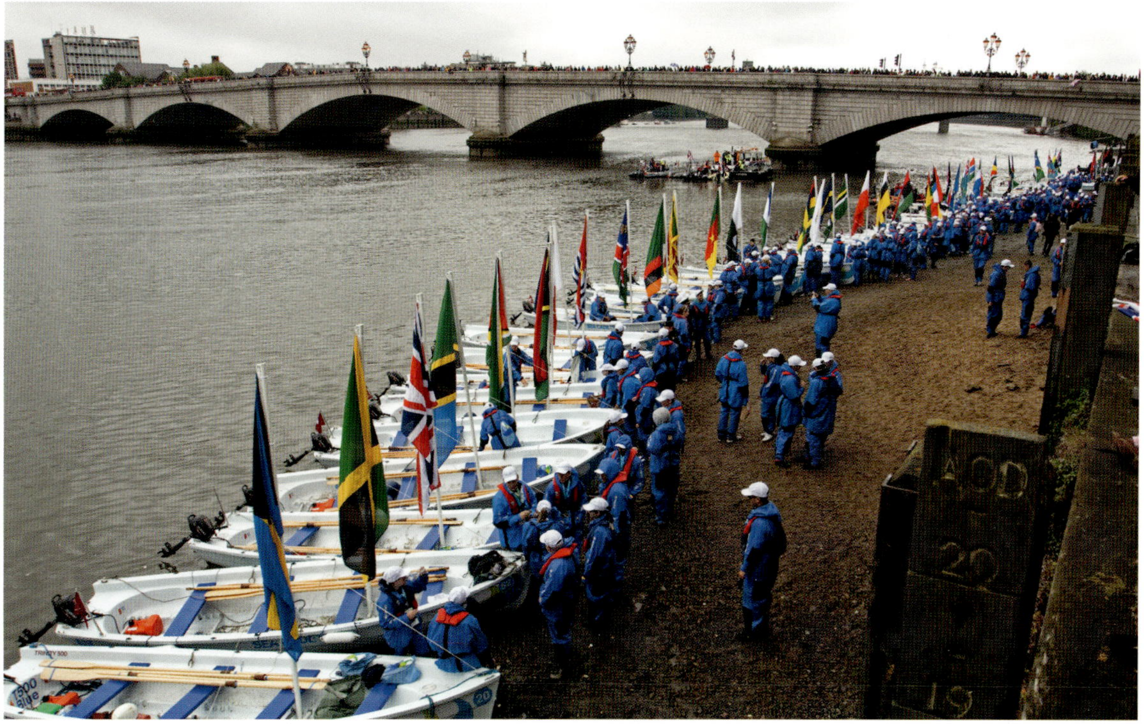

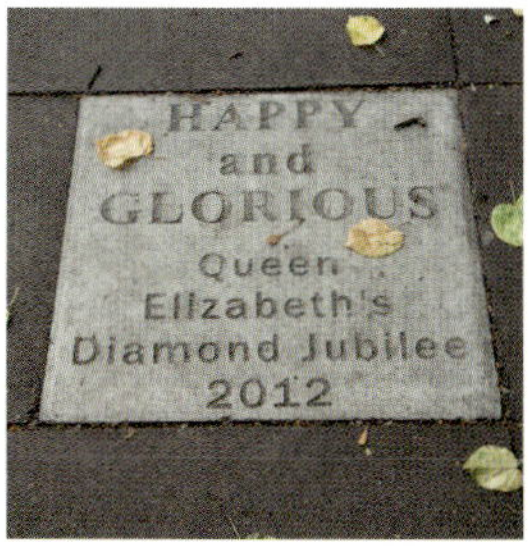

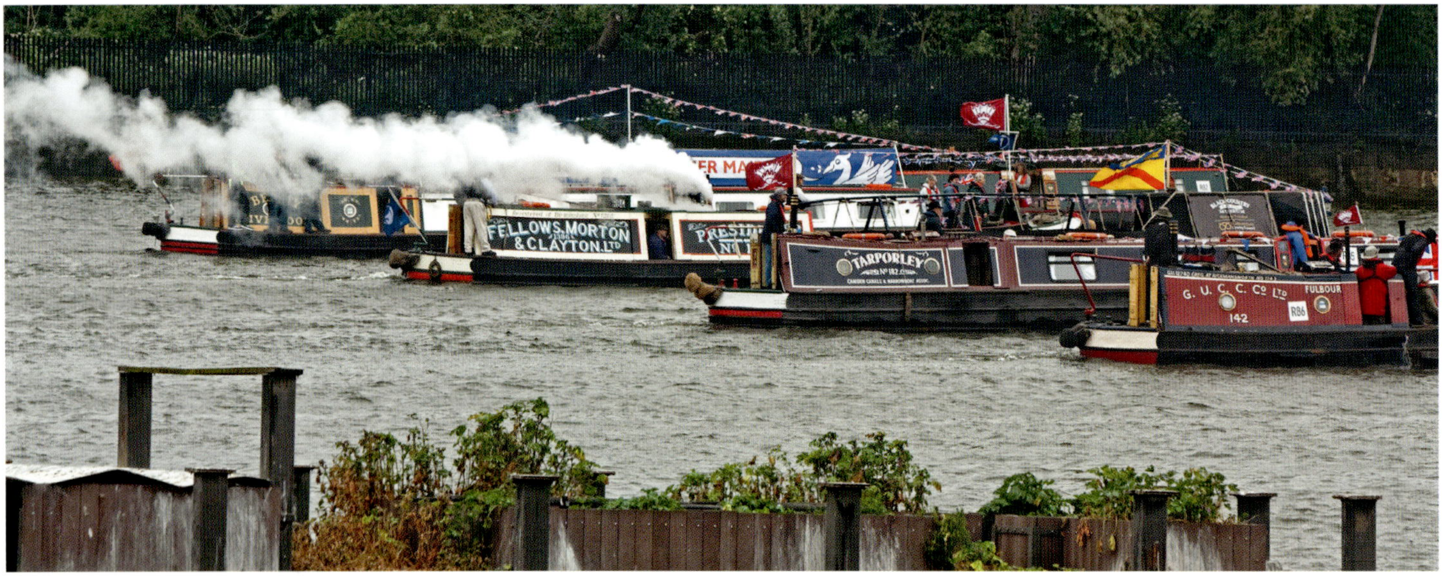

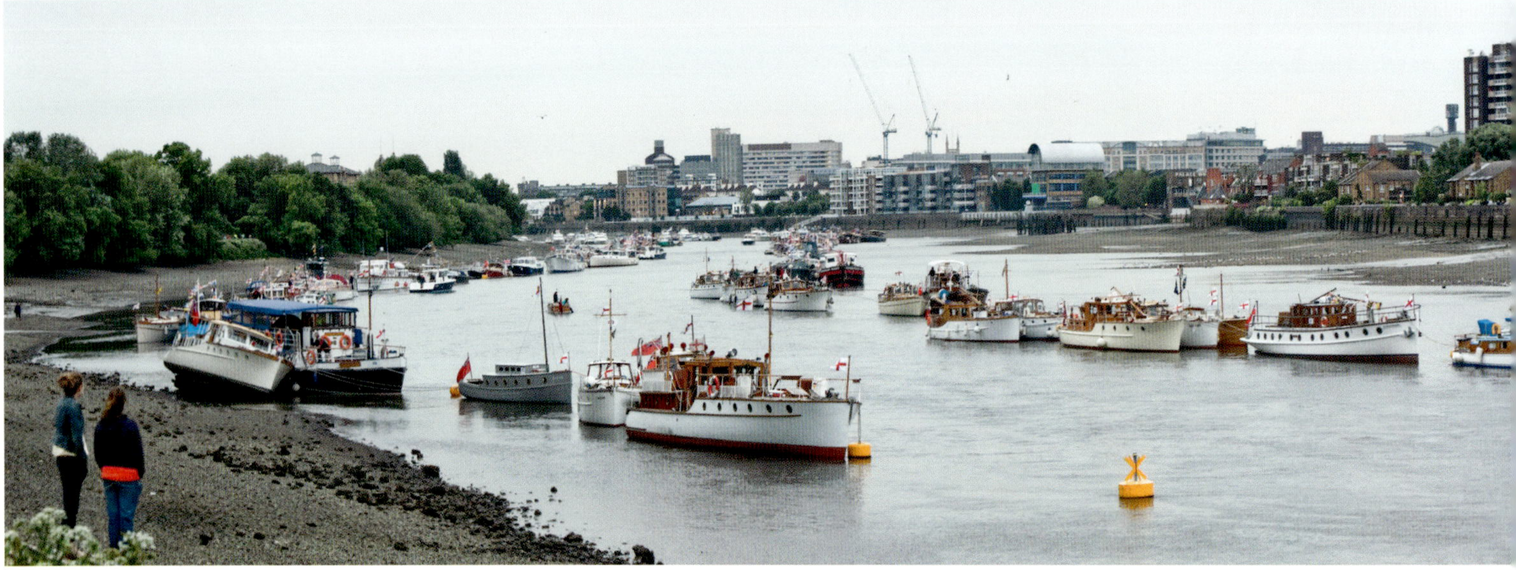

Top Left: All parts of the boating community took part. Here a group of Narrowboats pass Wandsworth Park.

Top Middle: The crowds in Wandsworth Park.

Top Right: Always a good view from Putney Bridge but the umbrellas tell you just what kind of day it was.

Above Left: Hundreds of small craft, some used in the evacuation of Dunkirk during the Second World War, moored up along the side of the river upstream of Putney and almost all the way to Hammersmith Bridge.

Bottom Right: The end of the day.

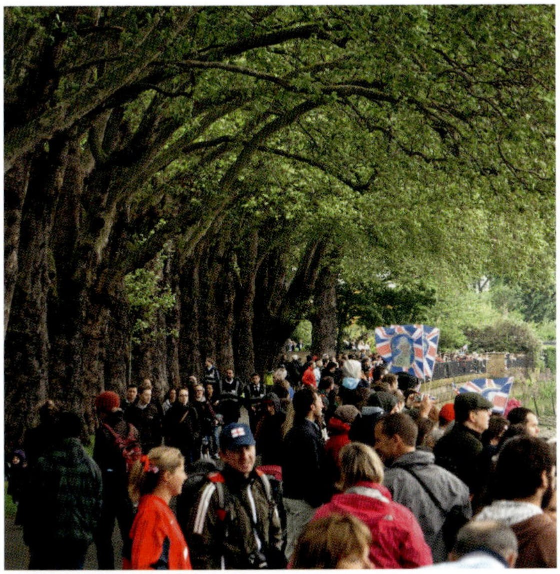

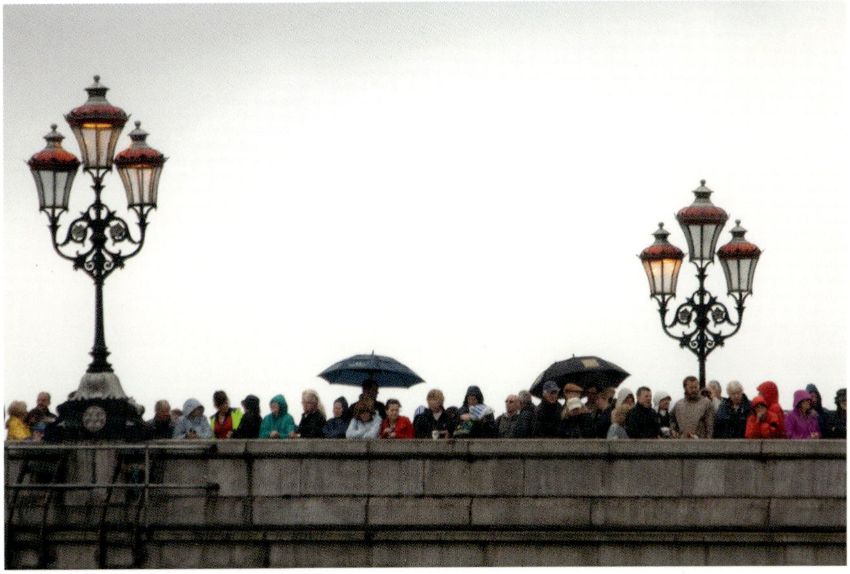

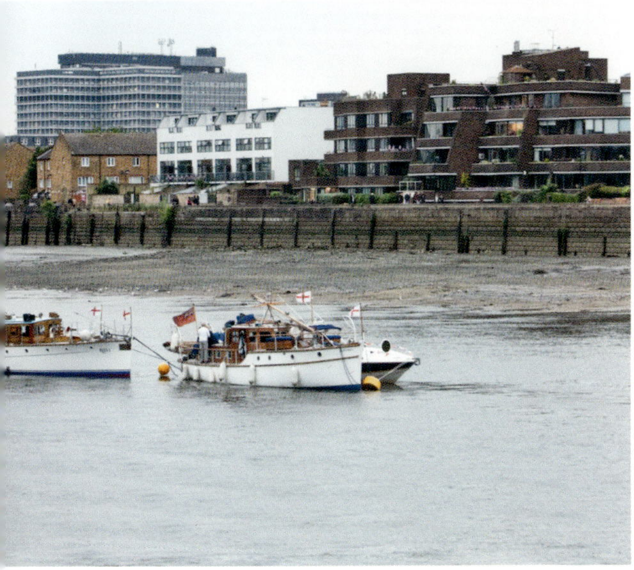

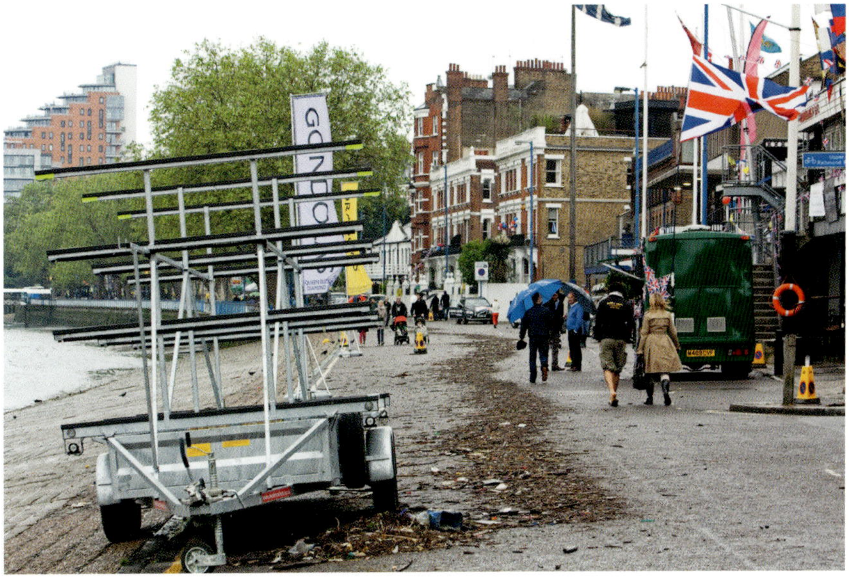

The Wharf

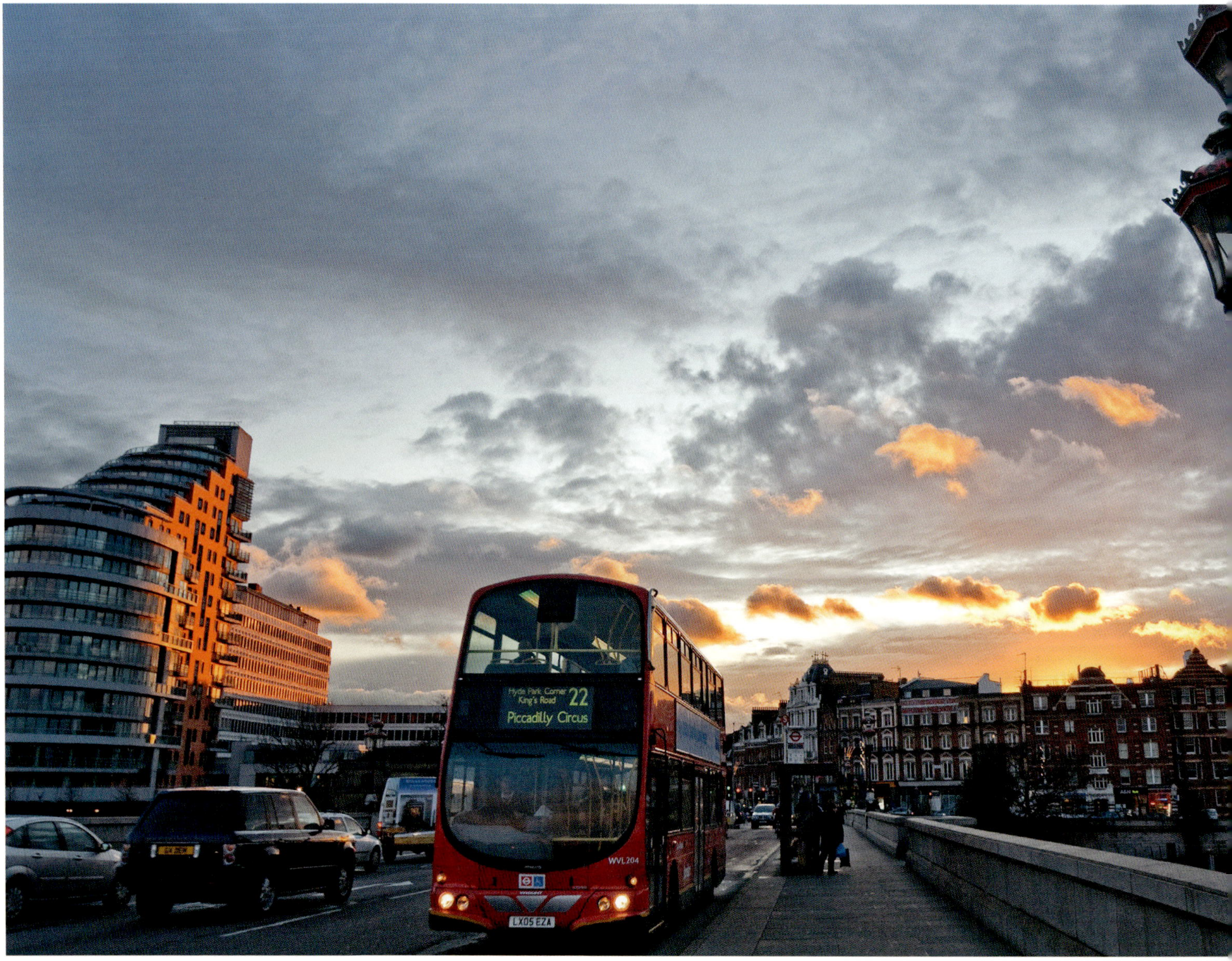
Hyde Park Corner
King's Road 22
Piccadilly Circus
WVL204
LX05 EZA

Given Putney's links with history, The Wharf Tower, with its striking design, is a recent addition to the river scene. Completed in 2004, this new building came as a redevelopment of an old office block, with the rather clever modification of a new curved piece to the front.

Left: Sunset over the Bridge.

Middle Top: The Wharf as viewed from the river.

Middle Bottom: The Wharf as viewed in the glass of a car parked in Deodar Road.

Overleaf: A spectacular sunrise in January.

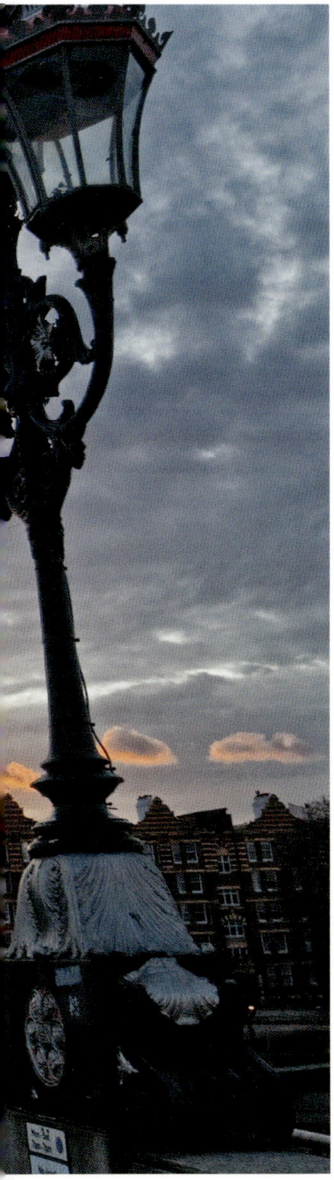

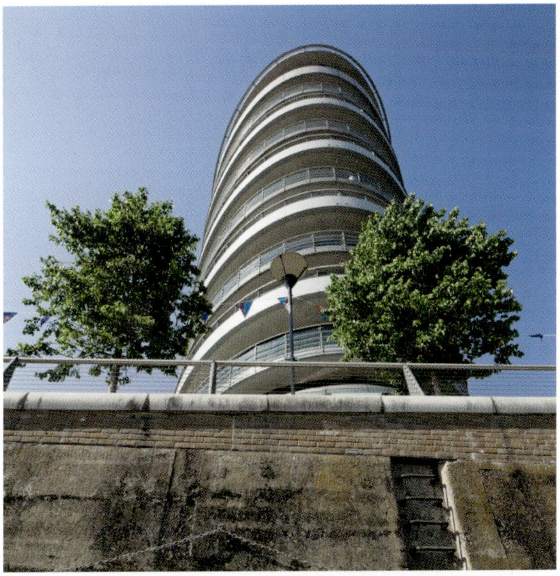

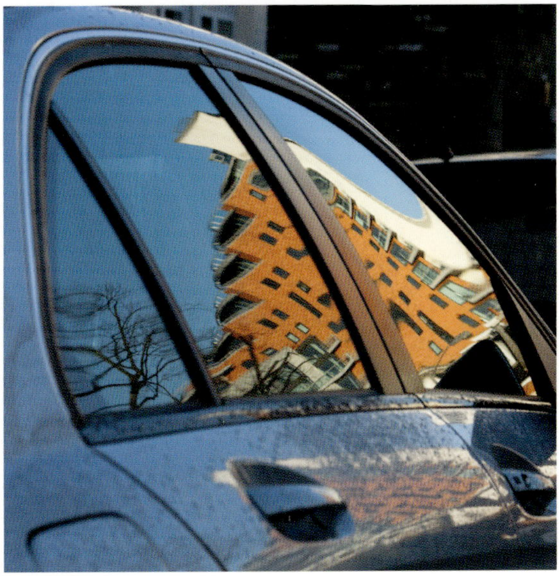

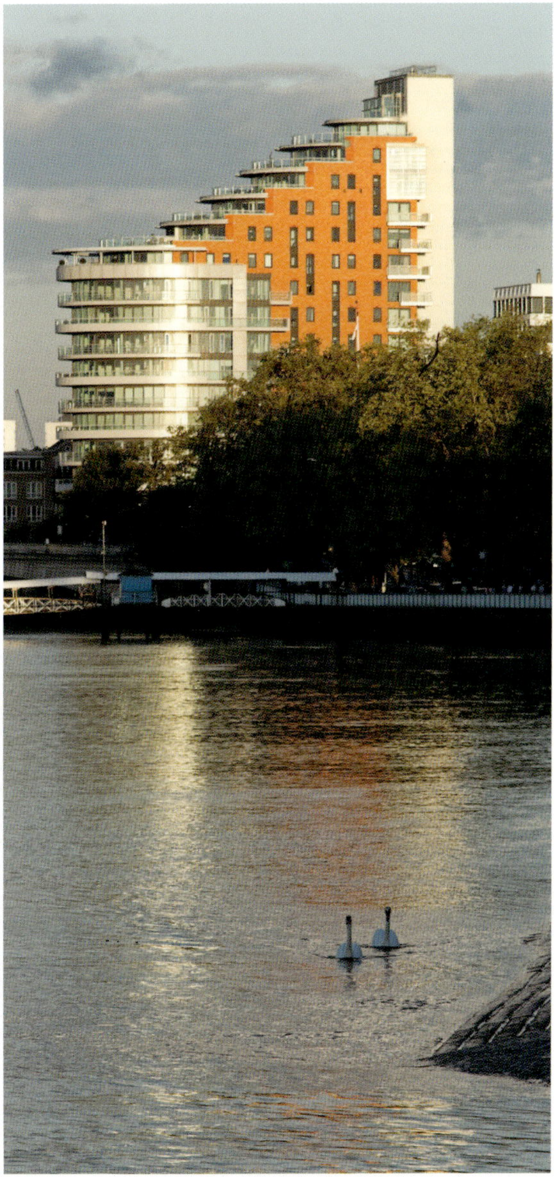

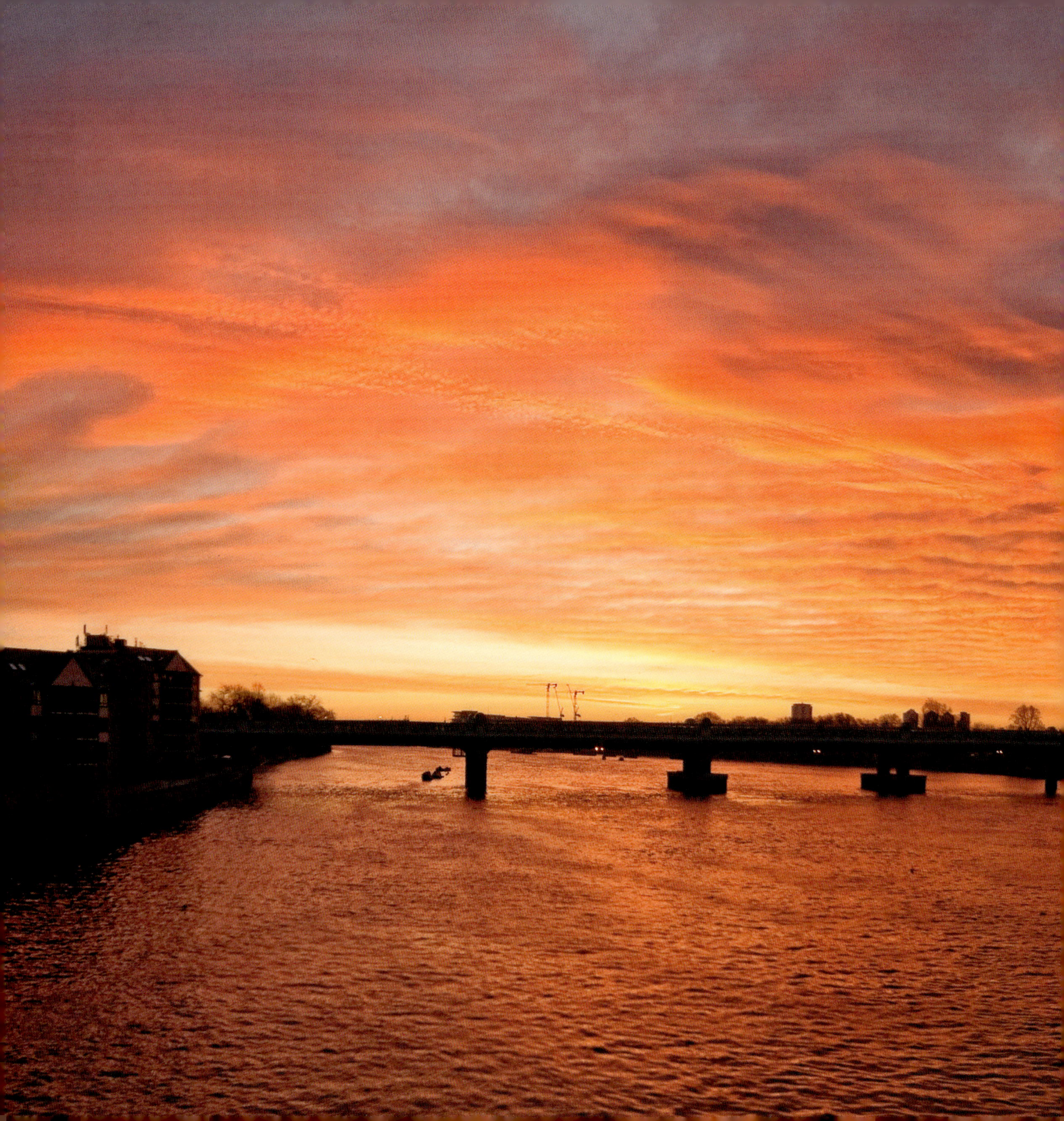

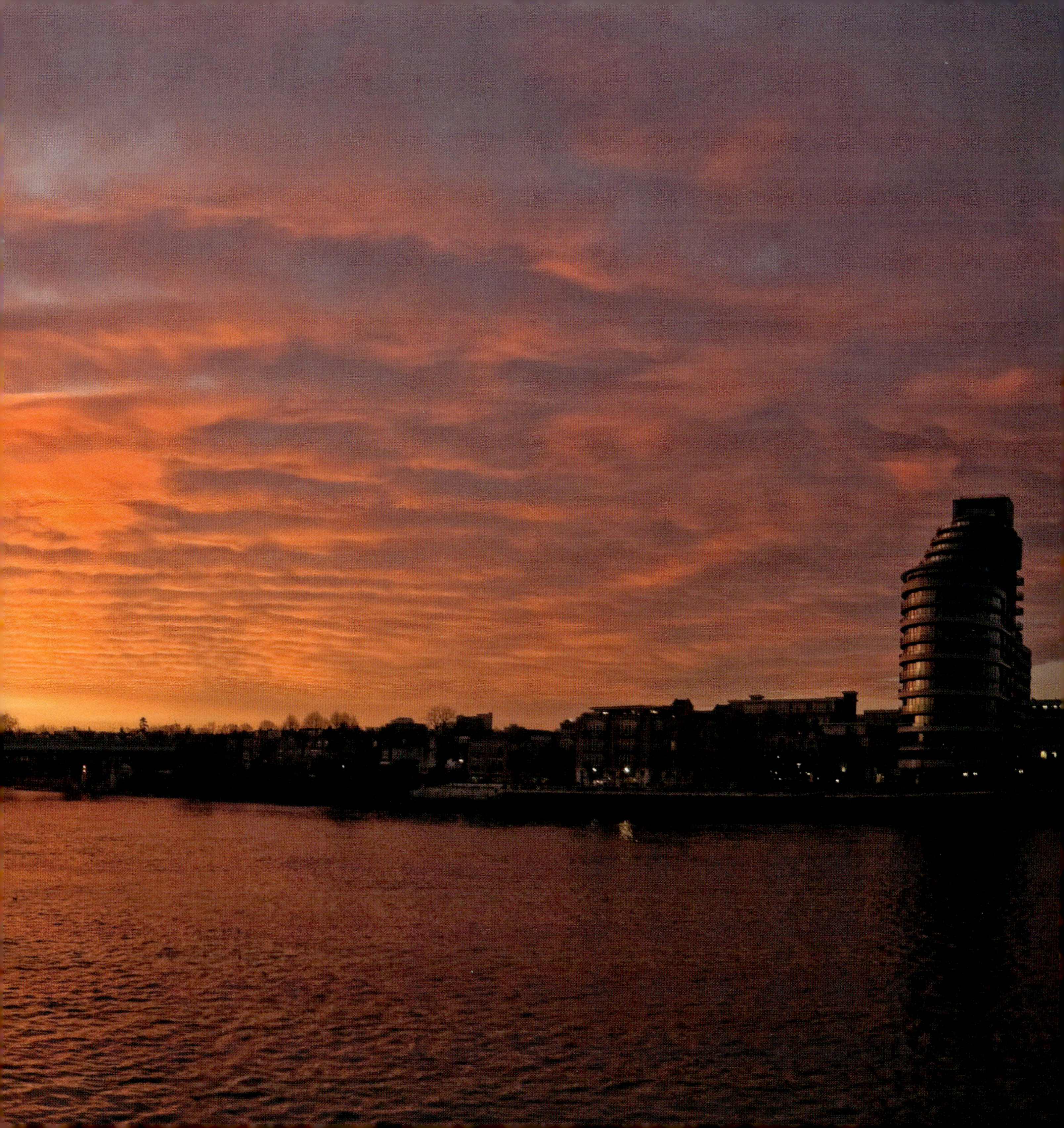

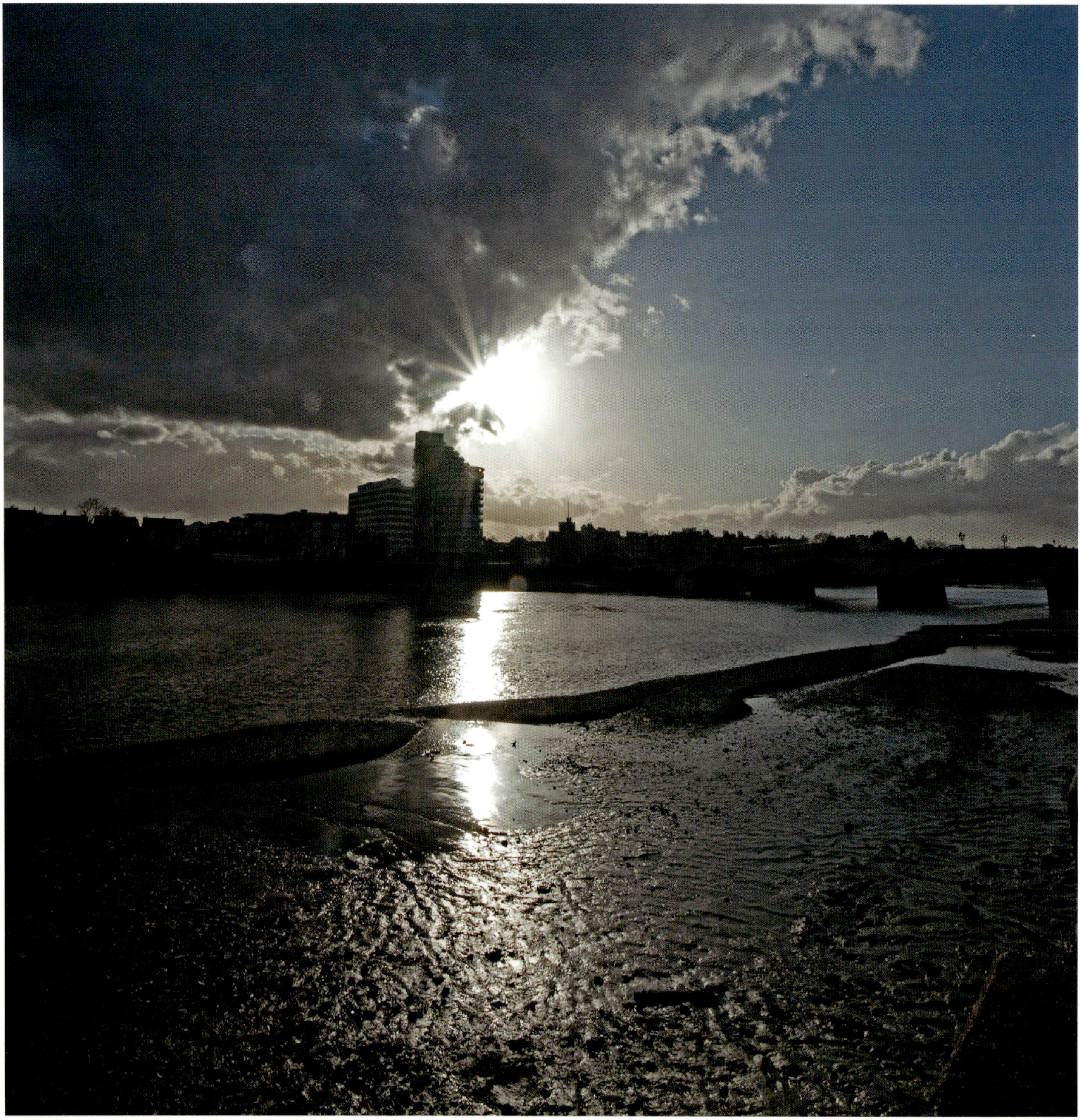

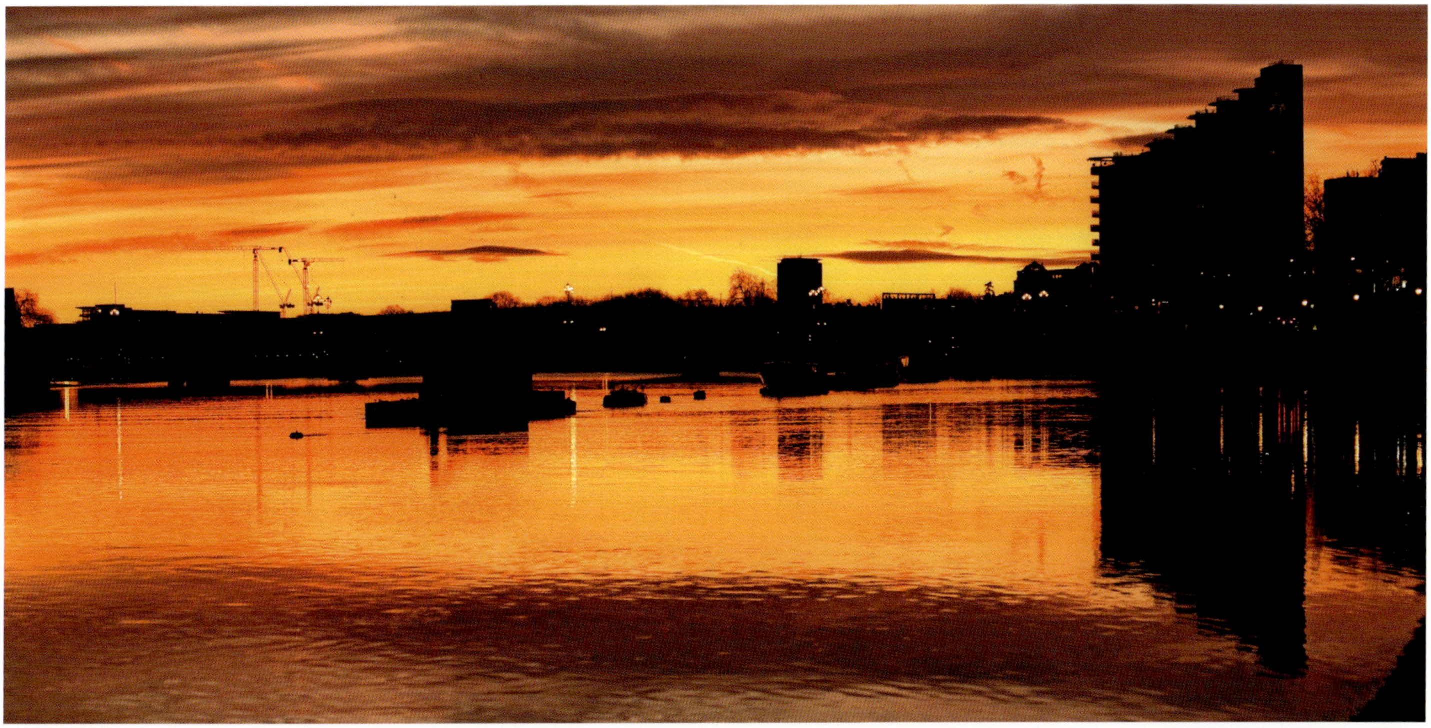

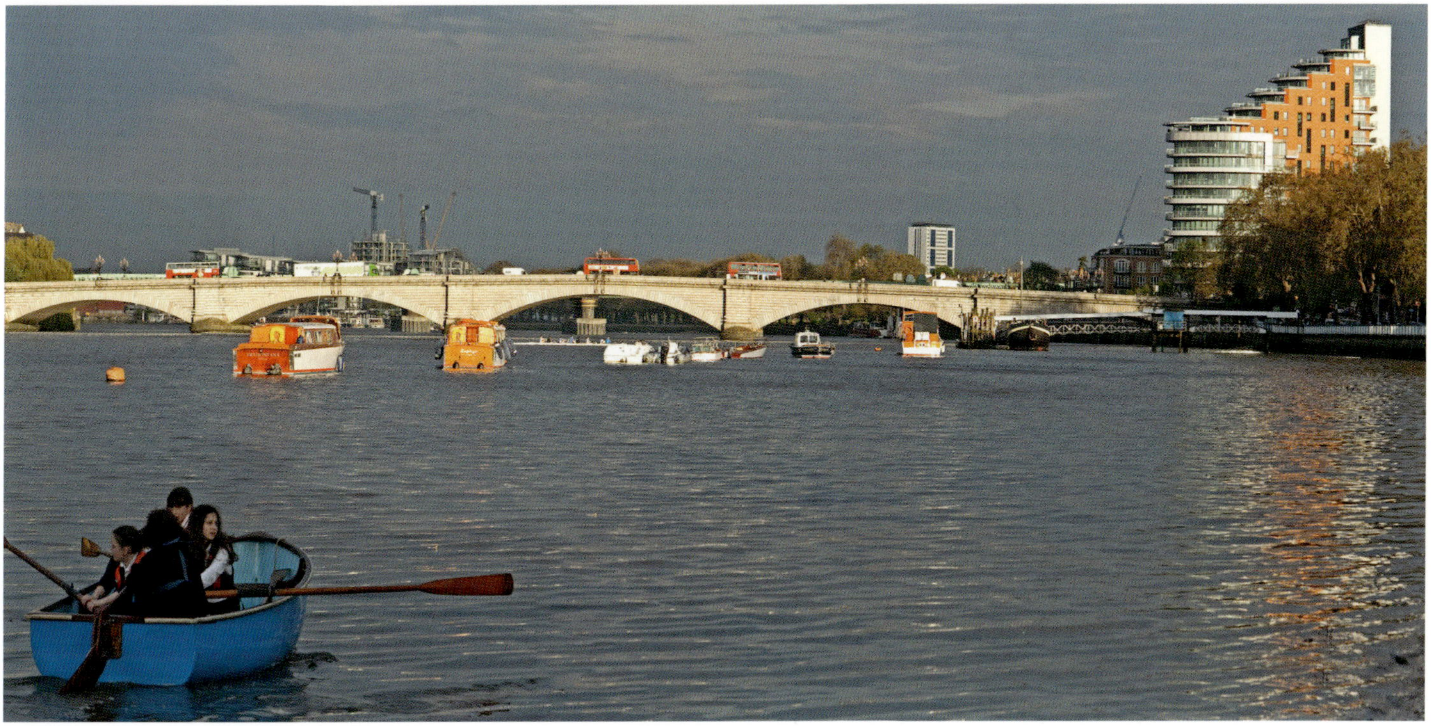

Street Scenes

Putney was for many years just a village on the Thames and for many Londoners, even a Queen (the first Elizabeth was a frequent visitor apparently), an escape to the fresh air from the nastier aspects of the old City of London. Thus it remained until rapid expansion in the 1800s, with the coming of the railway and the loss of the last 'great houses', bar Winchester (see page 82) in the 1880s. From the loss of these houses came five of the High Street's 'feeder roads' – Disraeli, Werter & Montserrat on the east side, and Norroy & Chelverton on the west. Despite this, Putney still retains a lot of character, from the charm of streets like Parkfields, Charlwood and the streets that make up the Riverside area to the wider expanses and larger houses of roads such as Chartfield Avenue. Take a closer look and further delights can be found: back on the High Street the handsome façade above Cashino Amusements, for example, site of Putney's first Boots store (1907), and the busts of Salisbury and Disraeli above the shops between Norroy & Chelverton Roads. The former Zeeta House (see page 62), at the south end of the High Street, Lloyds TSB, and the first floors above Paddy Power, Top Shop and Marks & Spencer all sport Art Deco features. Moreover, for those with eyes to seek and time to linger, the often tree-lined side streets offer examples of attractive, architecture and decoration, take the wonderful, if a little quirky busts off Deodar Road.

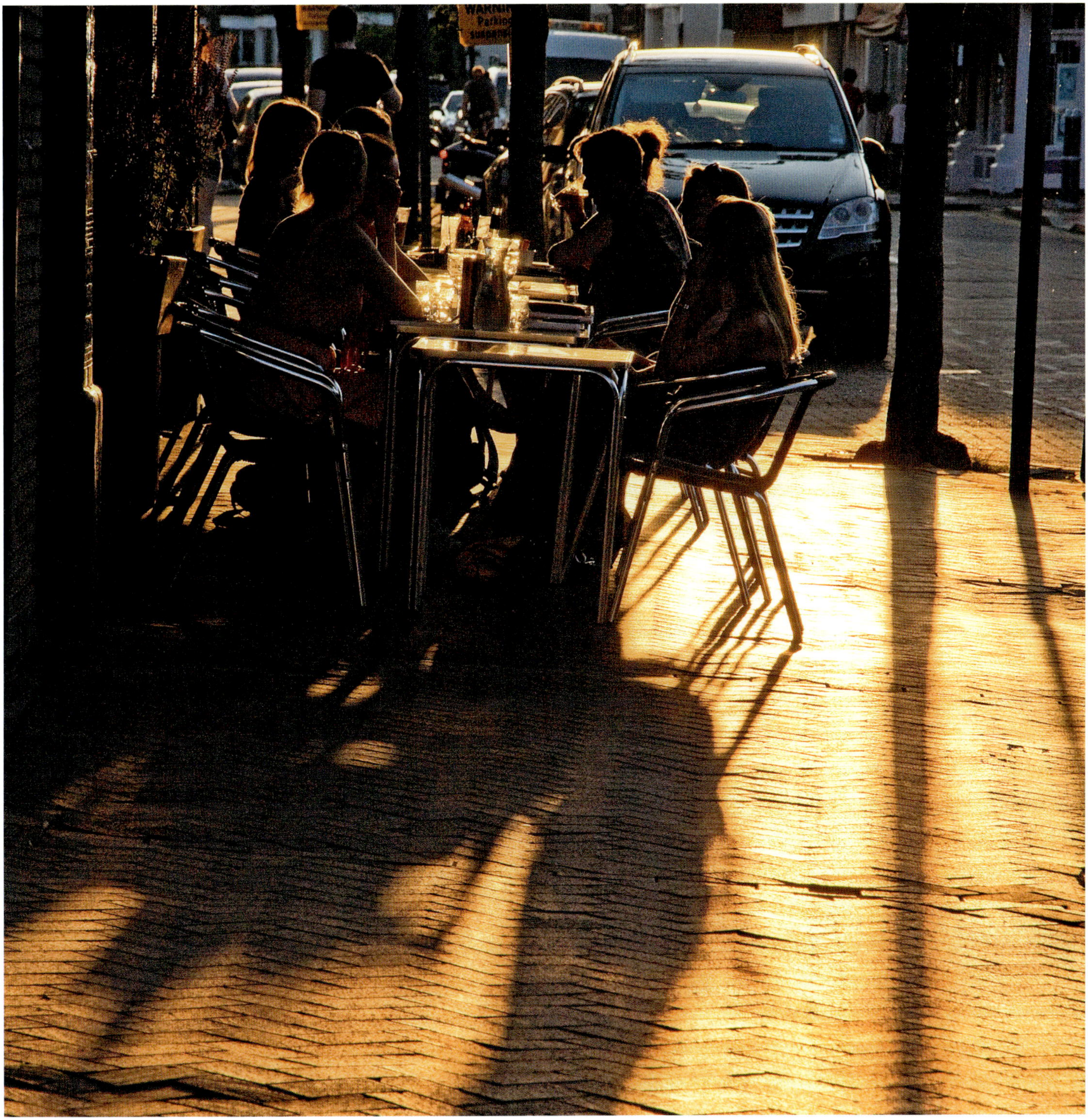

The Centre

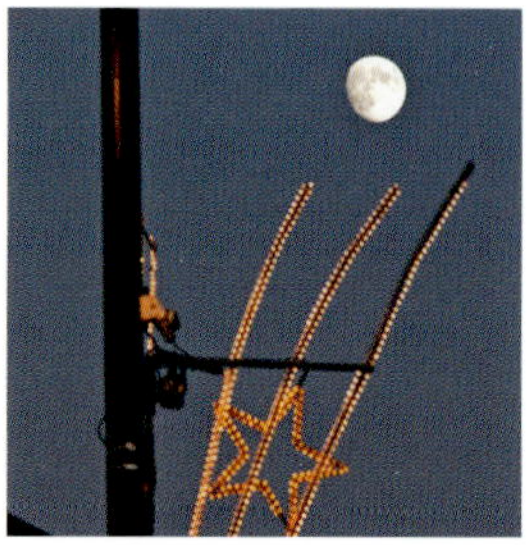

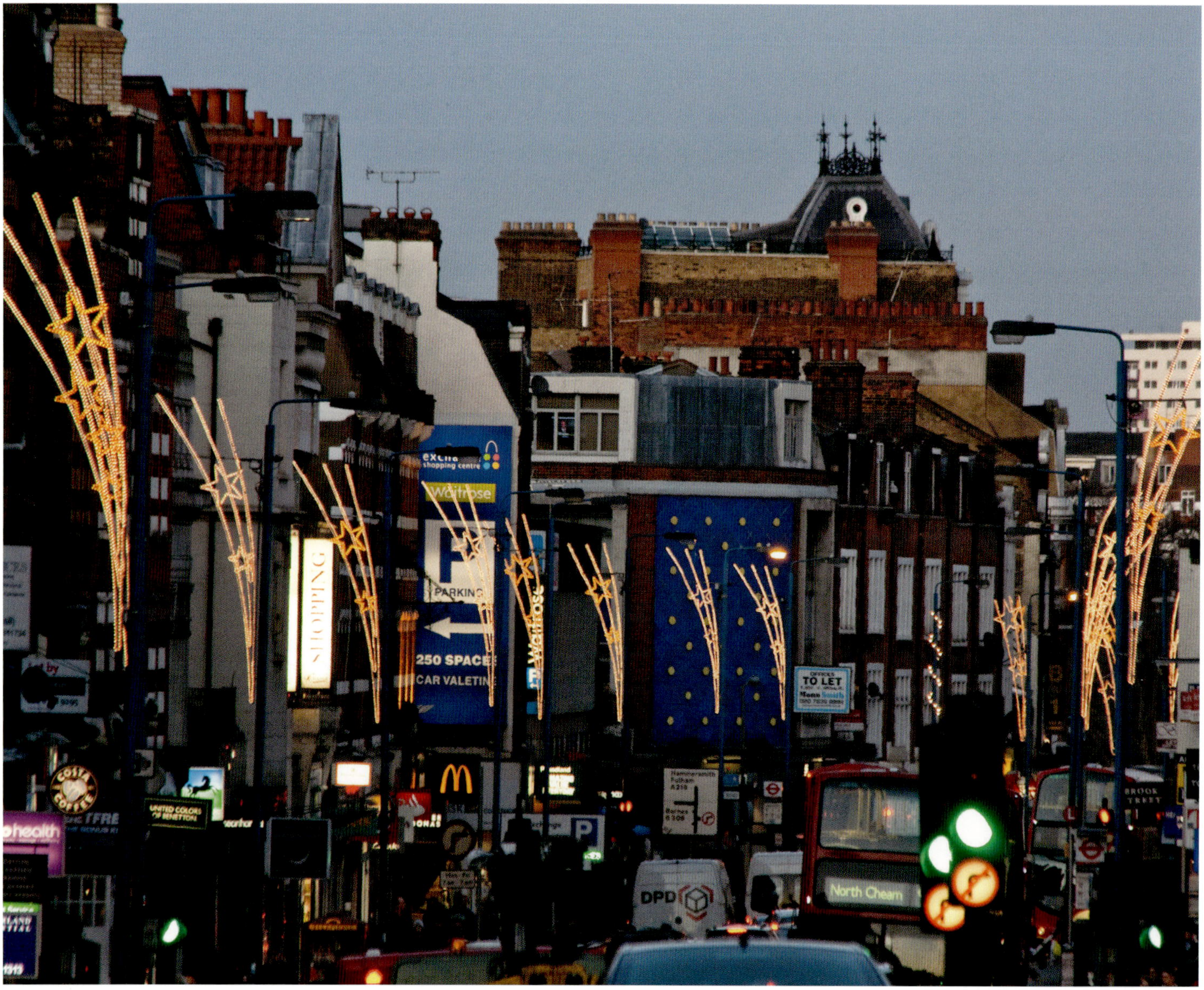
Waitrose
PARKING
250 SPACE
CAR VALETIN
SHOPPING
Waitrose
TO LET
North Cheam
DPD
COSTA COFFEE
UNITED COLORS OF BENETTON

Previous Page: Café life in Lacy Road late one summer's evening.

Opposite: Christmas Lights on Putney High Street.

This page: The railway line as it approaches Putney.The station has been radically transformed since these pictures were taken.

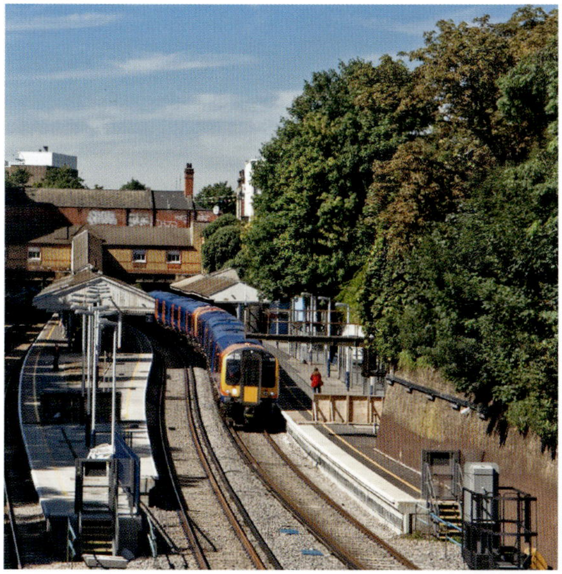

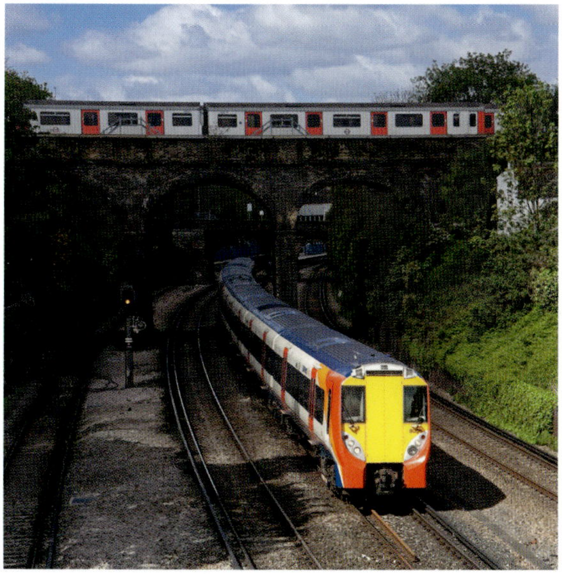

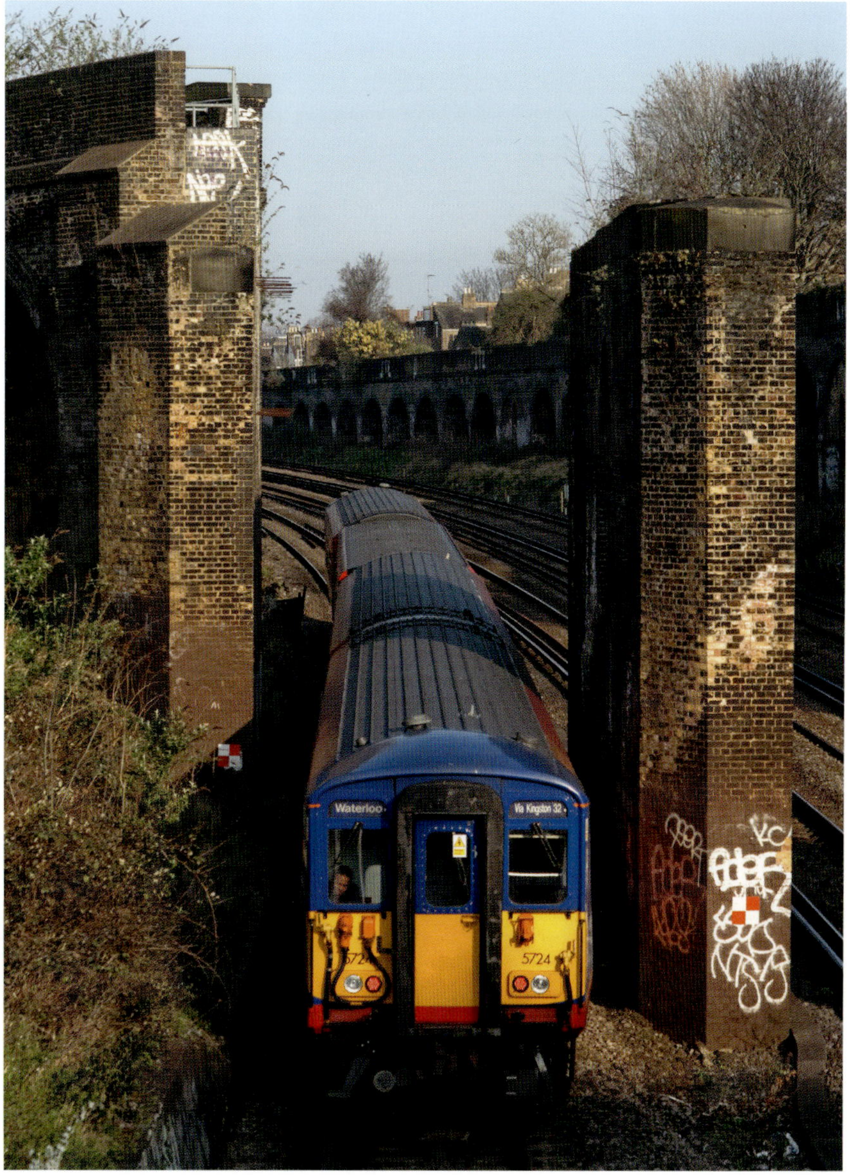

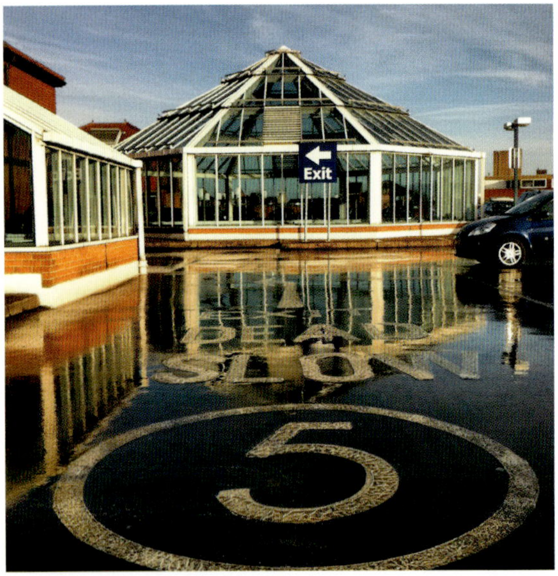

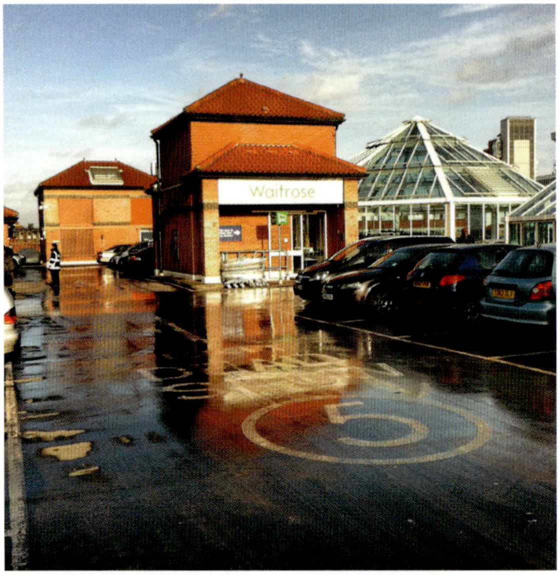

Top: Car park on top of the Exchange.

Below: The Library in Disraeli Road.

Opposite top left: Huttons in the Exchange.

Opposite top right: Shops on Upper Richmond Road just off the High Street.

Opposite bottom right: Waterstone's in the Exchange

Opposite bottom left: Vipul at the door of his shop Farrago in The Exchange; Vipul has been a great supporter of my book since it came out.

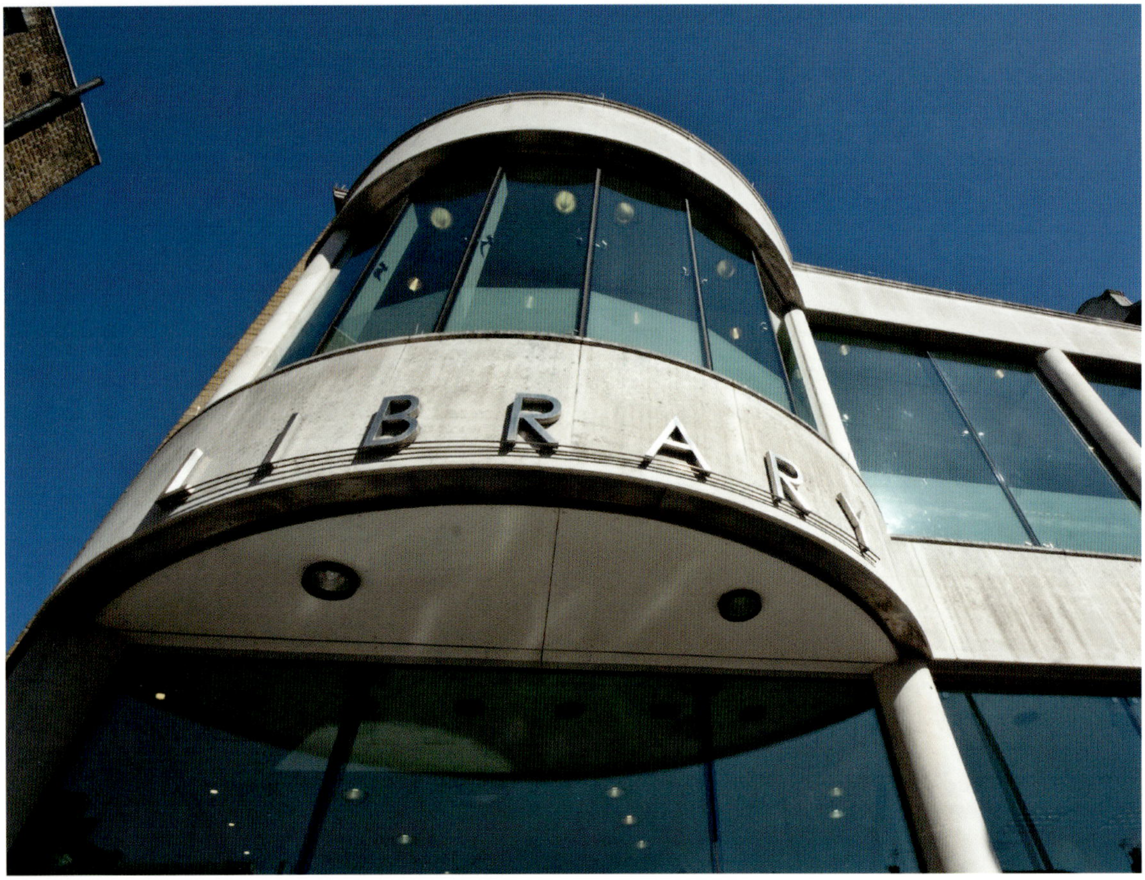

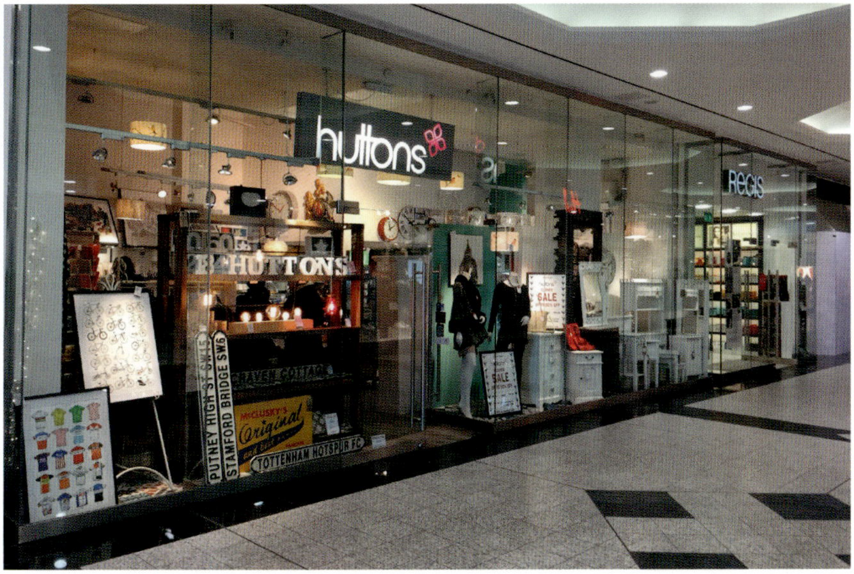
huttons
REGIS
PUTNEY HIGH ST SW15
STAMFORD BRIDGE SW6
TOTTENHAM HOTSPUR FC

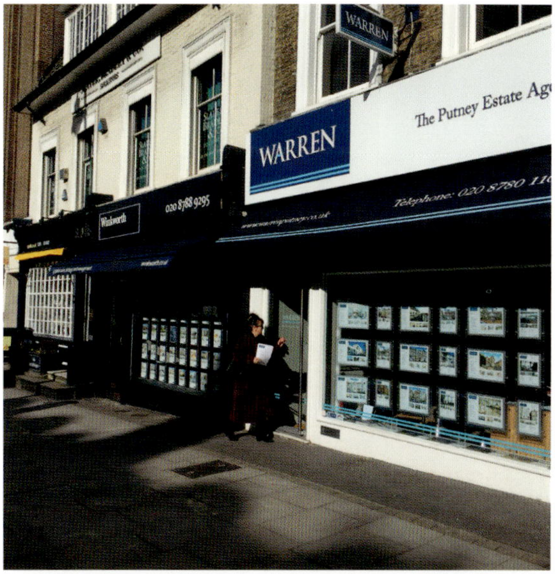
WARREN
WARREN
The Putney Estate

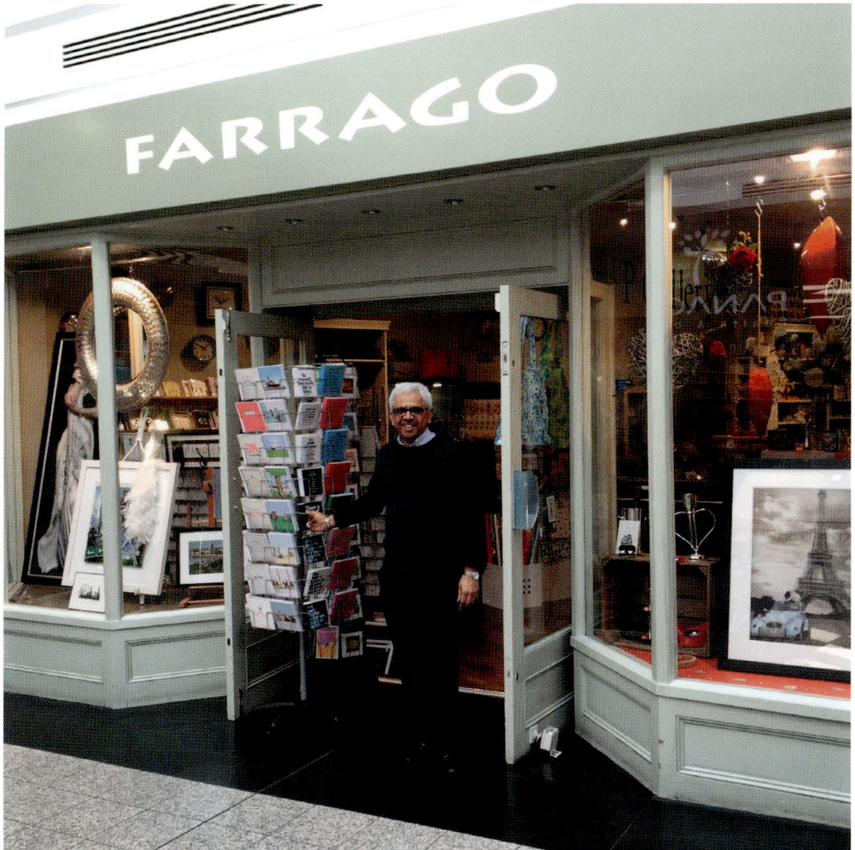
FARRAGO

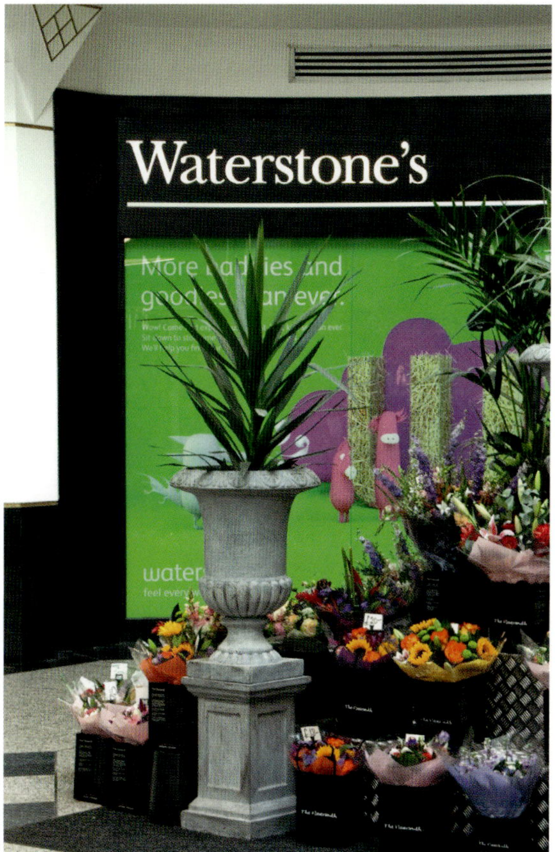
Waterstone's

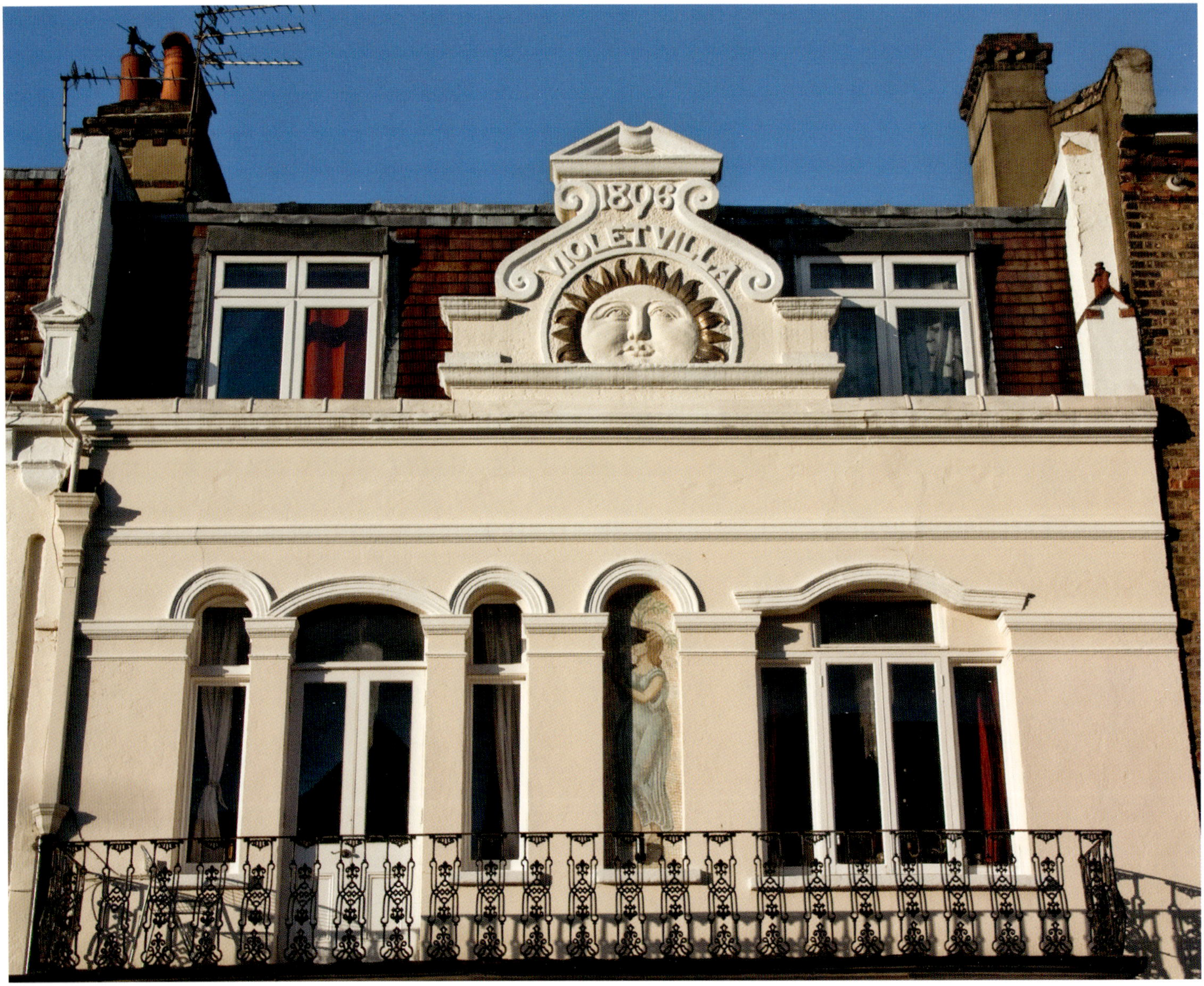

Above: The impressive
Violet Villa in Disraeli Road.

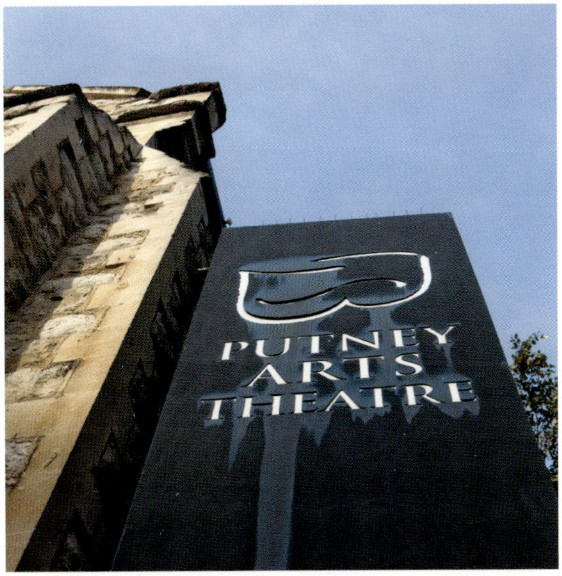

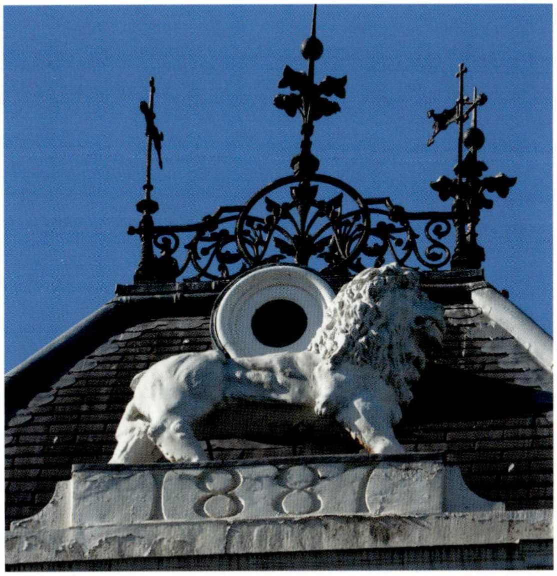

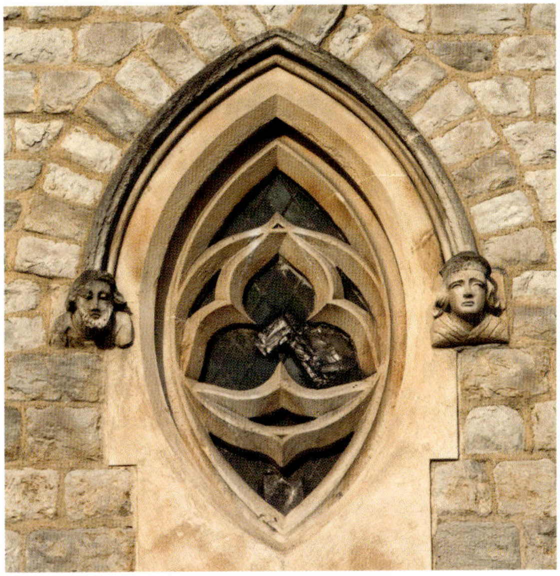

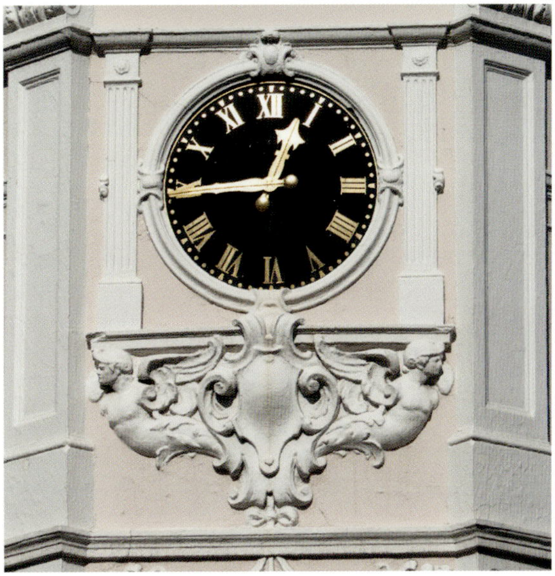

Above: The Putney Arts Theatre on the Upper Richmond Road. Formed in the early 1960s, the local arts group moved into the old Union Church in 1968, which by this time had become council property and who were only too pleased to support such an enterprise.

Top Right: The White Lion was a substantial 17th century (possibly earlier) inn close to the ferry landing, though subordinate in importance to its neighbour The Red Lion – venue for the annual parish dinner and sessions of the manor court. It was rebuilt in the 1870s and again, as we see it now, in 1887. Tradition has it that the splendid lion sculpture which adorns its façade was transferred from building to building, though subtle differences suggest that the present version was newly created. As is now the trend, its name has morphed through Slug & Lettuce, Litten Tree, Walkabout and Wahoo and, as at late 2012, it had closed. Since closing Wahoo is likely to re-open as a 'boutique' hotel.

Above: The clock on the corner of Norroy Road and Putney High Street.

The Olympic Games

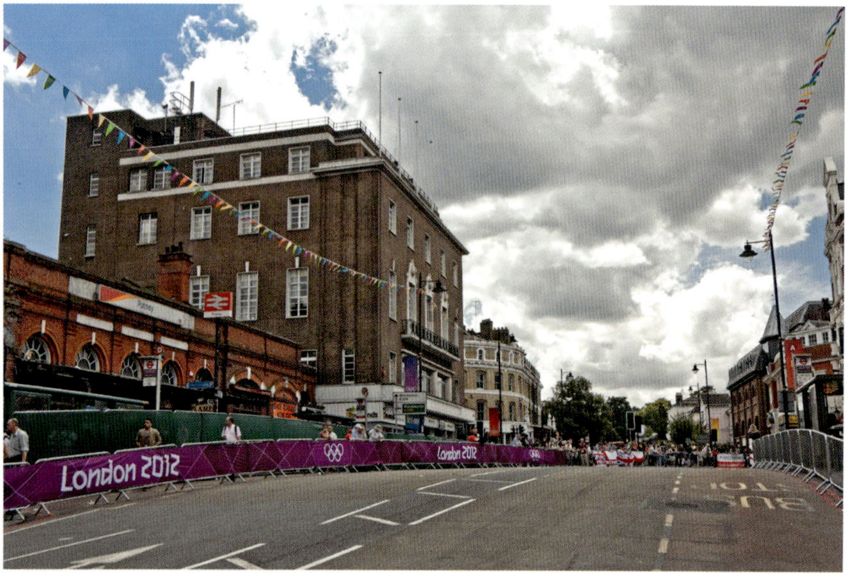

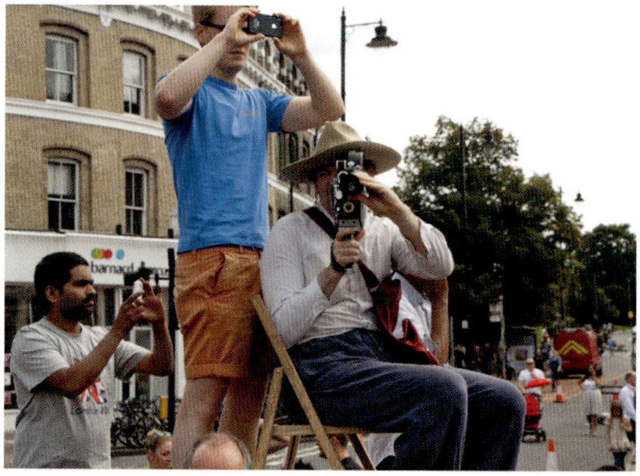

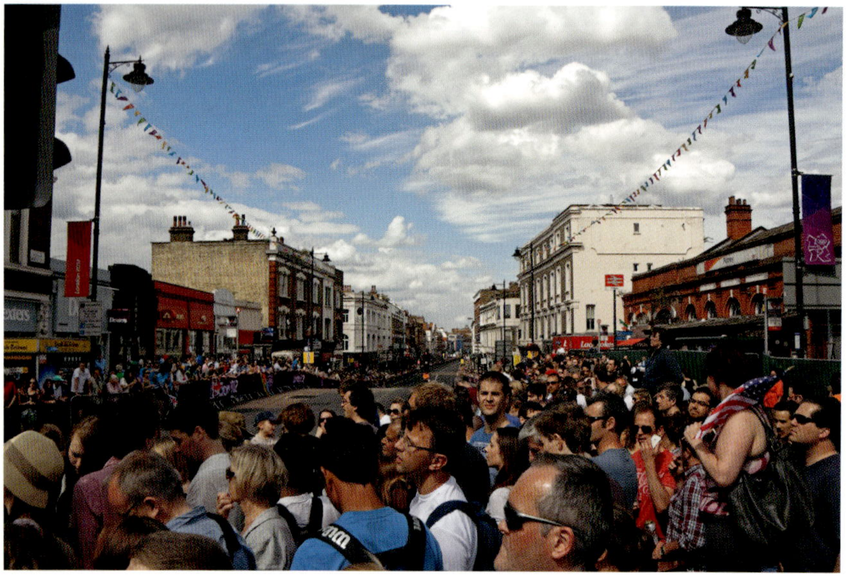

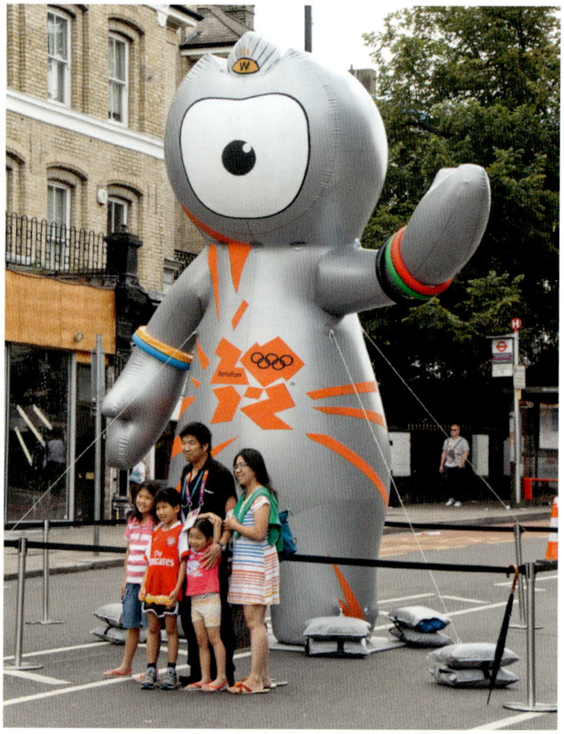

Opposite Page Top Left: On the left is the Art Deco-influenced former Zeeta House, designed by Bernard George FRIBA and opened in 1938.

One exciting aspect of the London Olympics was the cycle races, which came straight through the centre of Putney. The roads were closed and thousands of people came out to cheer. Even the sun came out on the first day.

Overleaf: The returning pack of cyclists as viewed along the Upper Richmond Road as they approached the turn on to the High Street, including out front two of our British heroes, Bradley Wiggins and Mark Cavendish.

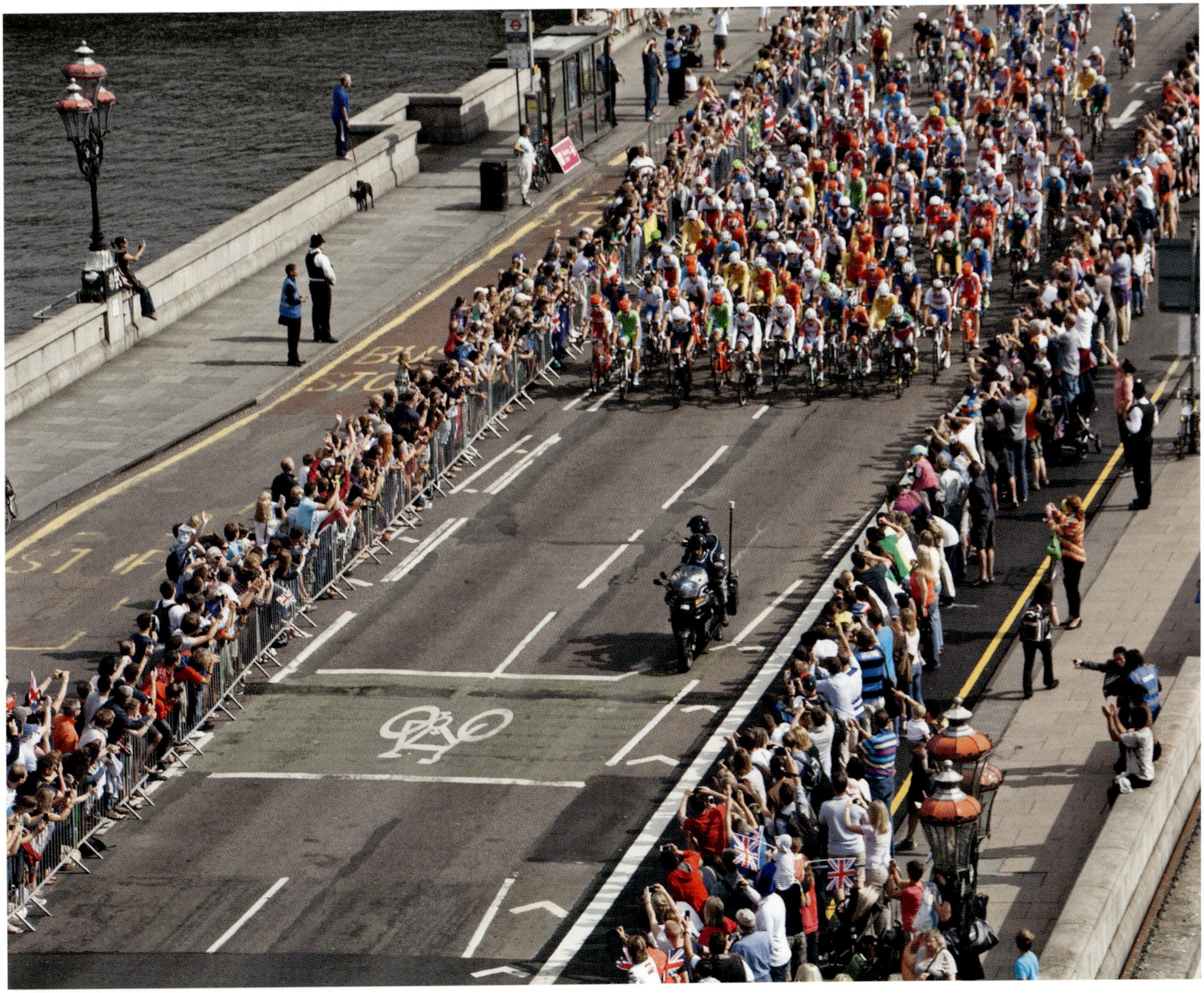

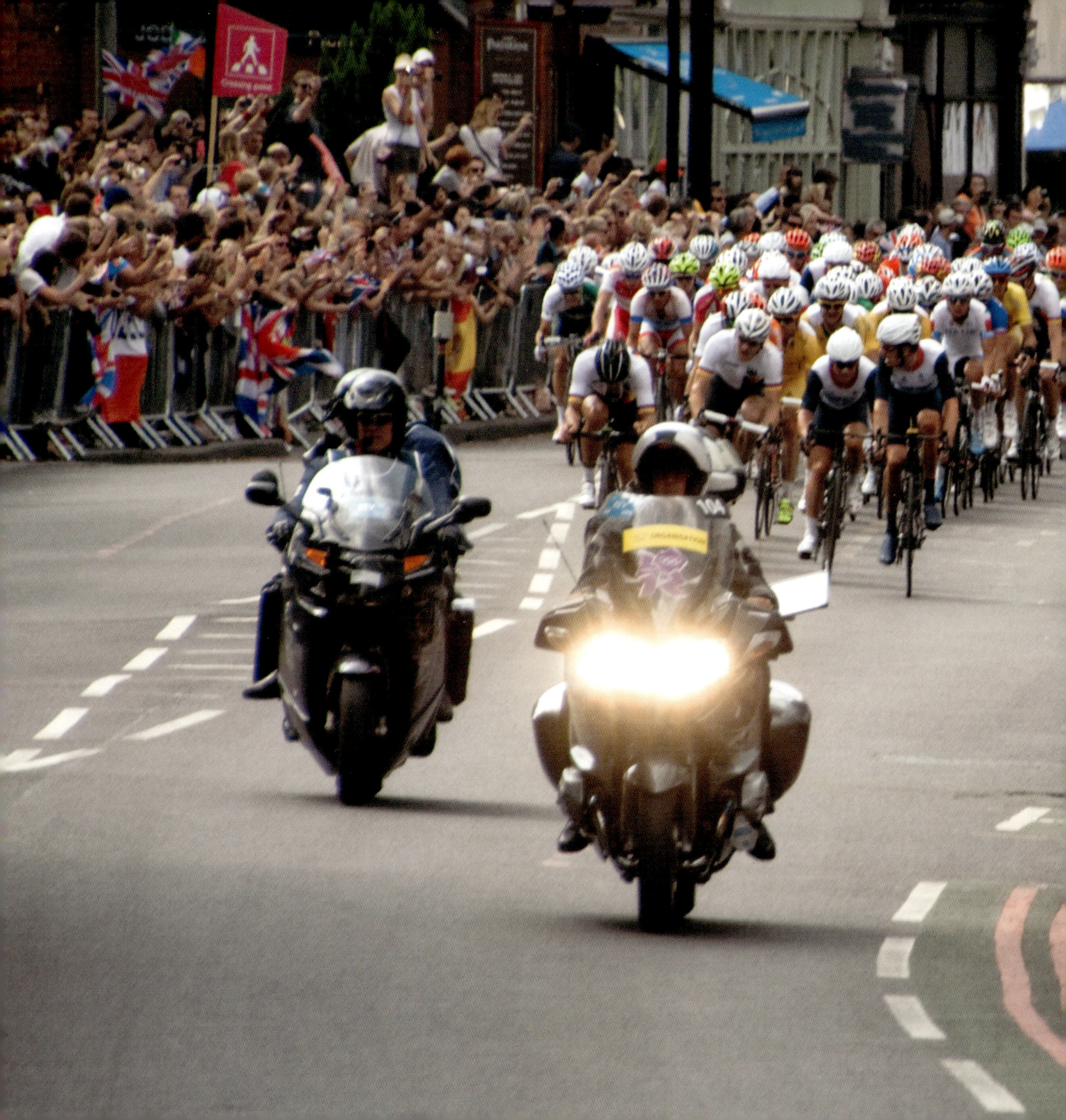

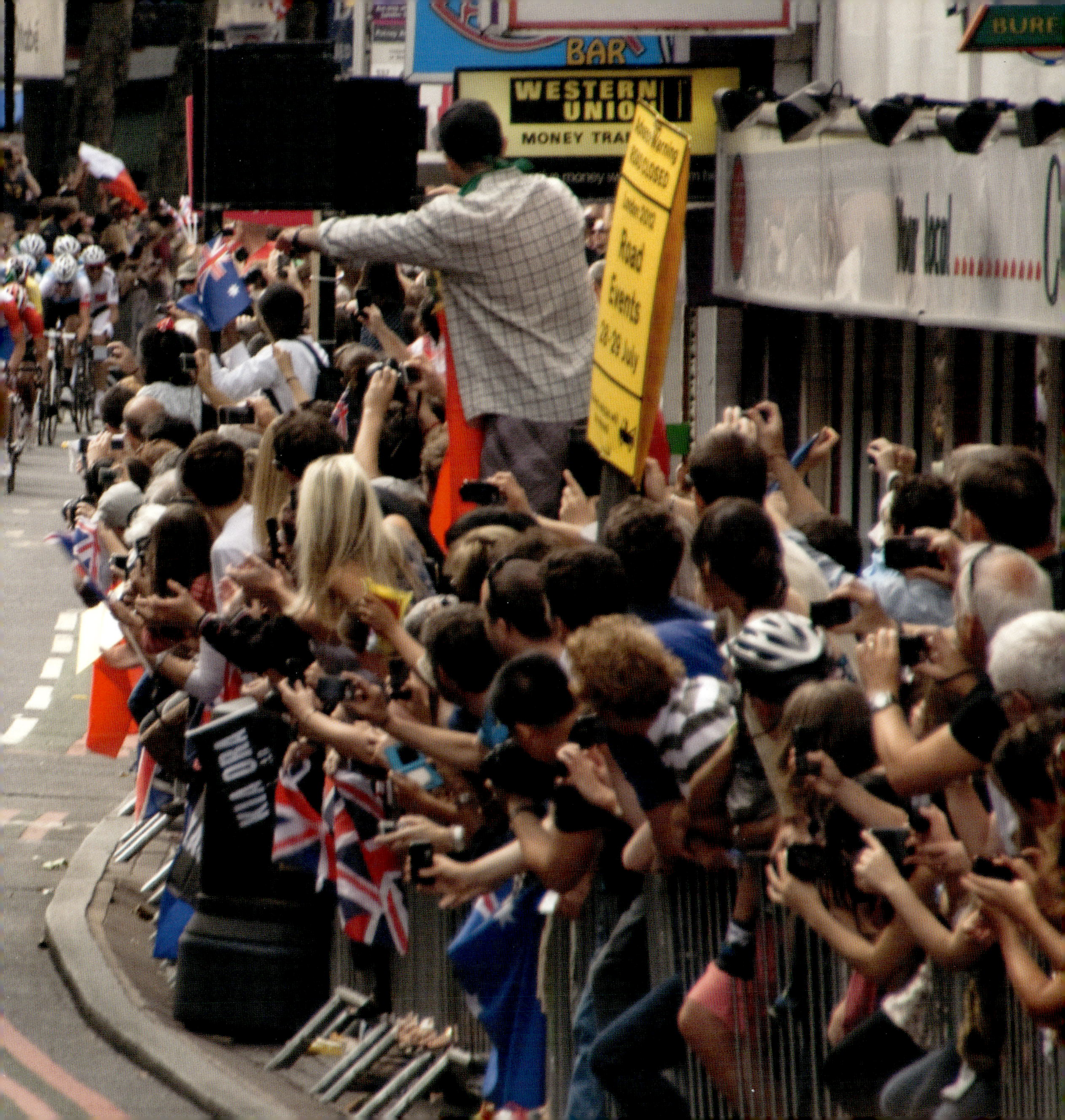
BAR
WESTERN UNION
Road Events
28-29 July
KIA ORA

As part of the Olympic festivities, the organisers funded a London-wide cultural event and here beside Putney Wharf is some cycling inspired performance art.

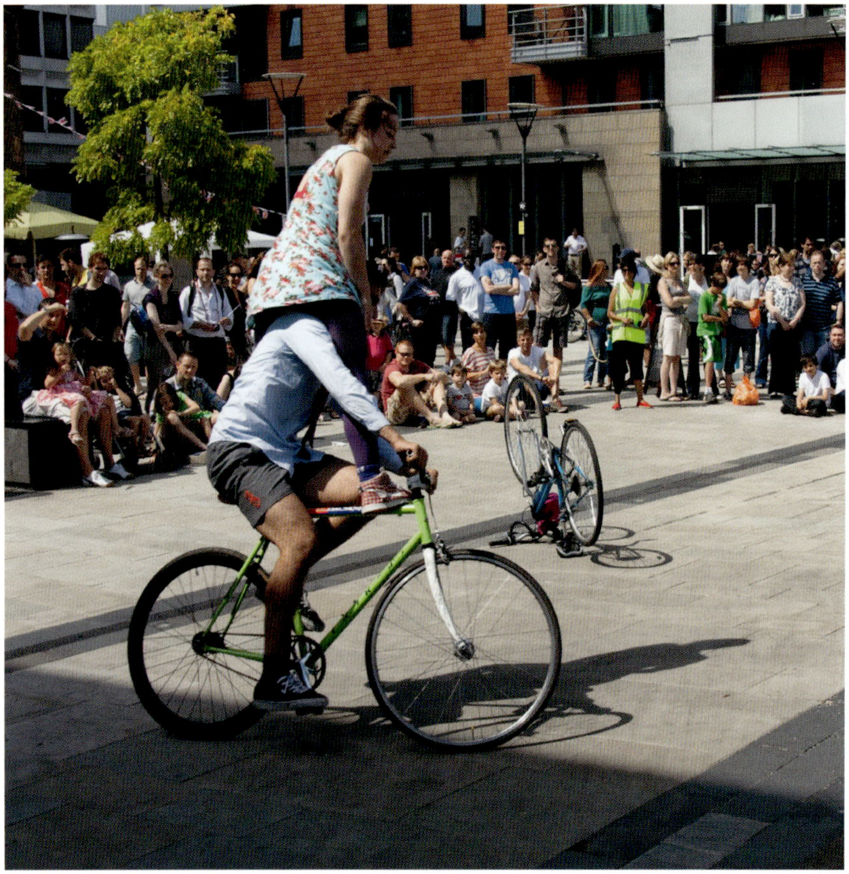

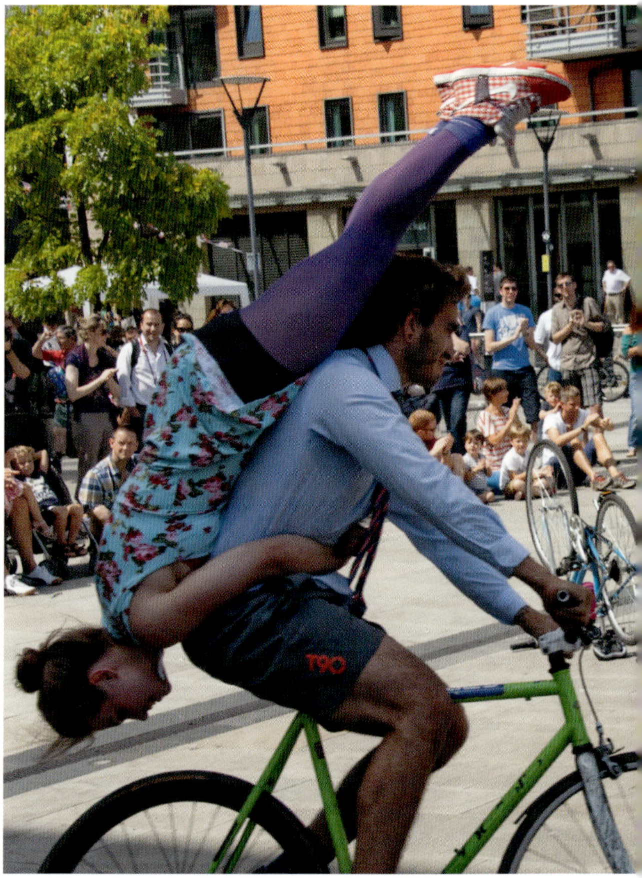

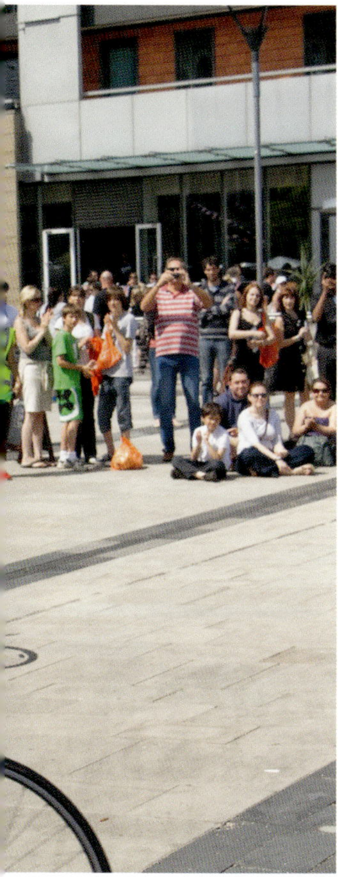

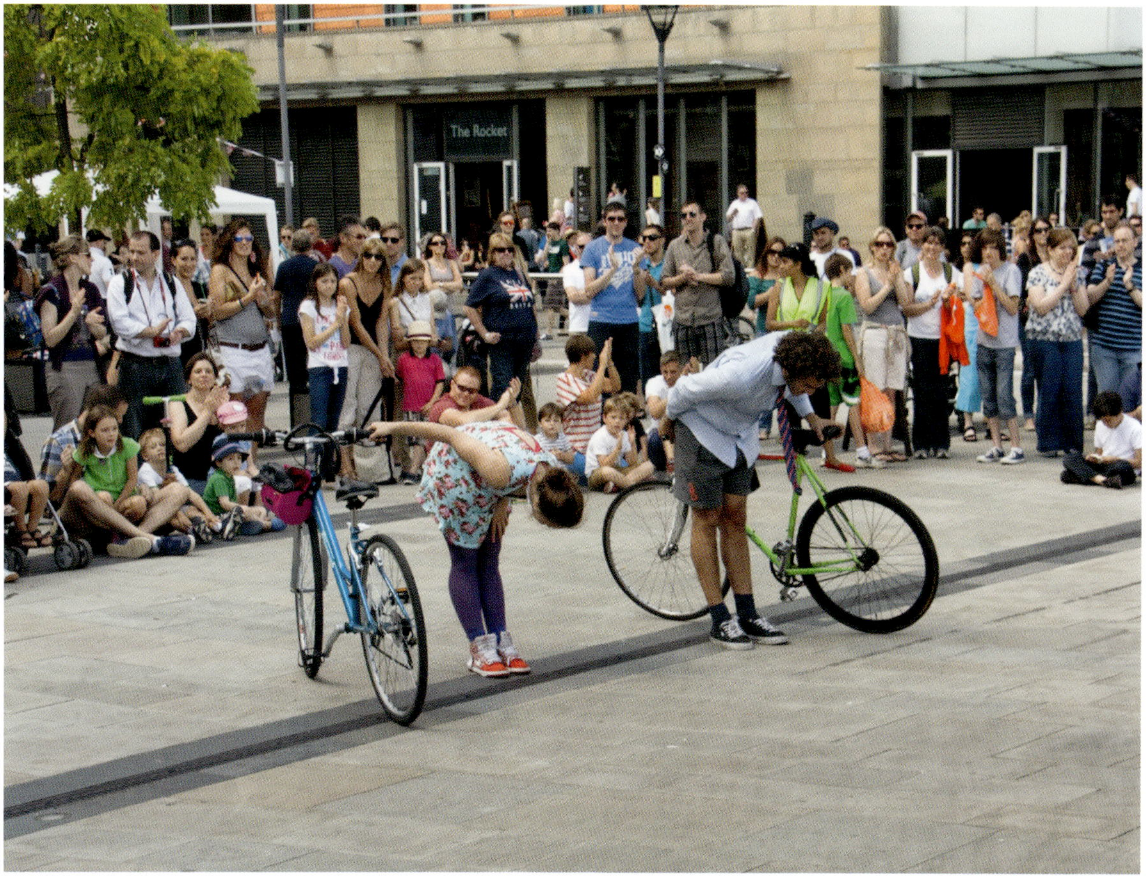
The Rocket

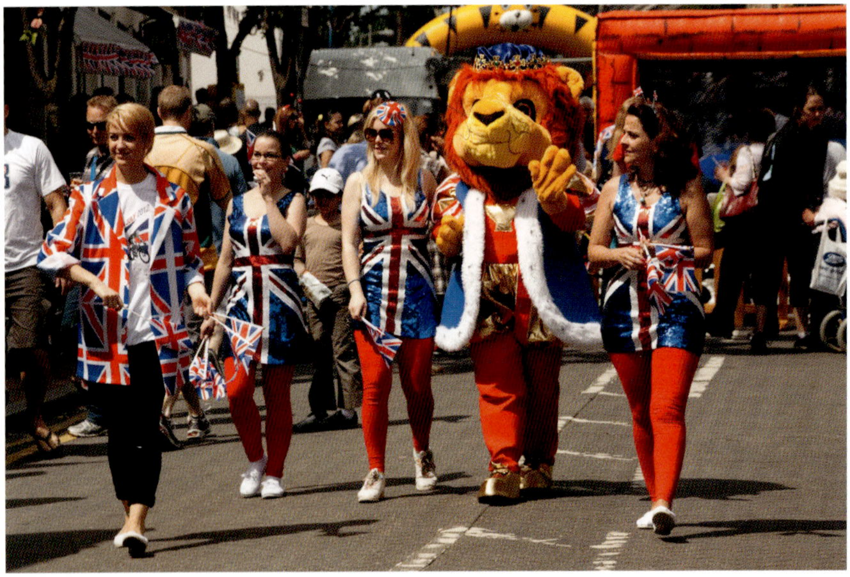

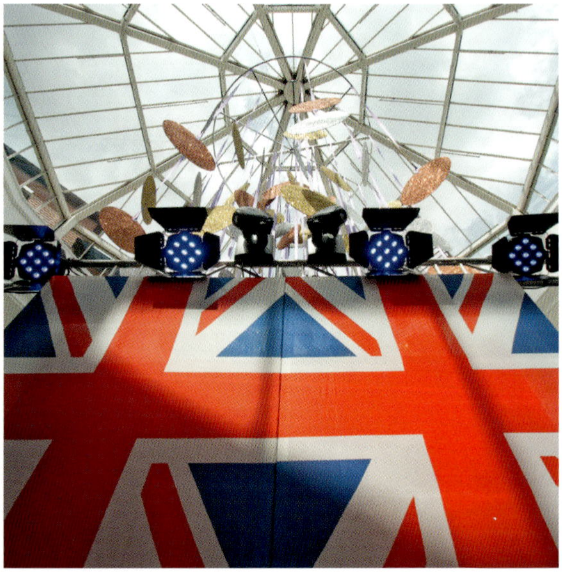

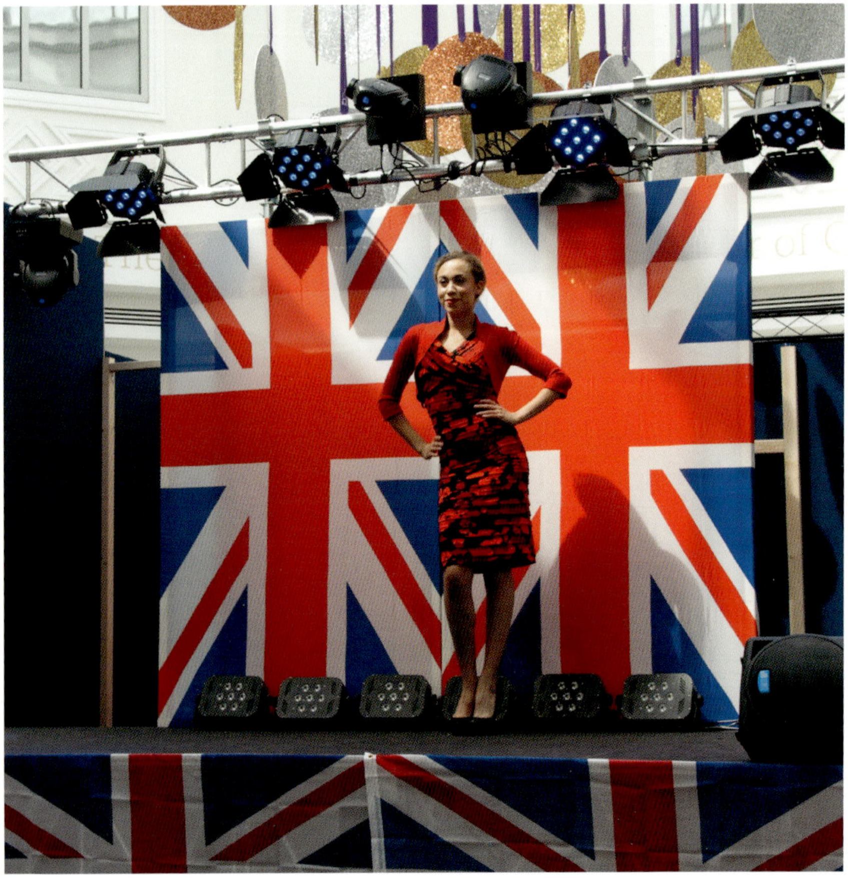

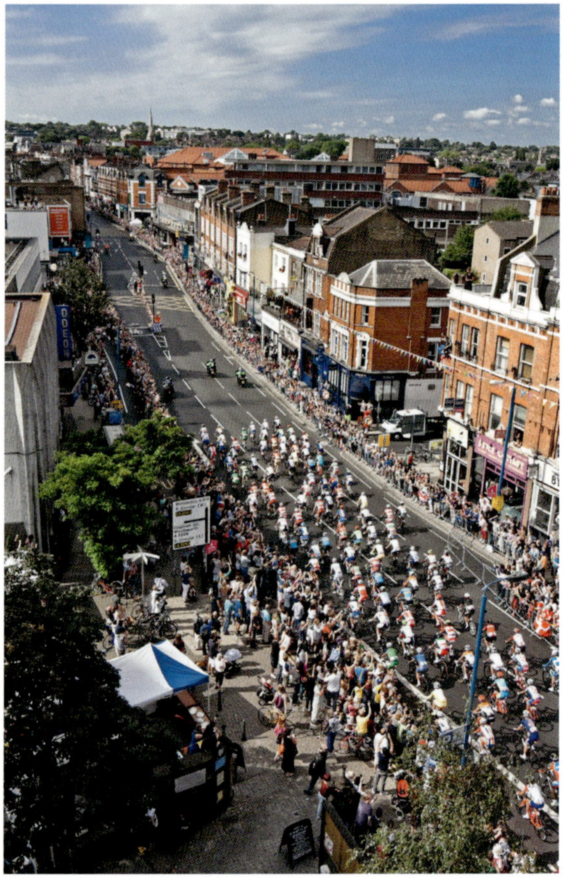

Page Opposite: Union Jacks everywhere, other local events during the first Olympic weekend included a fashion show in The Exchange and some stalls down Lacy Road.

Page Opposite Bottom Right: The Men's Cycle Race as seen going up Putney High Street.

This Page: Just before the Games got underway, the Olympic Flame was carried down the Thames on the Royal Barge *Gloriana*, passed Putney on its way to East London and the Olympic Park.

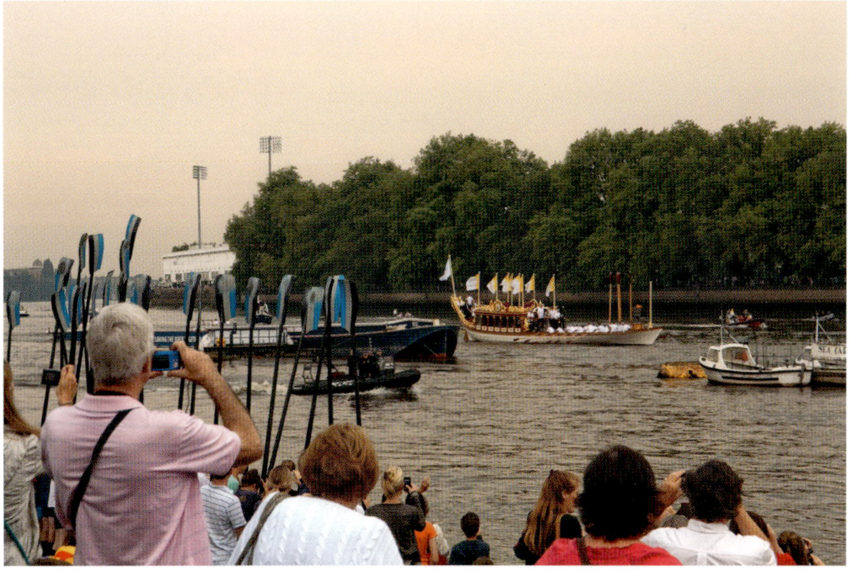

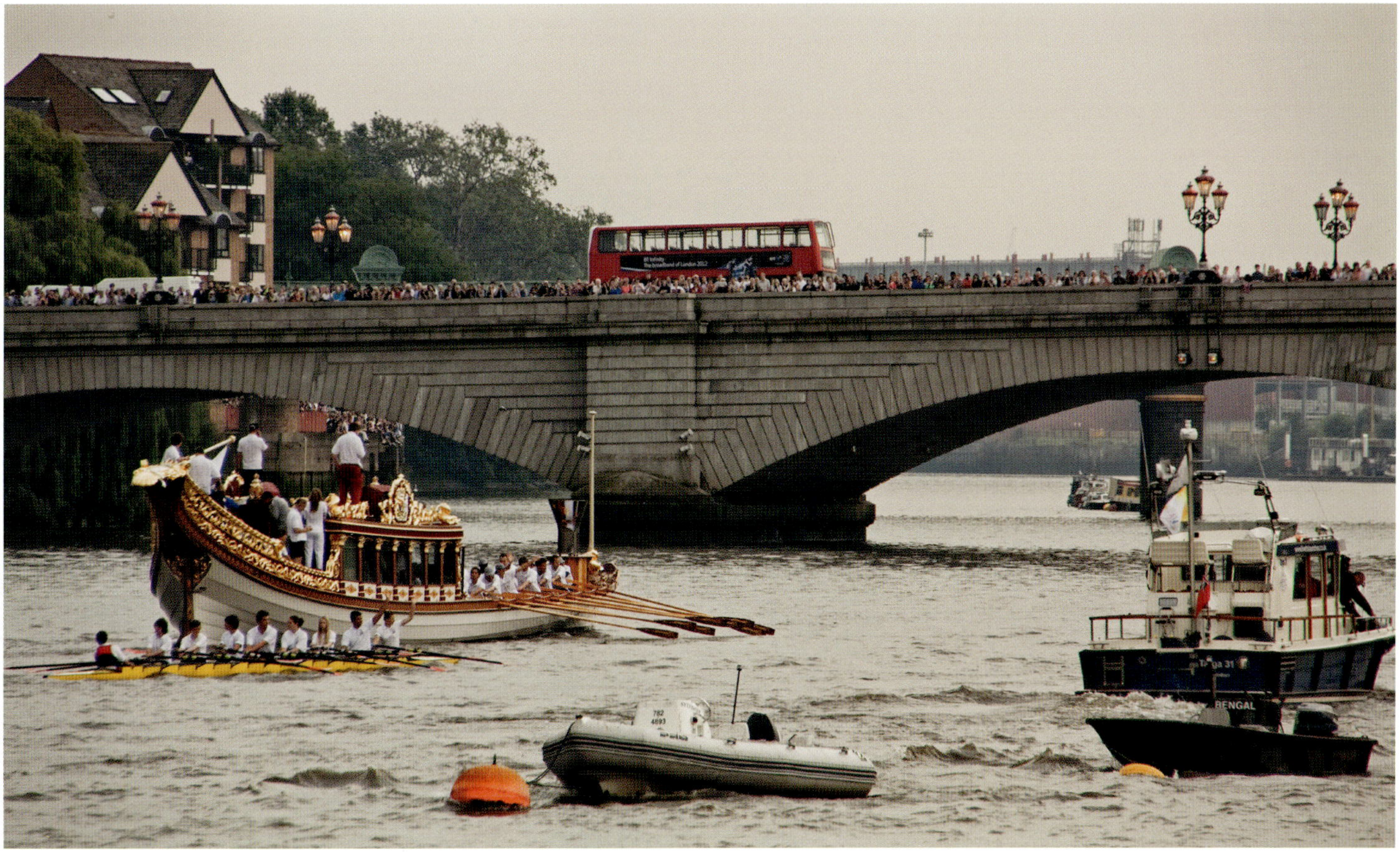

East Putney

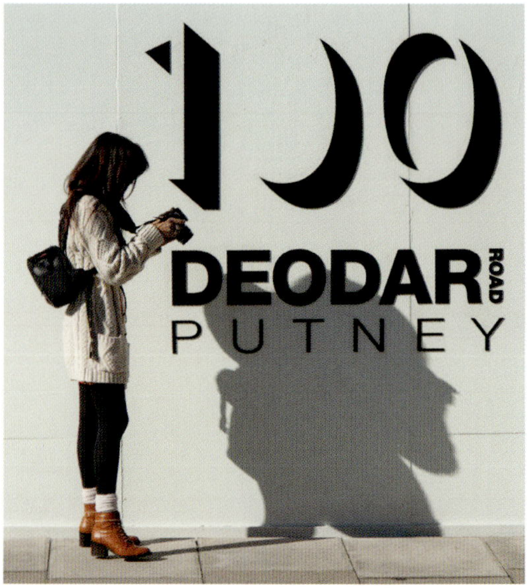

Below: The King's Railway Arches off Deodar Road.

Page Opposite: East Putney Underground Station. Opened in 1889, it serves the District Line, which runs from Earls Court to Wimbledon.

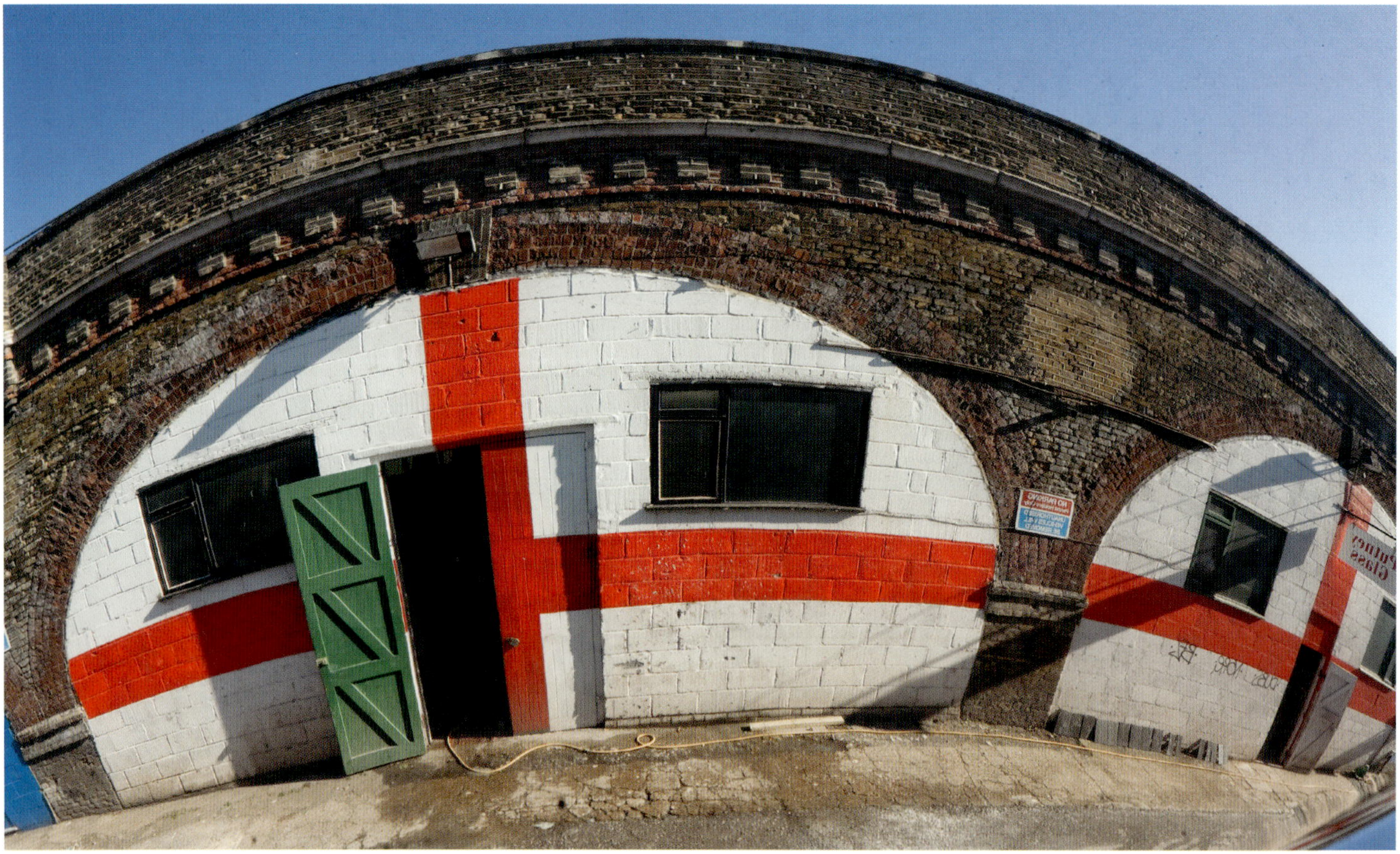

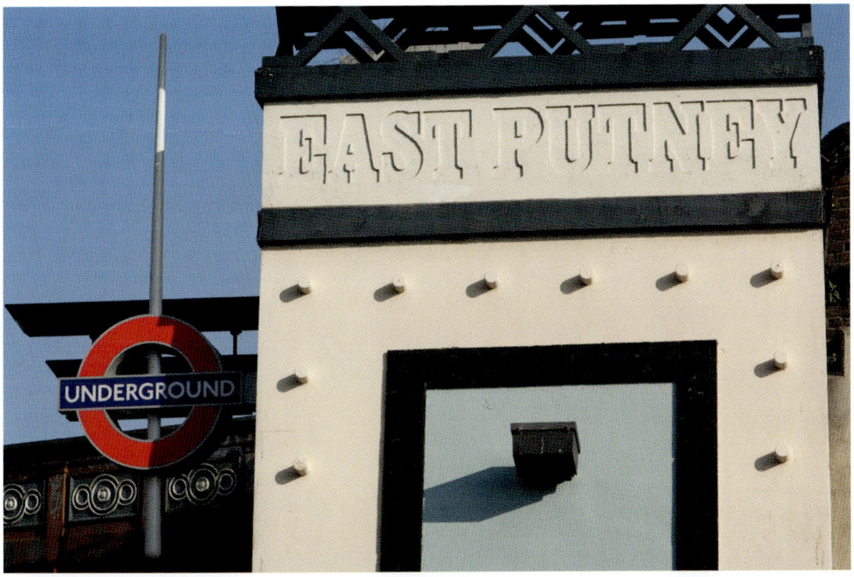
EAST PUTNEY
UNDERGROUND

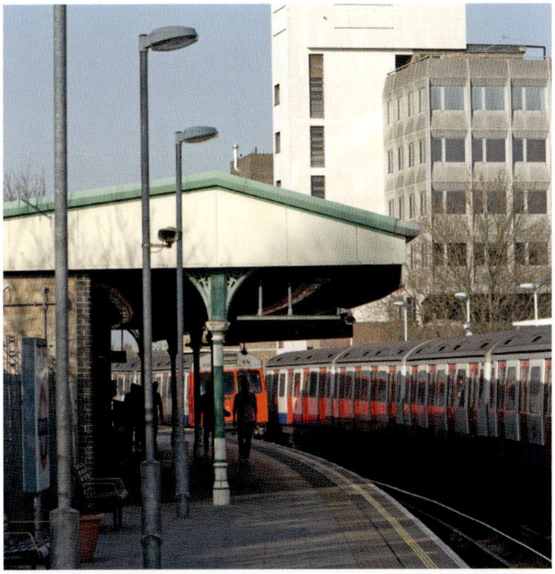

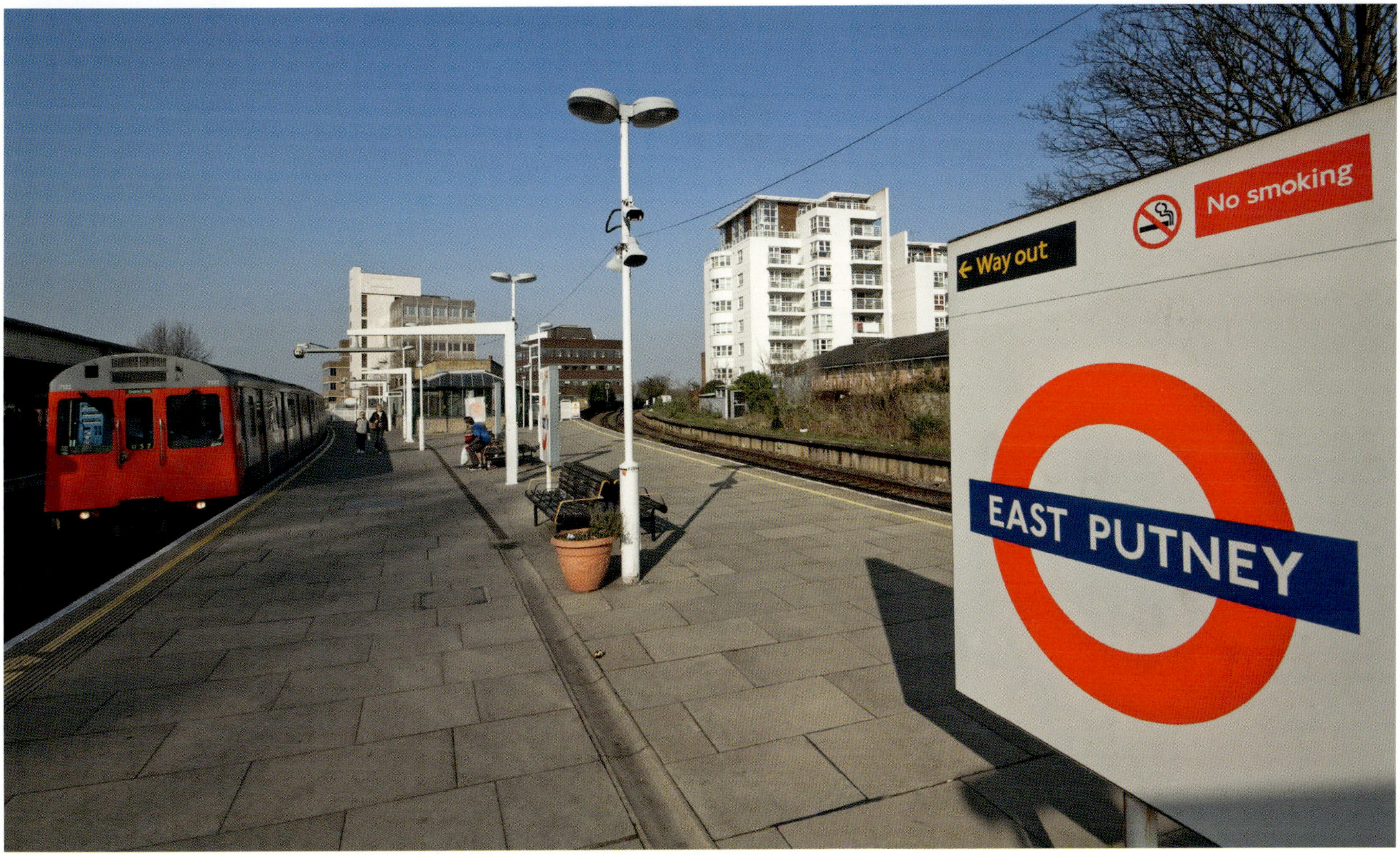
No smoking
Way out
EAST PUTNEY

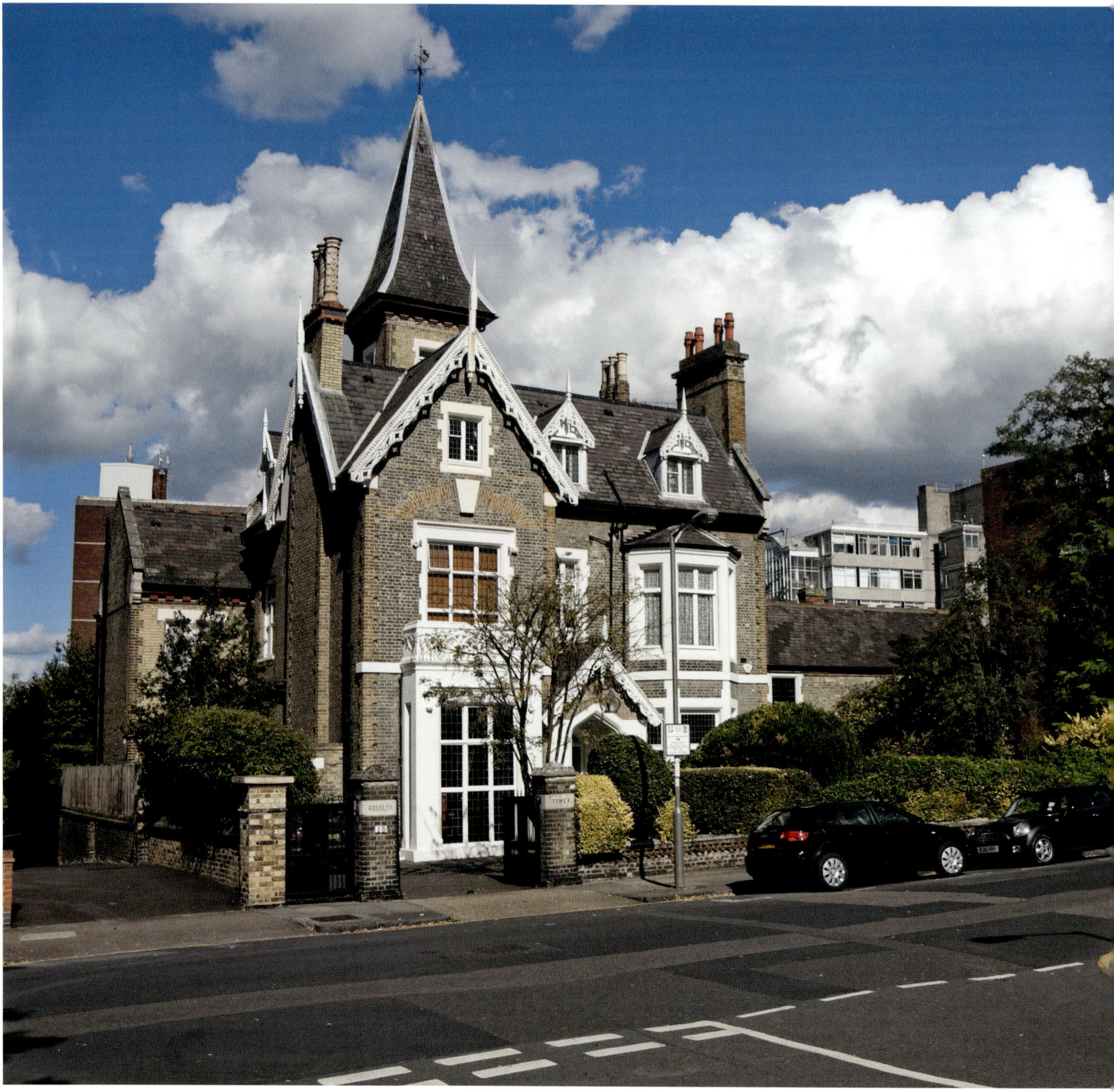
ROSSLYN
TOWER

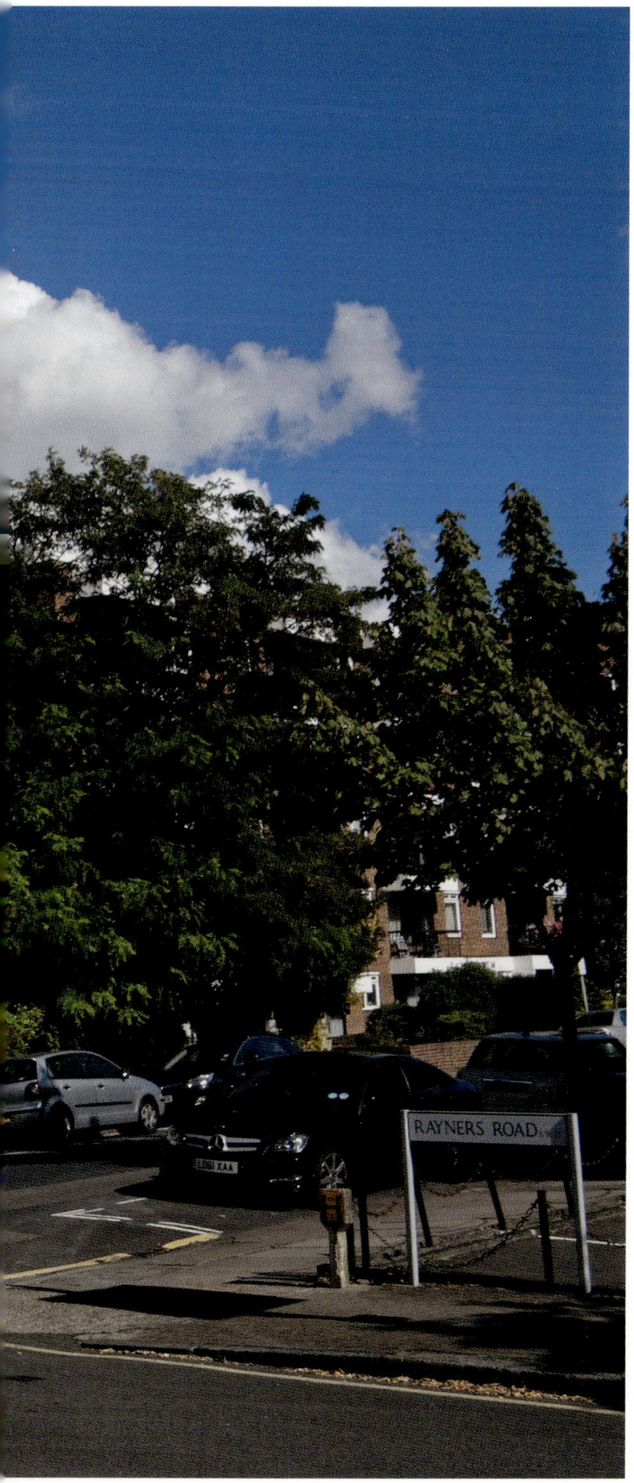

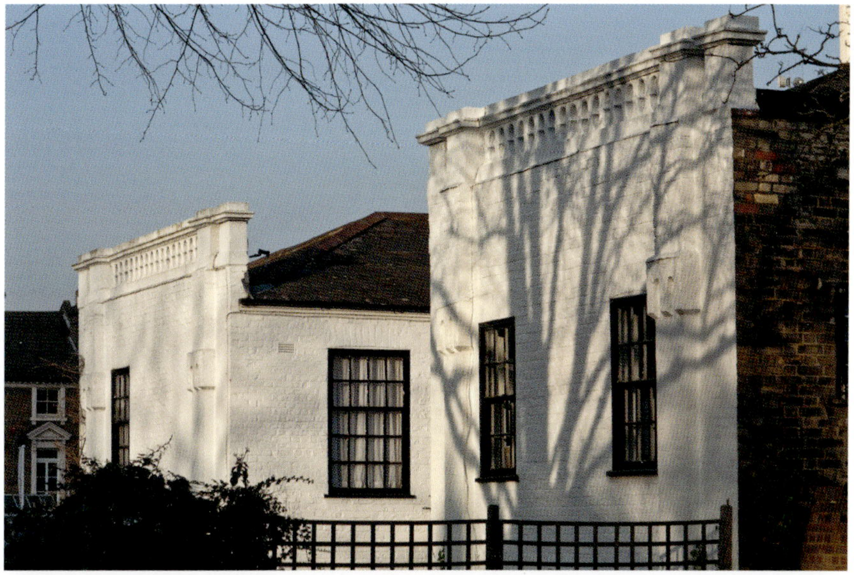

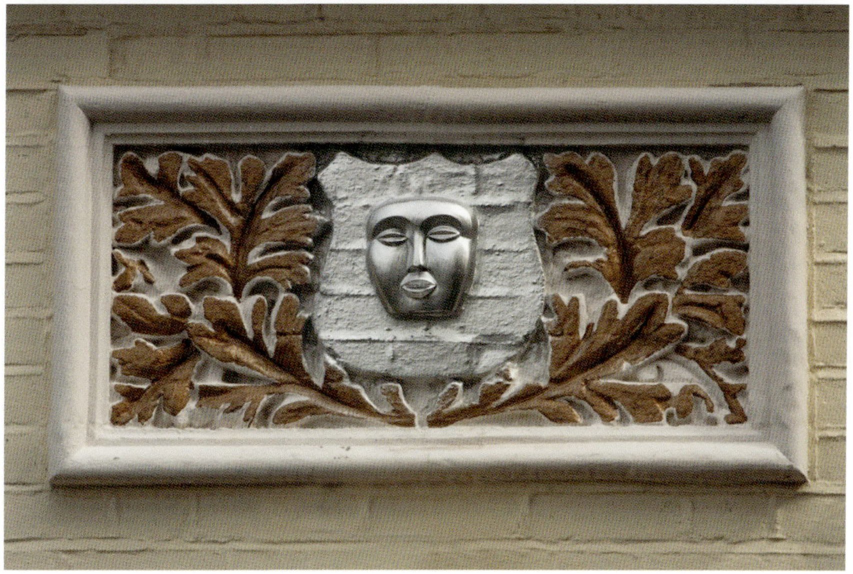

Left: Rosslyn Tower, situated on St John's Avenue.

Top right: Ernshaw Place, off Carlton Drive, an attractive mews.

Bottom right: An amusing detail on a house found in Deodar Road.

Overleaf: One of a series of quirky sphinxes capping the roofs off Deodar Road.

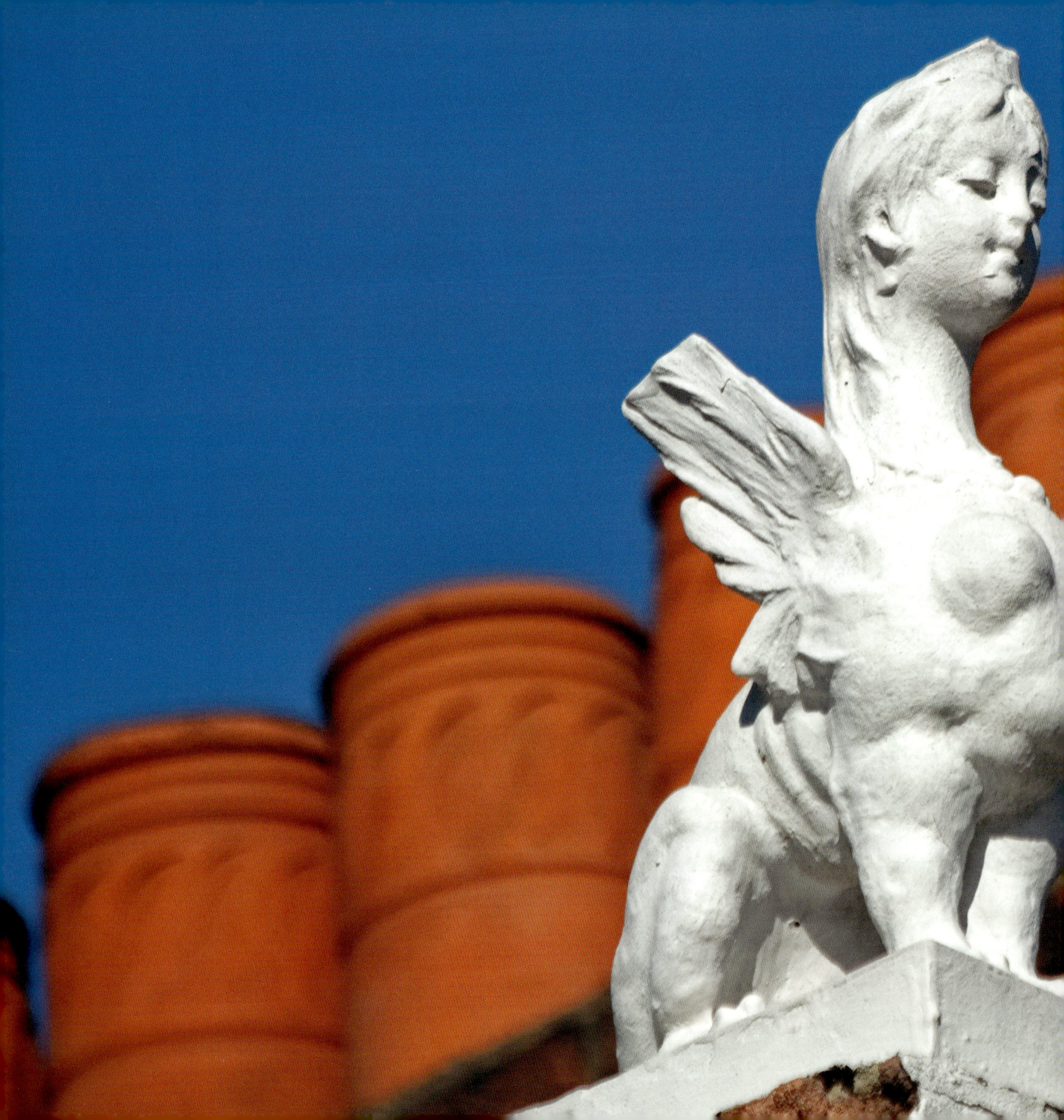

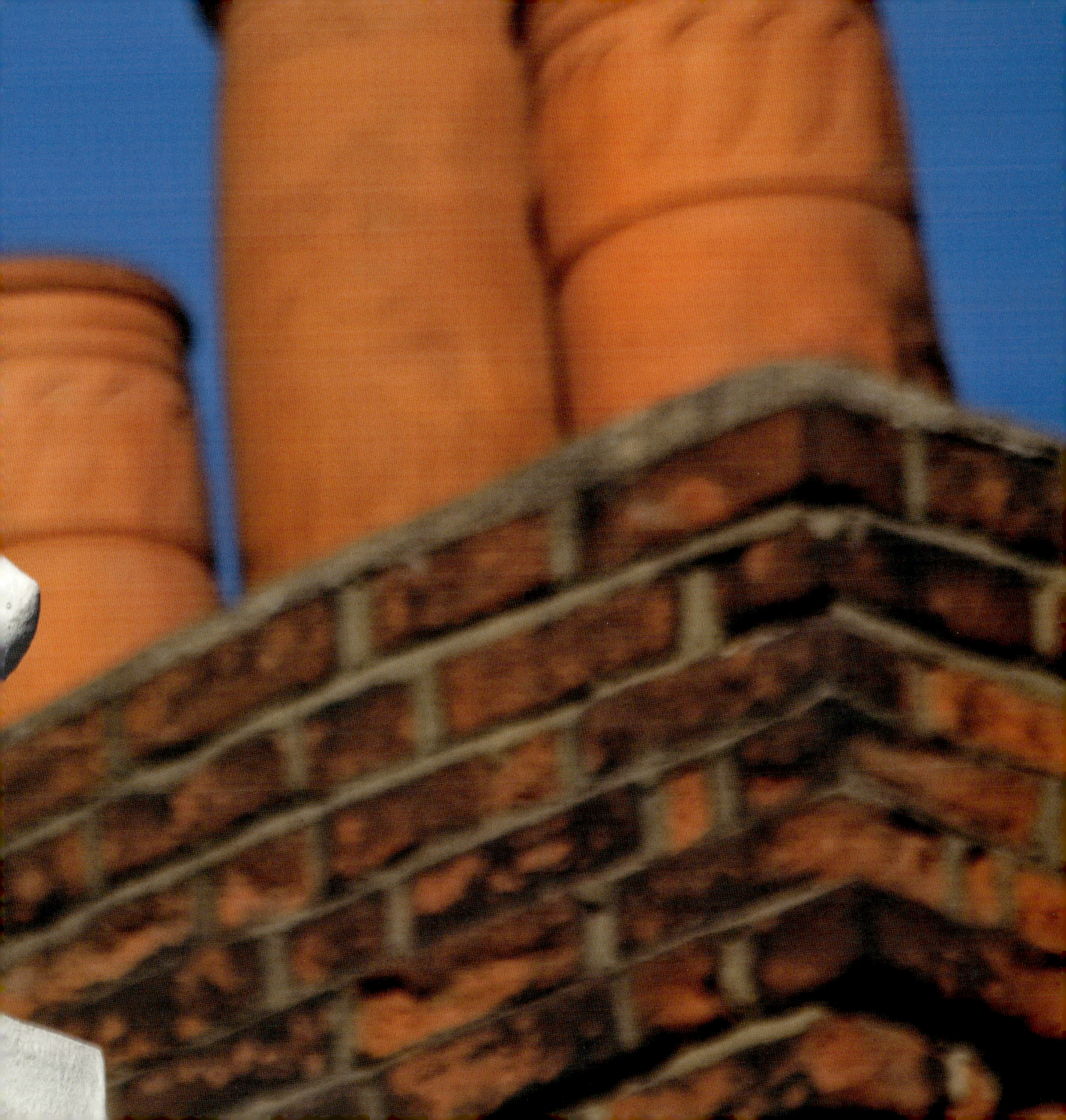

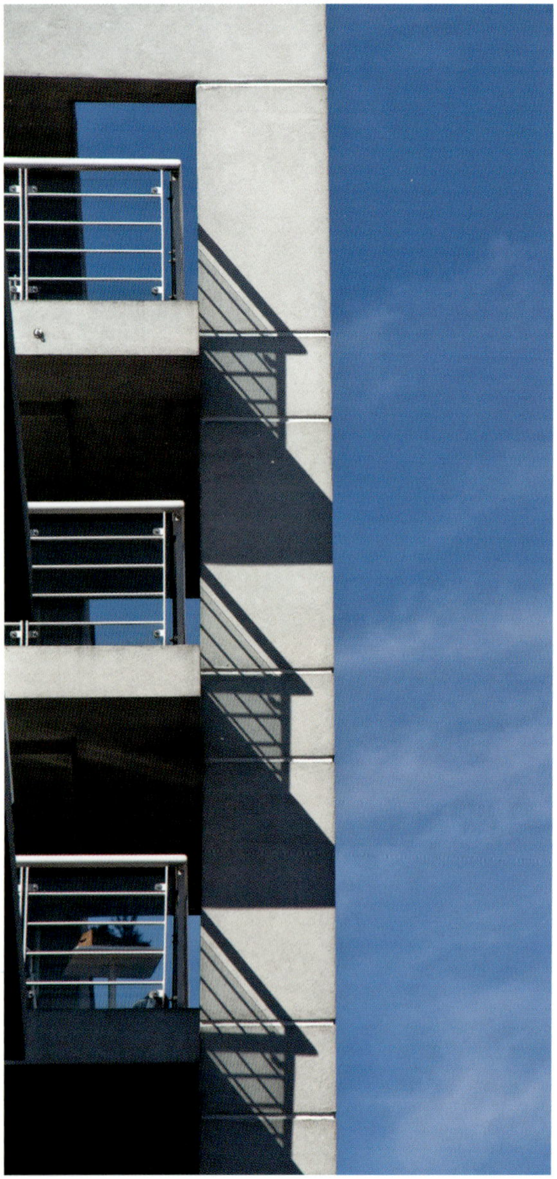

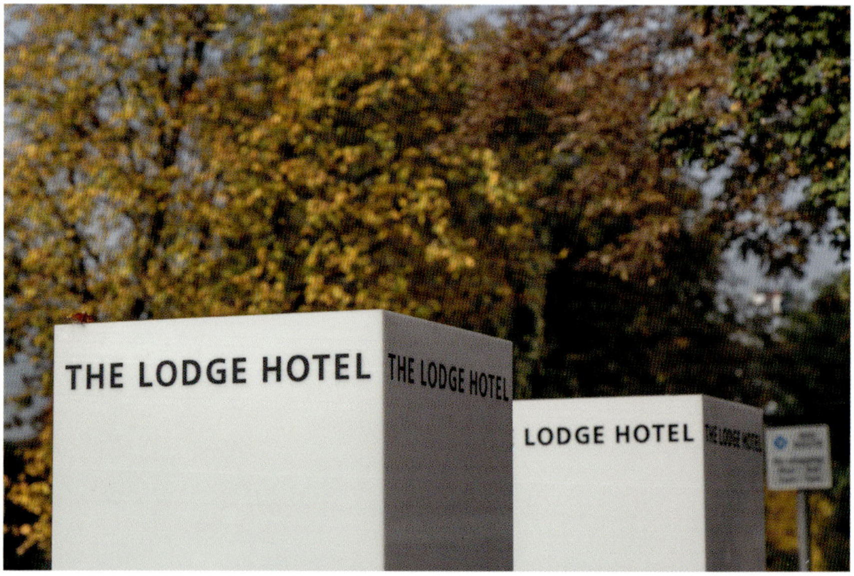

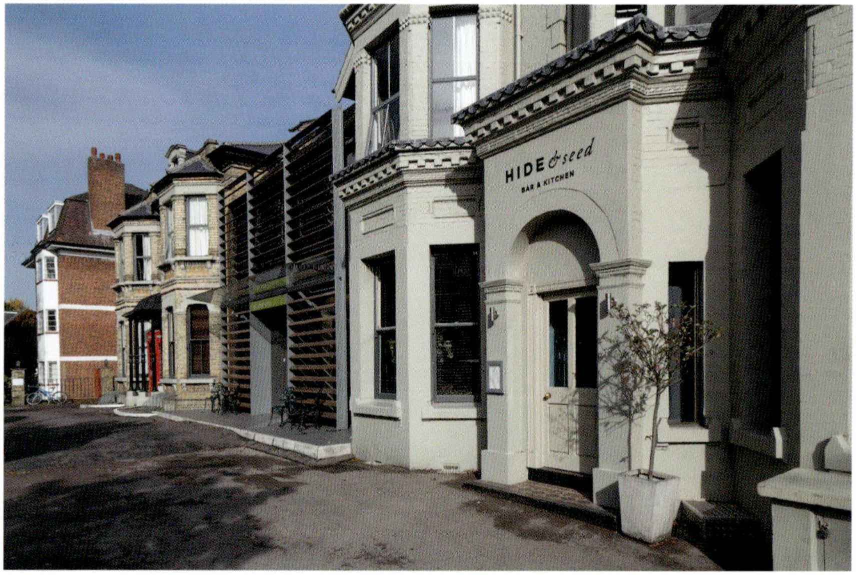

Above Left and Opposite: The flats on the Upper Richmond Road just past East Putney Tube Station, with the particularly impressive curved building on the corner of Keswick Road.

Above: The Lodge is a boutique hotel, located on the Upper Richmond Road as you leave Putney on the way to Wandsworth. Since featured in my first edition, they have greatly expanded with the addition in 2015 of a new wing, which is ideal for events, meetings and weddings.

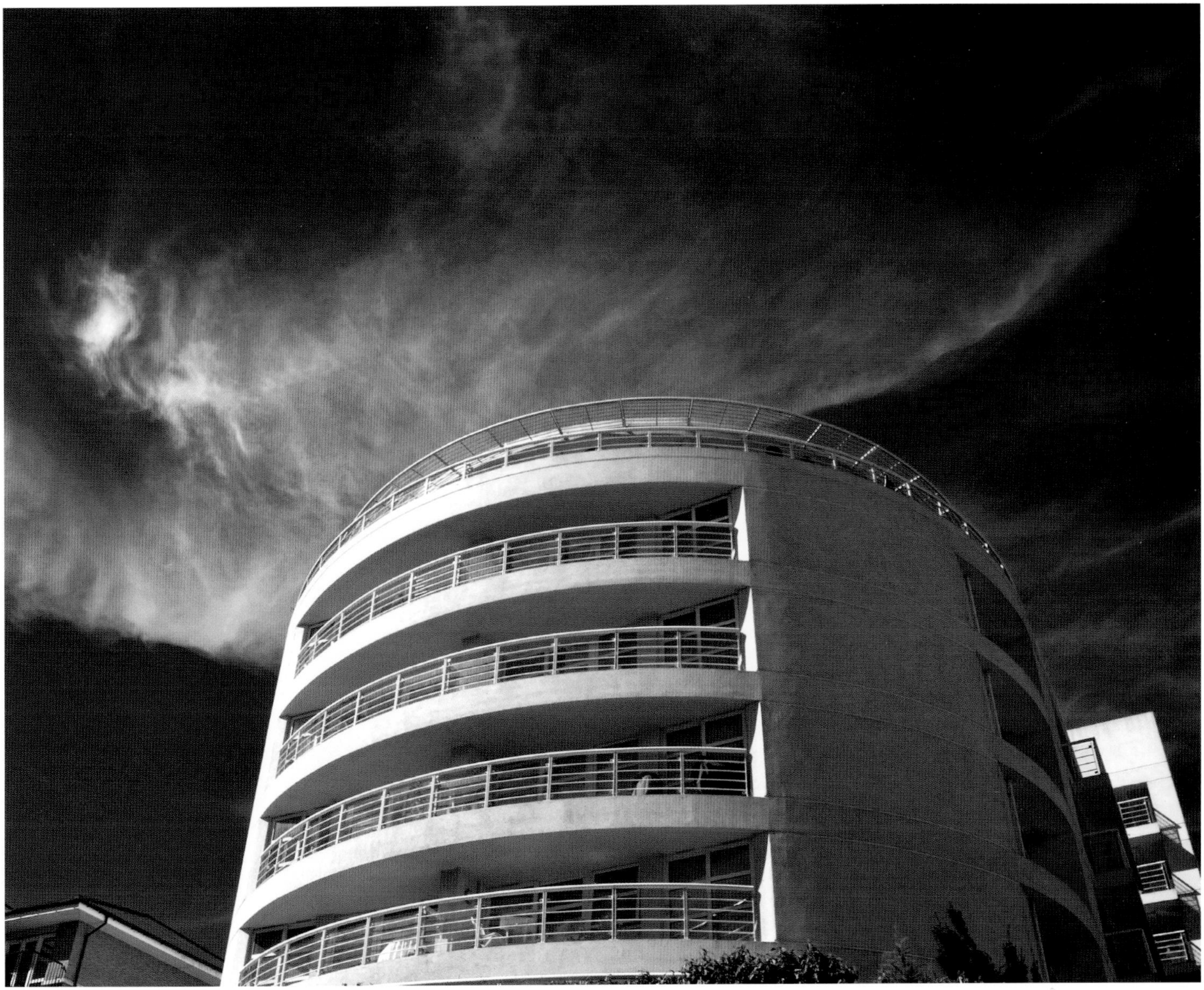

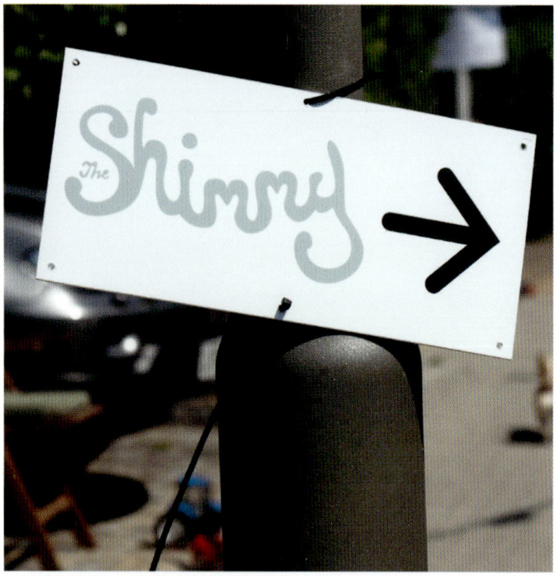
The Shimmy

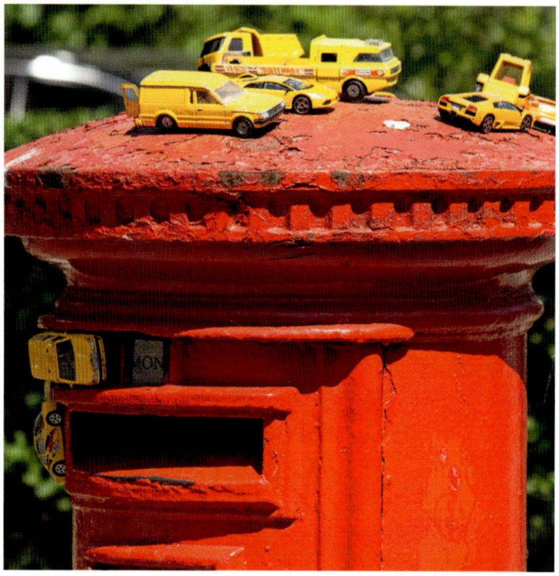

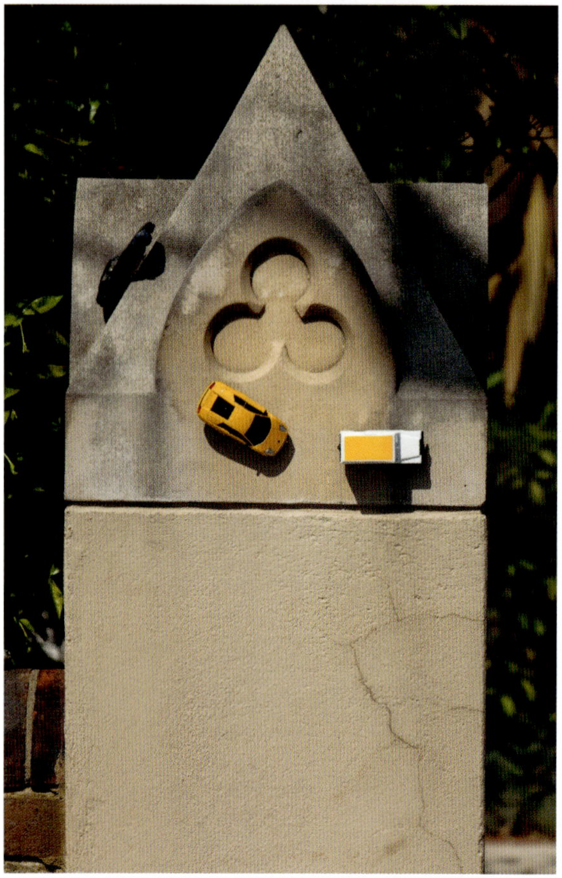

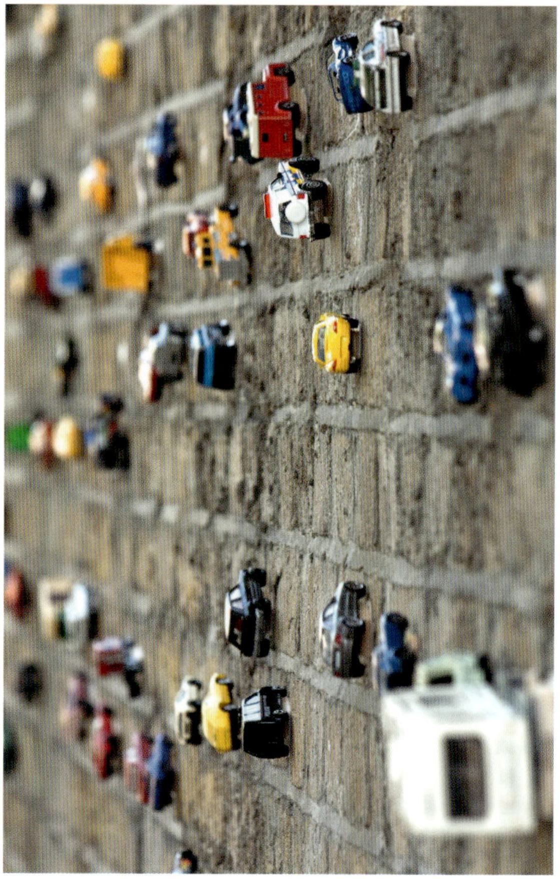

Opposite: The Shimmy was the final part of 2012's Wandsworth Arts festival, which included an ambitious exhibition in Deodar Road, made up of hundreds of dinky cars. I still don't profess to fully understand what was going on but it was very impressive, if a little unusual.

Below: The King's Arches, off Deodar Road.

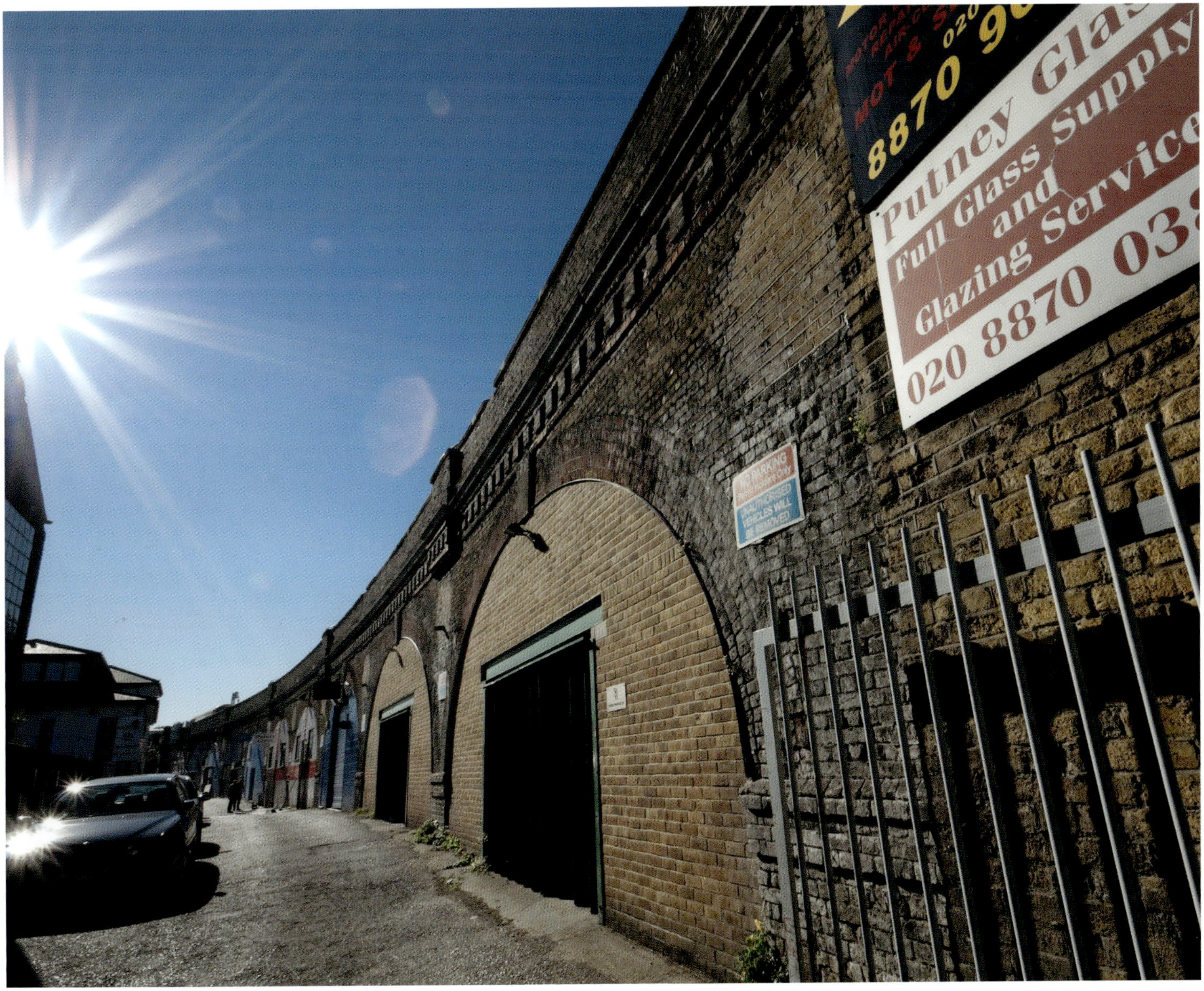

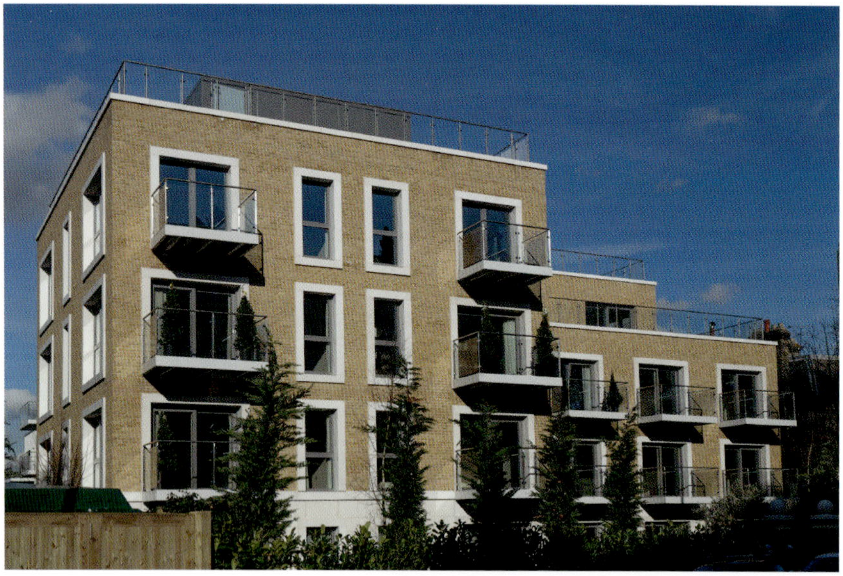

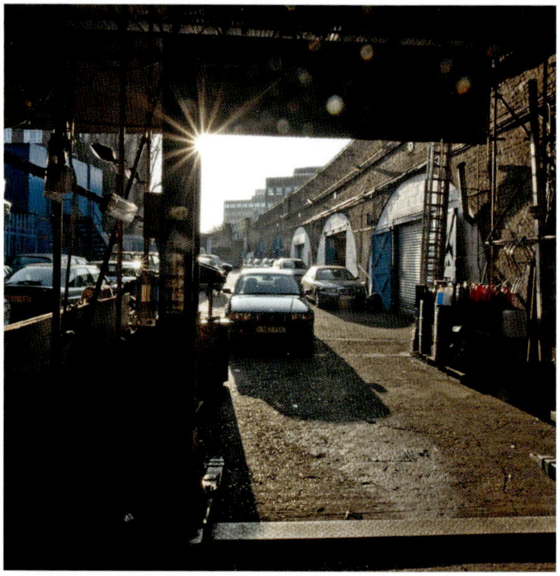

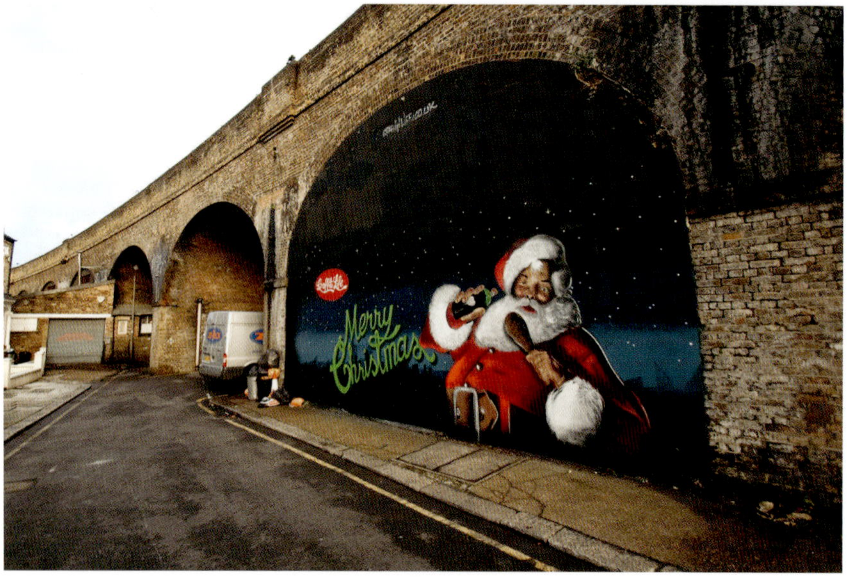

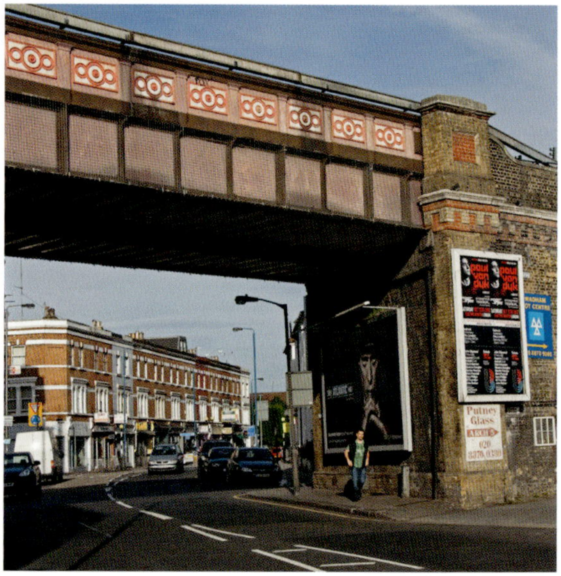

Top: The District Line as it crosses Putney Bridge Road.

Above: Arches in Winthorpe Road.

Top Right and Opposite: Ferny Parry, quite a character, ran his garage, FC Parry Motors, in Woodlands Way, amongst the railway arches for over 40 years. He retired in 2014 and a new development, Oakhill Park (top left) has been constructed on the site of the old garage.

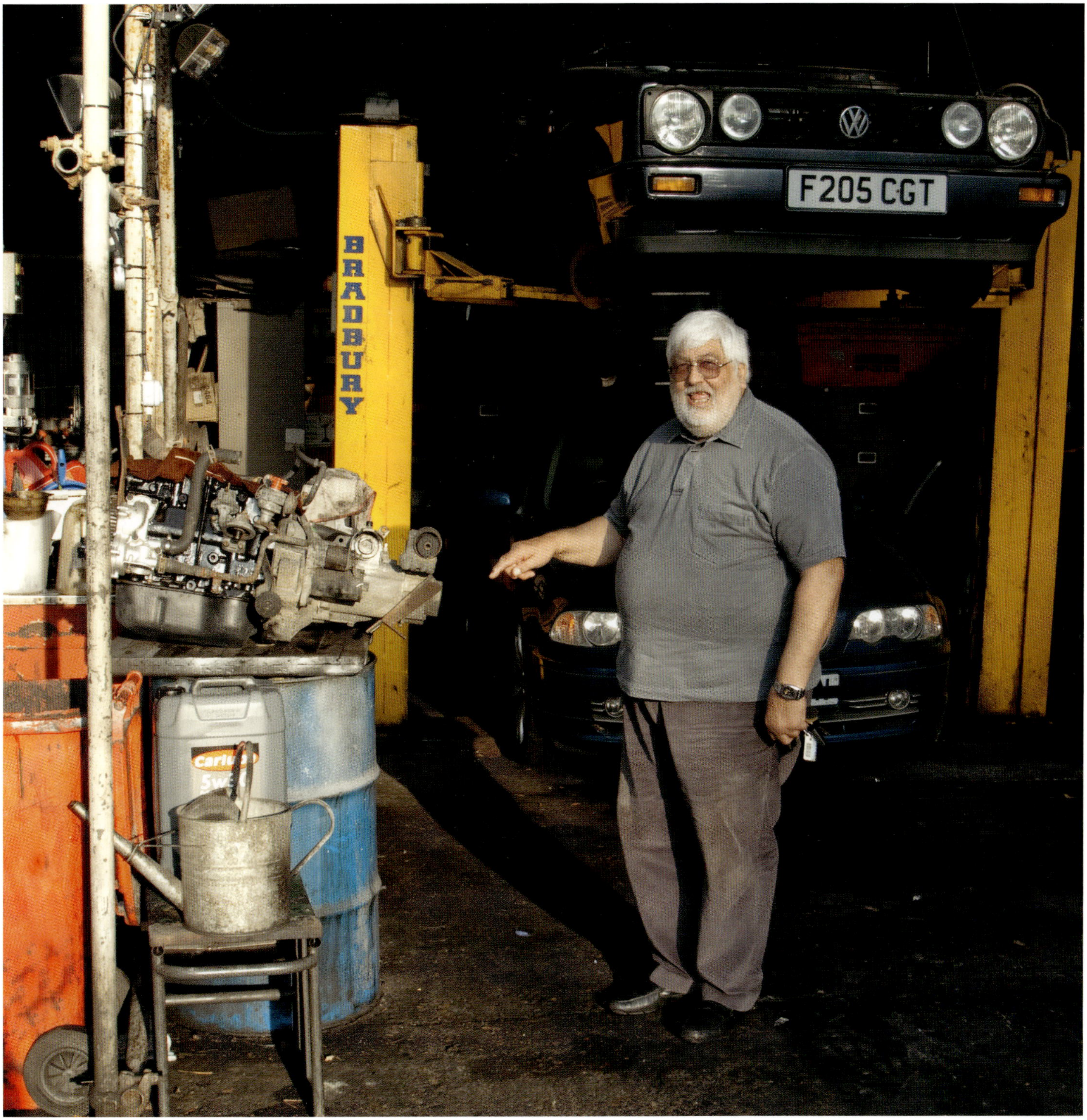
BRADBURY
F205 CGT

Riverside

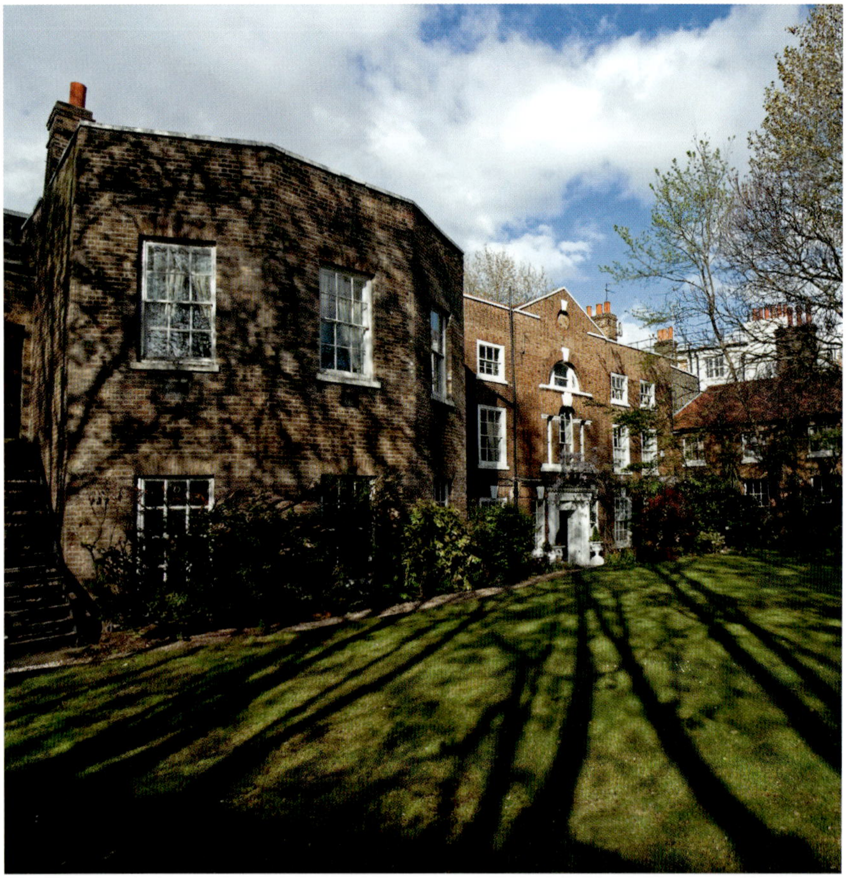

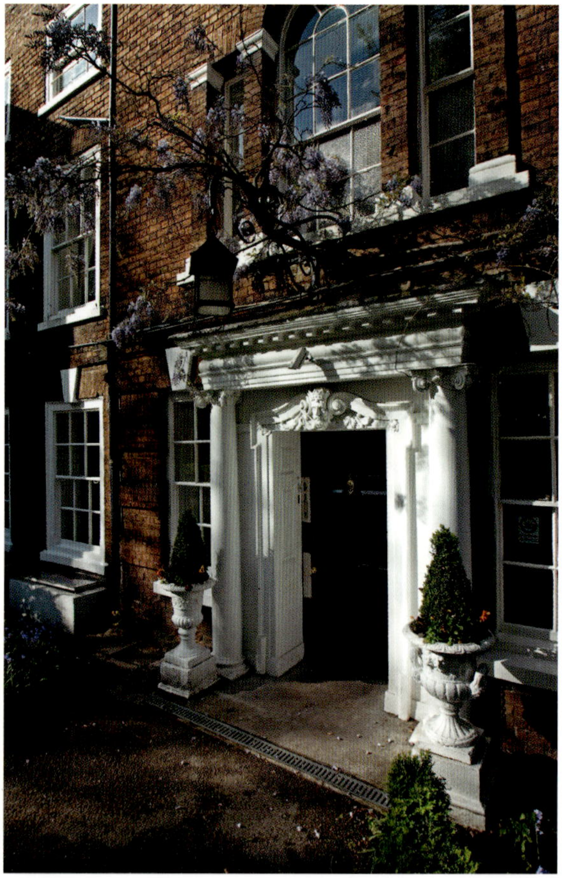

This Page: Winchester House Club (previously Constitutional Club) in Lower Richmond Road is a popular venue for functions including wedding receptions, with a lawn fronting the Embankment. It dates from c. 1730, possibly even earlier, is Grade II-listed and is the sole survivor of Putney's once numerous 'great houses'.

Page Opposite: These imposing flats were built c. 1901–3 and replaced a row known as The Terrace, built c. 1800. Residents commemorated by blue plaques (see page 7) have included former Putney MP Lord Jenkins, poet Gavin Ewart, and the 'father of modern ventriloquism', Fred Russell! Close to, if not exactly on the site, once stood clothmaker John Lacy's mansion, later known as Putney Palace to which Queen Elizabeth I was a frequent visitor. The mansion was owned for most of the 18th century by the wealthy d'Aranda family.

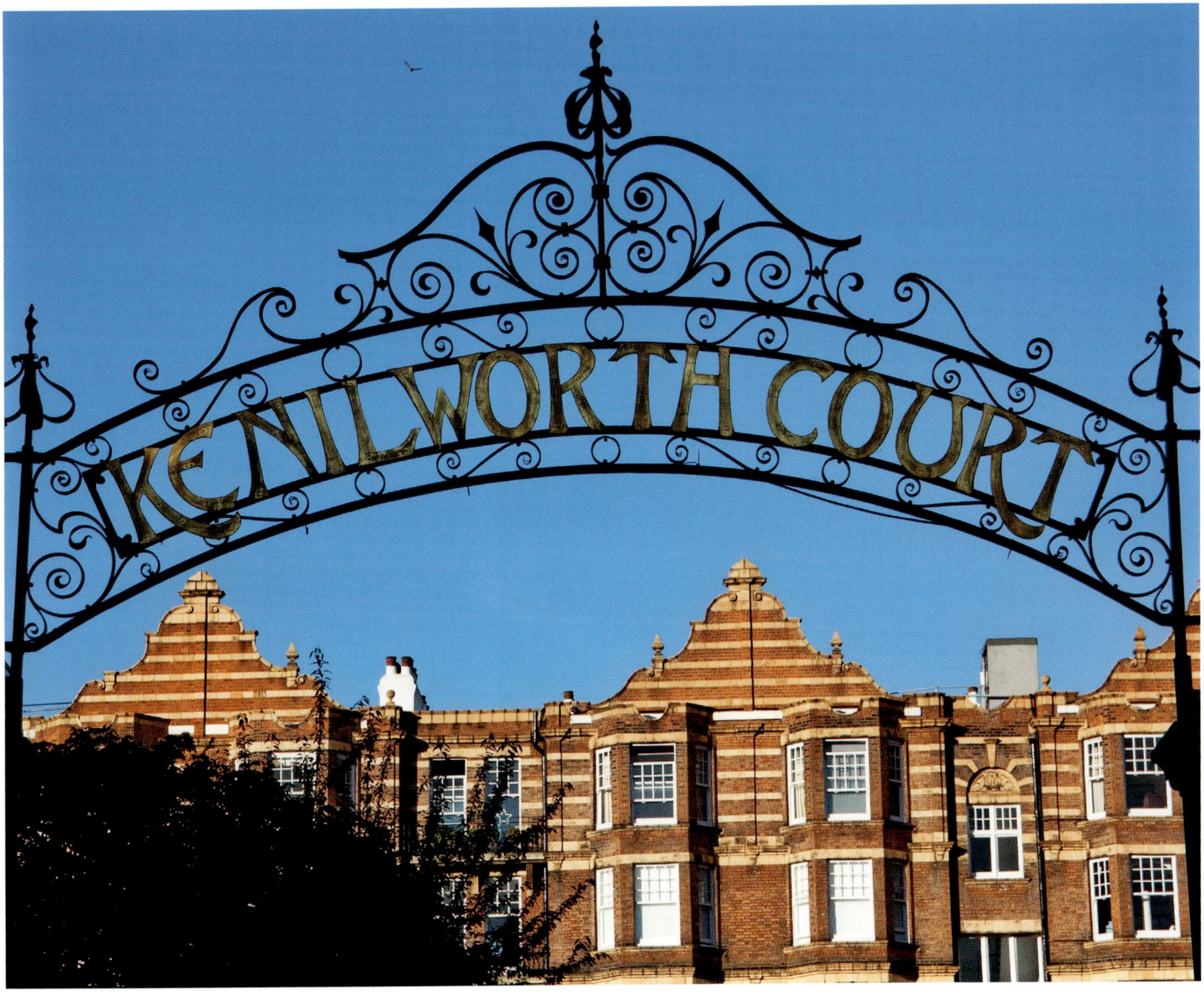
KENILWORTH COURT

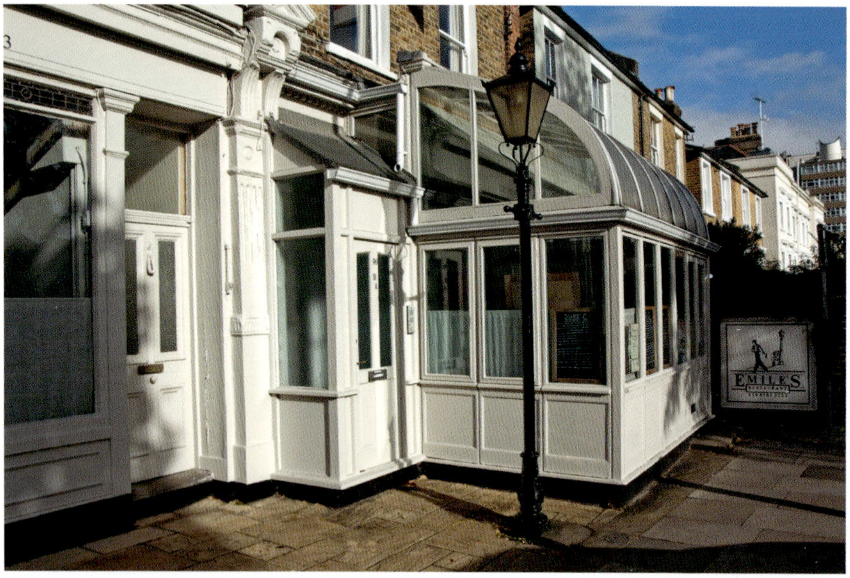

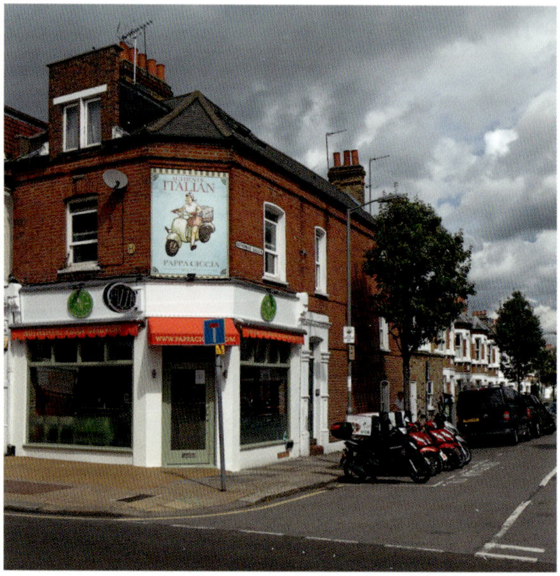

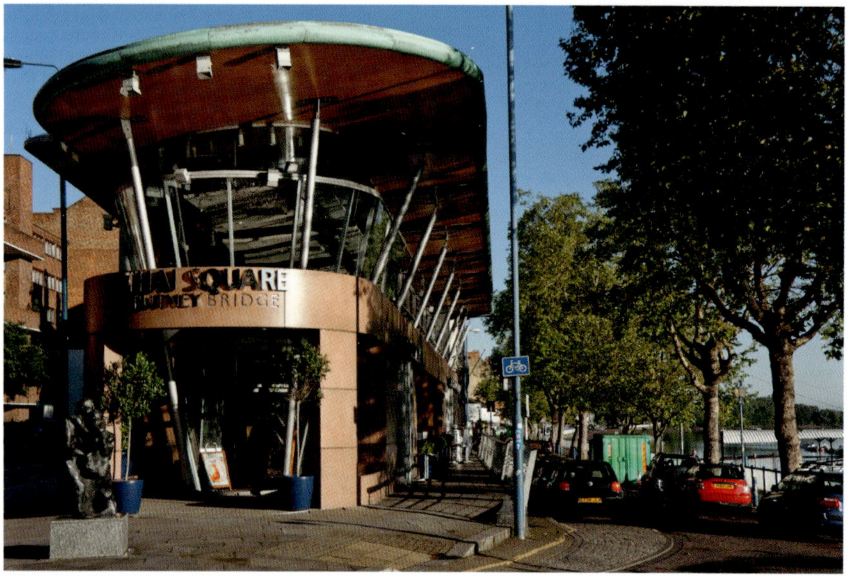

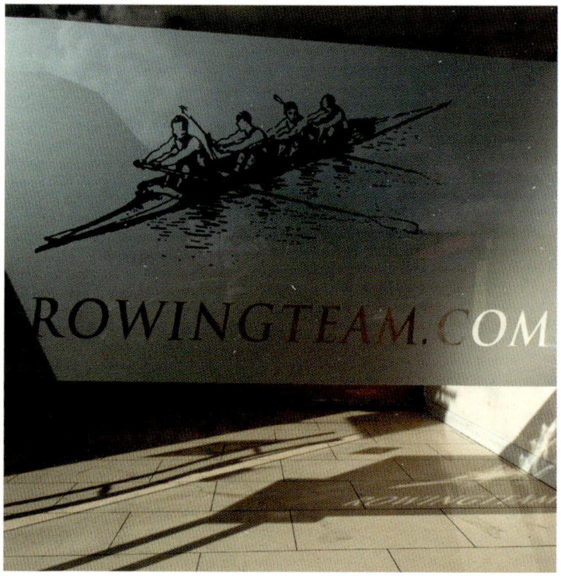

This Page: Eating out in or around Lower Richmond Road. Clockwise from Top Left: Emile's Restaurant in Felsham Road; Pappa Ciccia, Raja Rowing Team and Thai Square, all on Lower Richmond Road.

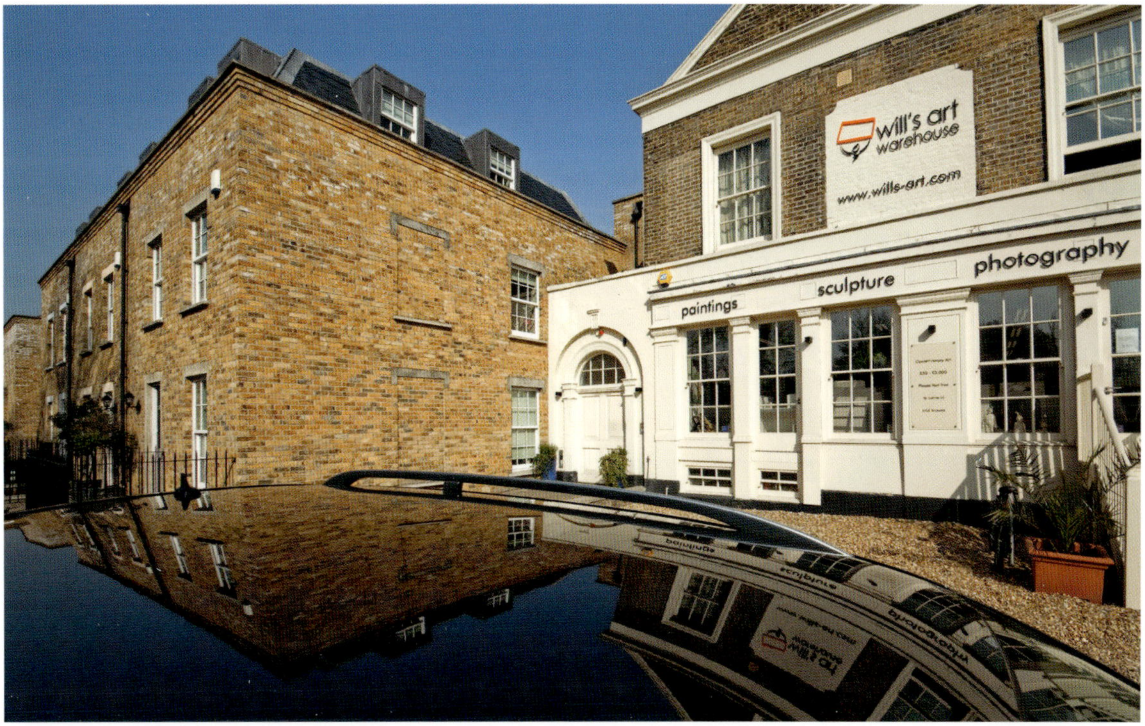

Right: Will's Art Warehouse on Lower Richmond Road used to be 'The Cricketers' pub.

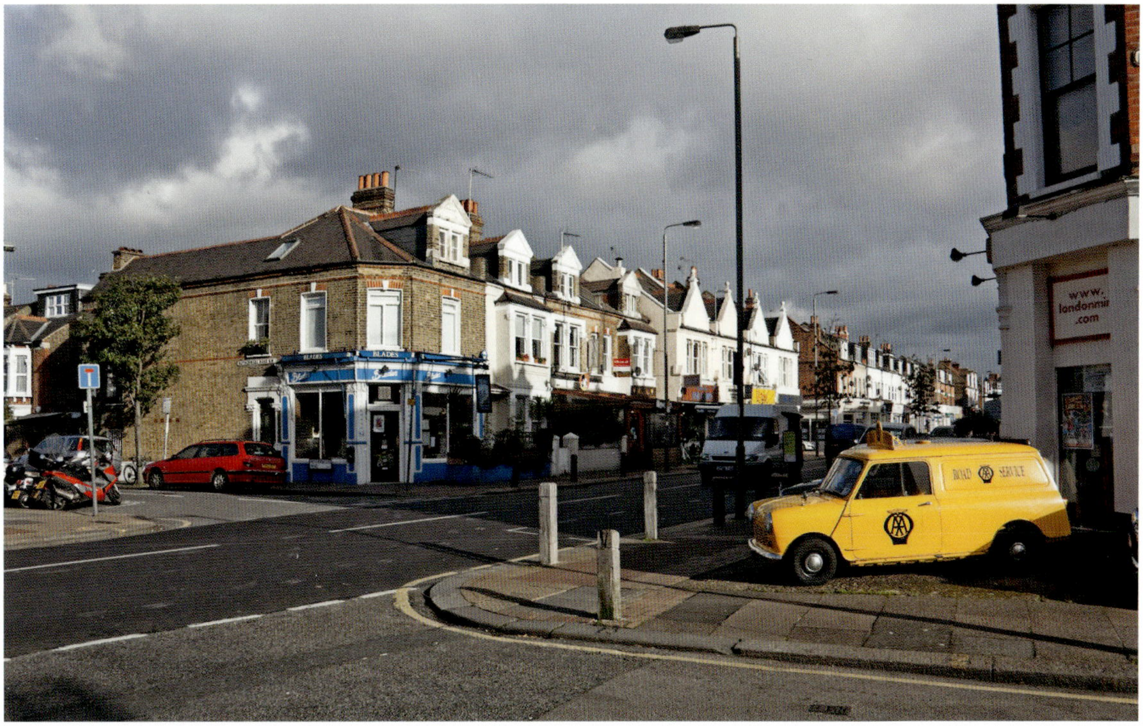

Bottom Right: The London Mini Centre on the corner of Roskell Road and Lower Richmond Road.

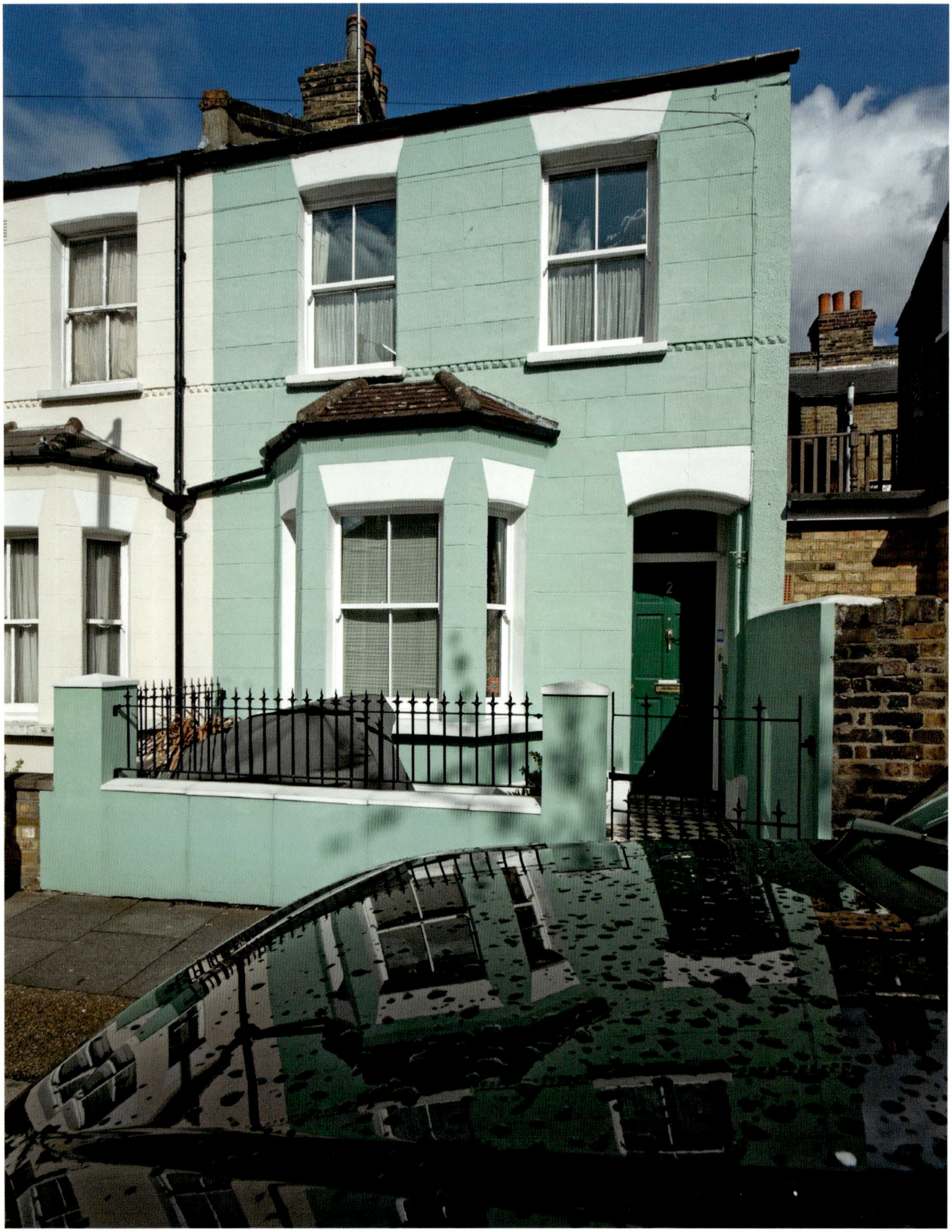

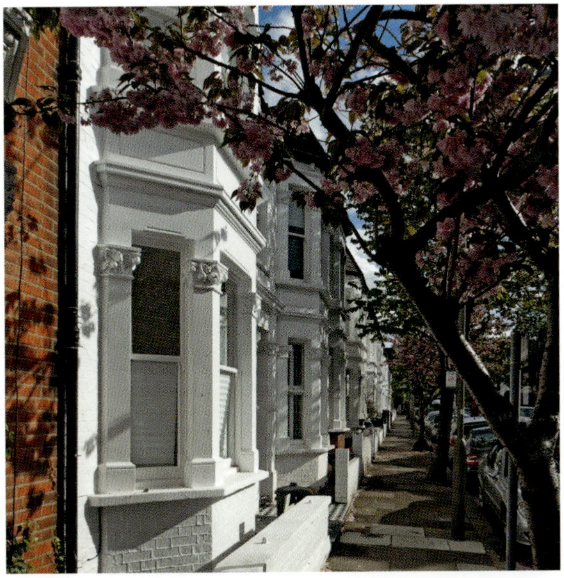

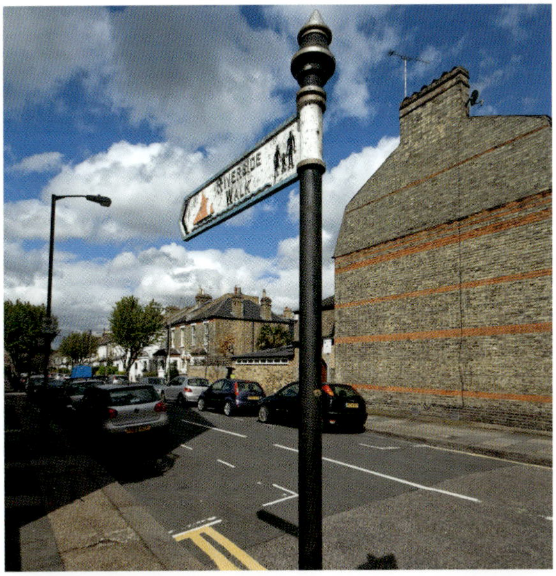

Opposite: Sefton Street.

Top Left: Glendarvon Street.

Top Right: Festing Road.
Bottom Left and Right
Bendemeer Road.

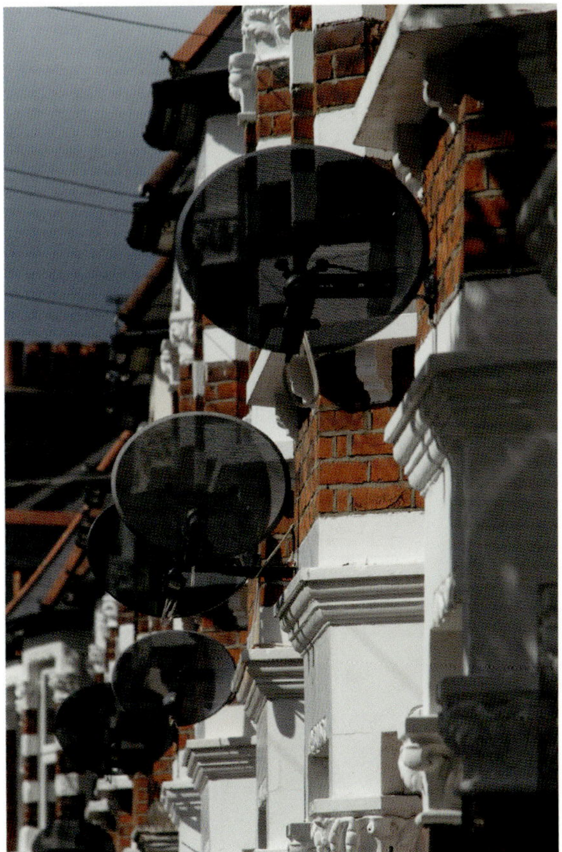

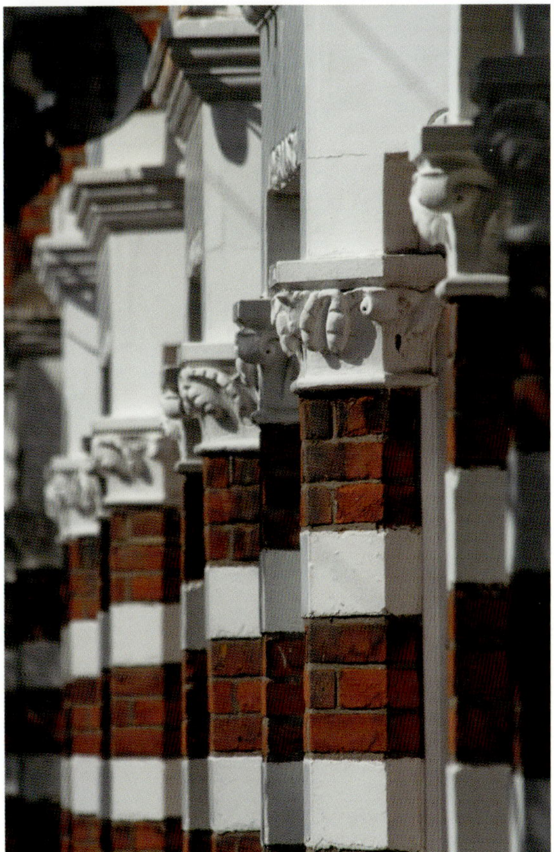

West Putney

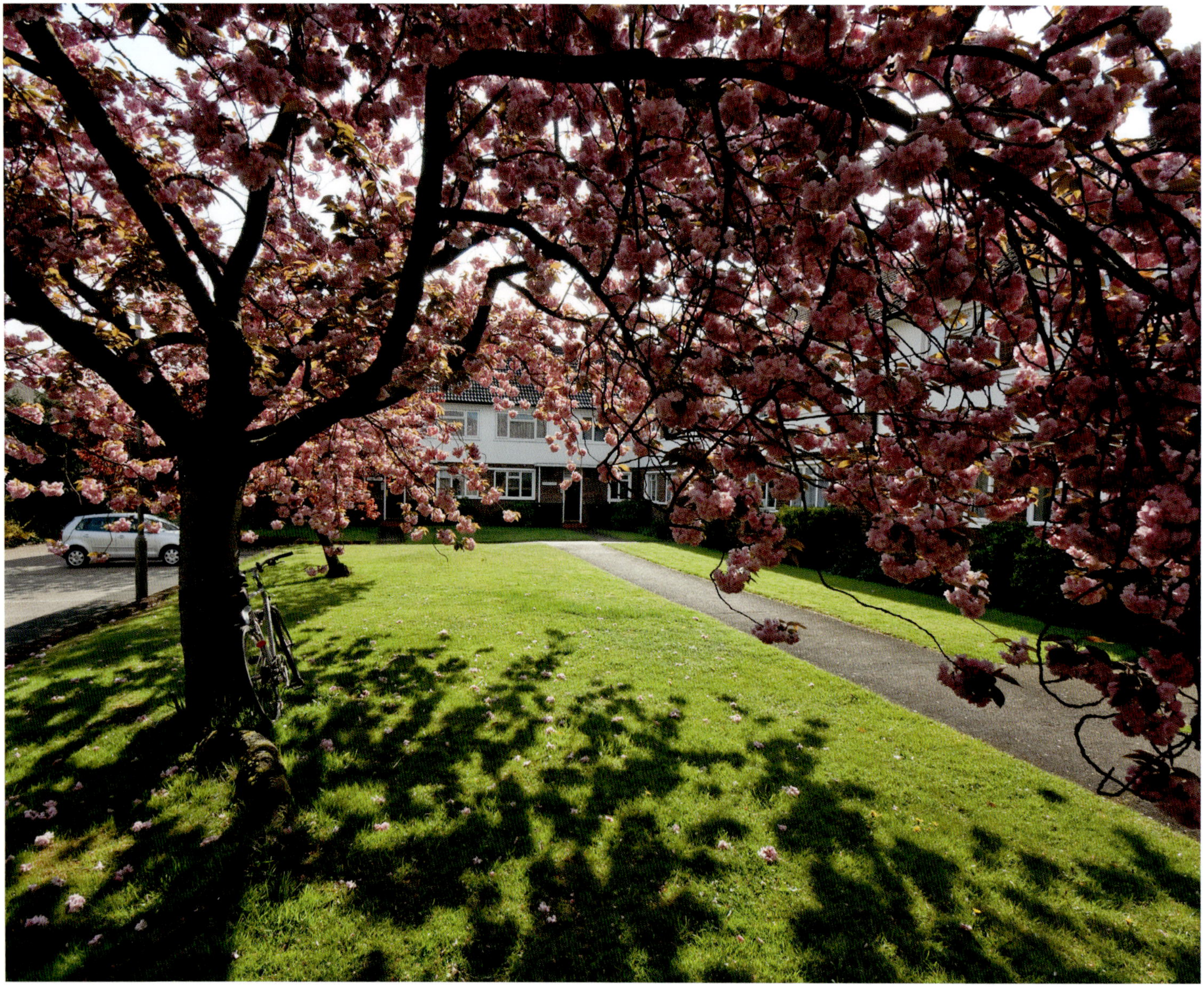

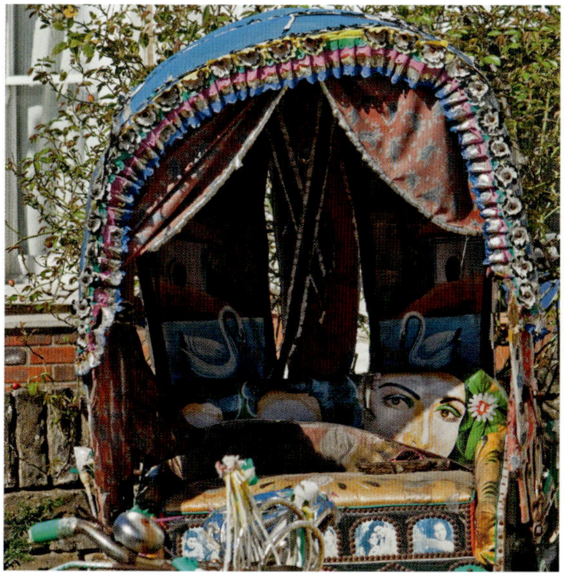

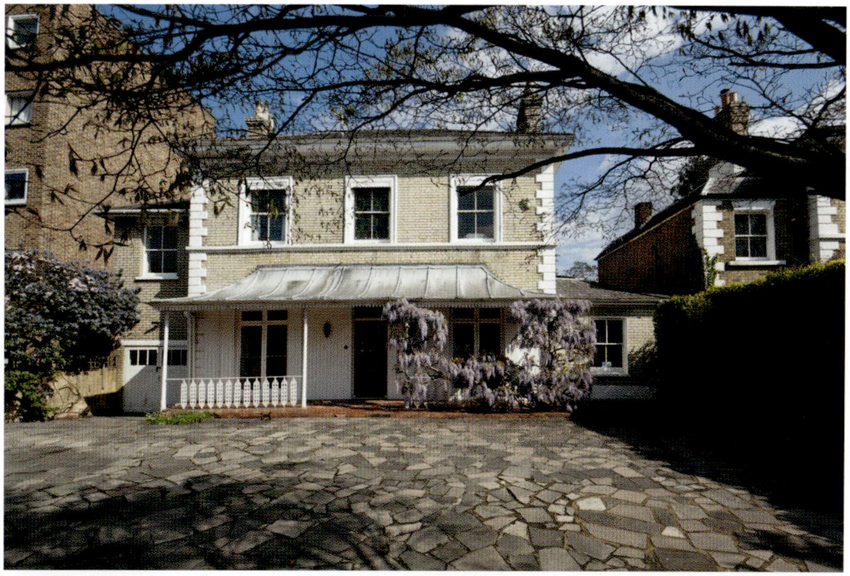

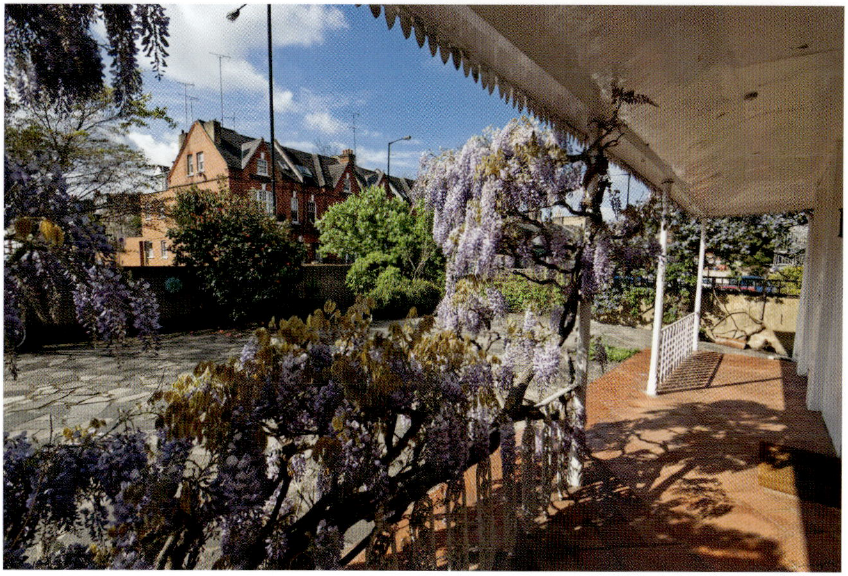

Page Opposite:
Radcliffe Square, off Putney Hill is not strictly West Putney, but what a beautiful display of blossom they had back in the spring.

Top Left: This Indian rickshaw in Norroy Road is a funny thing to have in your front garden.

Right: Some of the houses along the northern side of the Upper Richmond Road have beautiful awnings and if that wasn't enough, the owners of this one kindly let me photograph the gorgeous Wisteria they have.

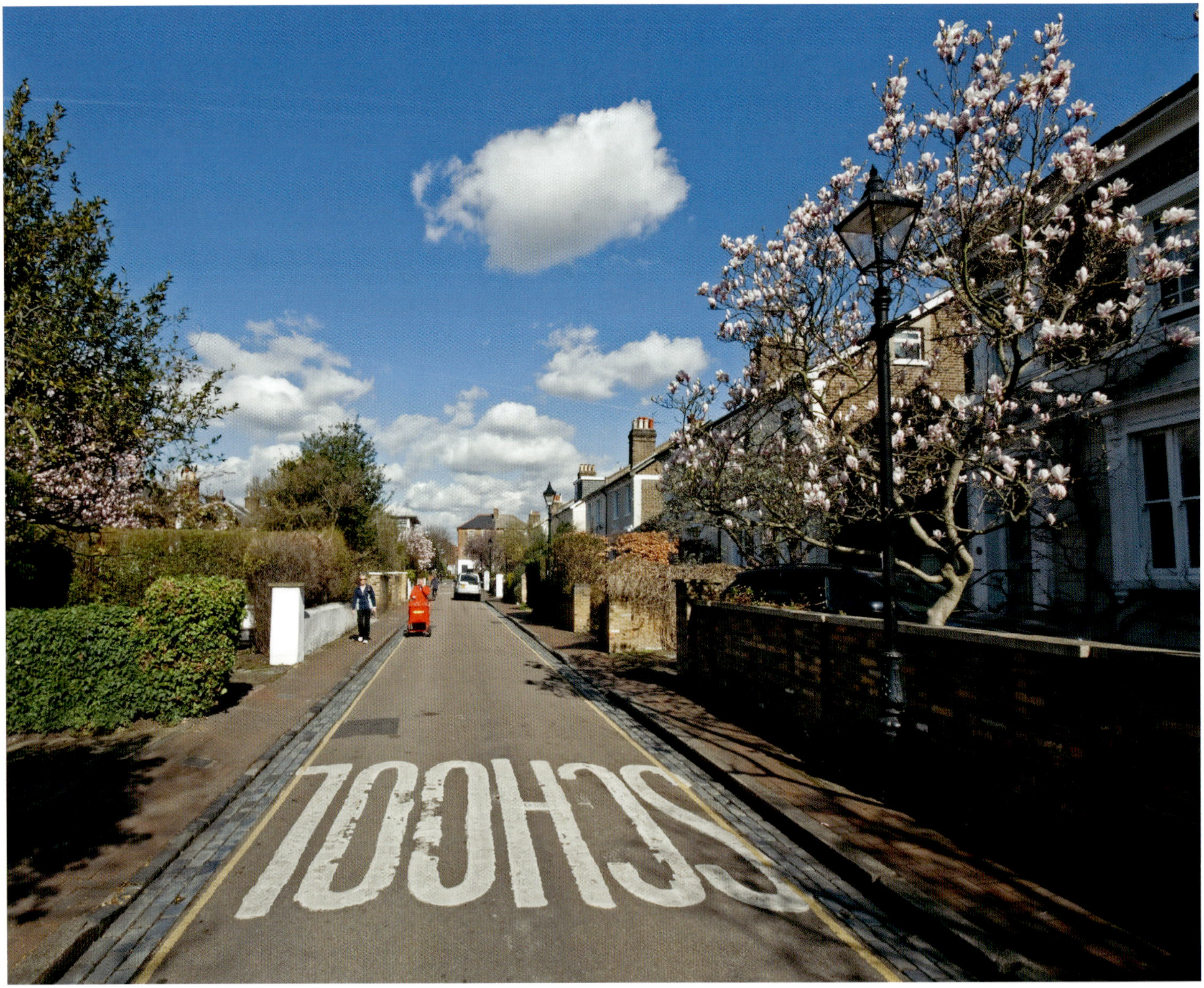
SCHOOL

Page Opposite: Charlwood Road.

Below Left: Quill Lane.

Bottom Left: The RSPCA Animal Hospital in Clarendon Drive.

Top Right: Putney Old Burial Ground, created due to overcrowding in St Mary's Church and churchyard. It was provided by Rev Roger Mortlock Pettiward DD and conecrated 2nd Nov 1763 by Archbishop of Canterbury, Thomas Secker. It is the burial place of several local 'notables', including explorer & MP Robert Wood, novelist Harriet Thomson, and Stratford Canning, uncle of Putney Heath duellist, then later Prime Minister, George Canning. Converted to present open space in 1963.

Bottom Right: Cherry blossom on Cambalt Road.

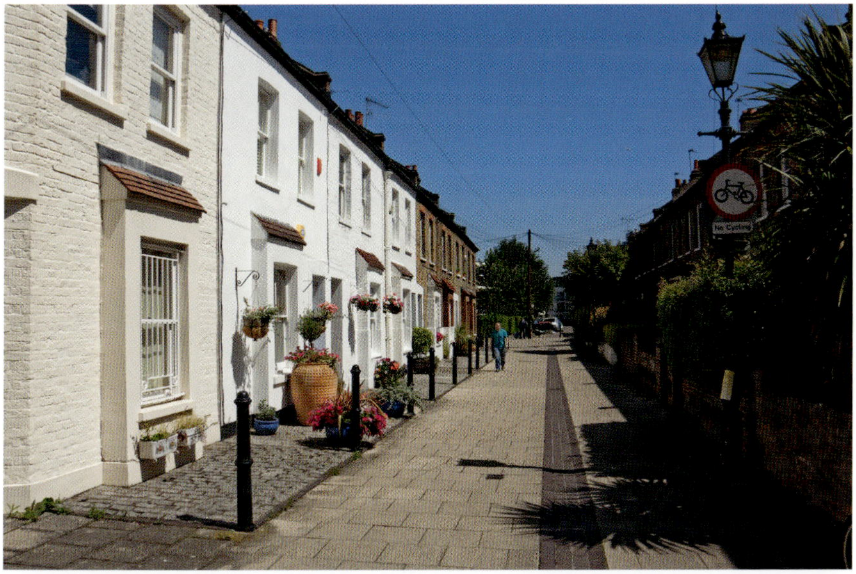

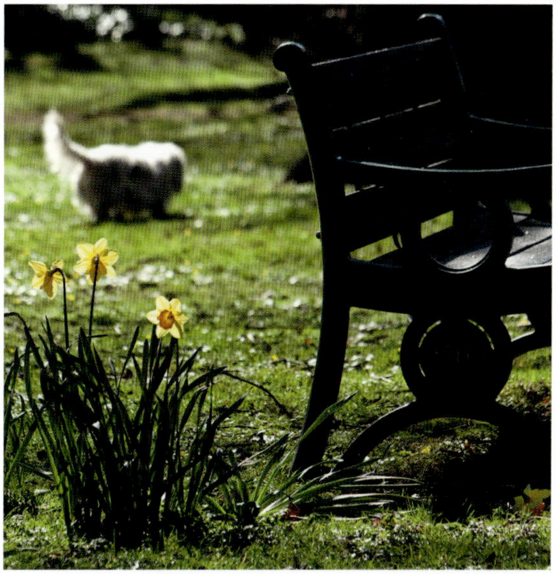

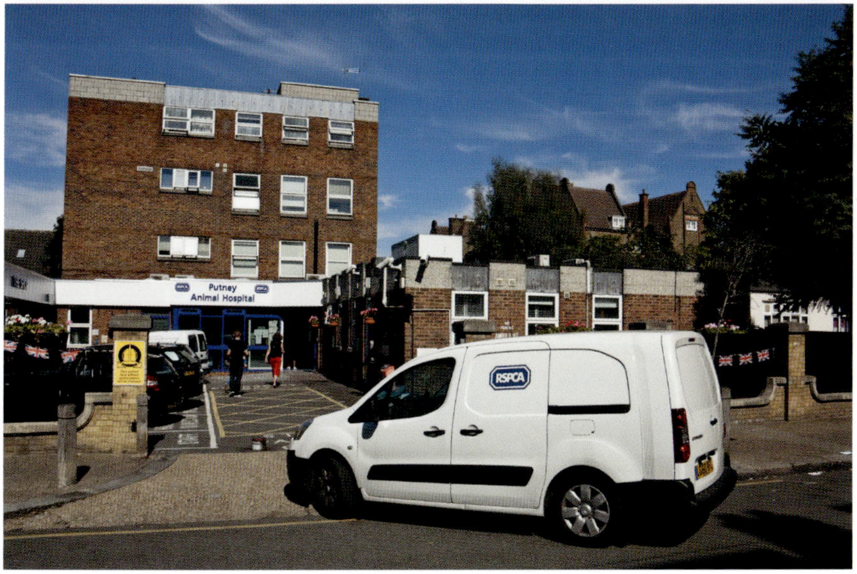

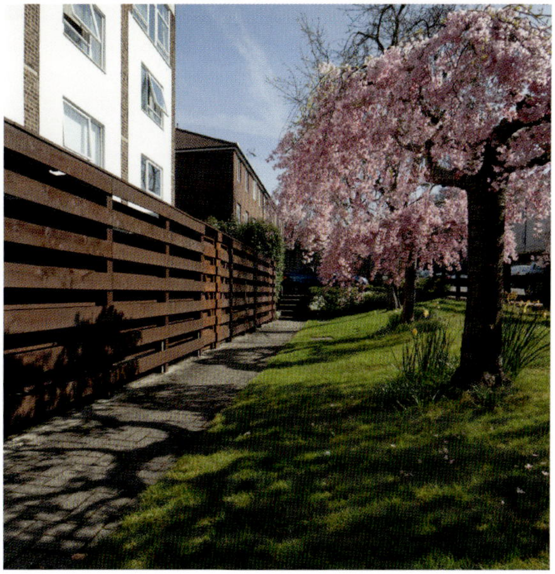

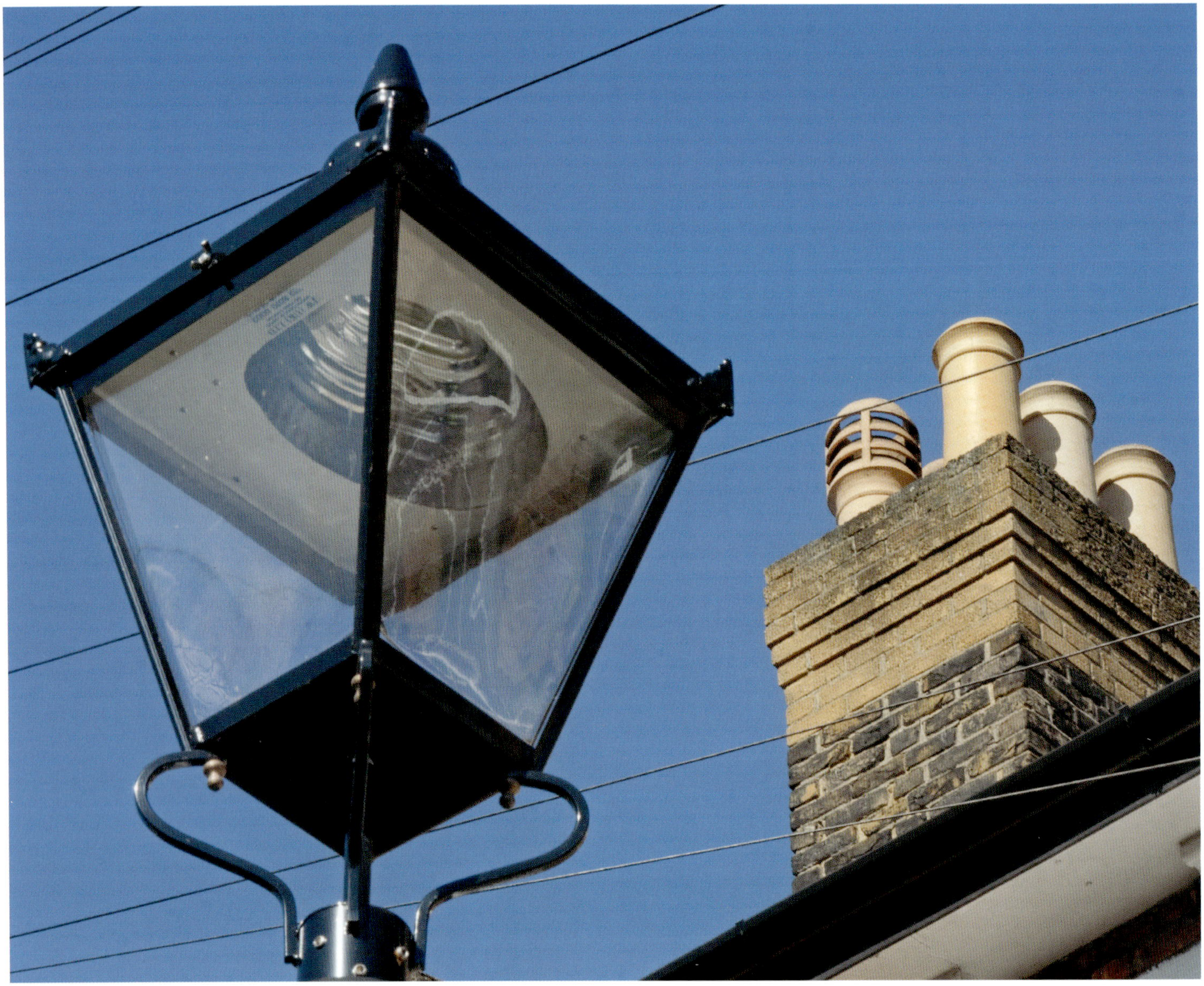

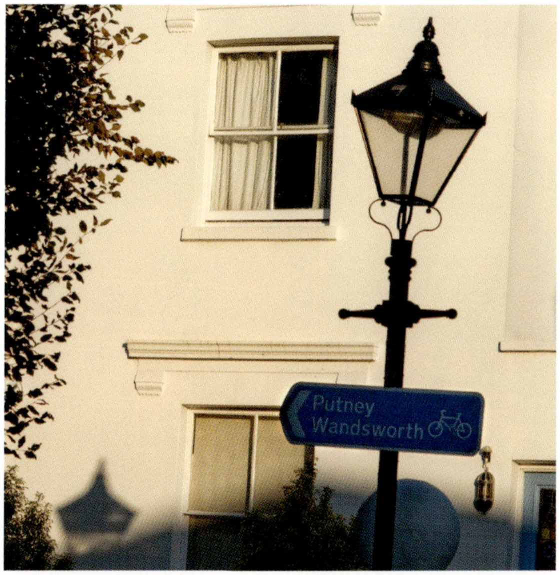

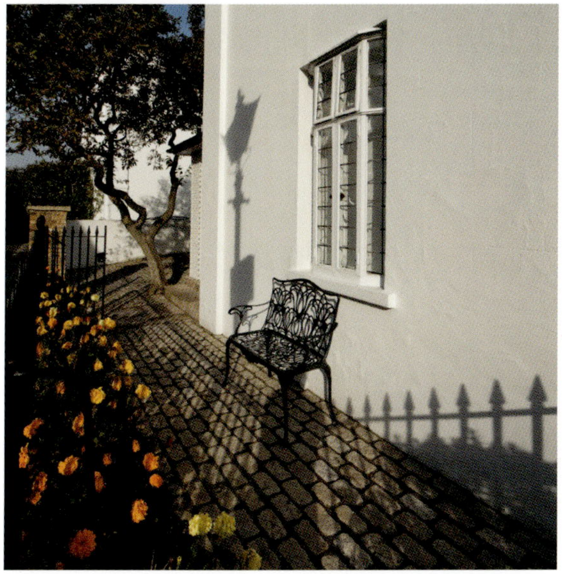

Wherever you go throughout Putney, there are still many original light fittings.

Opposite: Spencer Walk.

Top Left: Charlwood Road.

Bottom Left and Right: Parkfields.

Overleaf (Left to Right): March Court; Putney Leisure Centre, both on the Upper Richmond Road.

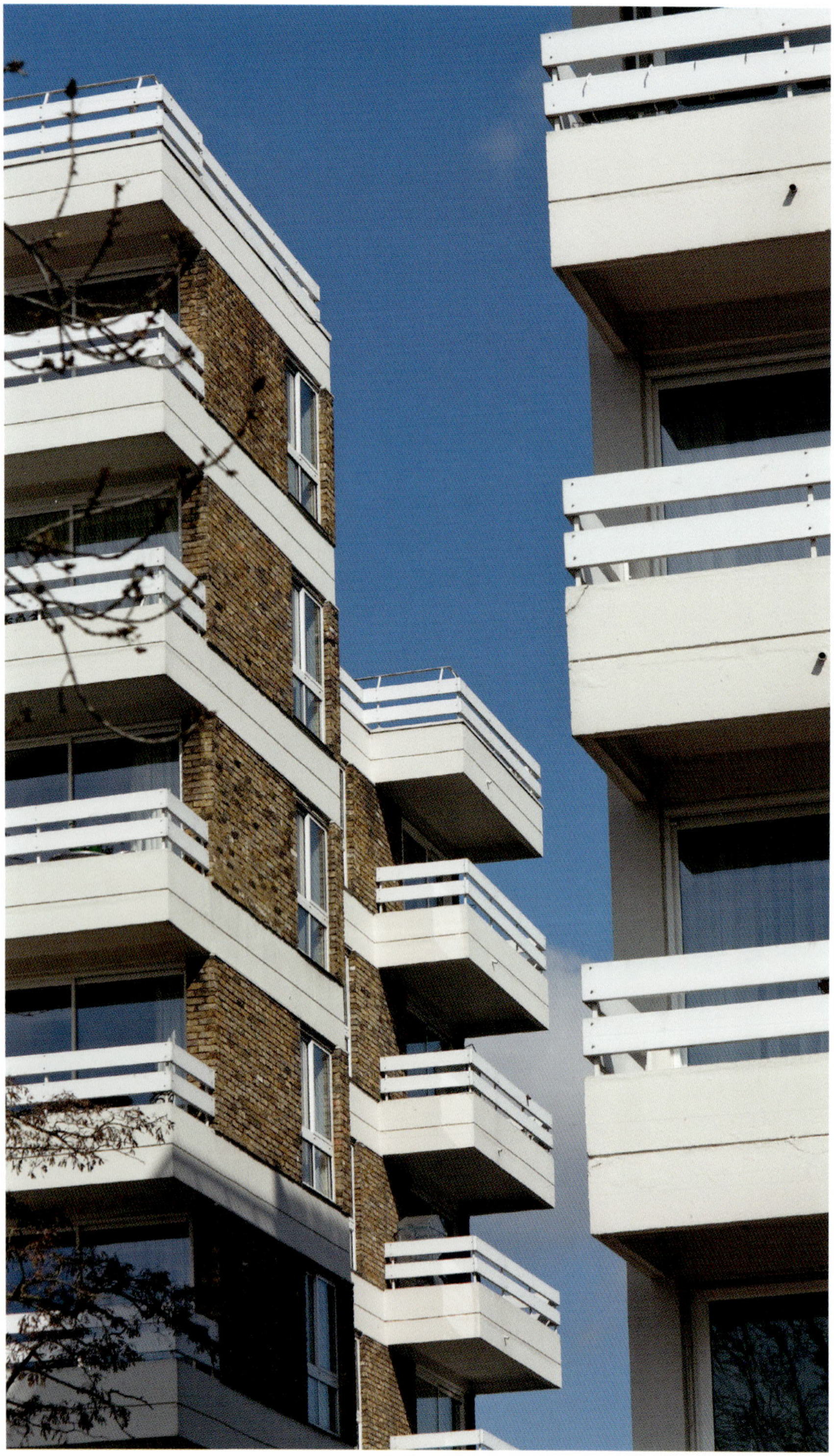

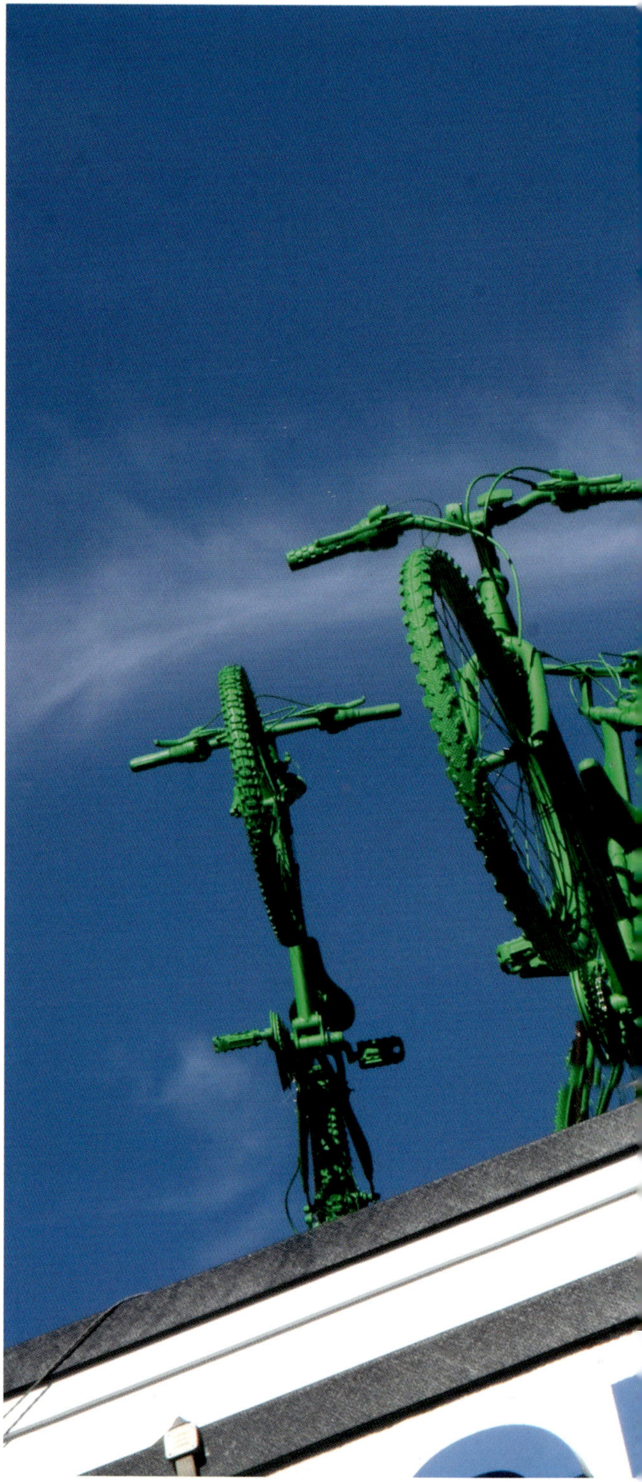

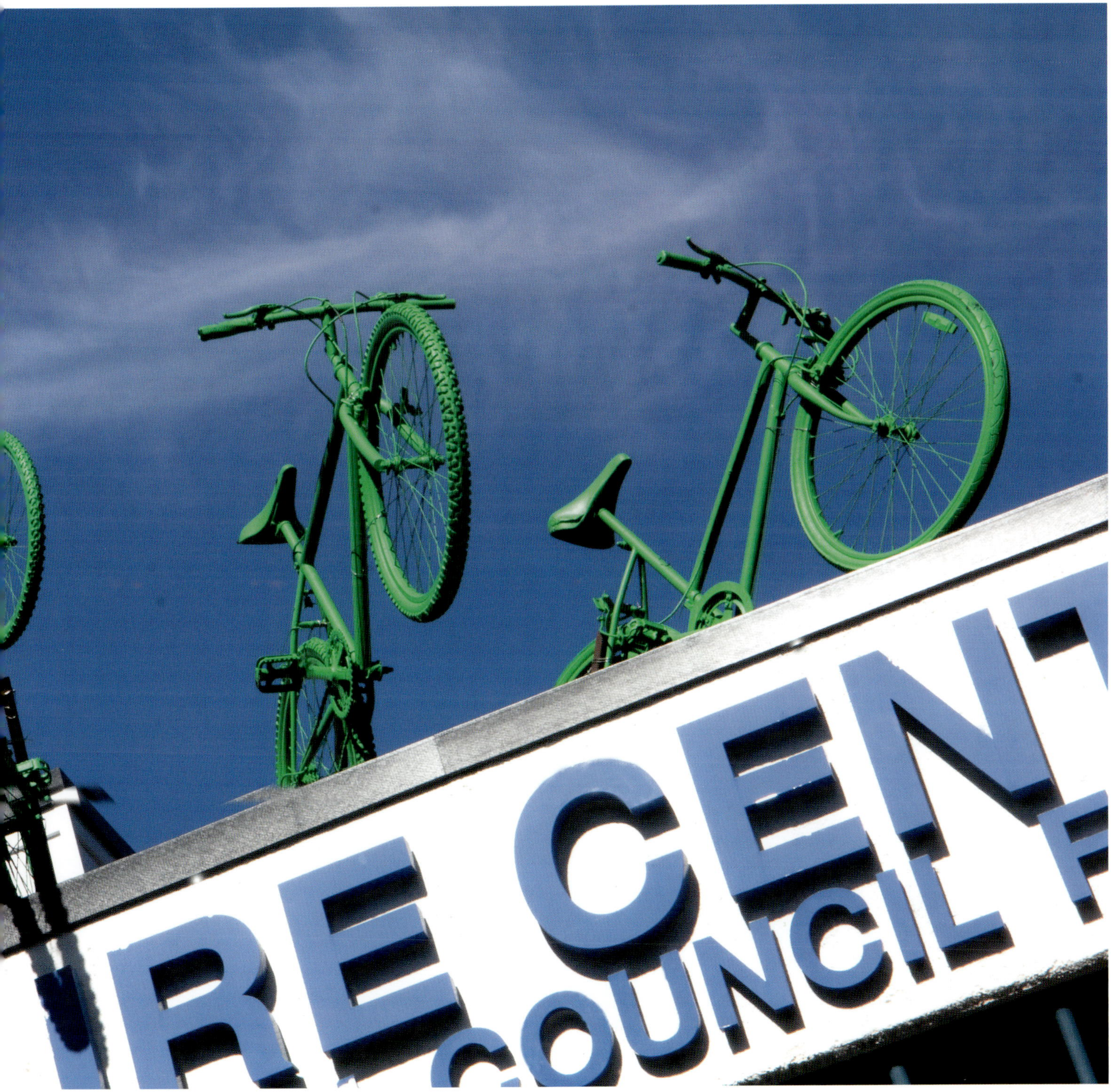
RE CEN
COUNCIL

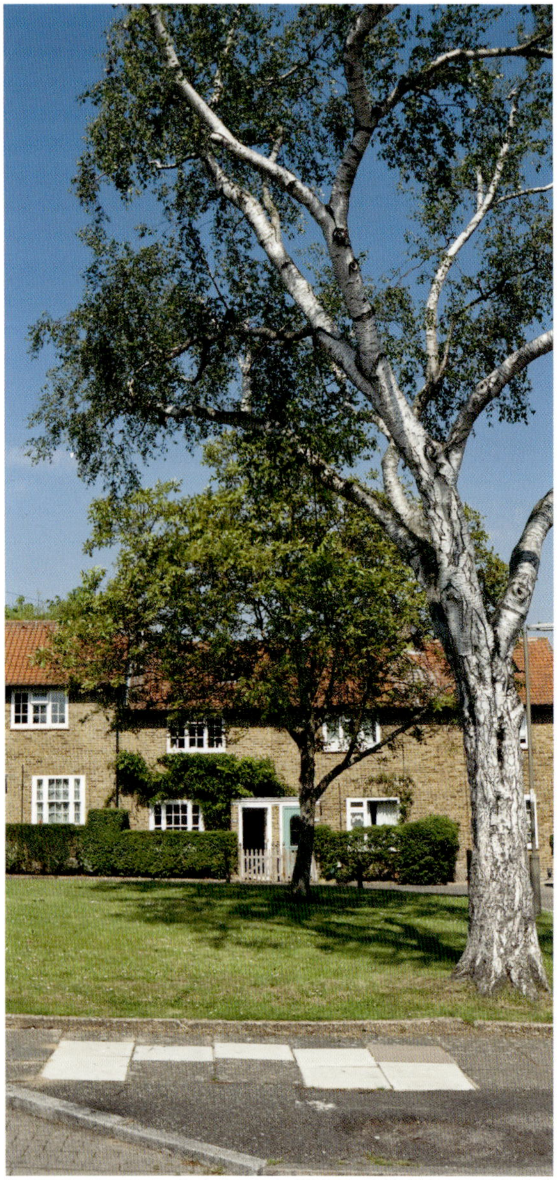

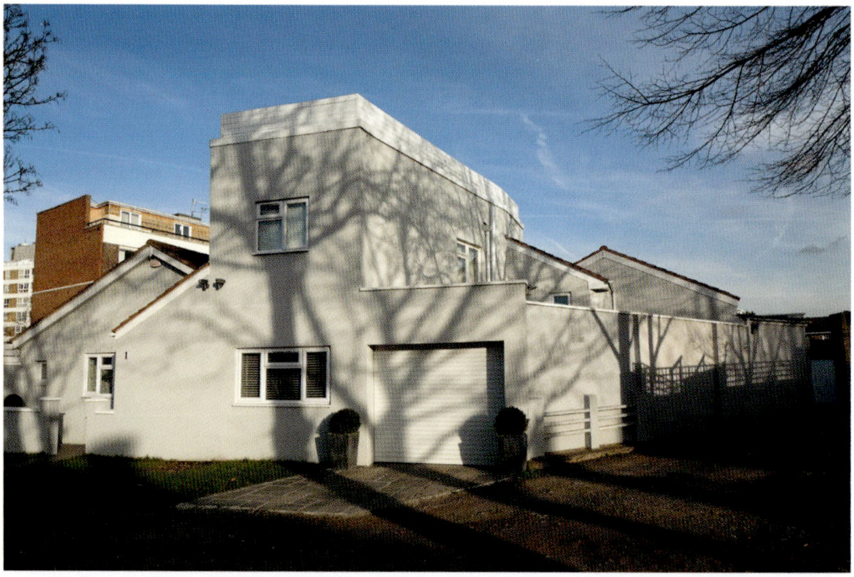

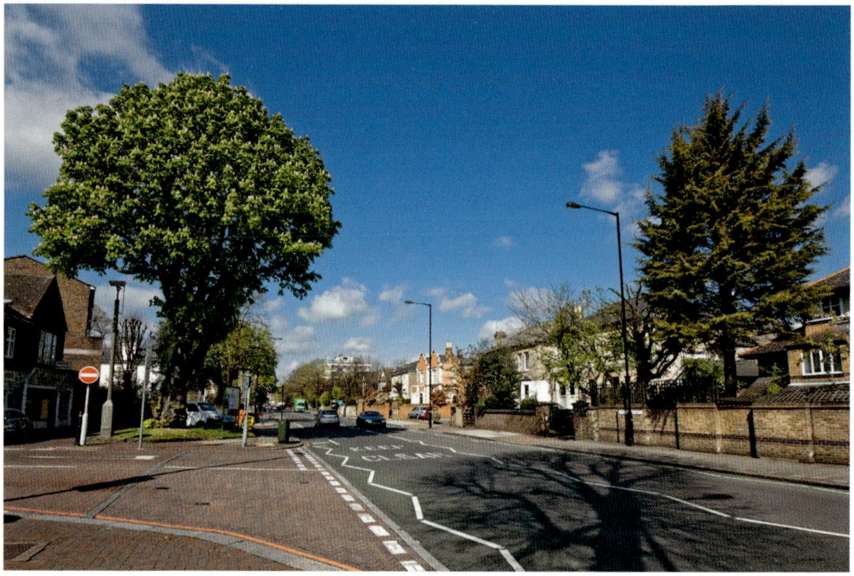

Above Left: Huntingfield Road.

Top: Putney Park Lane.

Above: Upper Richmond Road, where it meets Dover House Road.

Opposite Top: Dover House Road.

Right: Putney Park Lane.

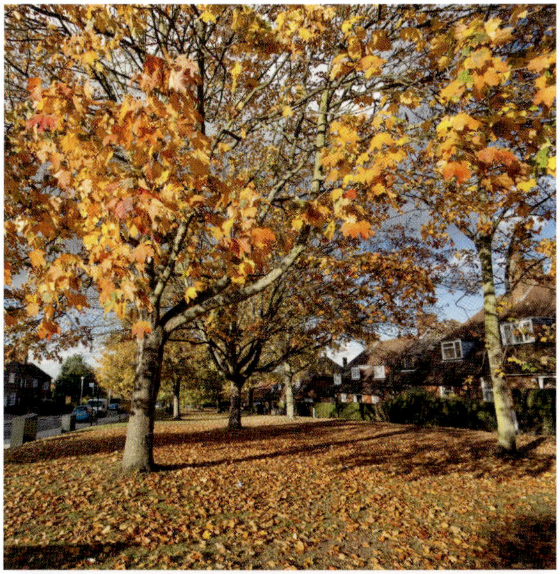
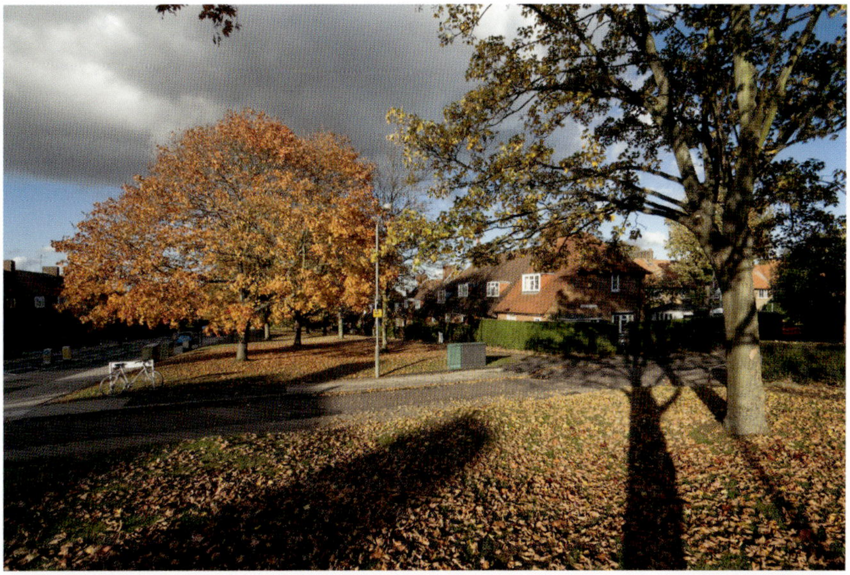
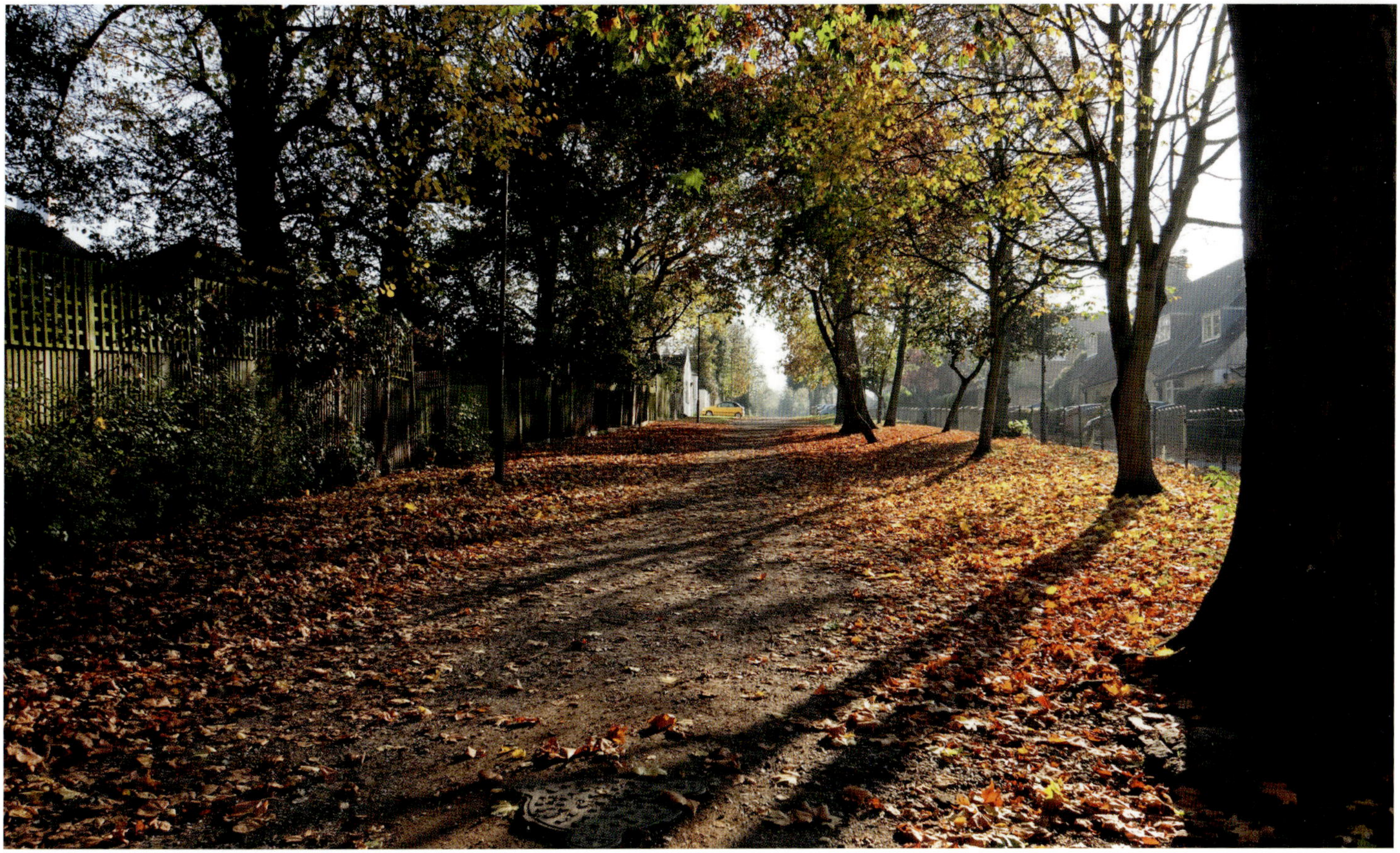

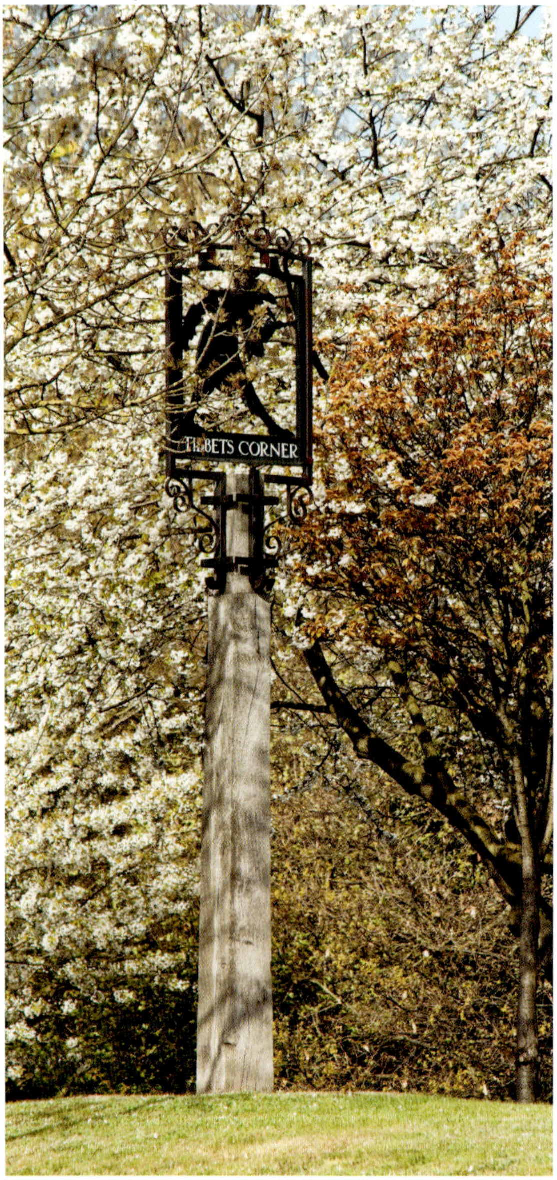

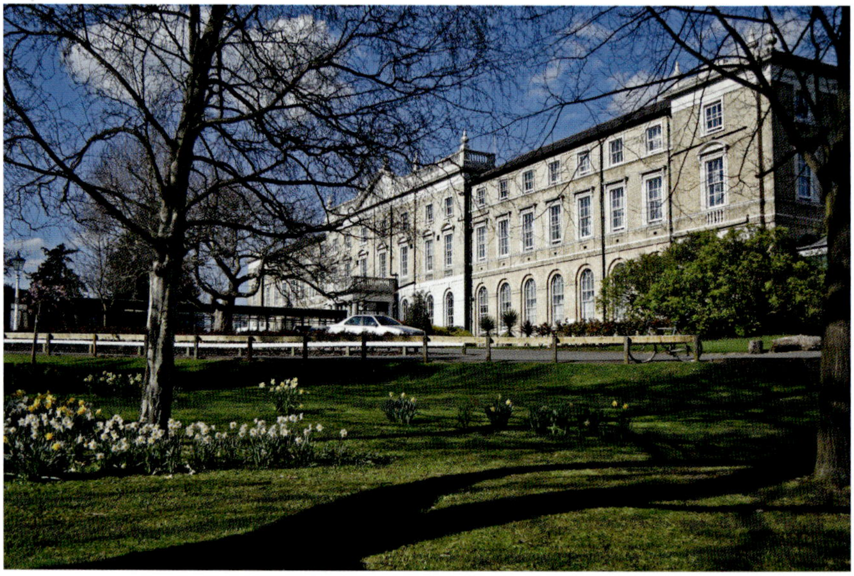

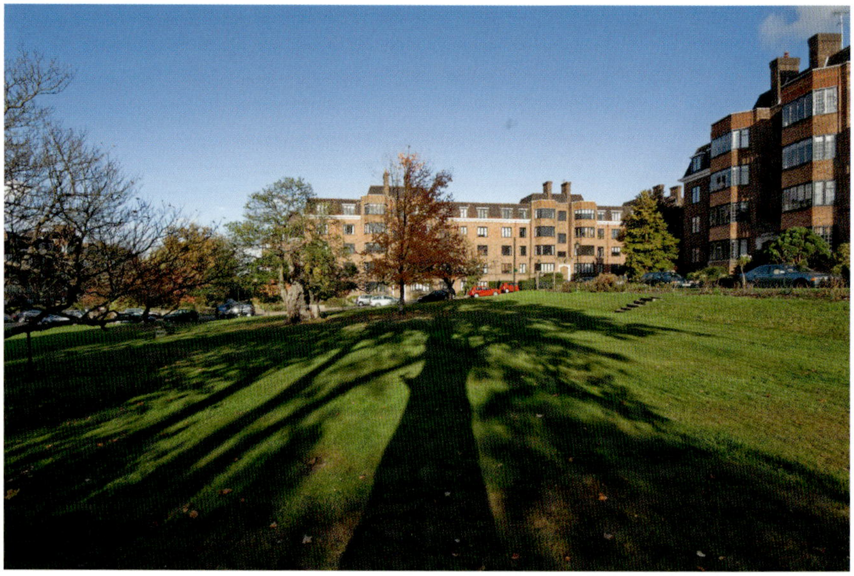

Above: Tibbet's Corner, where Putney Hill meets the A3 out of London.

Top: The Royal Hospital for Neuro-Disability, West Hill. This impressive building was part of Lord Spencer's original Wimbledon Park and has been successfully helping the sick for over 150 years.

Above: The Manor Fields Estate off Putney Hill, consists of two hundred and thirty flats of differing sizes in 14 houses and was built in the early 1930s on twelve acres of landscaped gardens adjacent to Putney Heath.

Opposite Page: The beautiful Beech Tree in Roehampton Close, off Roehampton Lane.

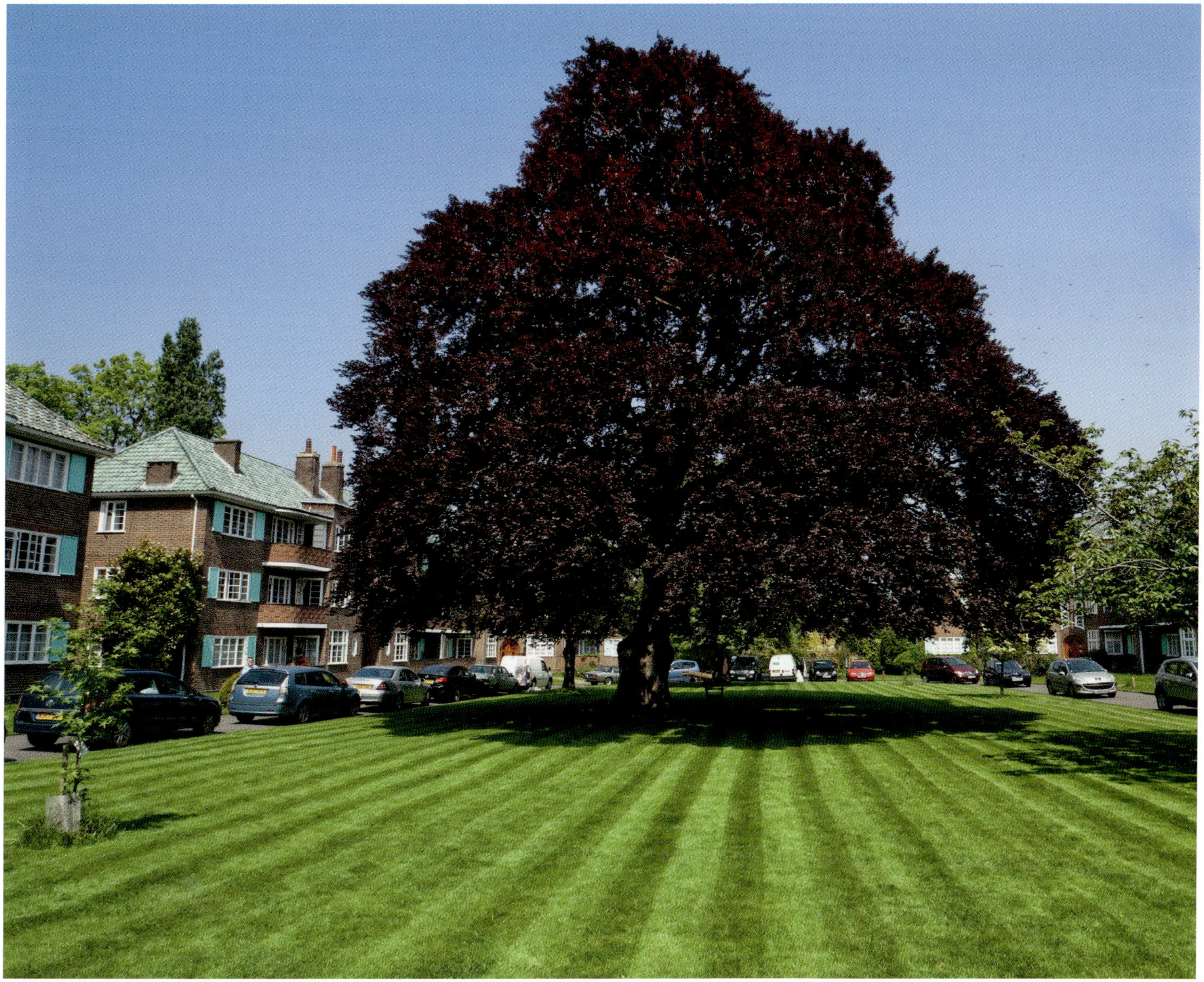

The Ashburton Estate

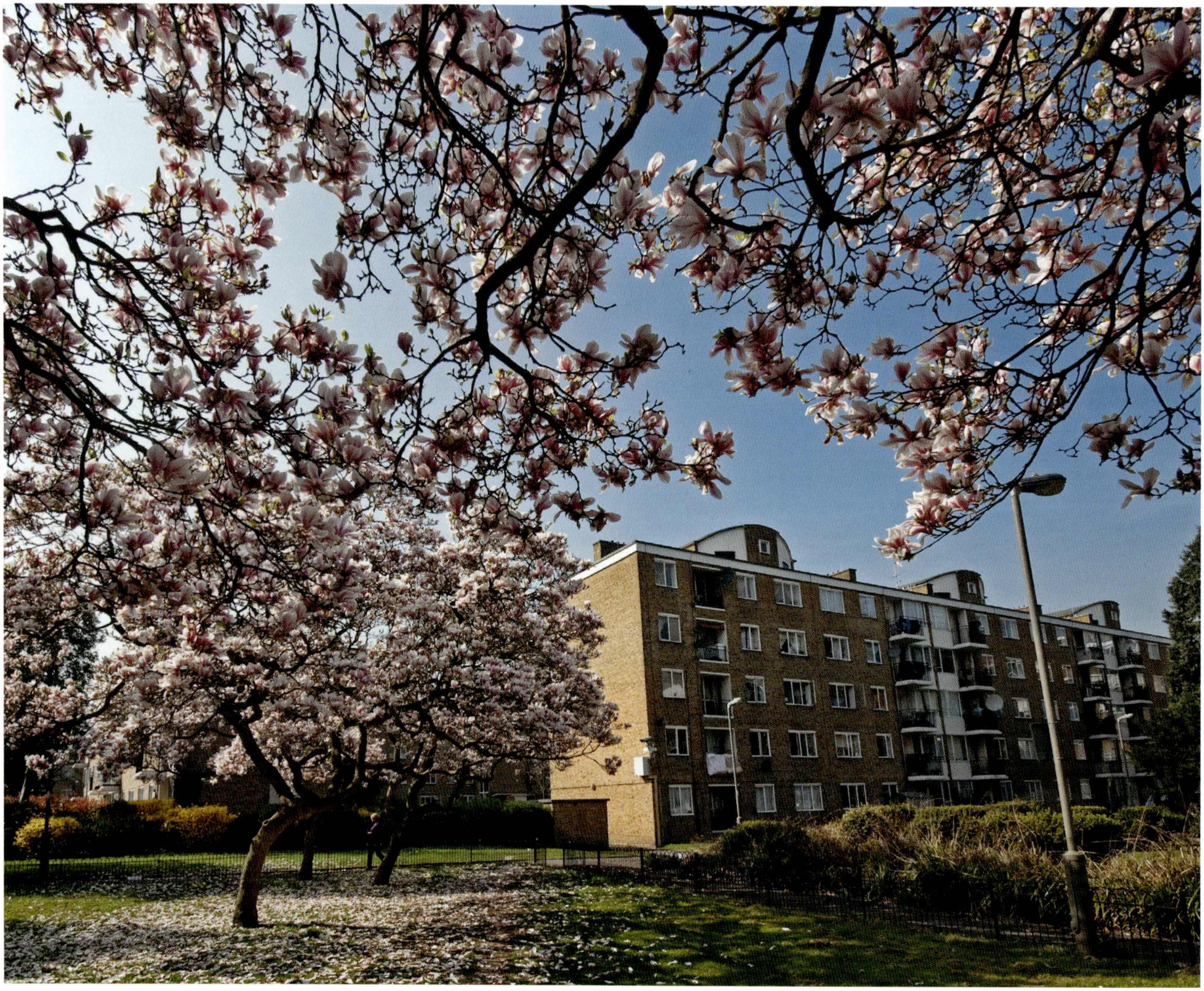

Covering a large area near Putney Heath, the Estate, with its distinctive arched roofs, covers land where once stood some of the grander houses of Putney, such as Ashburton House and Exeter House. The green spaces in between with lovely cedar trees hint at what was there before.

Bottom Right:
Ashburton Youth Club.

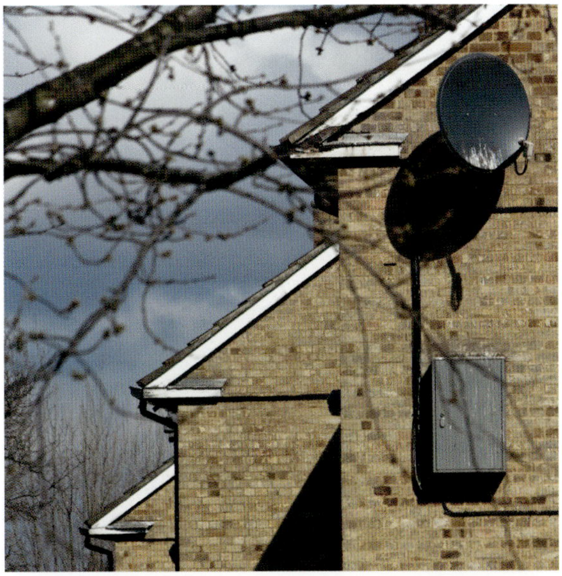

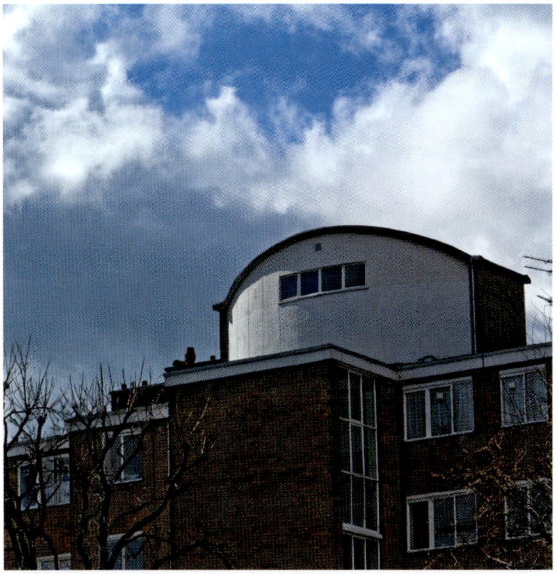

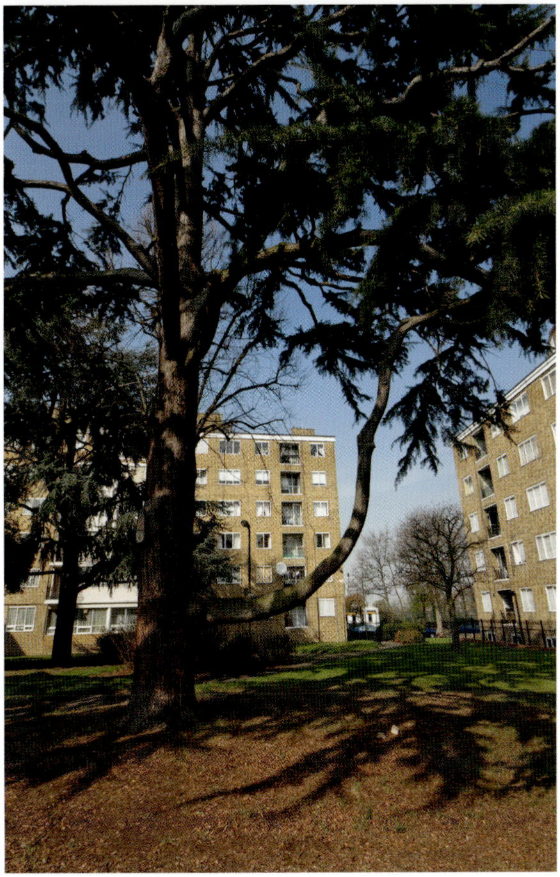

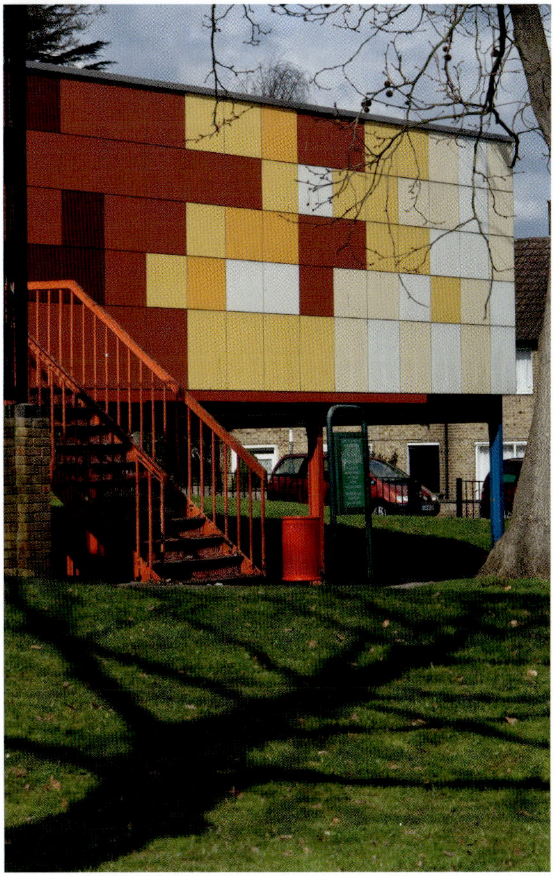

Roehampton Allotments, Dover House Road

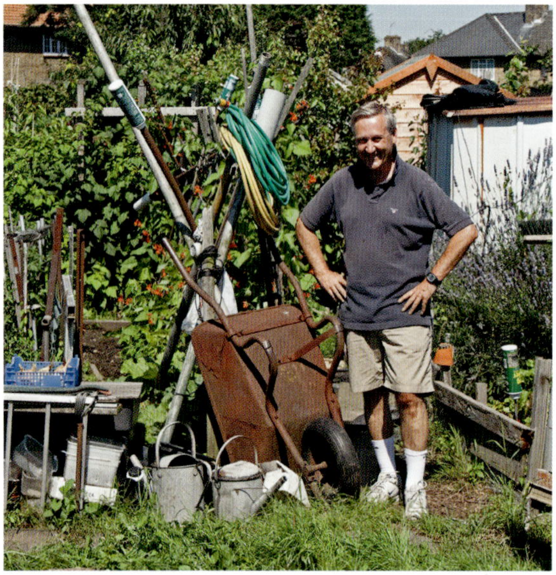

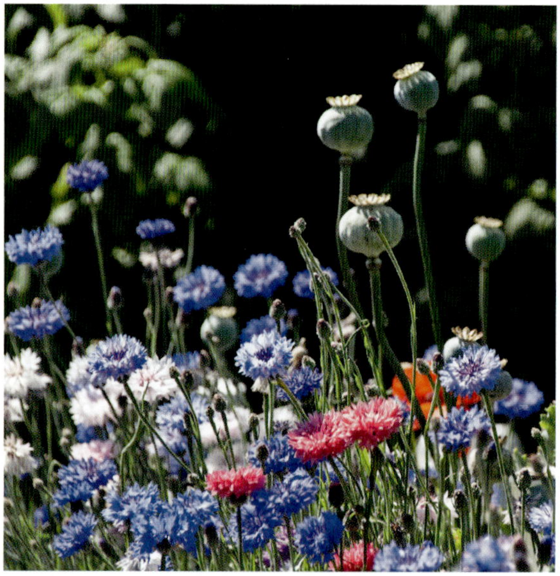

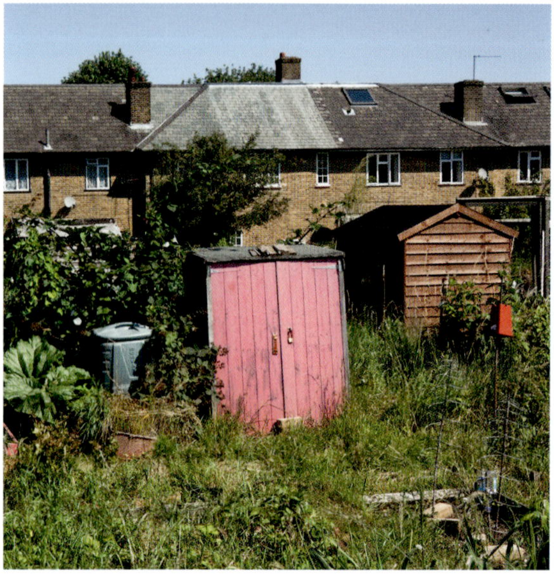

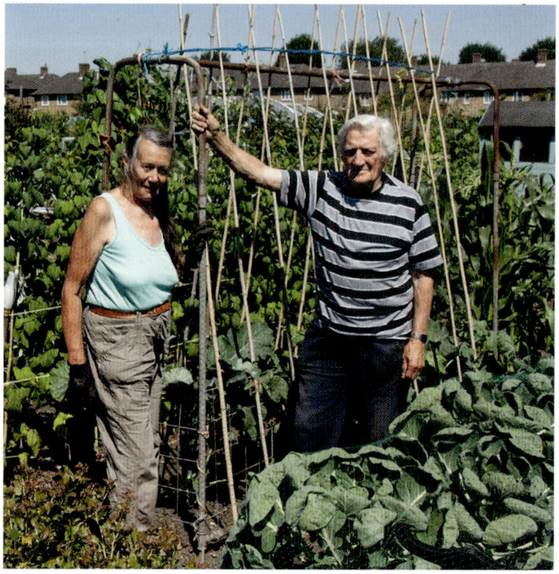

This marvellous green space is hidden behind the houses of the Dover House Estate, where there are approximately 180 plots of varying size. Managed by the Roehampton Garden Society, who together with such organisations as The Putney Society, have kept the allotments from being developed over the years. The allotments can trace their history back to 1922, when the surrounding estate was built (from what was originally the lands of Dover House and Putney Park House). When I was kindly invited to visit by my friend Stewart (top left), I was fortunate to meet some of the other characters, such as Paula and Frank (below left) who help to run the allotments. Another interesting fact that I learnt on my visit is that there are several Anderson Shelters still being used as sheds by people (see right). Anderson Shelters were used in the War to try and protect people during the Blitz.

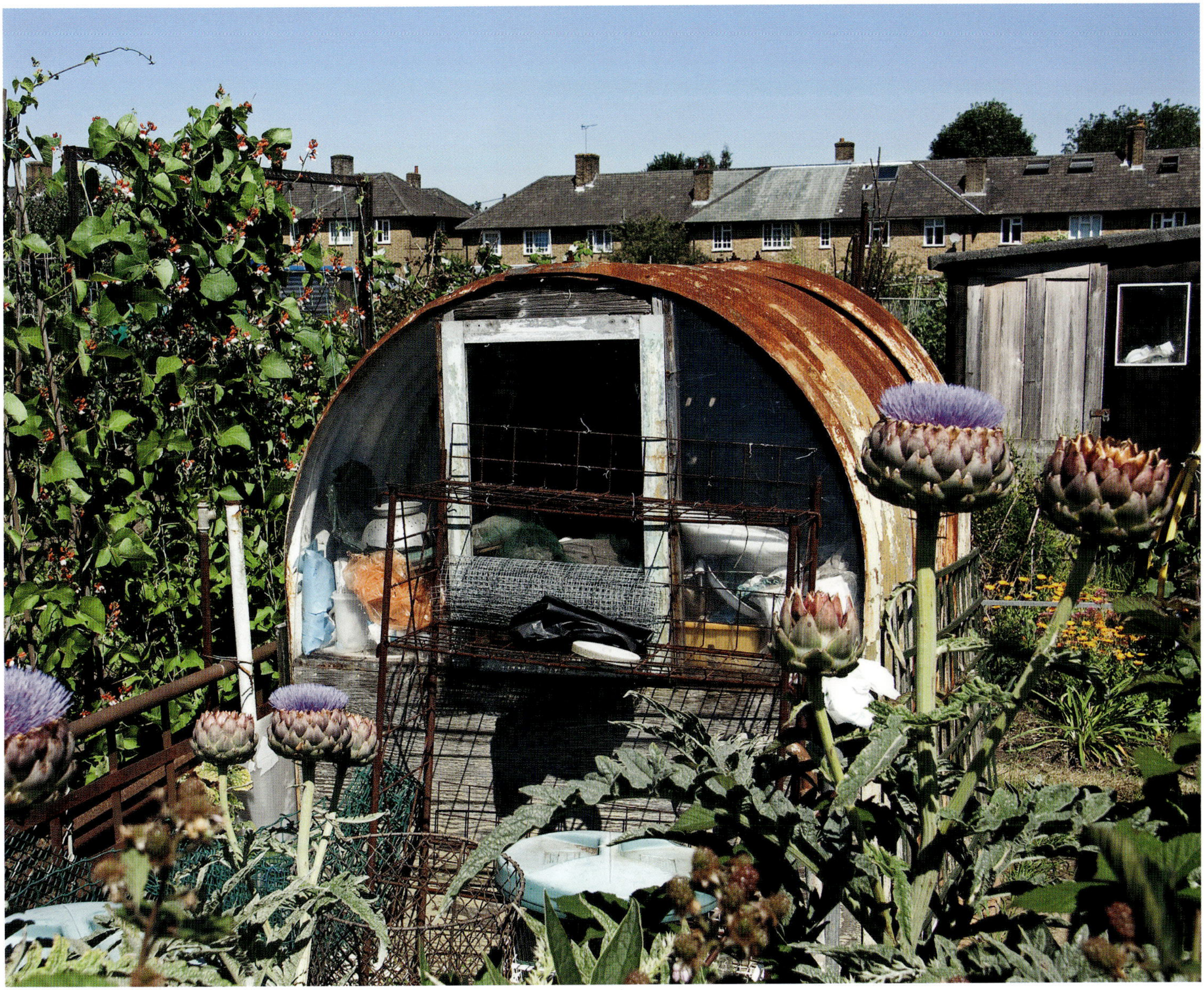

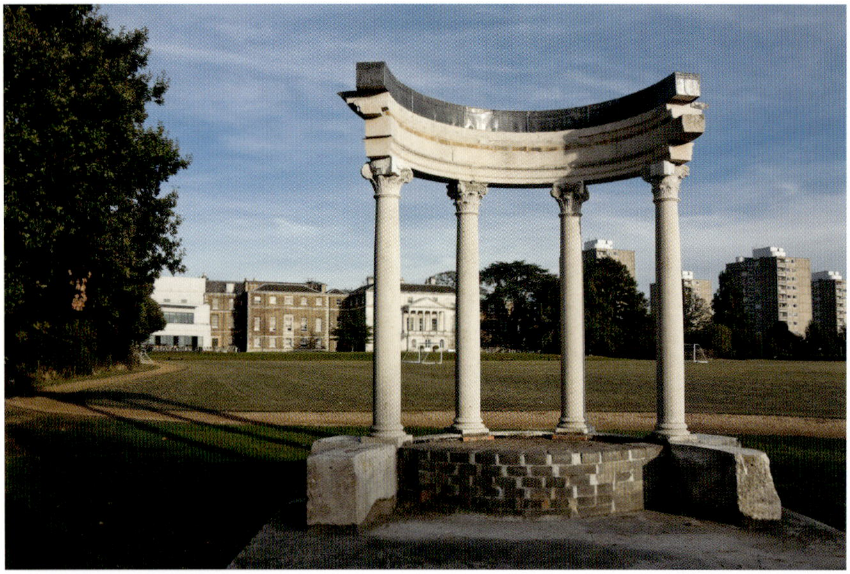

The Alton Estate, Roehampton

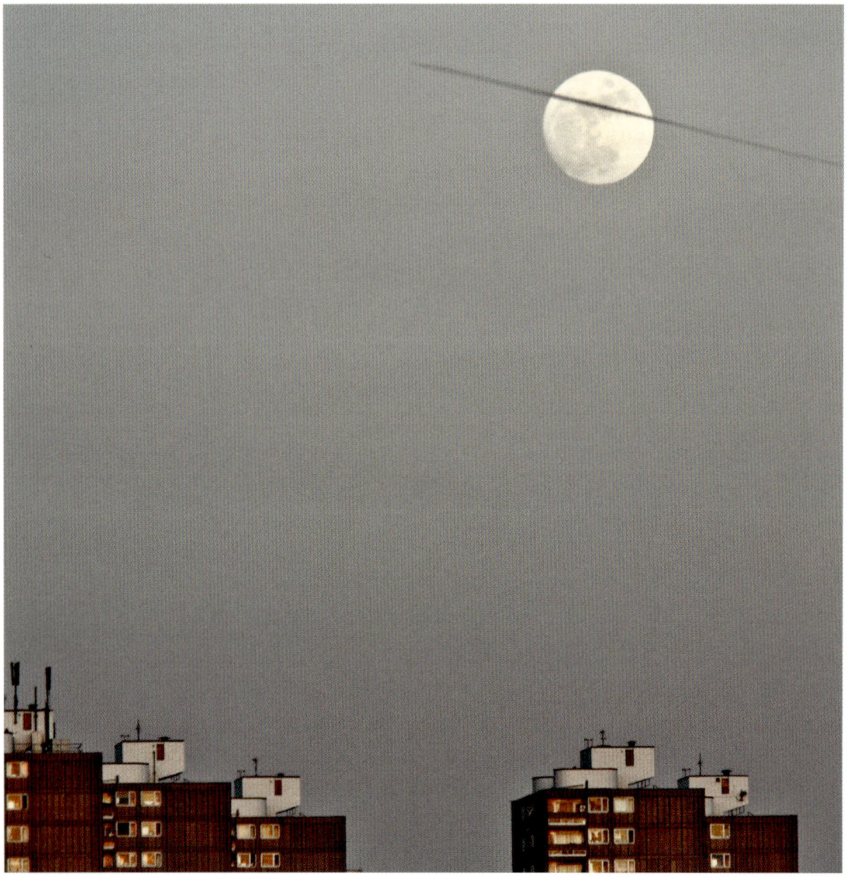

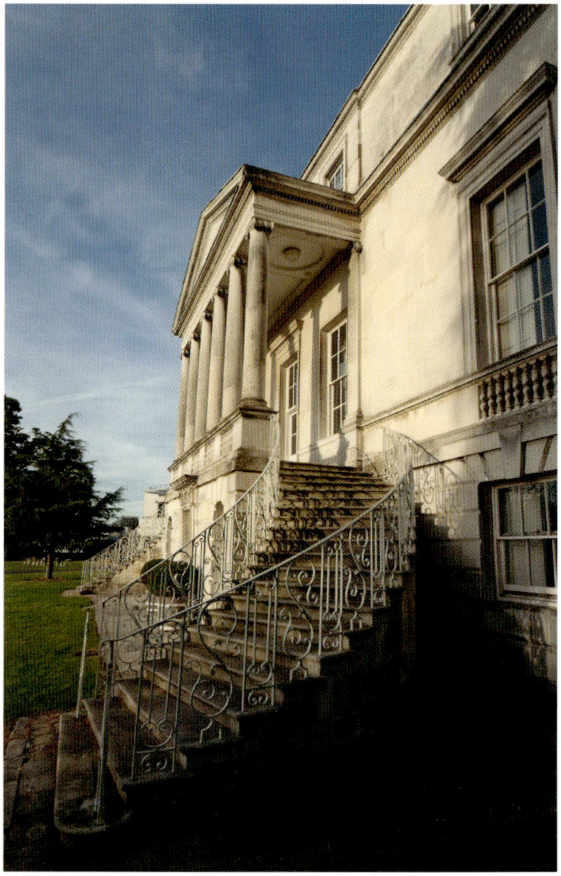

Page Opposite Top: Parkstead House, part of Roehampton University, with the Alton Estate in the background.

Page Opposite Bottom Left: The Alton Estate as seen from Richmond Park.

Page Opposite Bottom Right: Parkstead House.

Below: Part of the Wandsworth Arts festival 2012 took place on the Alton Estate, where one particular artist placed green coloured bicycles on the sides of blocks in the Estate, which was an inspired idea. This one was on the Library in Danebury Avenue, with Holy Trinity church behind.

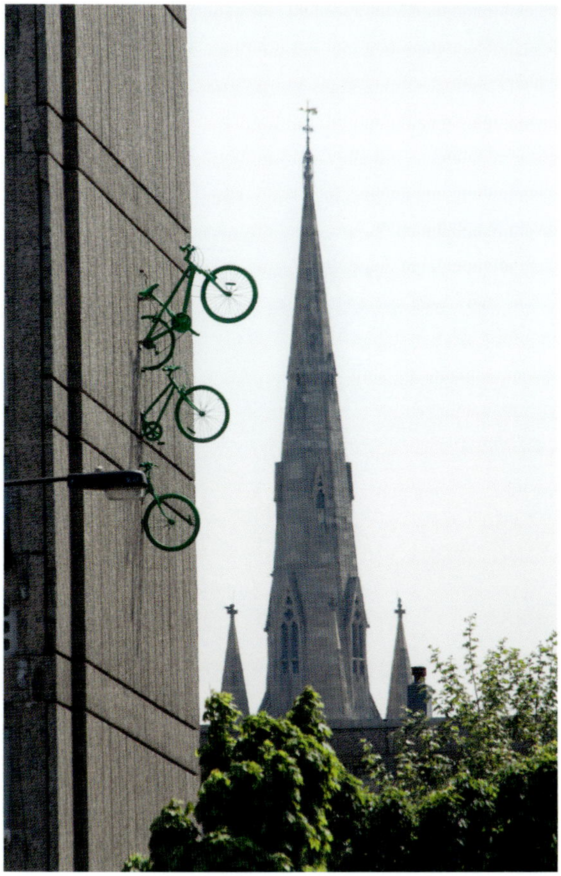

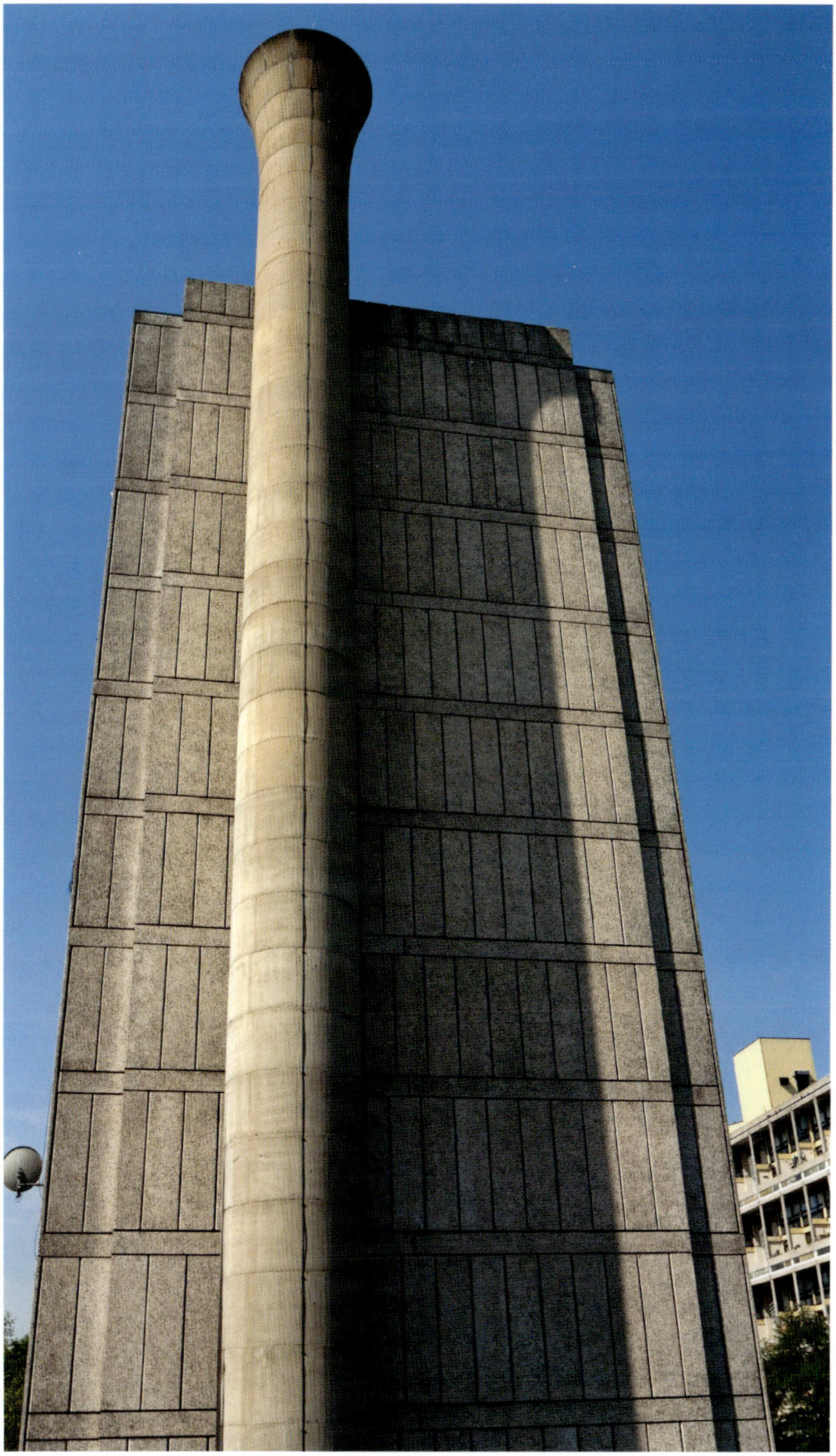

Churches

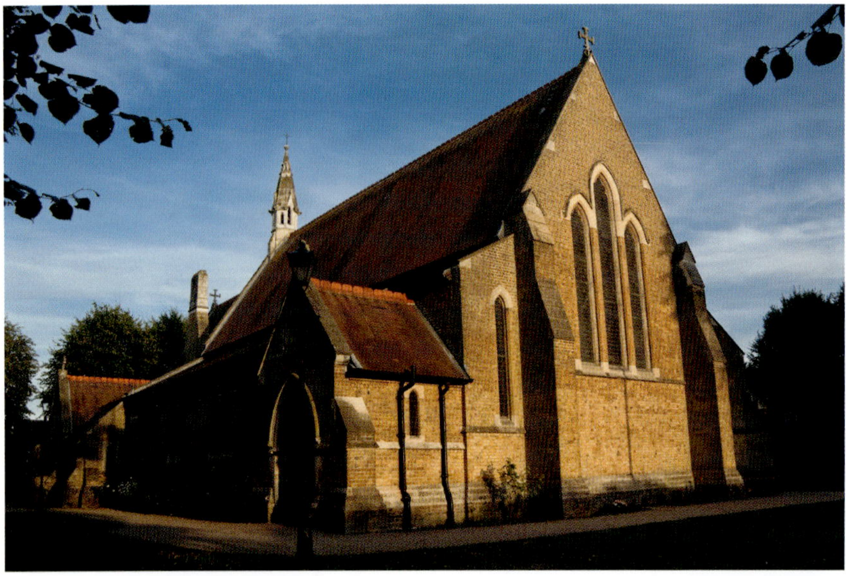

All Saints Putney Common. Built in 1874 and one of two churches in the Parish of Putney, the other being St Mary's. All Saints Church wasconsecrated on 25th April 1874.

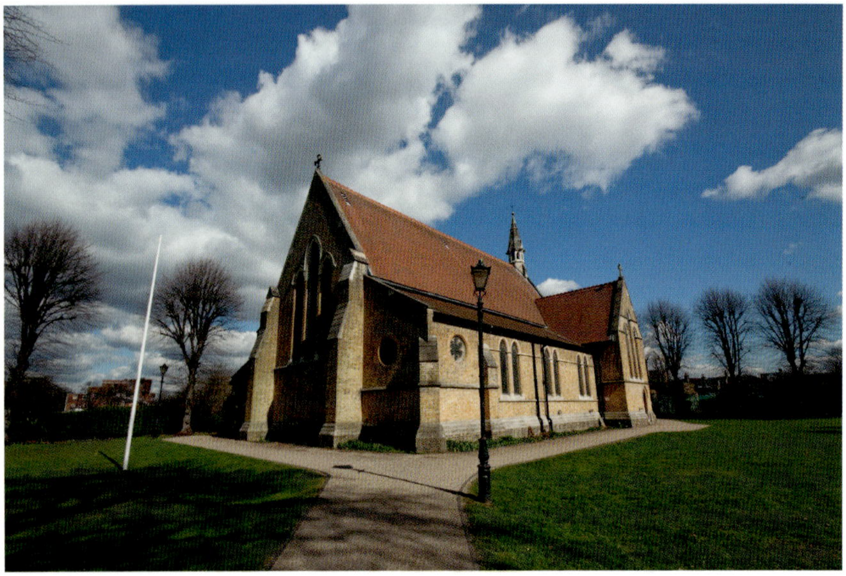

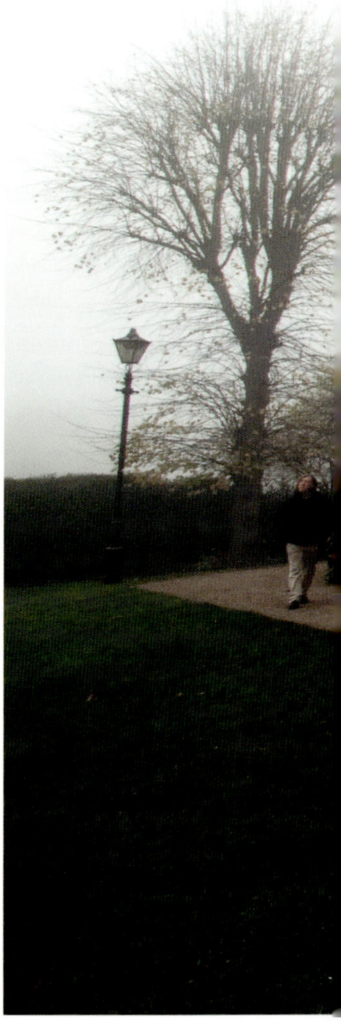

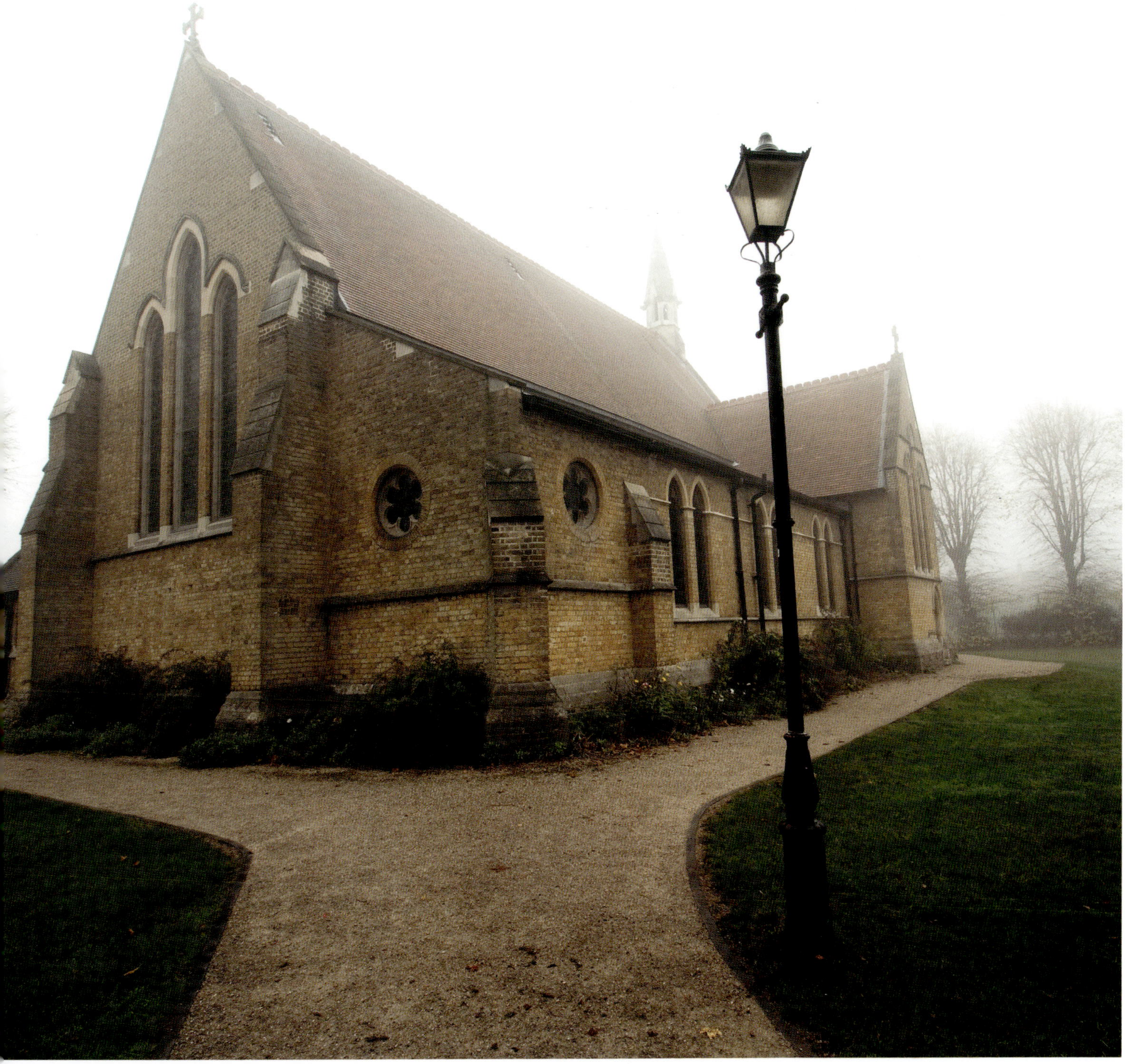

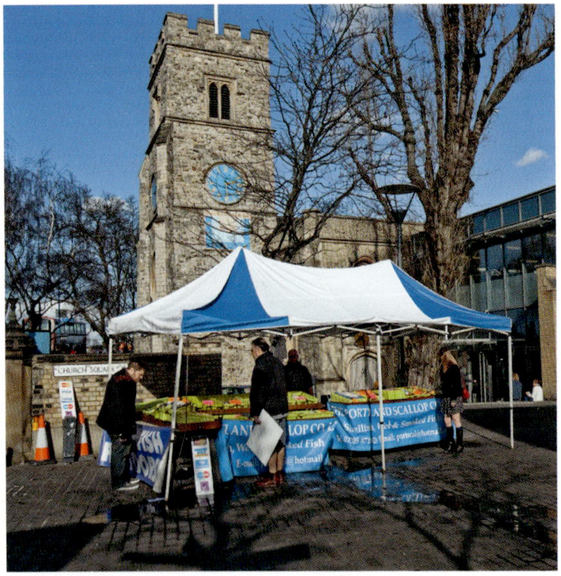

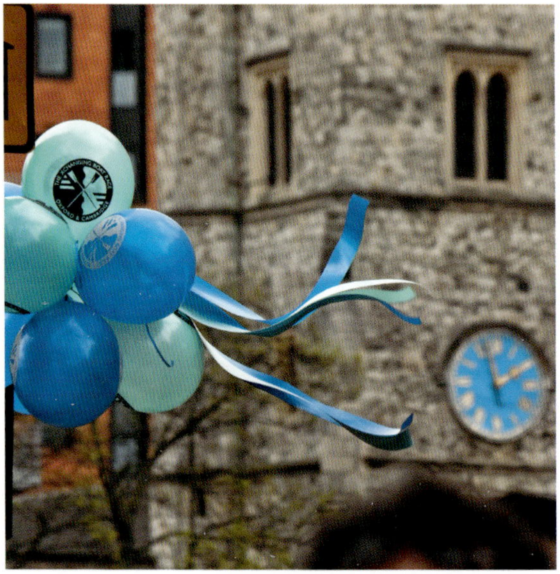

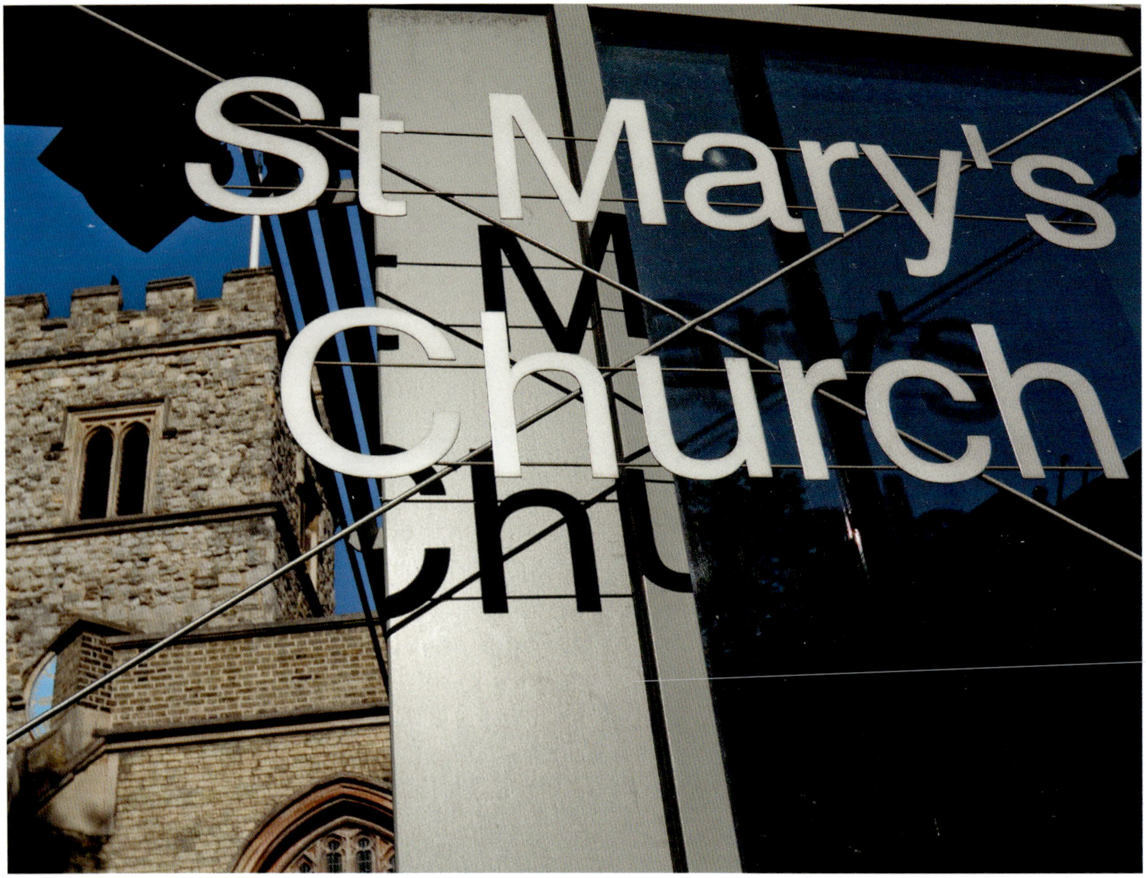

This Page: St Mary's, Putney Wharf. One of the most well known churches in Putney on account of its position. Steeped in history, the tower is 15th Century and the church was the site of the Putney Debates in 1647, during the English Civil War. St Mary's was rebuilt 1836, to a design by Edward Lapidge, extensively damaged by arson in June 1973 (tower, walls and pillars survived) and re-hallowed in 1982, with a new interior designed by Ronald Sim. Today, they have a modern extension, containing a café and regularly hold events and meetings for various local clubs and associations.

Opposite: St Margaret's in Putney Park Lane. Built in the 1800s, it became St Margaret's in 1912. It is thought to be named after the person who donated it to the local Church Council.

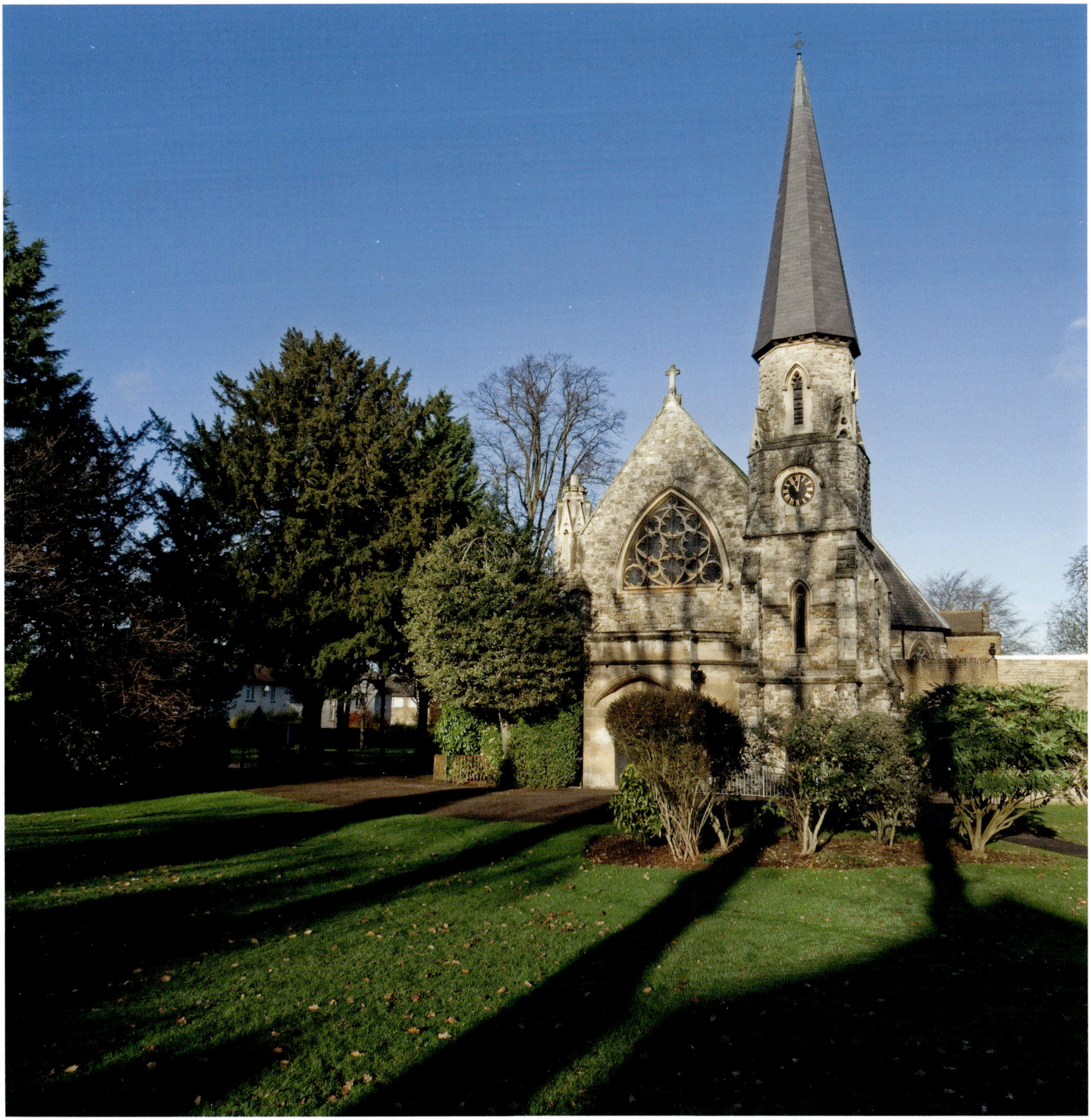

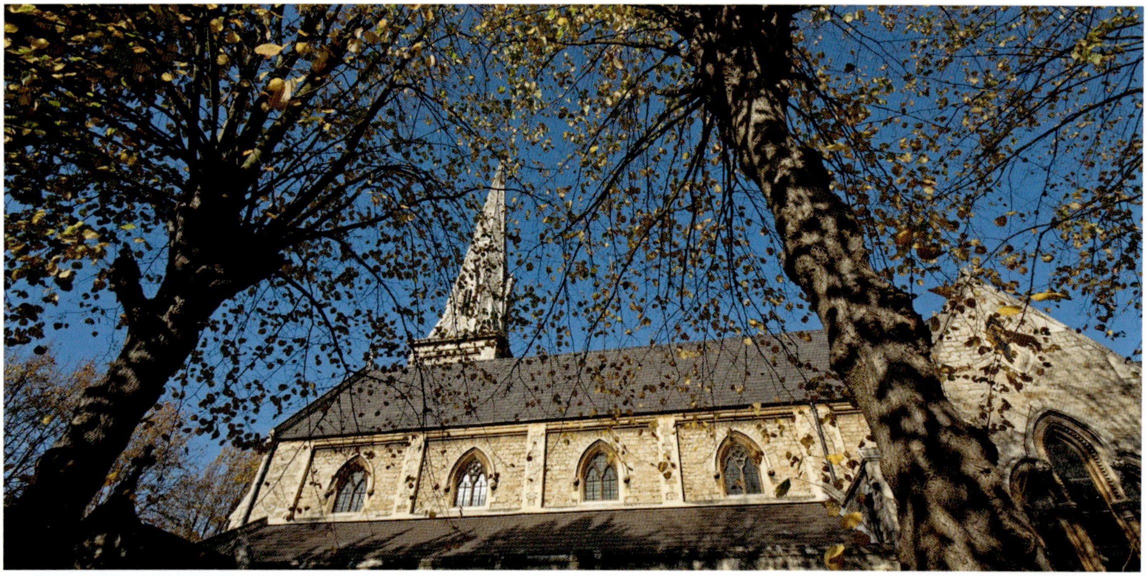

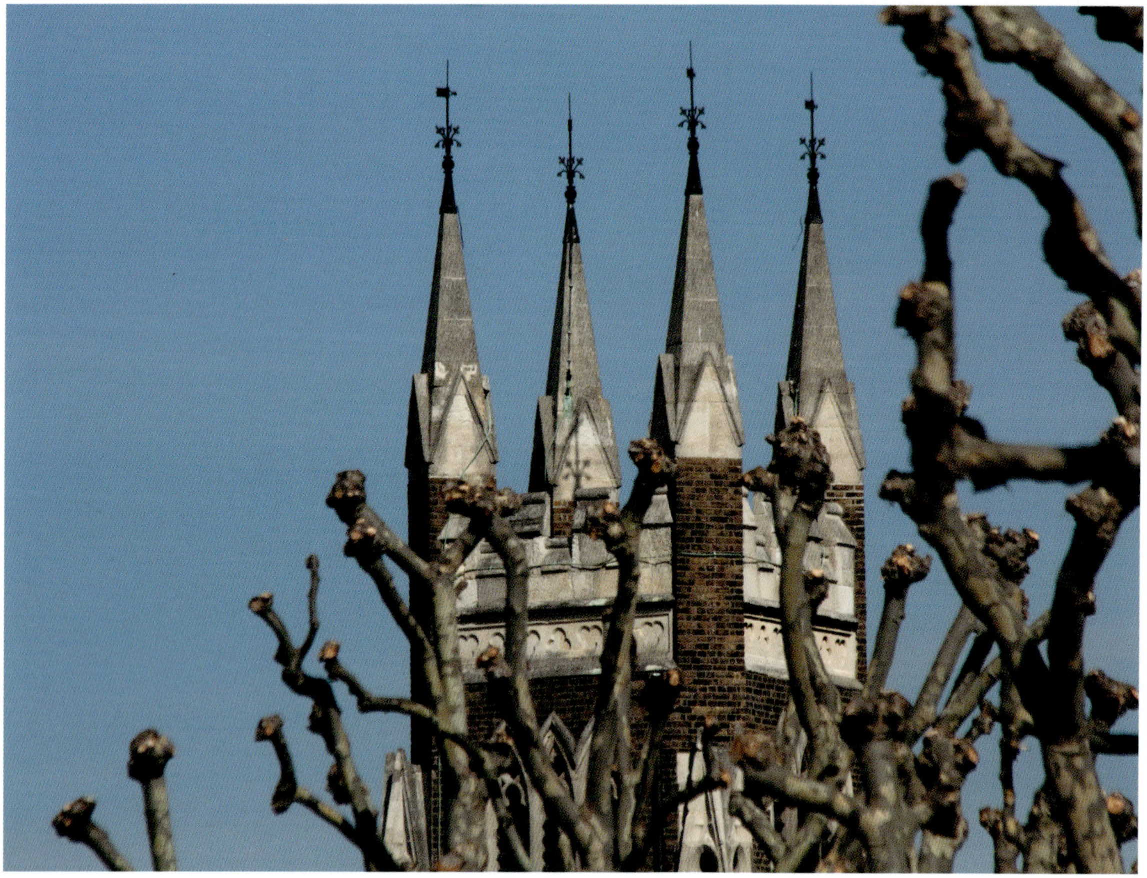

Left and Right Top and Bottom: aSt John's in St John's Avenue, dates from 1859 and is now a place of worship for the Polish Catholic community.

Below Left: Putney Methodist Church, on the corner of Upper Richmond Road and Gwendolen Avenue. The church dates from 1882, at about the time of the rapid expansion of Putney.

Far Right: Holy Trinity, Ponsonby Road Roehampton. Dating from 1898, there has most recently been a campaign to restore the wonderful spire, now complete.

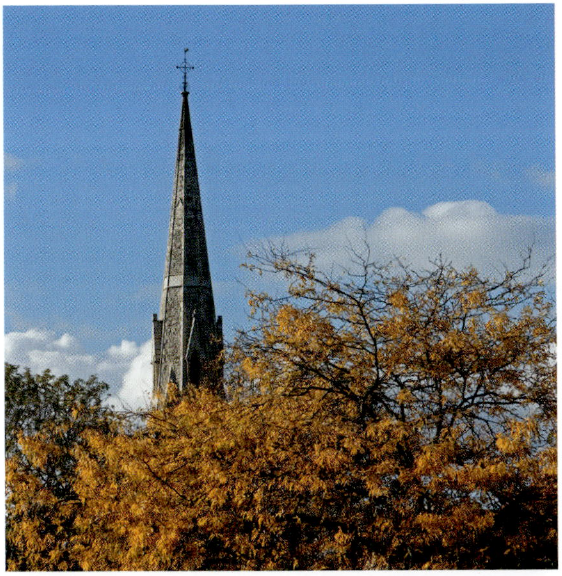

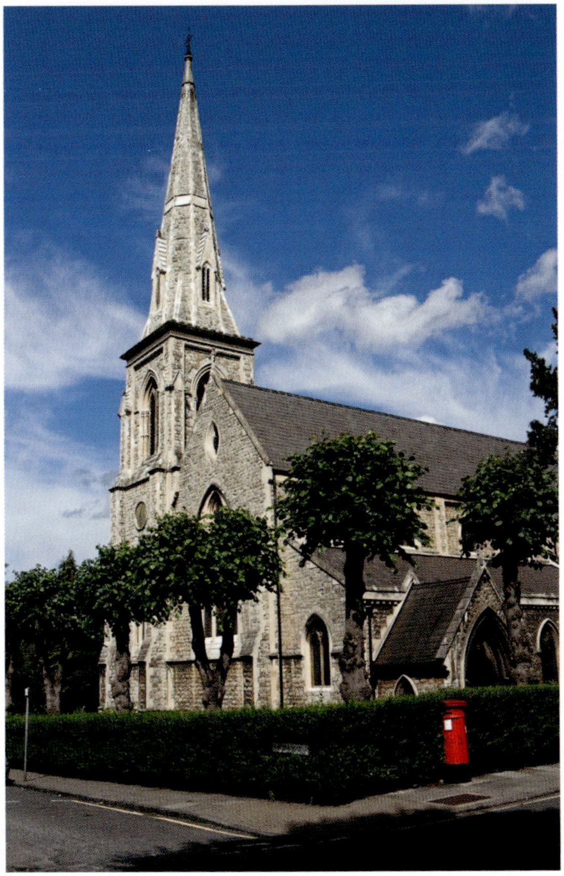

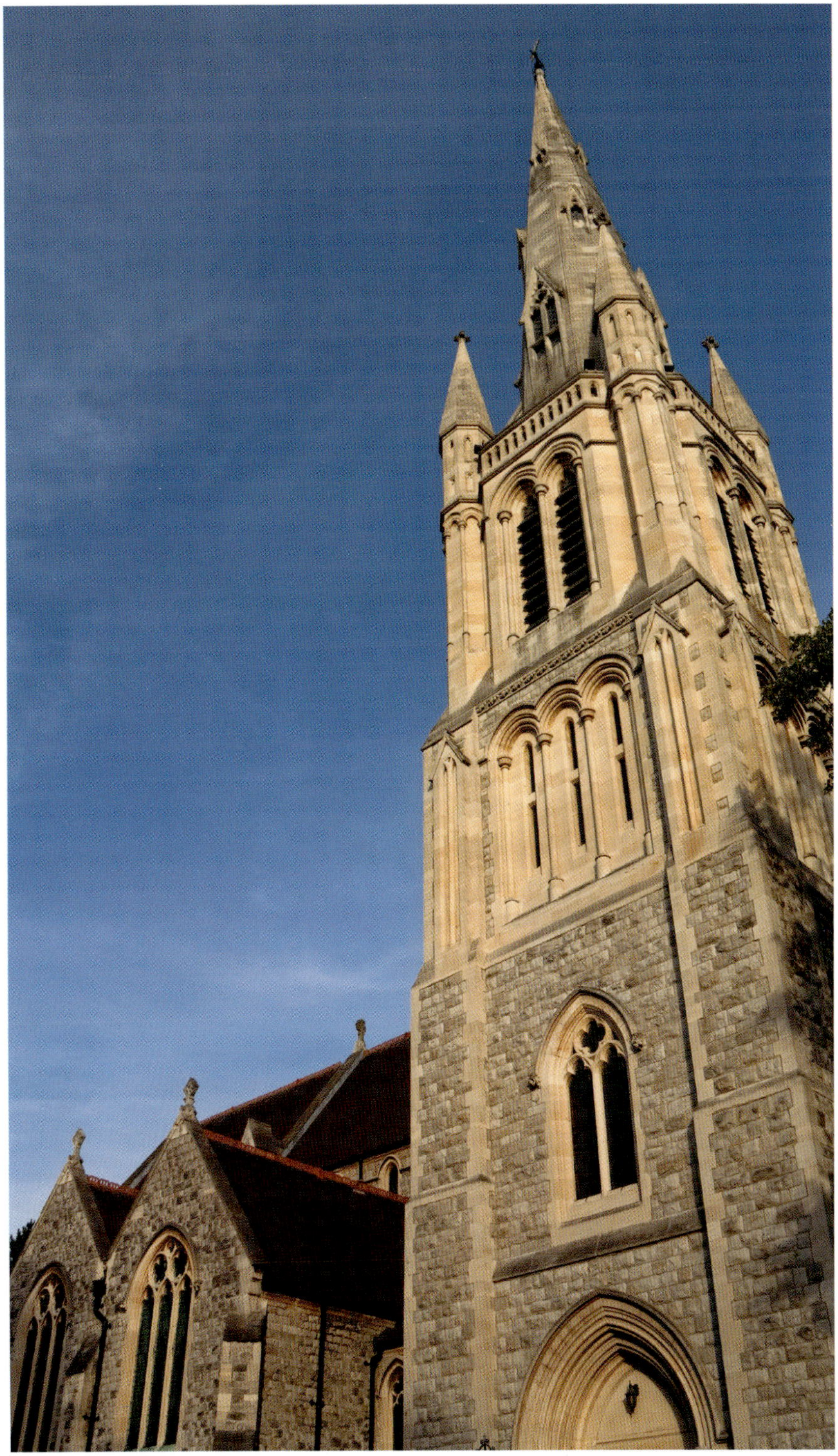

Schools

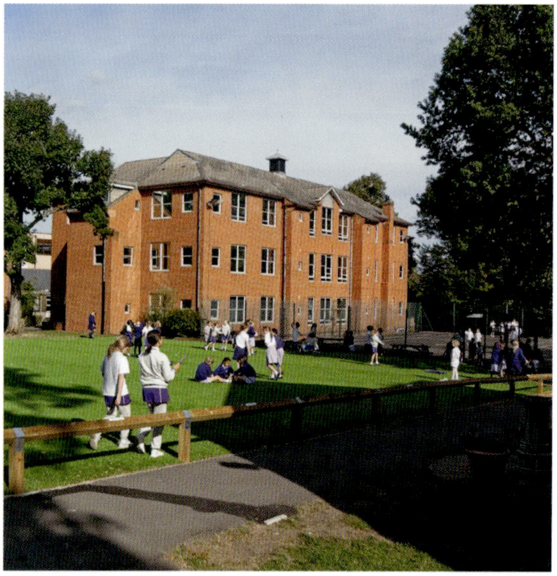

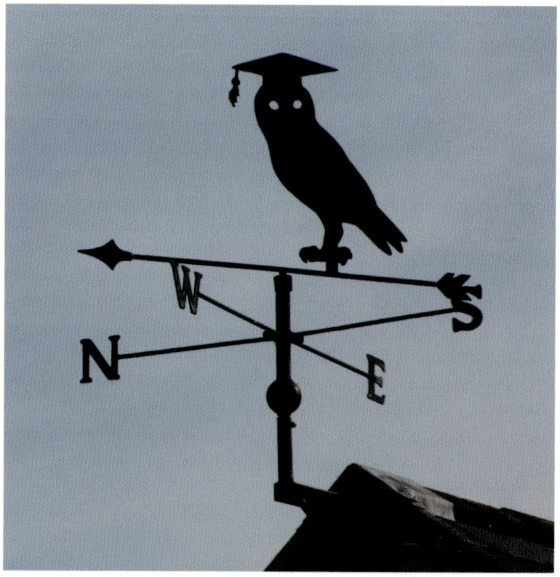

Putney High School dates from 1893, when it was known as East Putney High School. For girls aged 4 to 18, Putney High, located on Putney Hill, is one of the UK's leading schools. 2012 was an exciting year as they saw the opening of a brand new sixth form centre (see opposite bottom right).

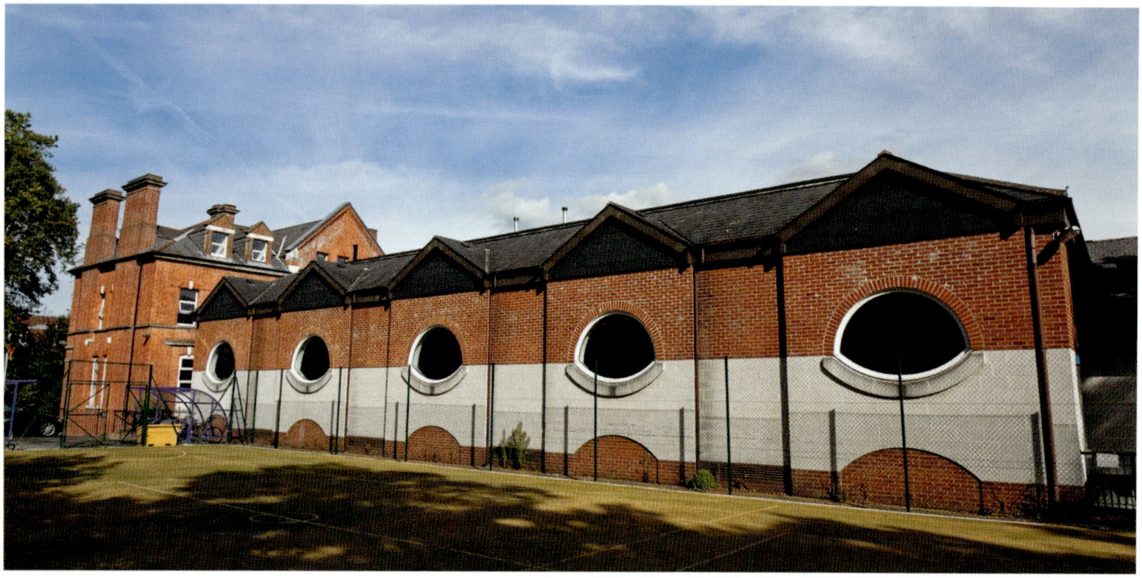

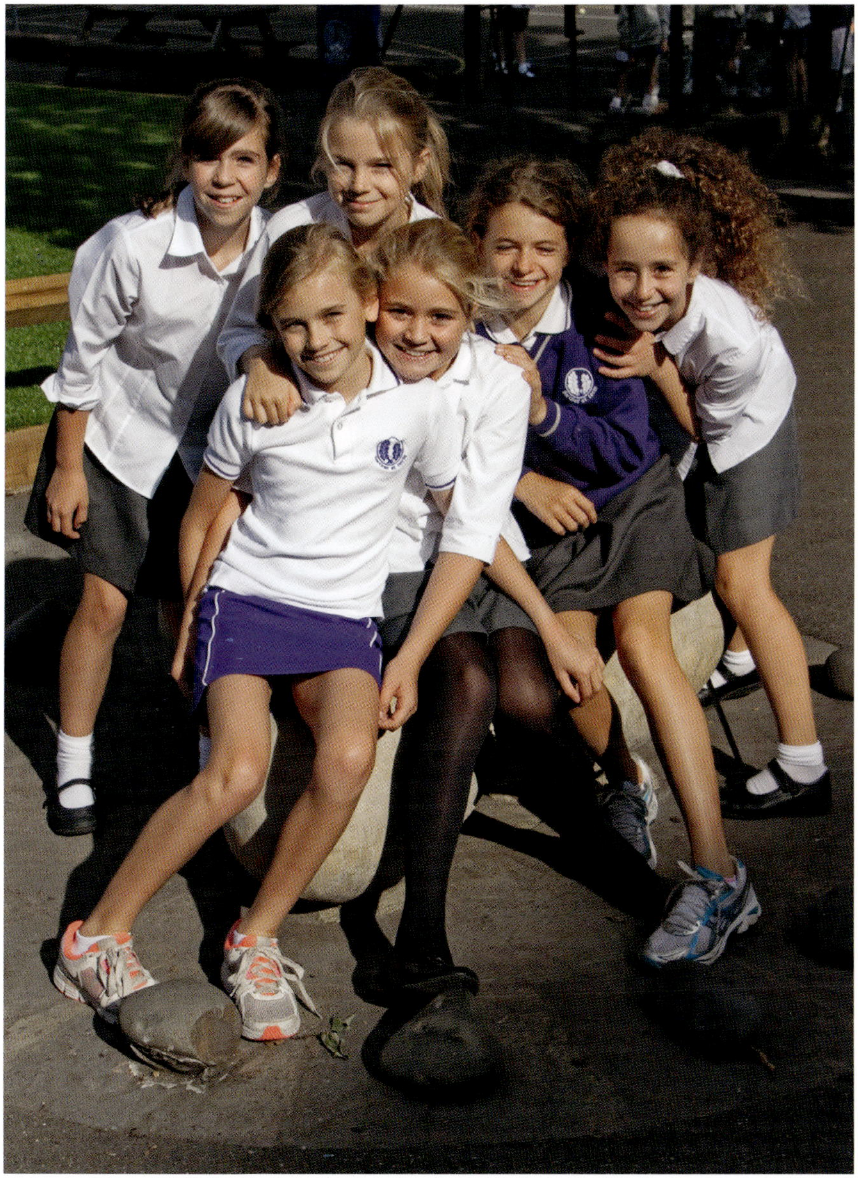

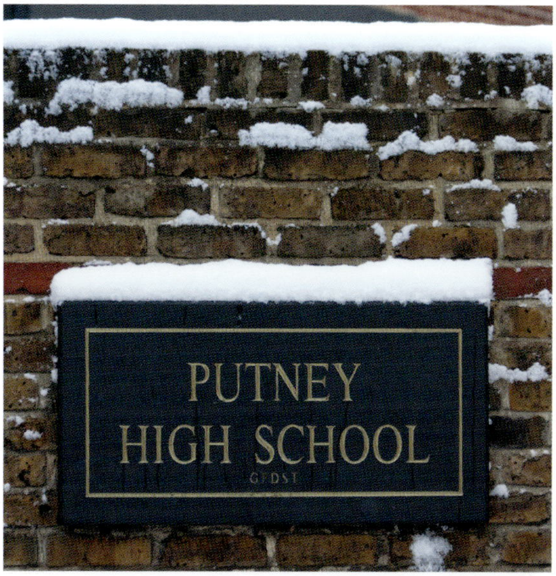
PUTNEY
HIGH SCHOOL

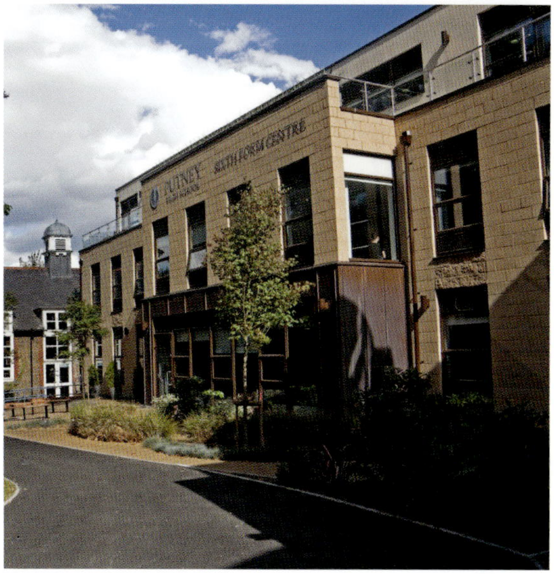

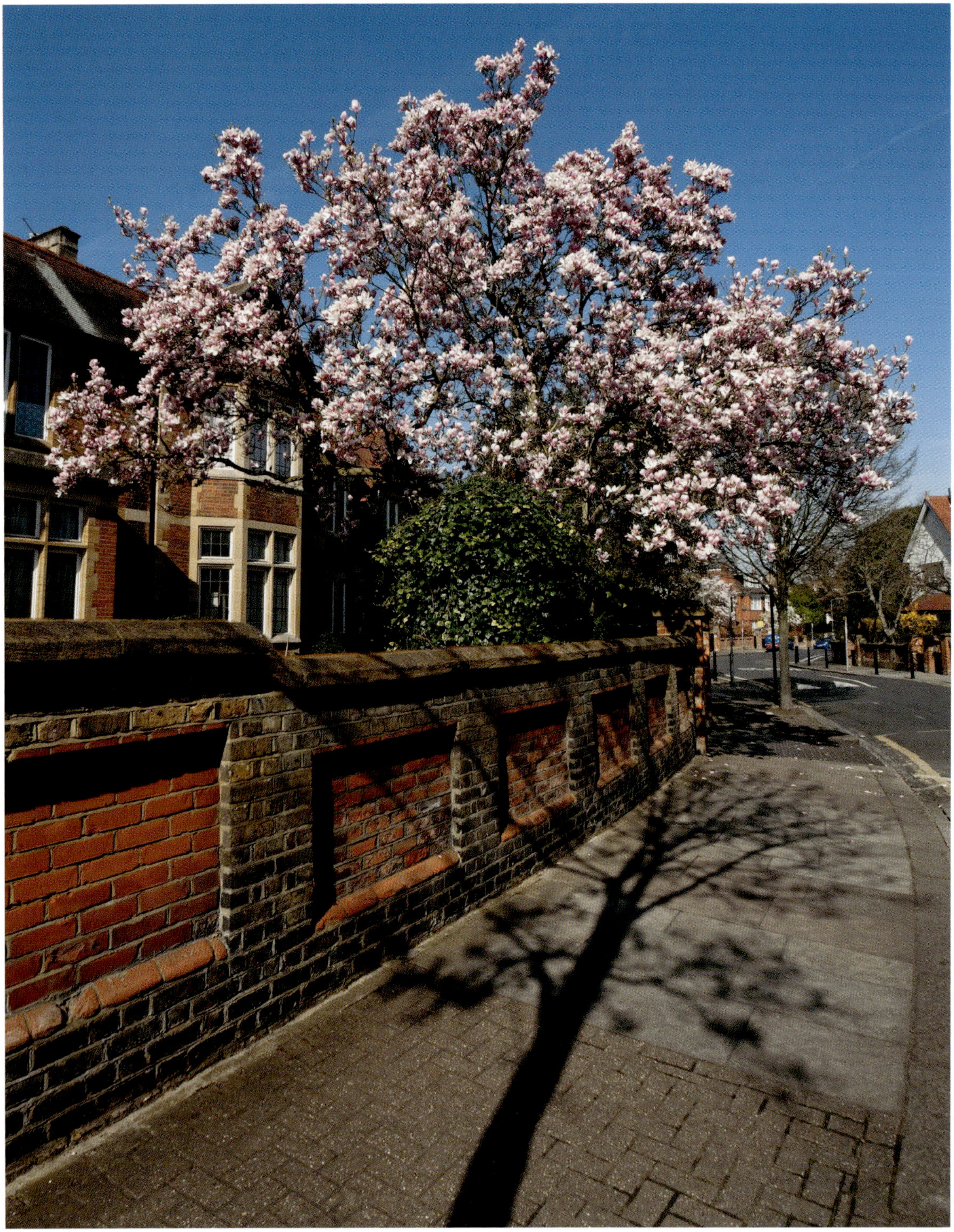

Putney Park School is now the Falcon School for Girls (see opposite bottom right) and is located in some charming Edwardian houses in Woodborough Road.

Overleaf Left: Granard Primary School in Cortis Road was opened in 1953 and is dominated by the most marvellous cedar tree, which is 300 years old.

Overleaf Top Right: ARK Putney Academy, formally Elliott School, is located in Pullman Gardens, part of the Ashburton Estate. In need of upgrading, the buildings still look impressive and are dominated by a large chimney, which is part of the old furnace and is a listed building.

Overleaf Bottom Right: Greenmead School in the foreground and Paddock School behind, in front of St Margaret's Church, Putney Park Lane. Greenmead and Paddock Primary schools share the same grounds and both cater for children with special needs.

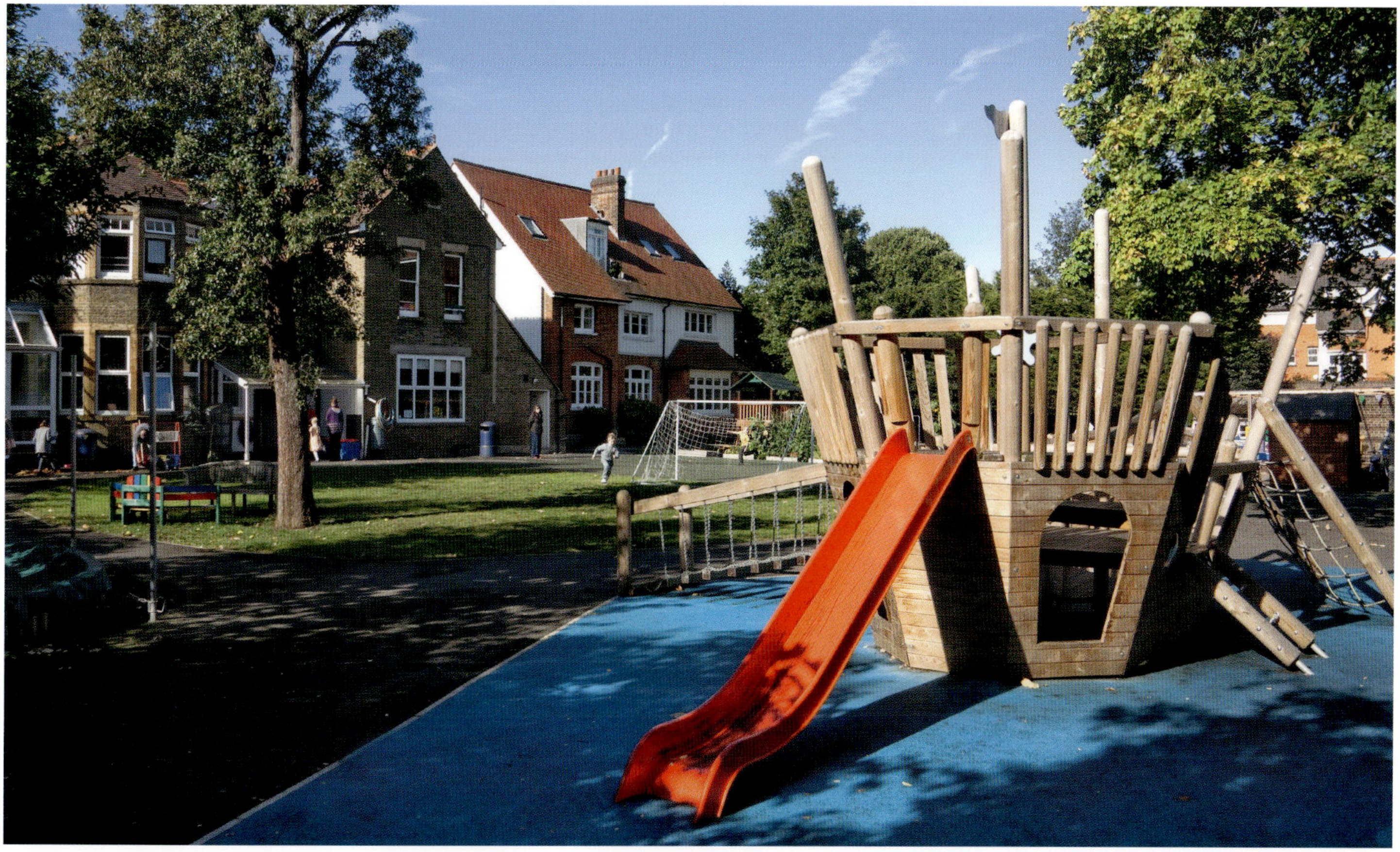

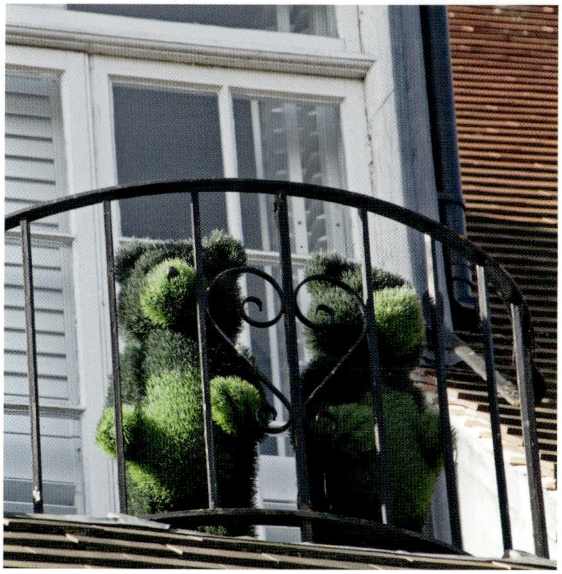

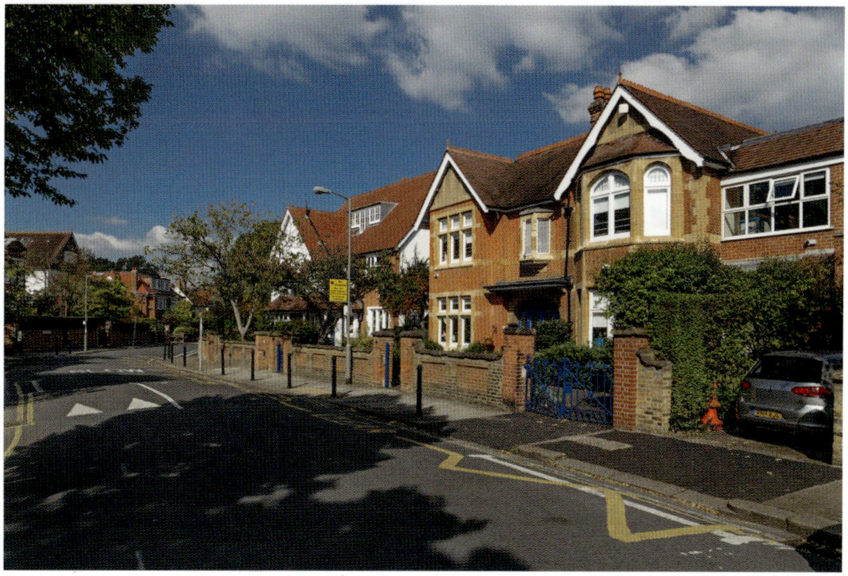

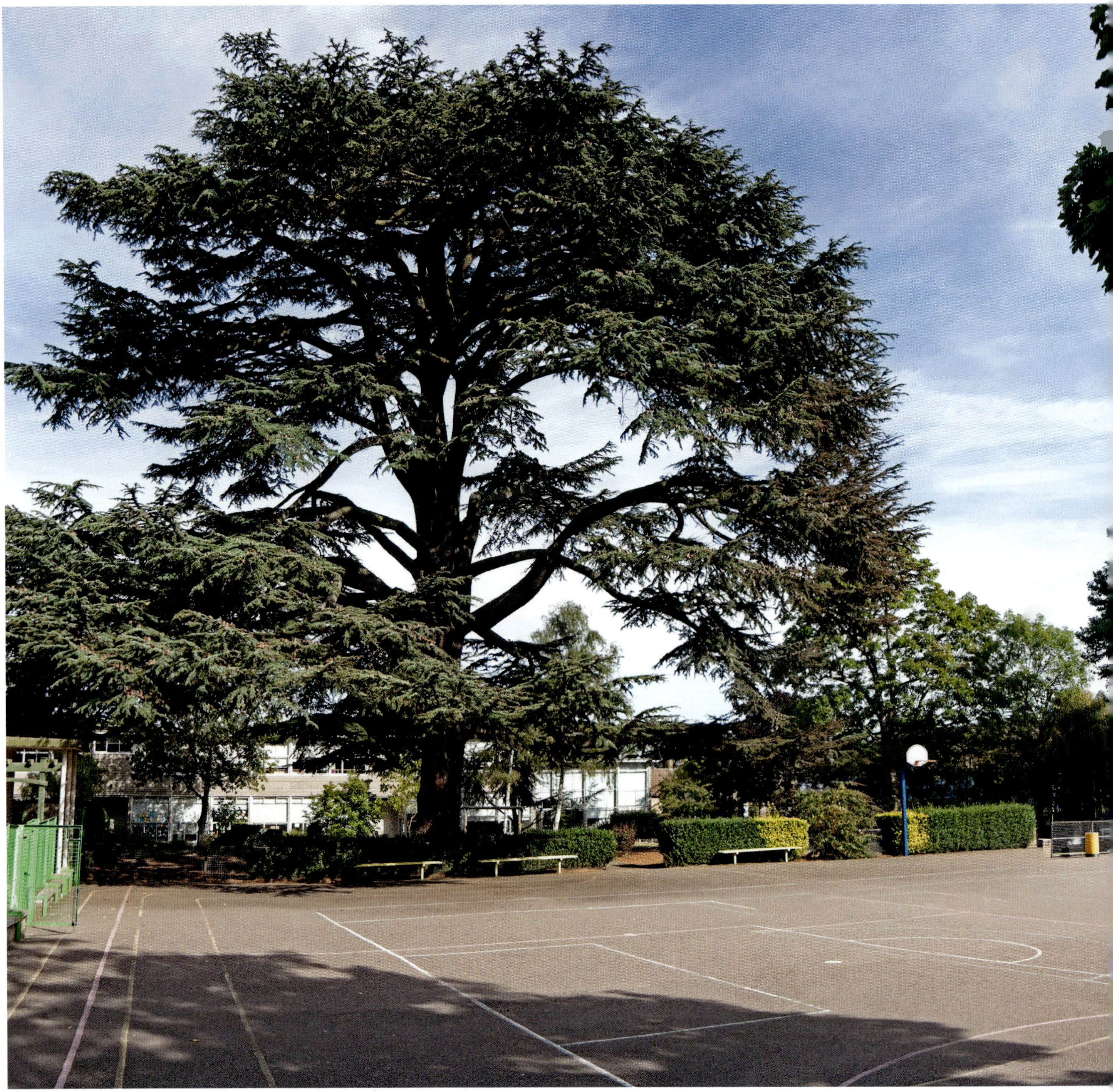

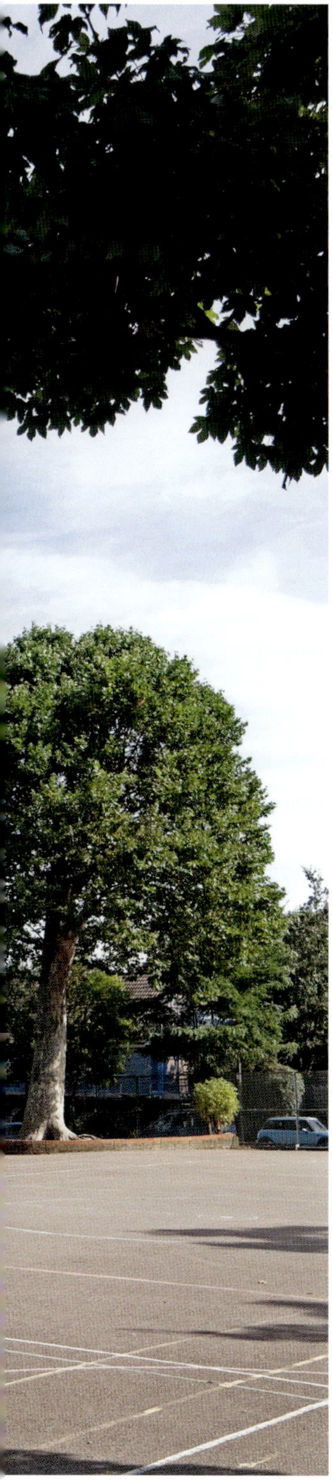

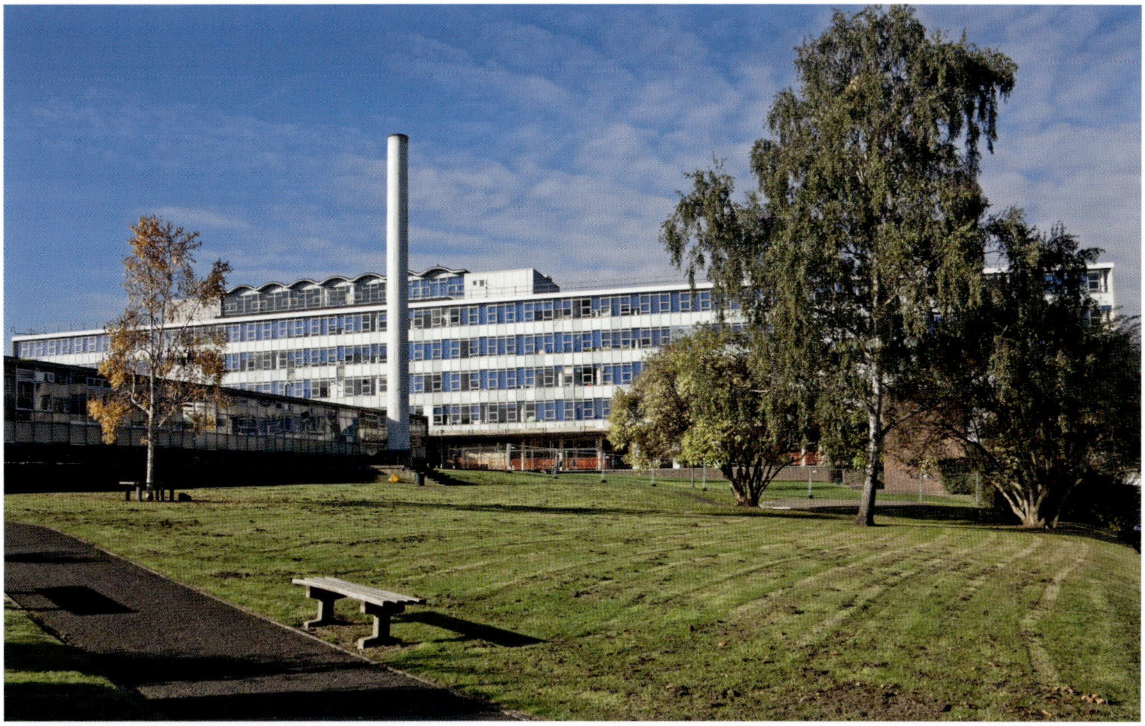

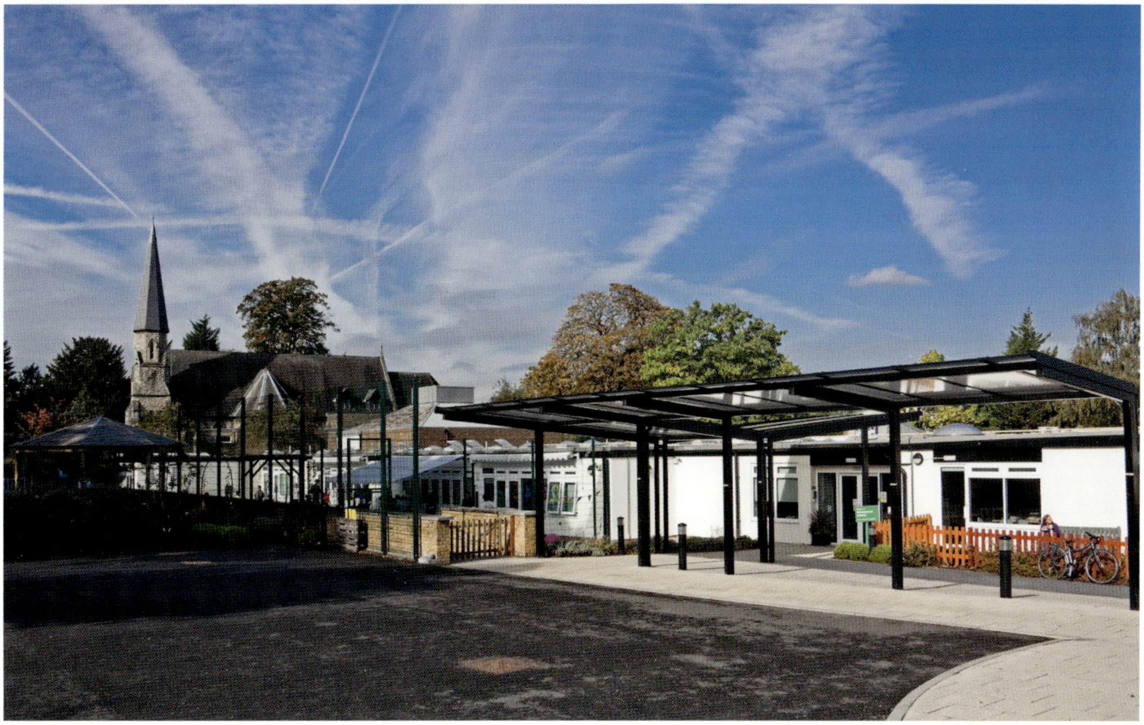

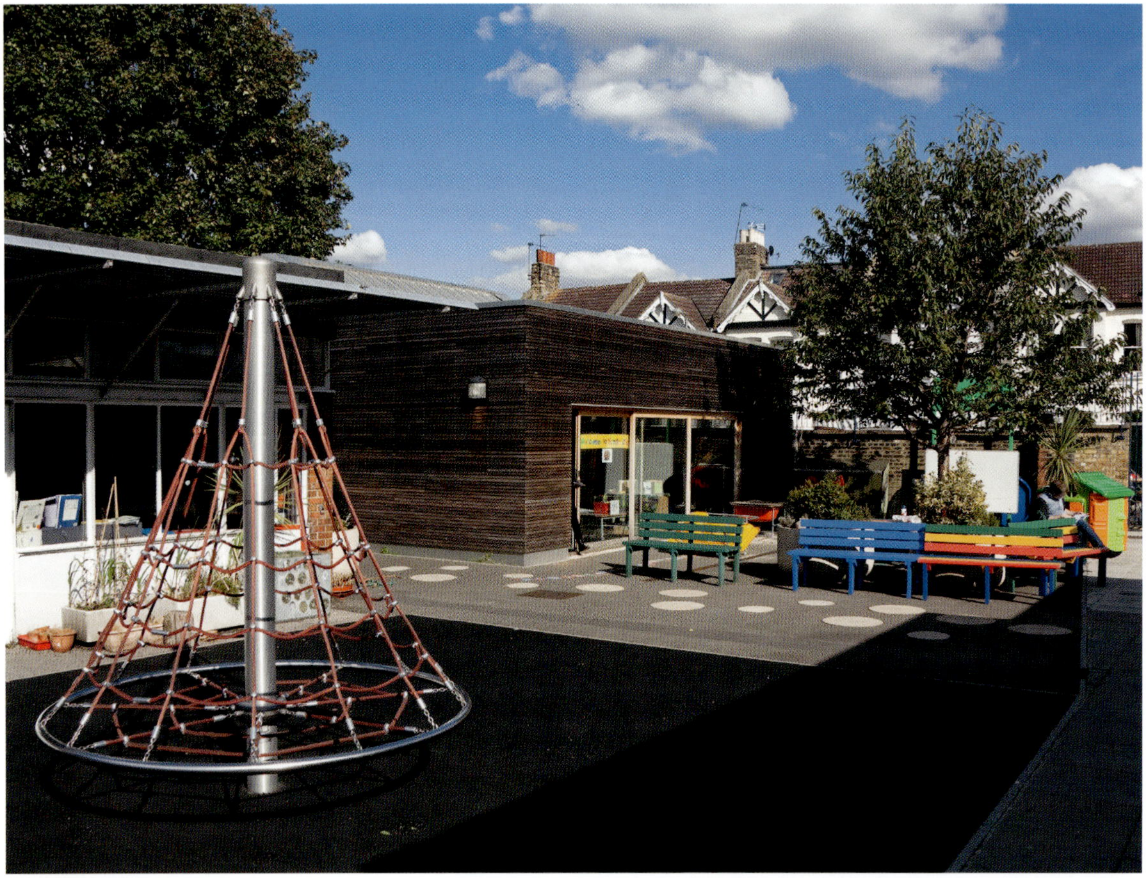

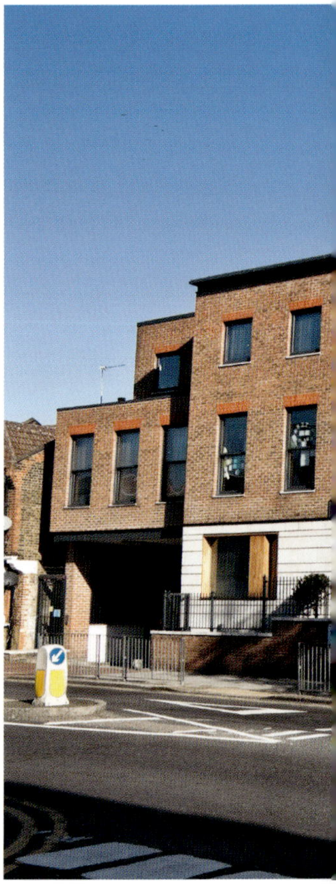

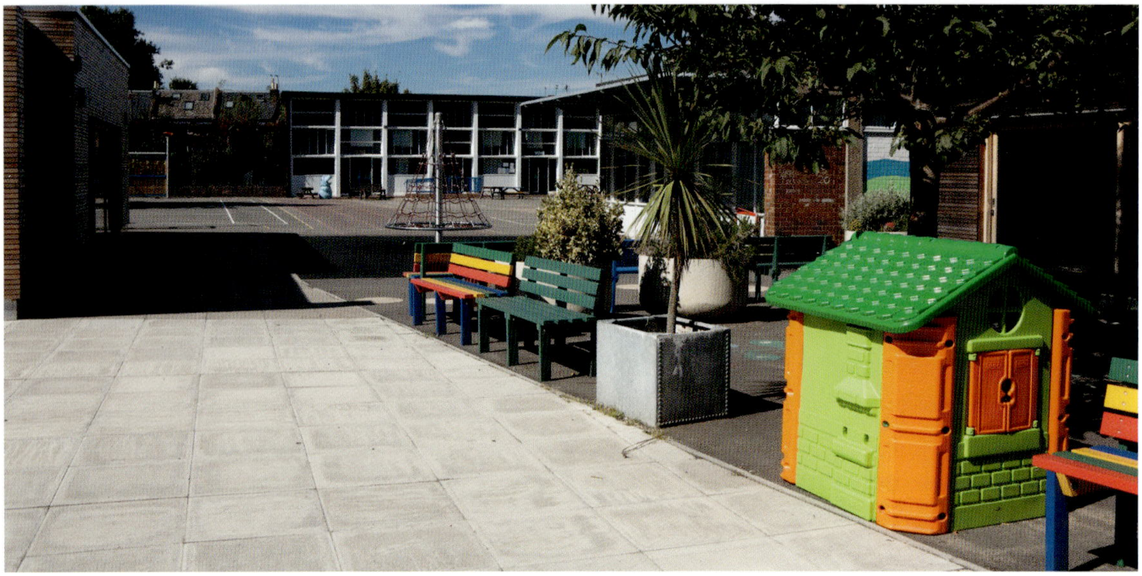

Above Left and Left:
Brandlehow Primary School, Brandlehow Road, off Putney Bridge Road, is noted for its unusual architecture and is a Grade II listed building. The school dates from 1902 but the original building was lost during WWII and replaced by a single story structure designed by the Hungarian born modernist architect Erno Goldfinger (see building in the background of the bottom picture). The top picture shows a new building commissioned to complement Goldfinger's, and was designed by team 51.5° architects.

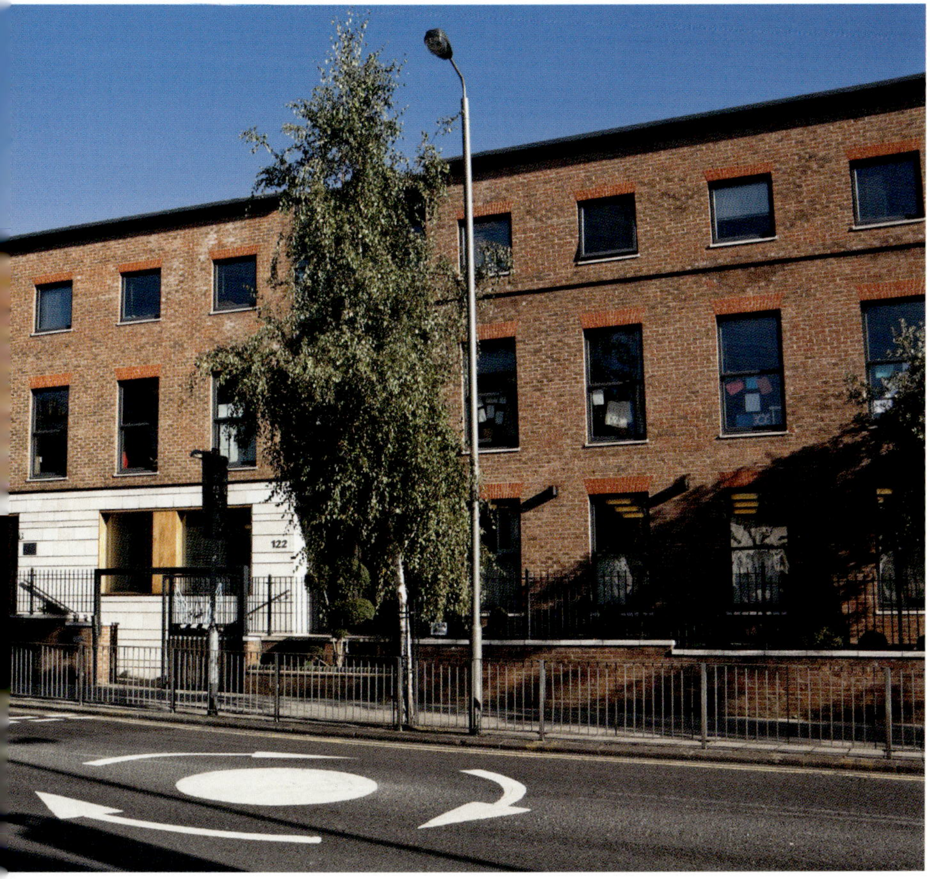

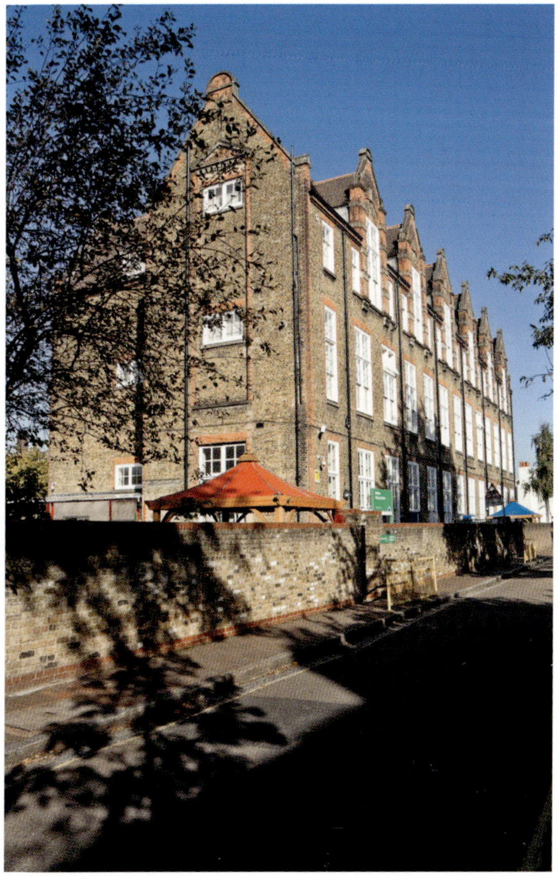

Above Left: Hurlingham Primary School, Putney Bridge Road, founded in 1947, is an independent co-educational school for children aged 4–11.

Above: Hotham Primary School, on Charlwood Road, celebrated their centenary in 2009. Although they retain the wonderful Edwardian Building, much else has changed.

Pubs

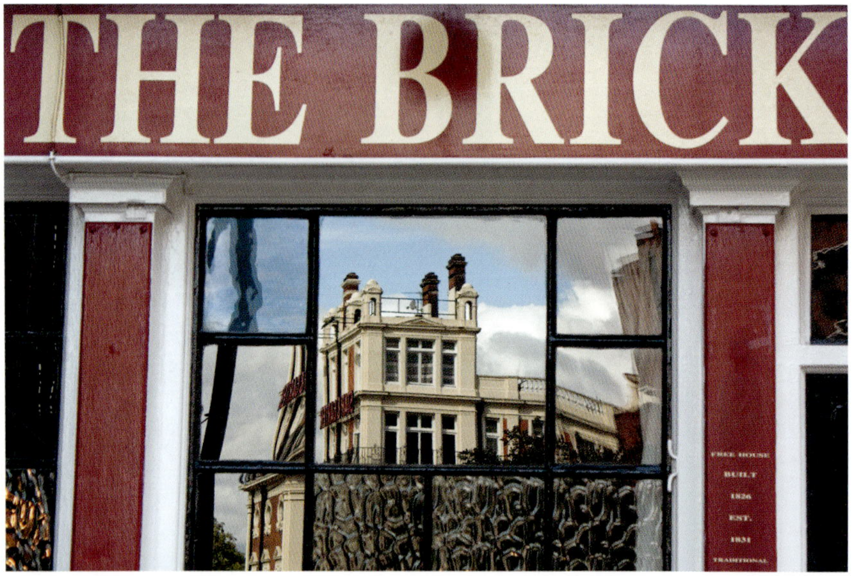

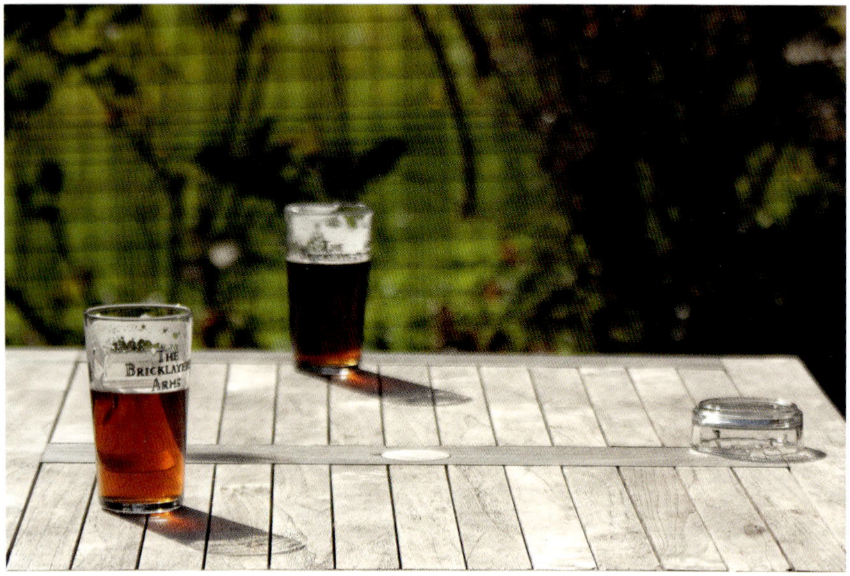

The Bricklayers: Built in 1826, it is one of Putney's oldest pubs, stands at the top of Waterman Street. A noted 'real ale' pub, it won SW London CAMRA Pub of the Year in 2006, 2008 & 2010 and CAMRA Greater London Regional Pub of the Year in 2007 and 2009.

The Duke's Head: A 'John Costrell, Victualler' is recorded at this location in 1665. The pub was first recorded by name in 1714 as the Duke of Ormonde's Head and later, until the late 1820s, as the Old Duke's Head. The present building dates from c. 1864 and is one of Putney's oldest operating pubs.

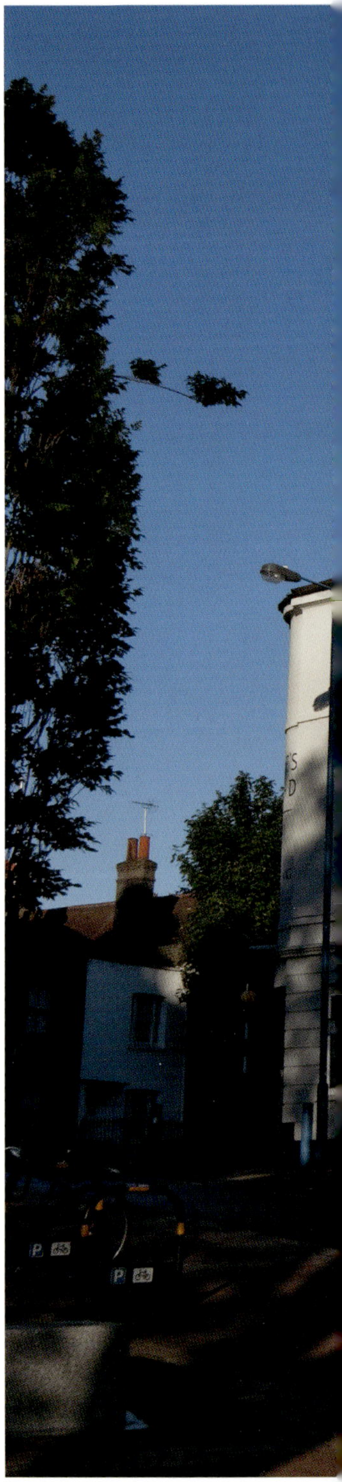

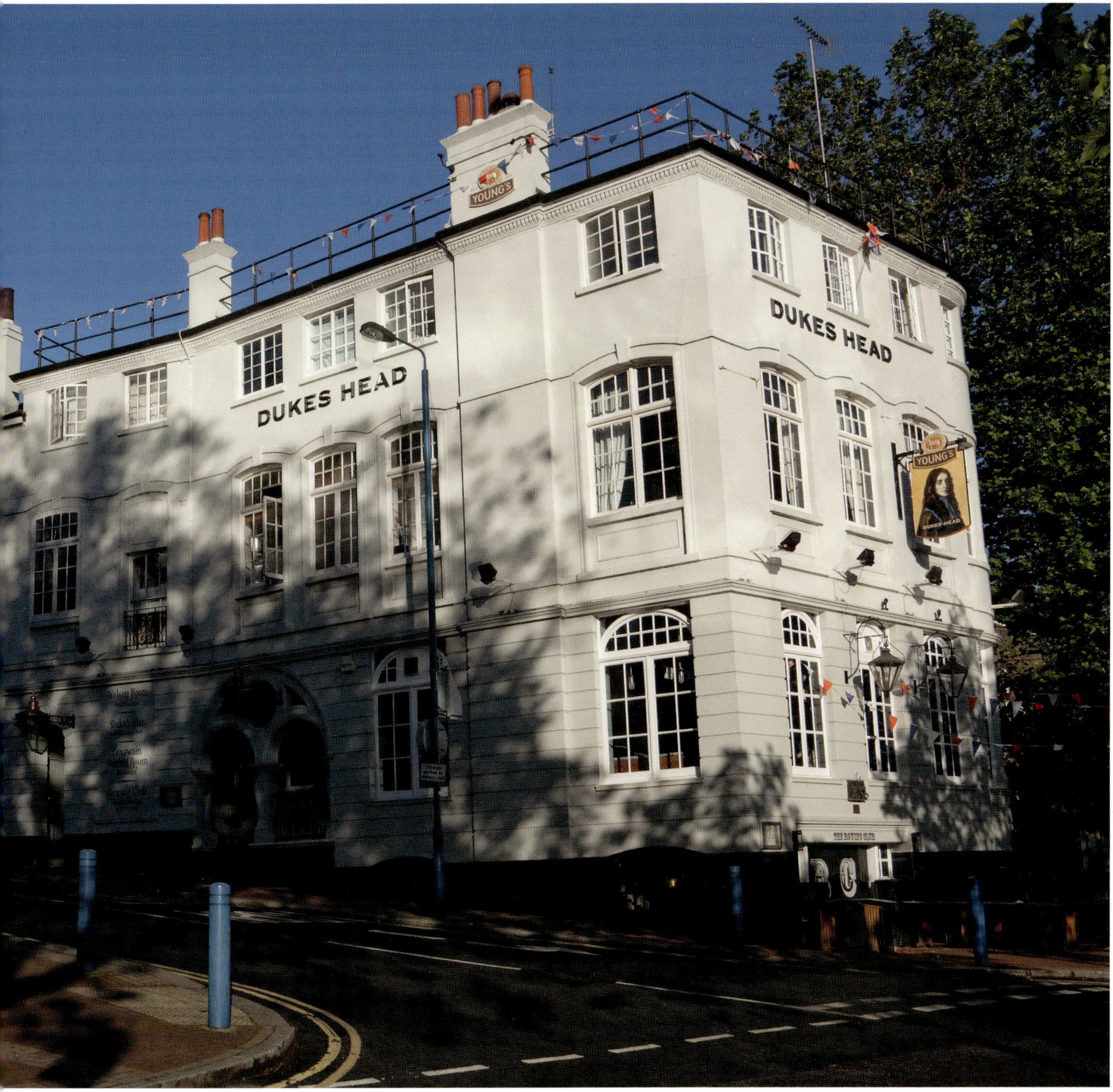
YOUNG'S
DUKES HEAD
DUKES HEAD
YOUNG'S
DUKES HEAD

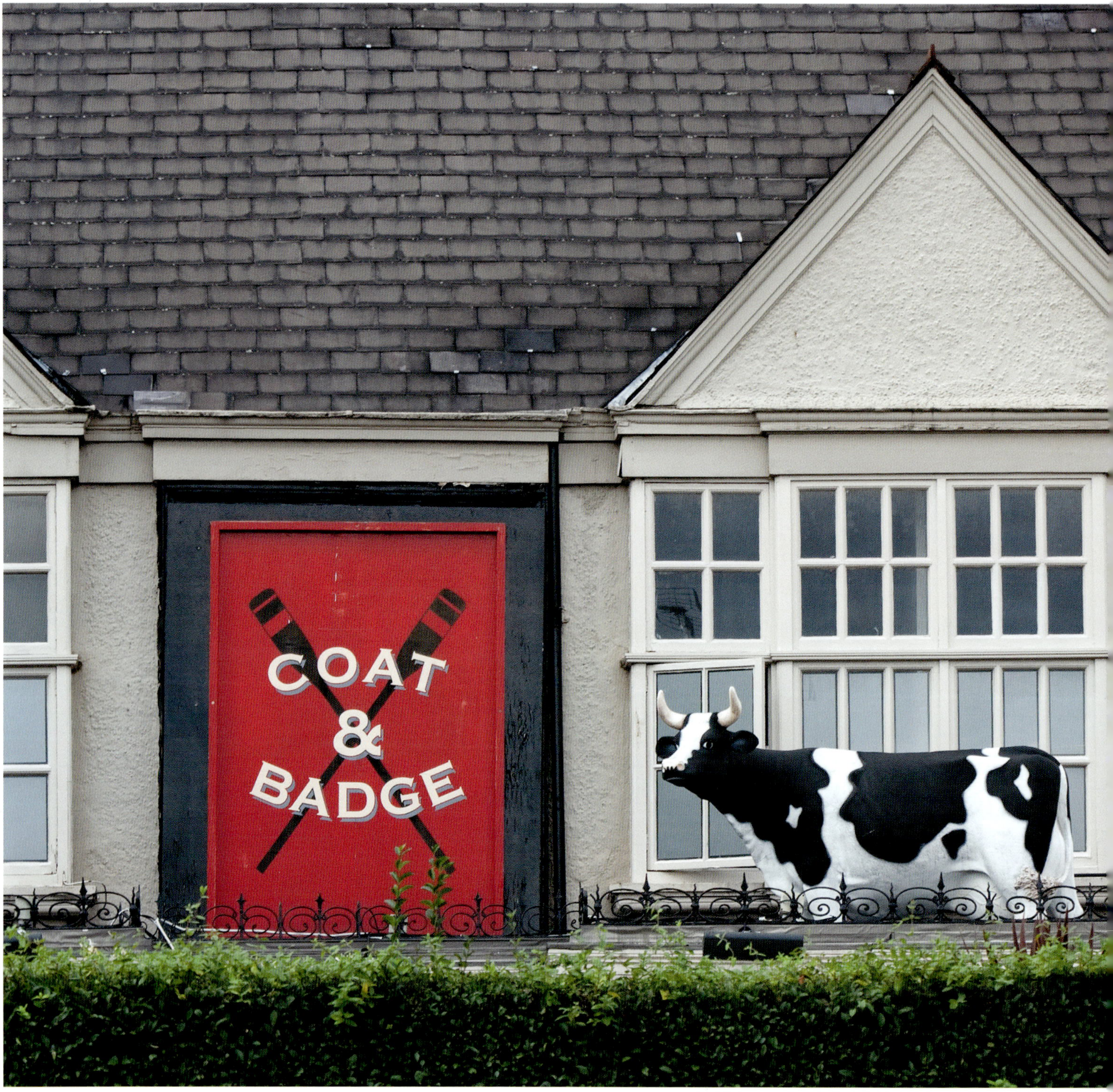
COAT
&
BADGE

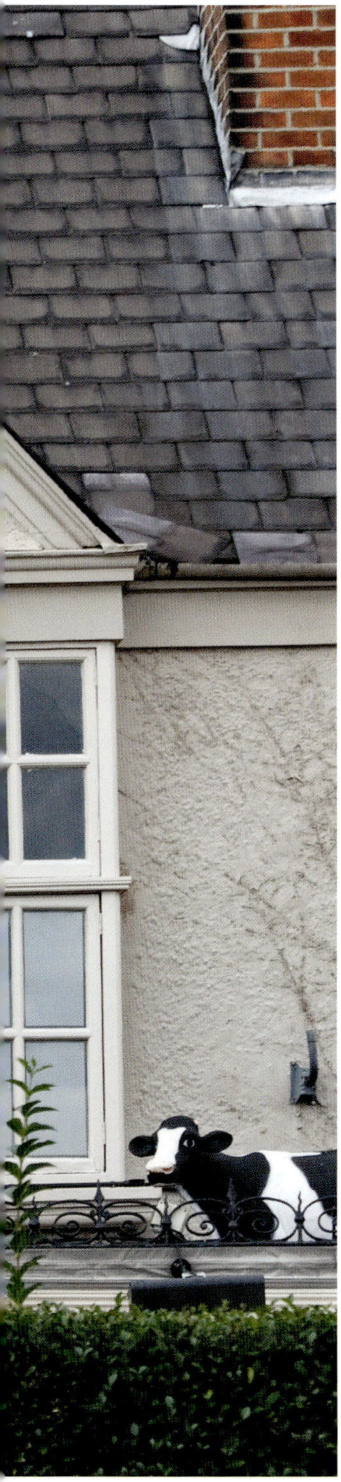

The Coat & Badge: First recorded in 1861, it was named after the annual Doggett's Coat & Badge rowing race for apprentice watermen, run from London Bridge to Chelsea and founded in 1715 by Irish actor and theatre manager Thomas Doggett. There have been more winners from Putney than from any other part of the river!

The Jolly Gardeners: Originally a beer shop from c. 1830, a full pub licence was finally obtained some 40 years later. The name reflects the fact that the area was once one of Putney's main market-gardening areas (near Felsham Road was formerly Gardener's Lane). The present building dates from 1938.

The Star & Garter: With it's Northern Renaissance and Queen Anne influence, The Star & Garter was first noted in 1787 and has undergone many transformations over the years. It was originally built as a hotel for the use of the boating and sailing community. In approximately 1870 they even had a boathouse on the ground floor. The name 'Star & Garter' relates to the Order of the Garter.

The King's Head: Newly refurbished, this 15th century landmark, formerly known as 'The Bull', is probably the oldest secular building in the Borough of Wandsworth. Situated on the corner of Roehampton High Street and Roehampton Lane, it has recently been renovated and brought back into use as a public house by the Roehampton Regeneration Scheme, involving Wandsworth Council and the St James' Group.

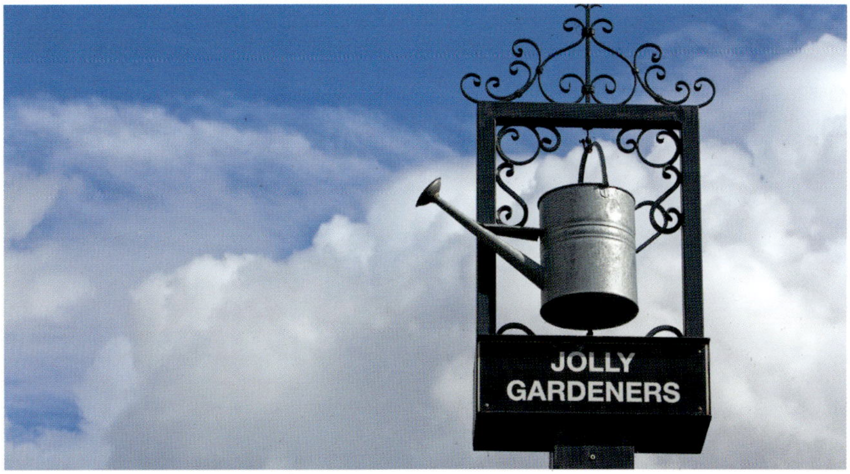

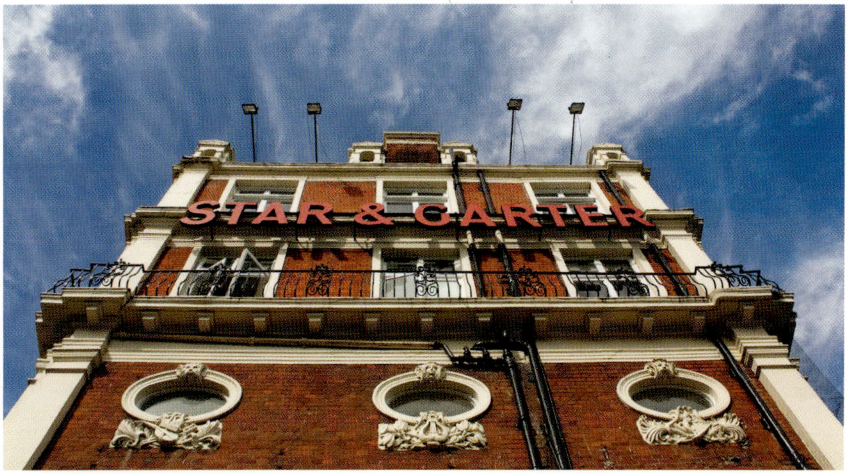

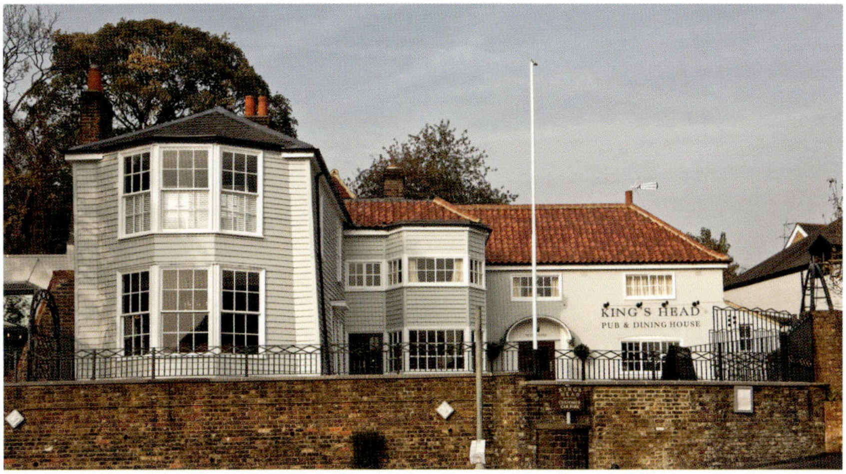

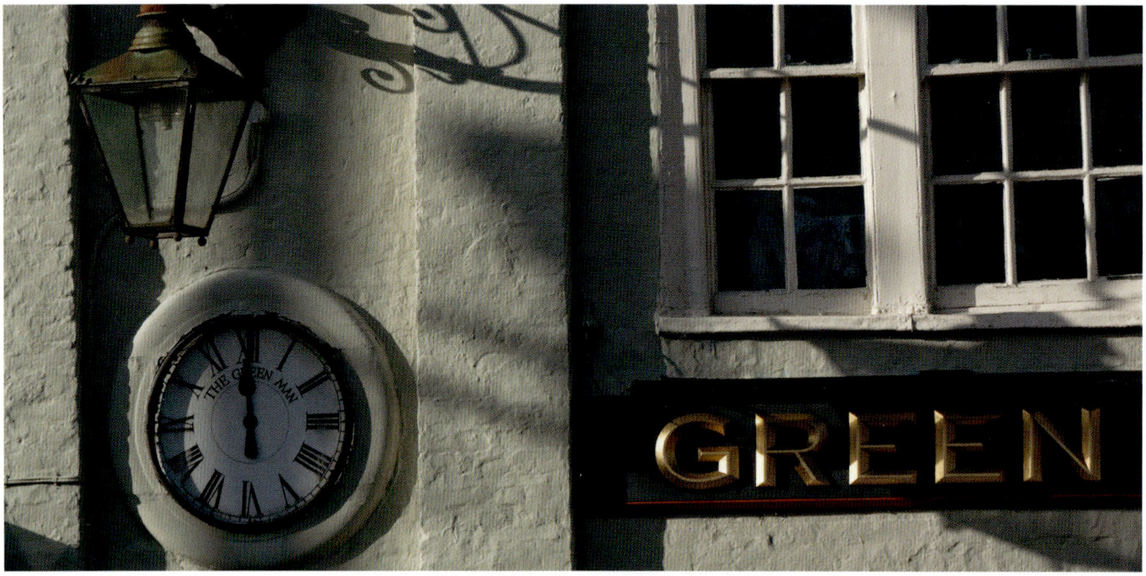

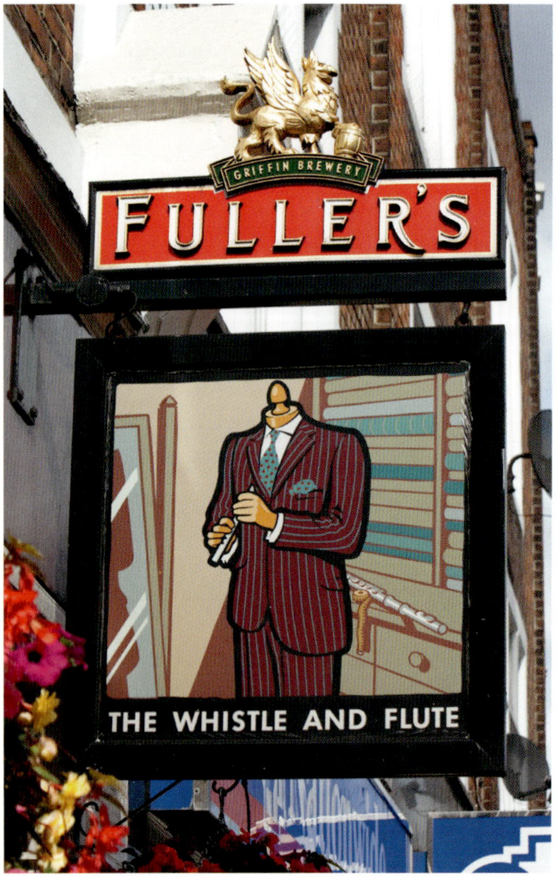

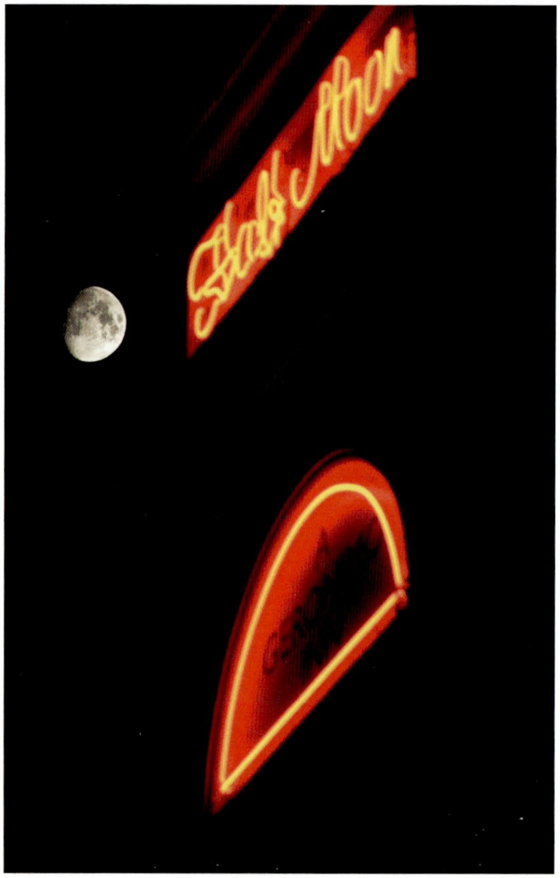

The Green Man: Almost certainly Putney's oldest pub, dating back to the early 1700s

The Whistle & Flute: The Whistle and Flute is now a Five Guys burger bar.

The Half Moon: Although it was first recorded in 1723, there may have been an alehouse on the site in the 17th century. The present building dates from 1903, and has been Putney's premier live music venue for half a century, featuring some of the country's major bands. The threat of closure, which emerged in late 2009, was thankfully averted.

The Normanby:
Its predecessor, the Cedar Tree, was built in the 1860s, demolished and rebuilt in 1936, and re-named a decade or so ago.

The Arab Boy: Built by local solicitor, landowner and developer Henry Scarth and opened in 1850, it was named after his Beirut-born servant Yussef Sirrie. A painted sign on the east wall, now painted over (see page 7) says cautiously "Probably the oldest pub in Putney", which it isn't, though it is arguably Putney's oldest purpose-built pub. They have recently changed their sign.

The Railway (Bottom Left): The railway came to Putney in 1846 and the first Railway Hotel, opposite the station, was opened in 1857. The present building dates from 1889.

The Prince of Wales:
As of January 2012, this pub became a member of the 'Food & Fuels' group, with a sharper focus on its food and drink.

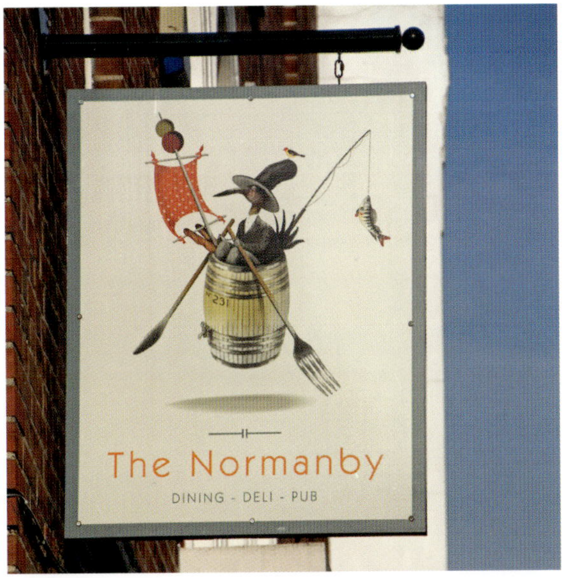

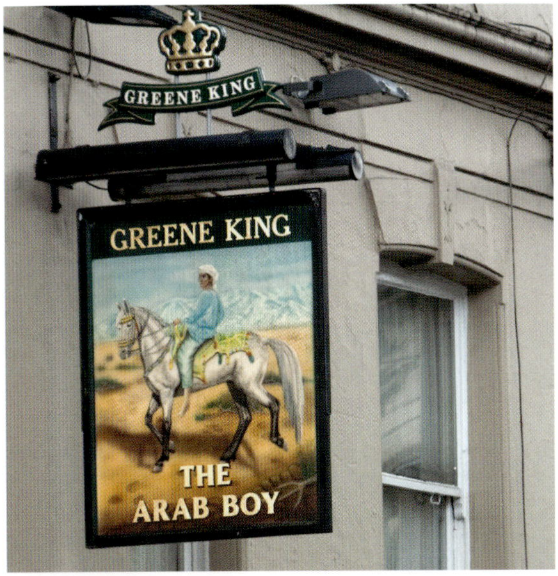

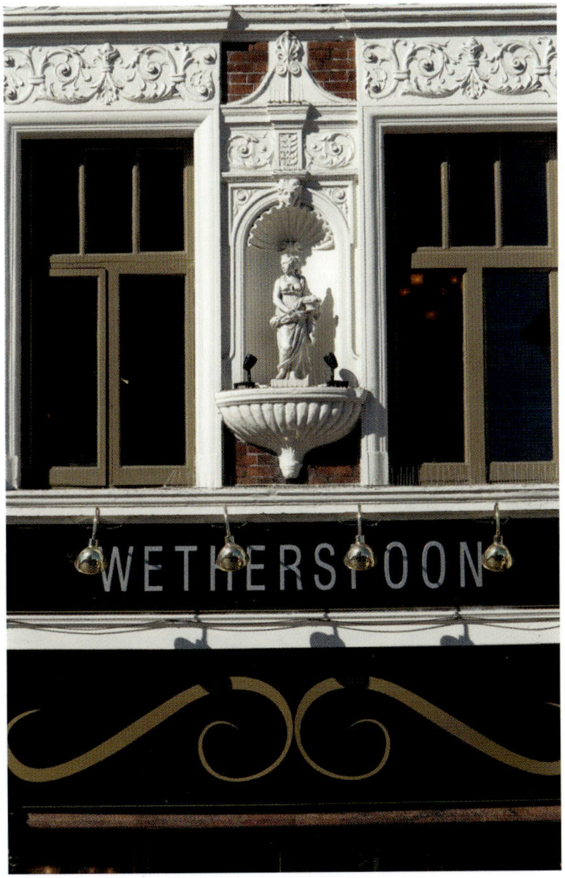

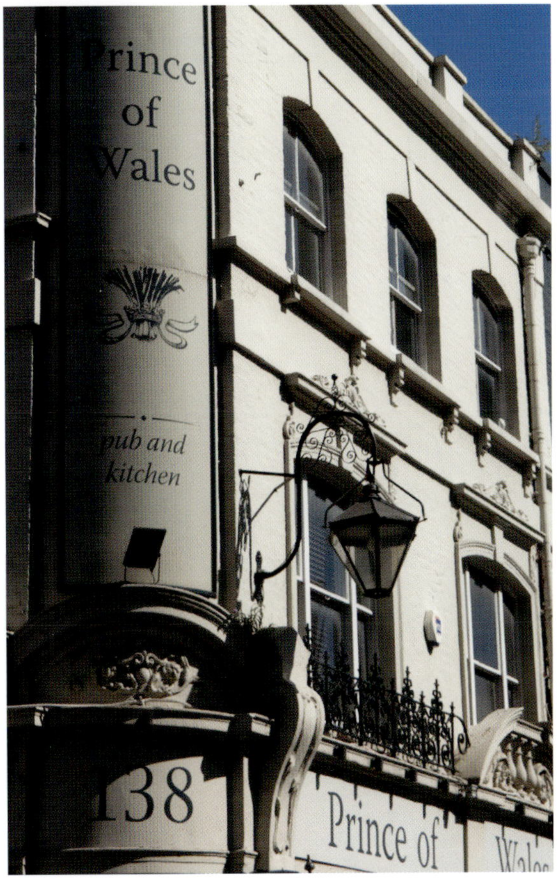

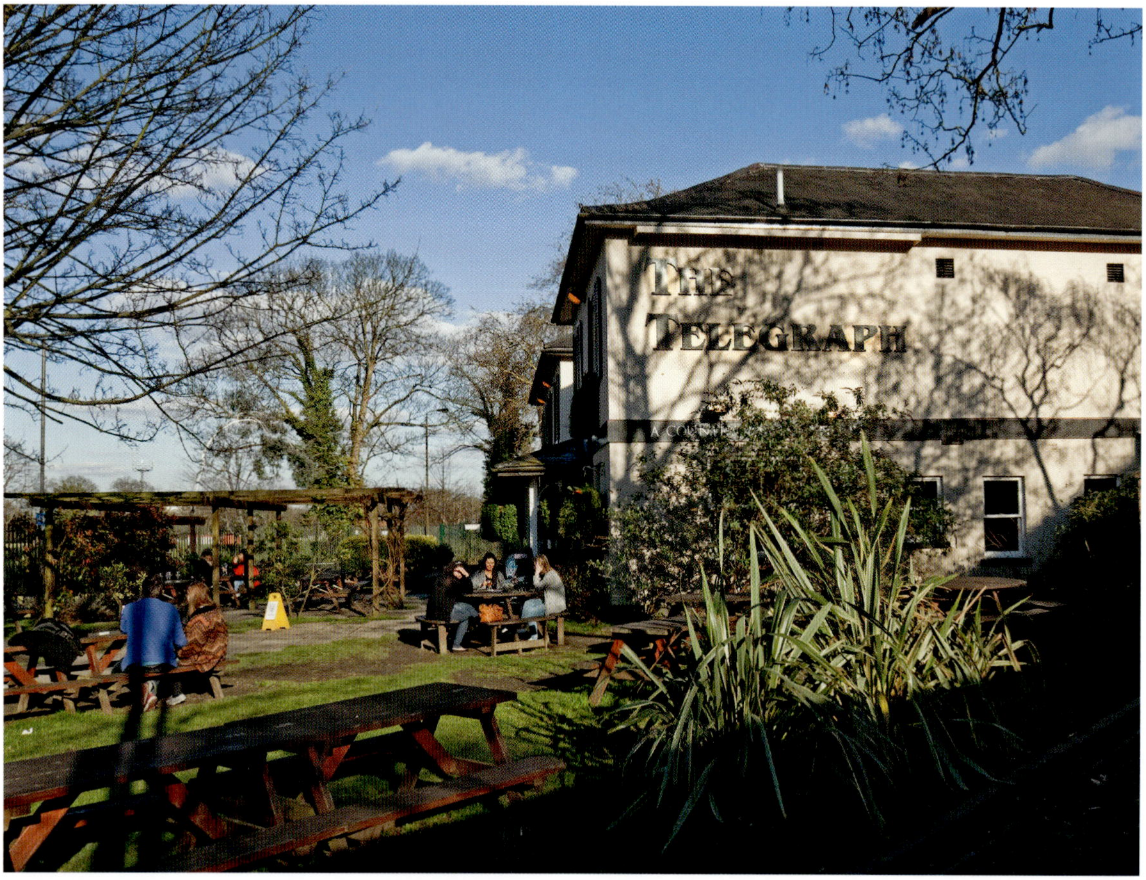

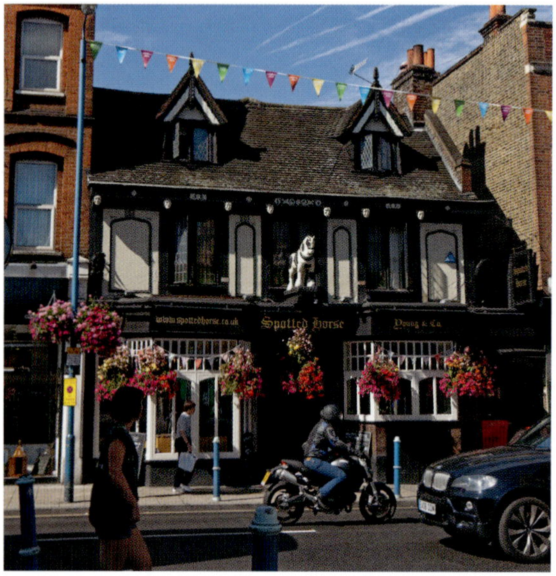

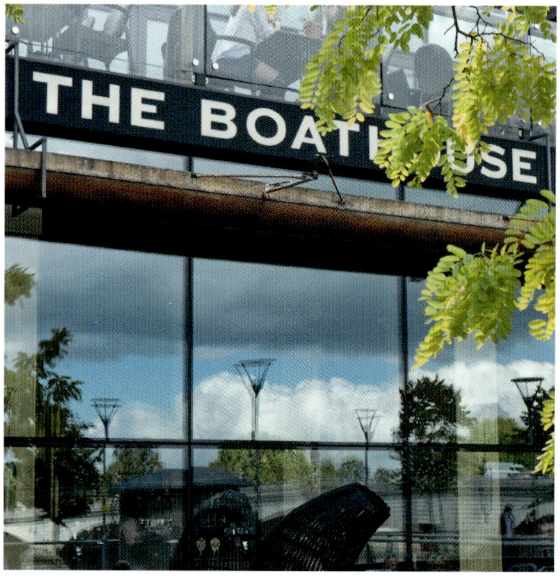

The Telegraph: The name reflects the fact that a telegraph station (originally shutter, later semaphore) stood nearby on the Heath in the early 19th century.

The Spotted Horse: First mentioned by its present name in 1754; the 'antique' frontage is a 20th century addition. It was here that spy Klaus Fuchs passed atomic secrets to his KGB contact in the 1940s!

The Boathouse: This was built to replace The Castle pub, at the other end of Brewhouse Lane. It is almost exactly on the site of one of Putney's earliest brewhouses, and Martin the Brewer is recorded in a 1332 tax list. In the late 15th century, the brewery and adjacent tavern were owned and run by Walter Cromwell, father of Thomas, who was born in the area around 1485.

The Rocket: Housed on the ground floor of the Putney Wharf tower, it was originally a wine bar and is currently a Wetherspoons outlet. The earlier tower, the core of which is contained within the present building, was previously the HQ of computer company ICL.

The Captain Cook: A late 19th century pub, originally called The Northumberland Arms closed in 2015 and has now become a Sainsbury's Local.

The Spencer: Formerly the Spencer Arms, it opened in 1898, replacing an earlier Spencer Arms from the 1860s. Its name reflects the family name of the Lords of the Manor of Wimbledon, ancestors of the late Diana, Princess of Wales.

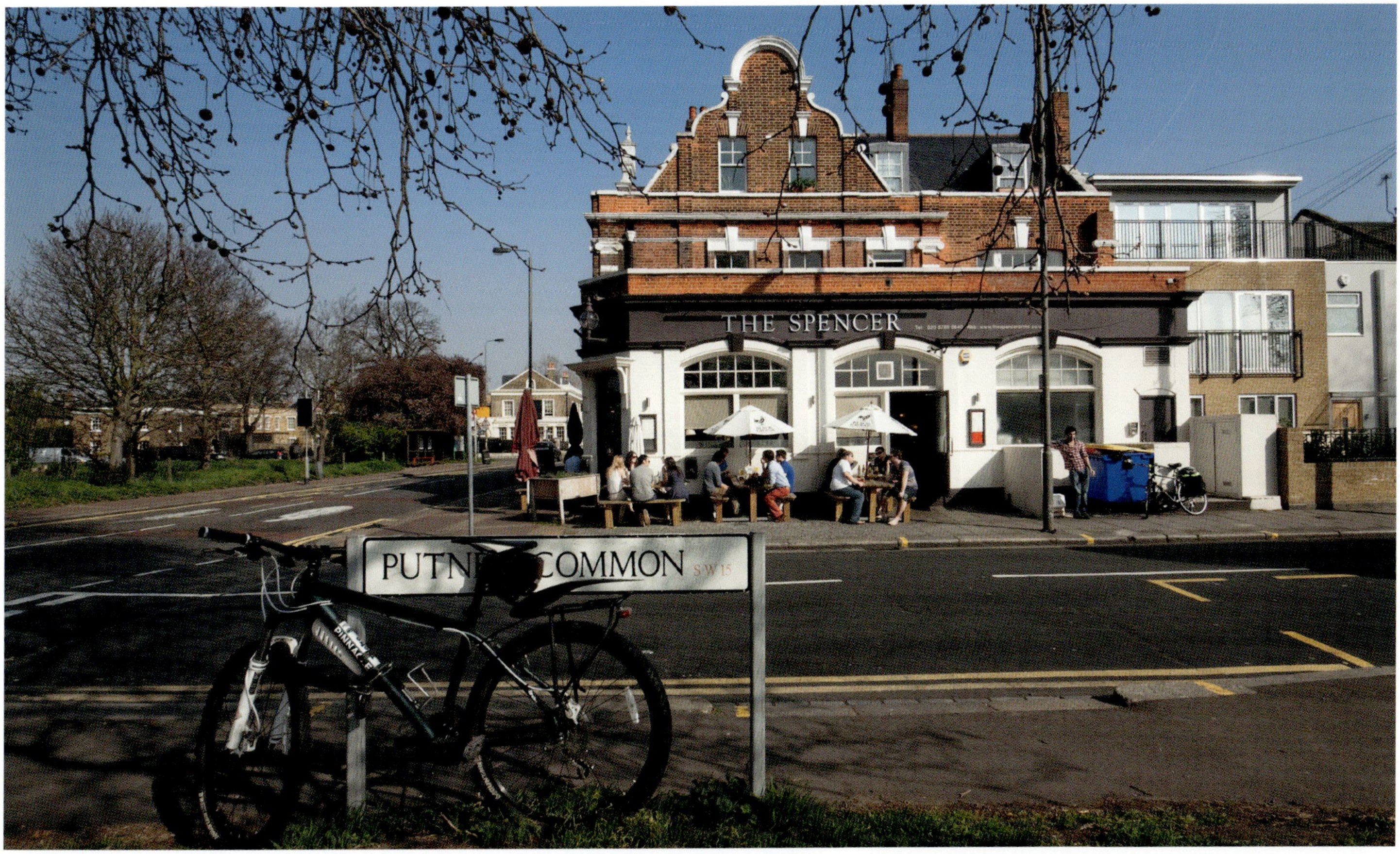
THE SPENCER
PUTNEY COMMON S.W.15

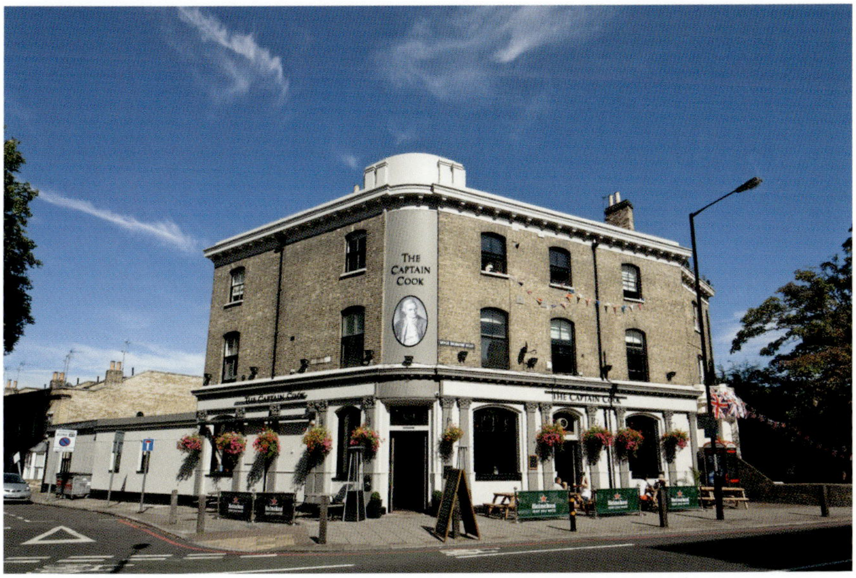
THE CAPTAIN COOK

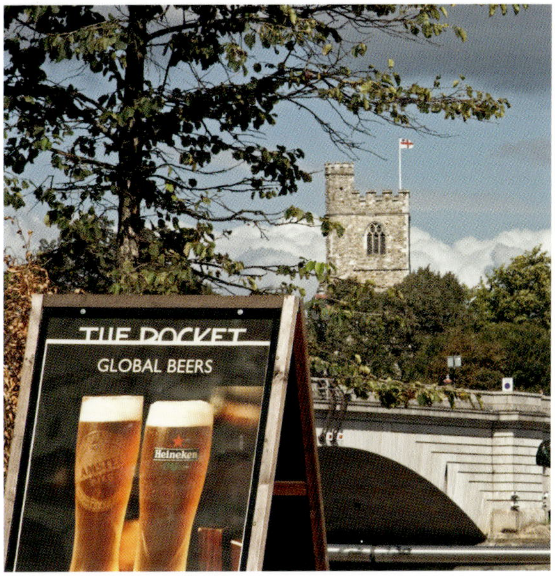
GLOBAL BEERS
Heineken

Open Spaces

In an increasingly urbanised and congested environment, open spaces supply welcome escape and recreation and Putney is greatly blessed in this regard. To the north-west is the great expanse of Putney Common, in parts of which (Heathrow approach-path permitting!) you can imagine yourself in the countryside. A great favourite with dog-walkers, it offers grass and woodland, the meandering Beverley Brook and, for those of a more macabre turn of mind, Lower Common Cemetery and the neglected and spooky Old Barnes Cemetery (technically not in Putney). Jilly Cooper's 1984 memoir The Common Years gives a good flavour. To the east is the much smaller, but still excellent, riverside Wandsworth Park. On the southern border, the wildness of Putney Heath, with its many historic associations. A telegraph station (originally shutter, later semaphore) stood there in the early 19th century – one of a chain stretching from London to Portsmouth – hence the pub name. David Hartley's experimental 'Fireproof House' was built in 1776, commemorated now by an obelisk. Several notable duels took place there, e.g. Castlereagh & Canning in 1809, from which both emerged more or less unscathed. Highwaymen, including the notorious Jerry Abershaw, haunted the Heath and, legend has it, slaked their thirsts (and eyed up potential victims!) in the Green Man, the oldest pub in Putney, dating from the early 1700s.

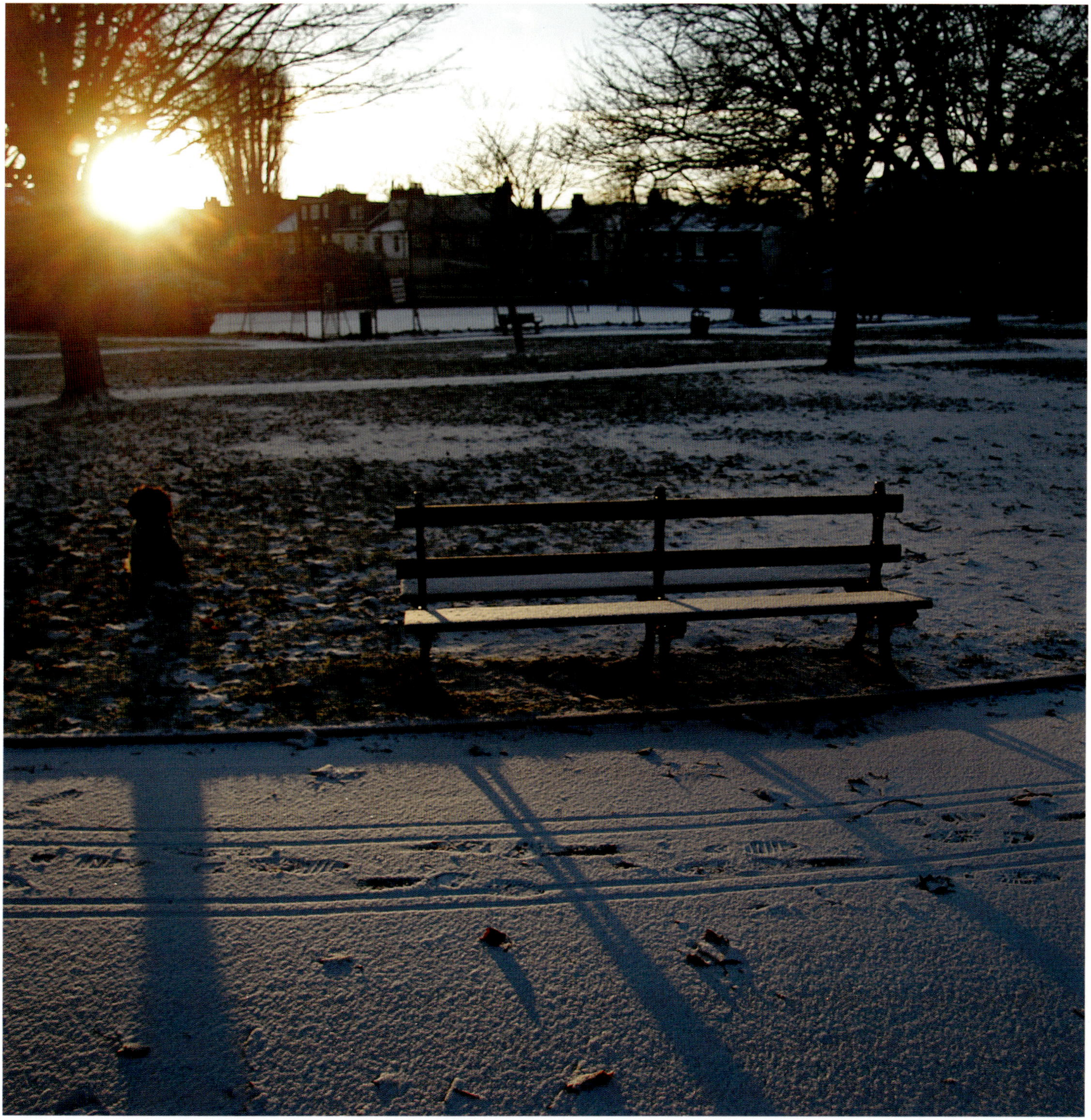

Putney Common

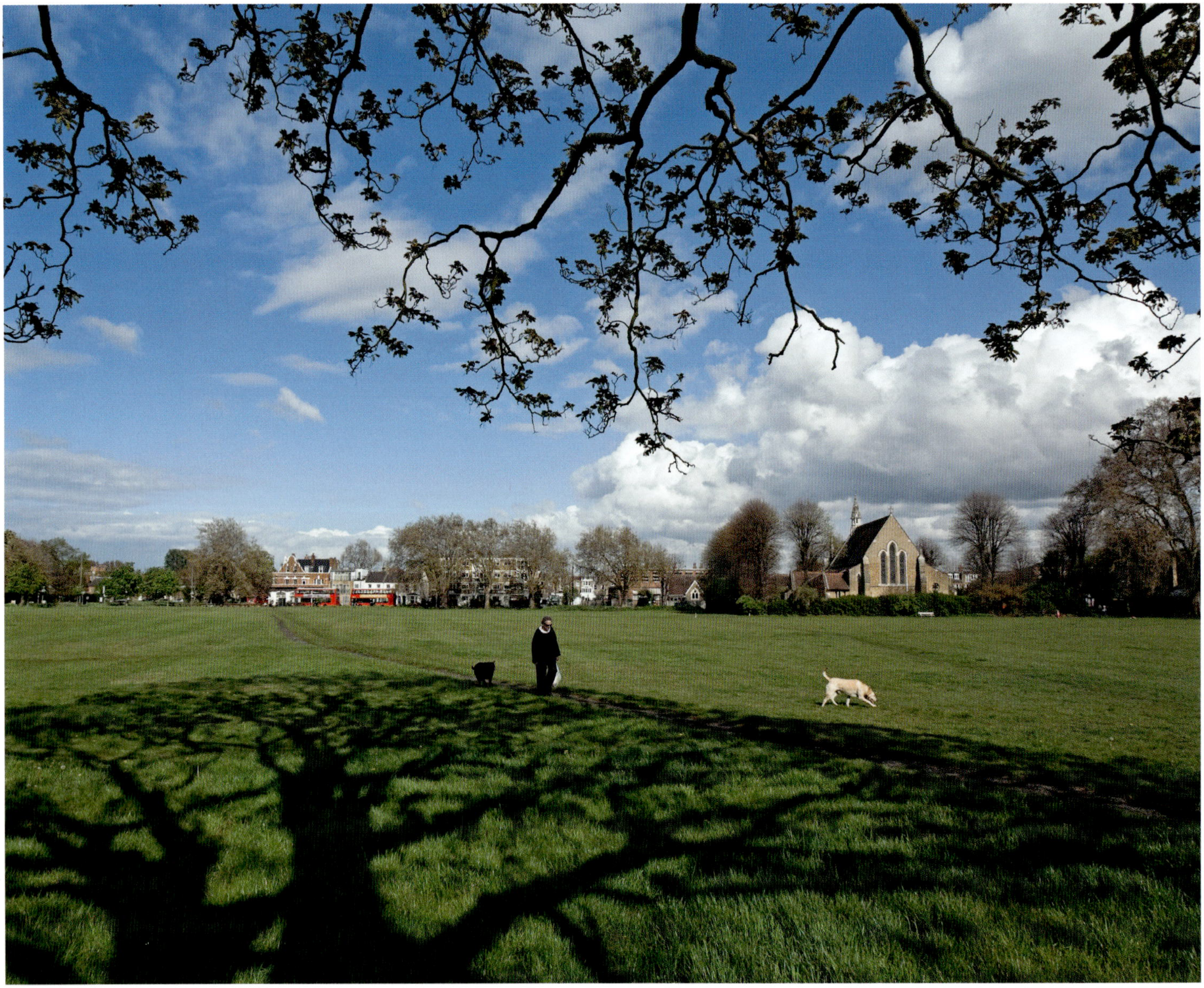

Opposite Page: The Common with All Saints church in the background.

Top Right: Lower Common South has some very distinctive houses, some of which have been sensitively renovated recently.

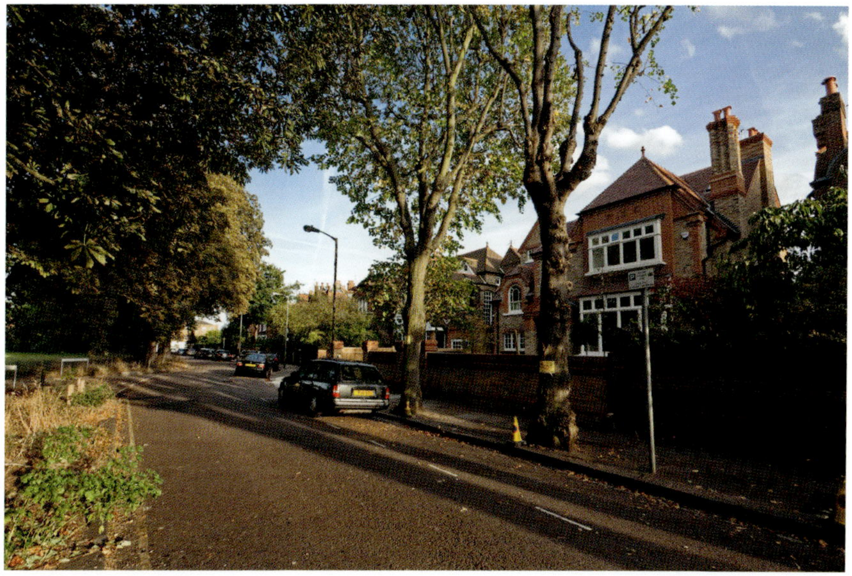

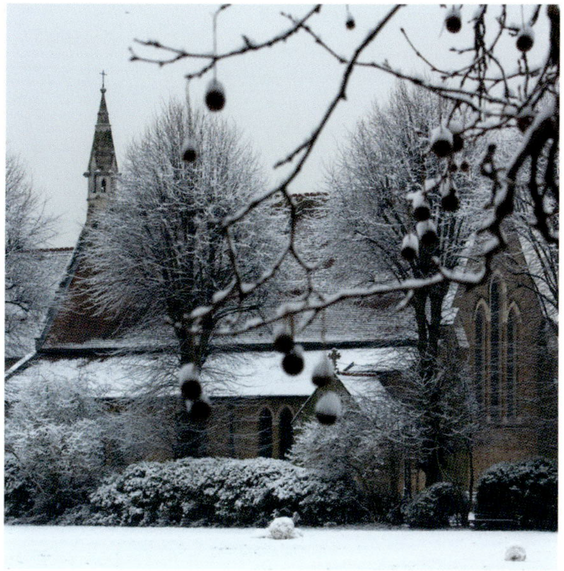

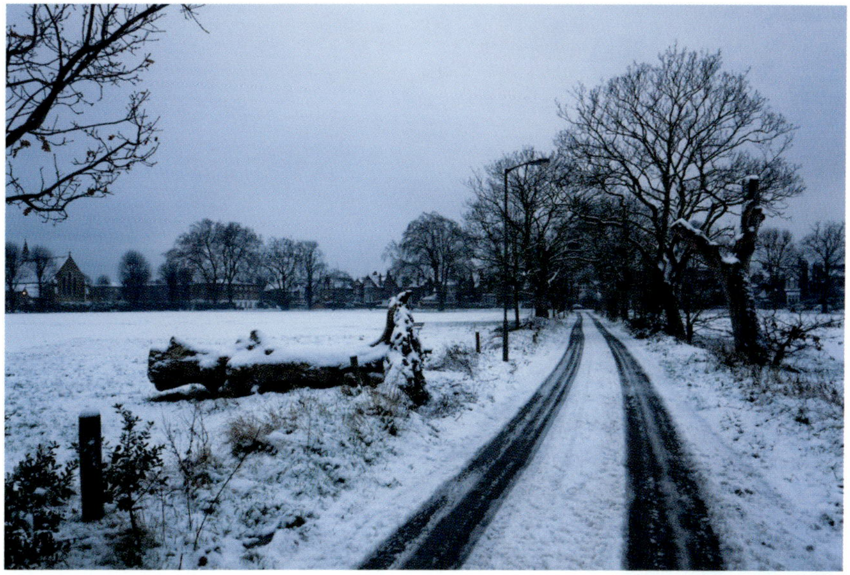

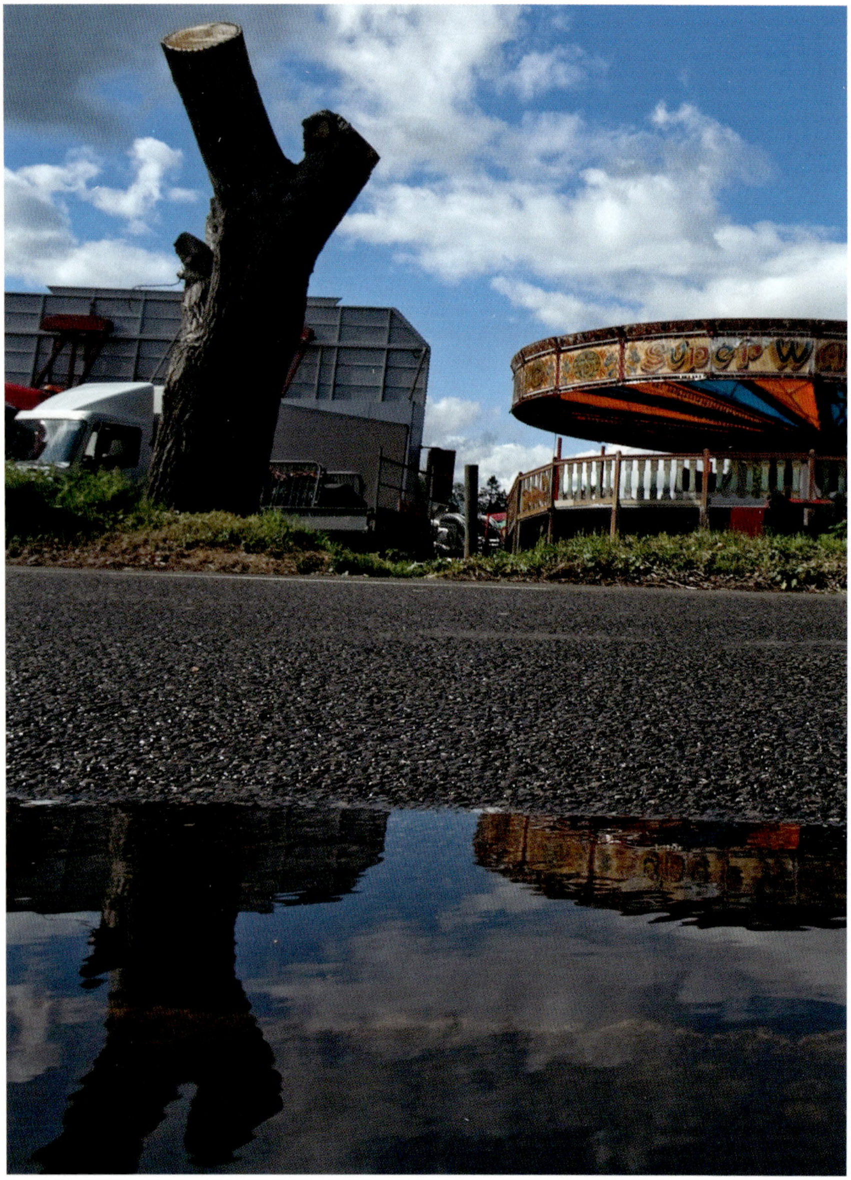

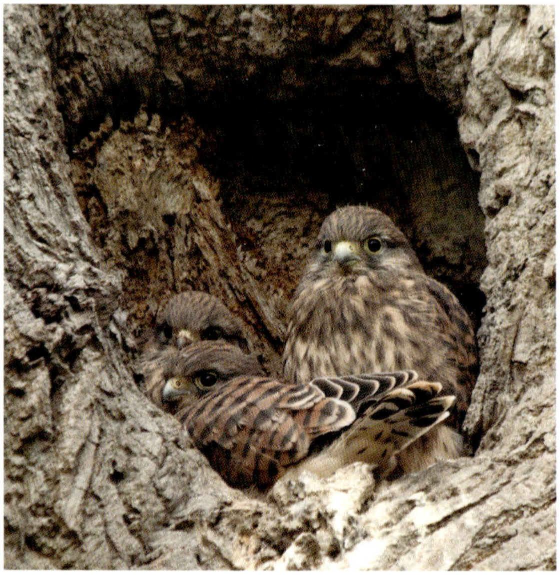

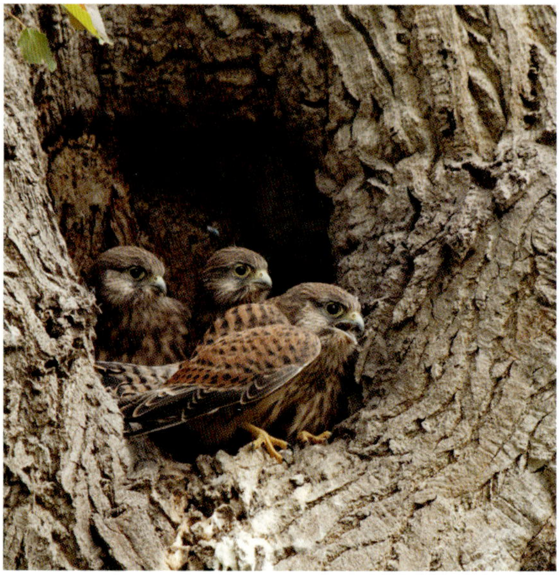

I was surprised to find that the old tree stump on Putney Lower Common had a kestrels' nest in it, despite there being a fair right outside.

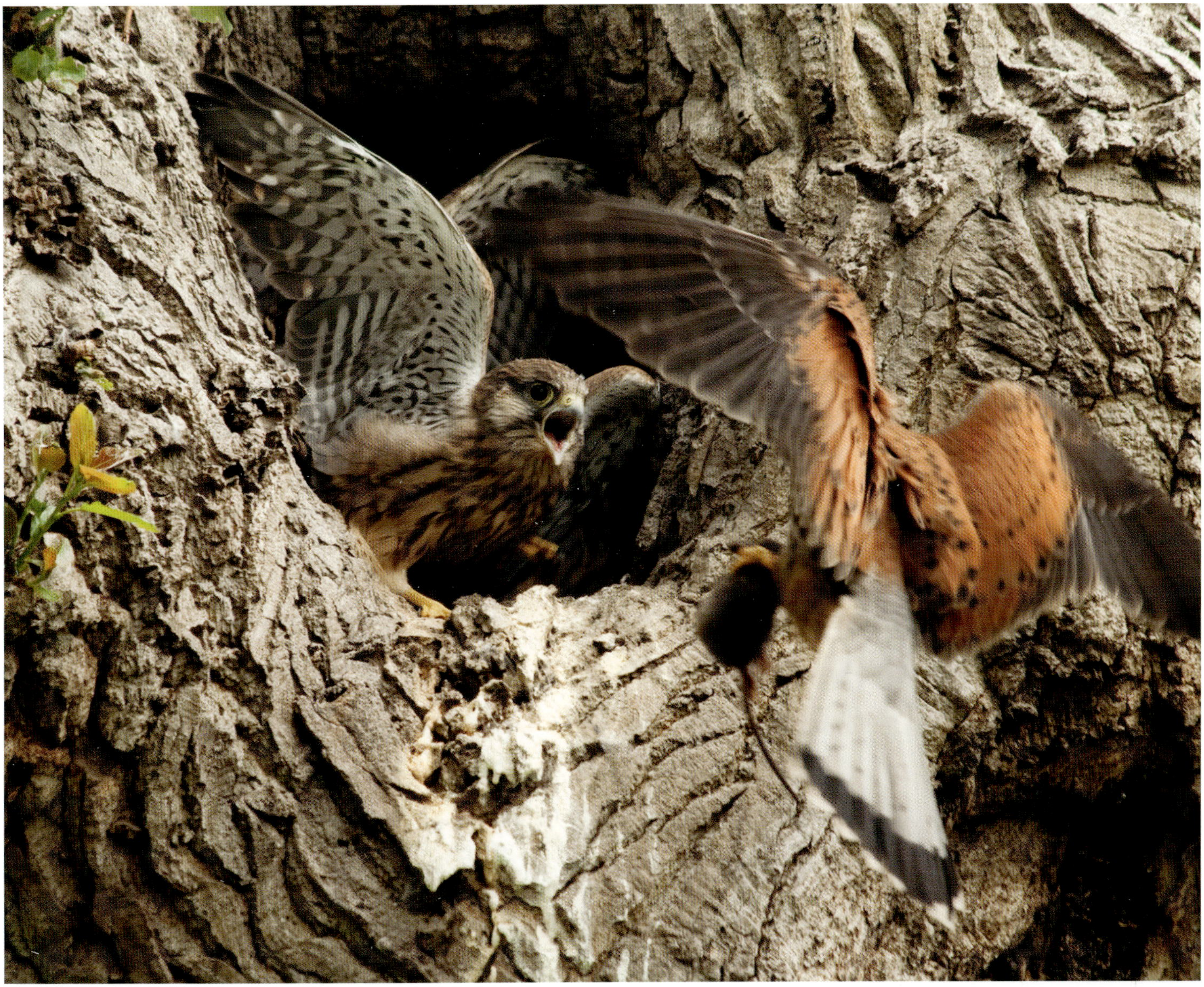

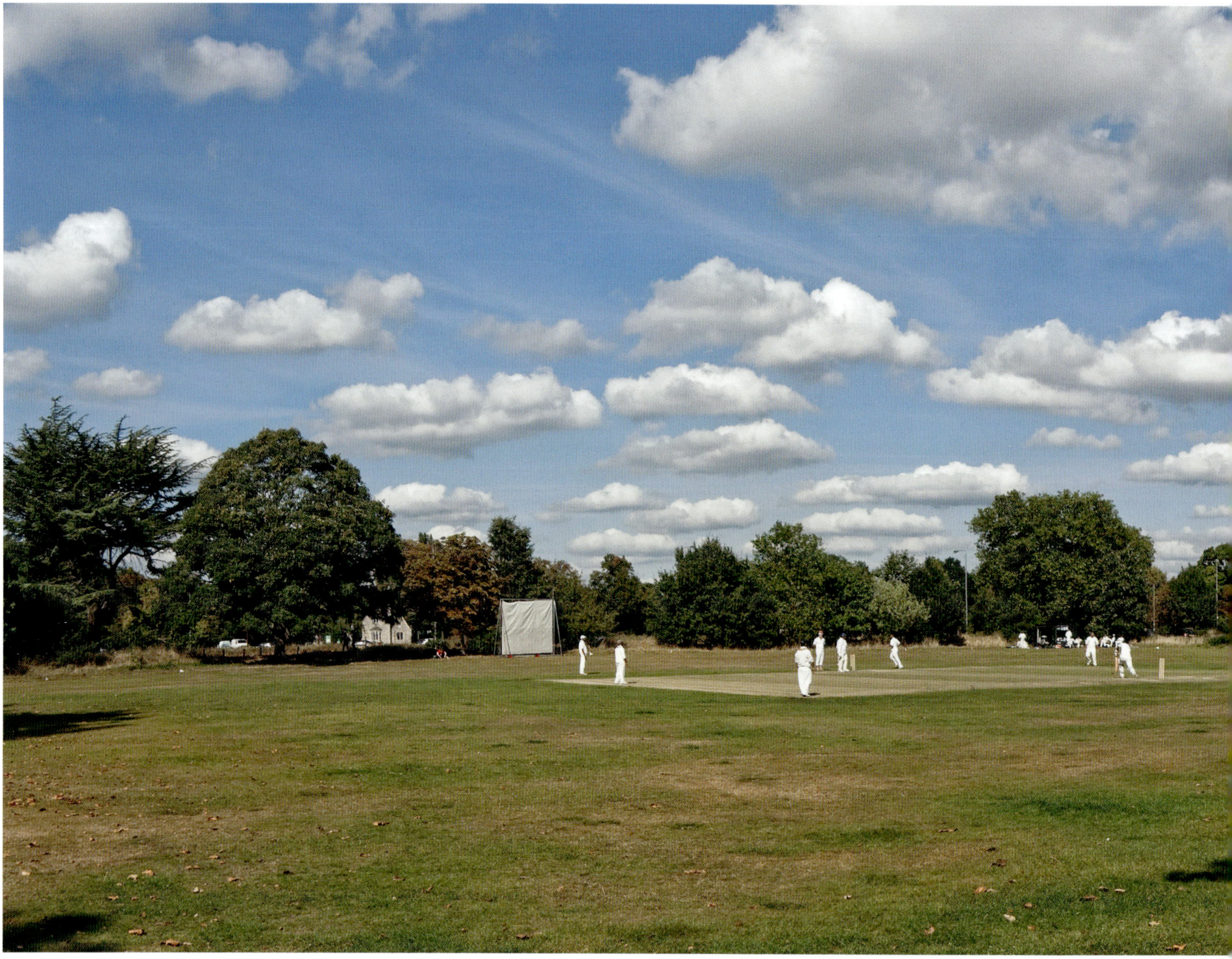

The cricket pitch on Lower Putney Common, the home of Putney Cricket Club. Formed in 1870, cricket has been played here for over 50 years.

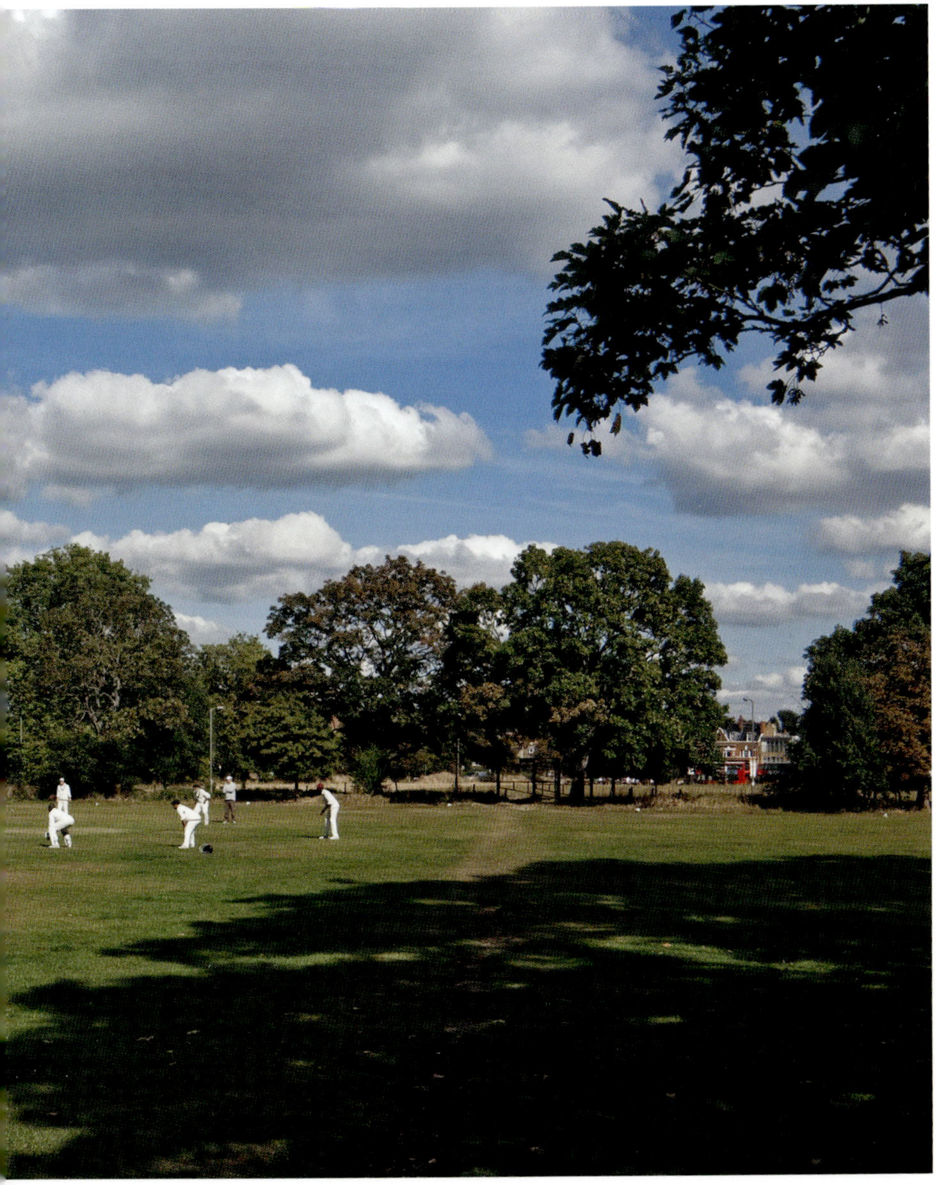

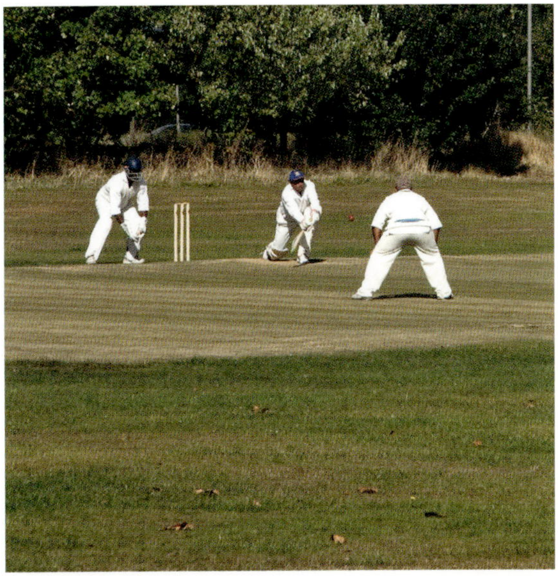

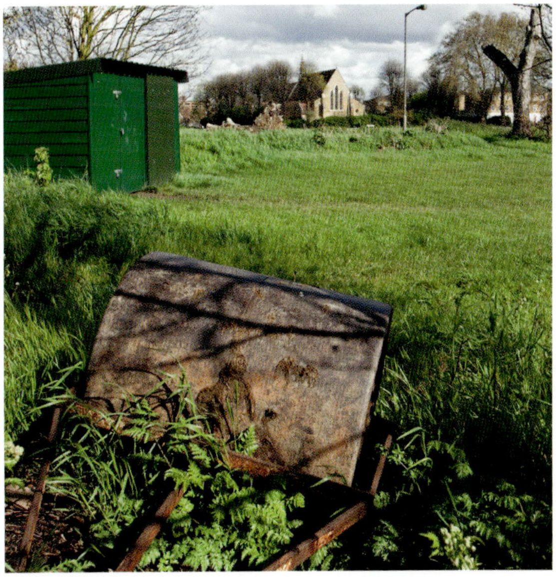

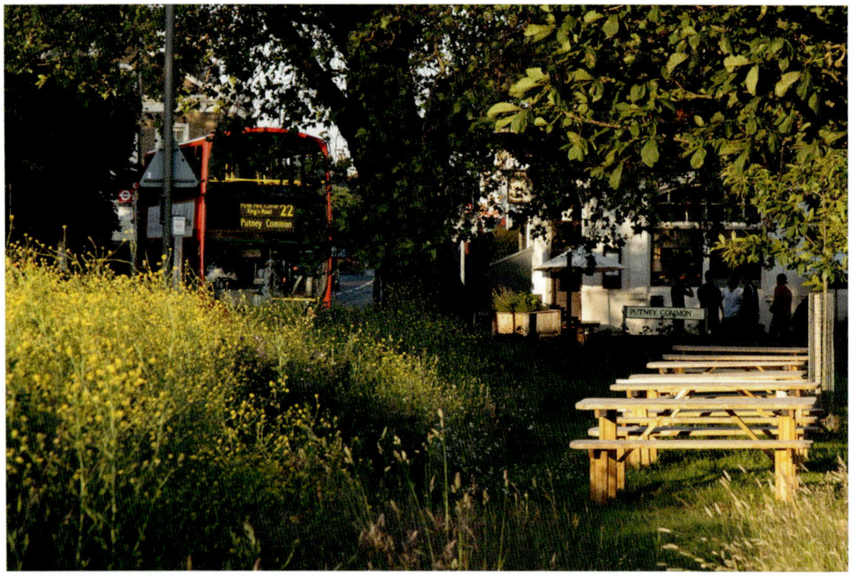

Left: The ever-popular number 22 bus that runs from beside The Spencer, travels between the Common and Piccadilly.

Below: Since this picture was taken, the old Putney hospital has been demolished and a new school and housing development has replaced it.

Right Top and Bottom Right: Beverley Brook, that rises in Worcester Park, runs across the Common and enters the Thames by Leader's Gardens. Popular with dog walkers, this end of the stream is very much affected by the tides on the Thames.

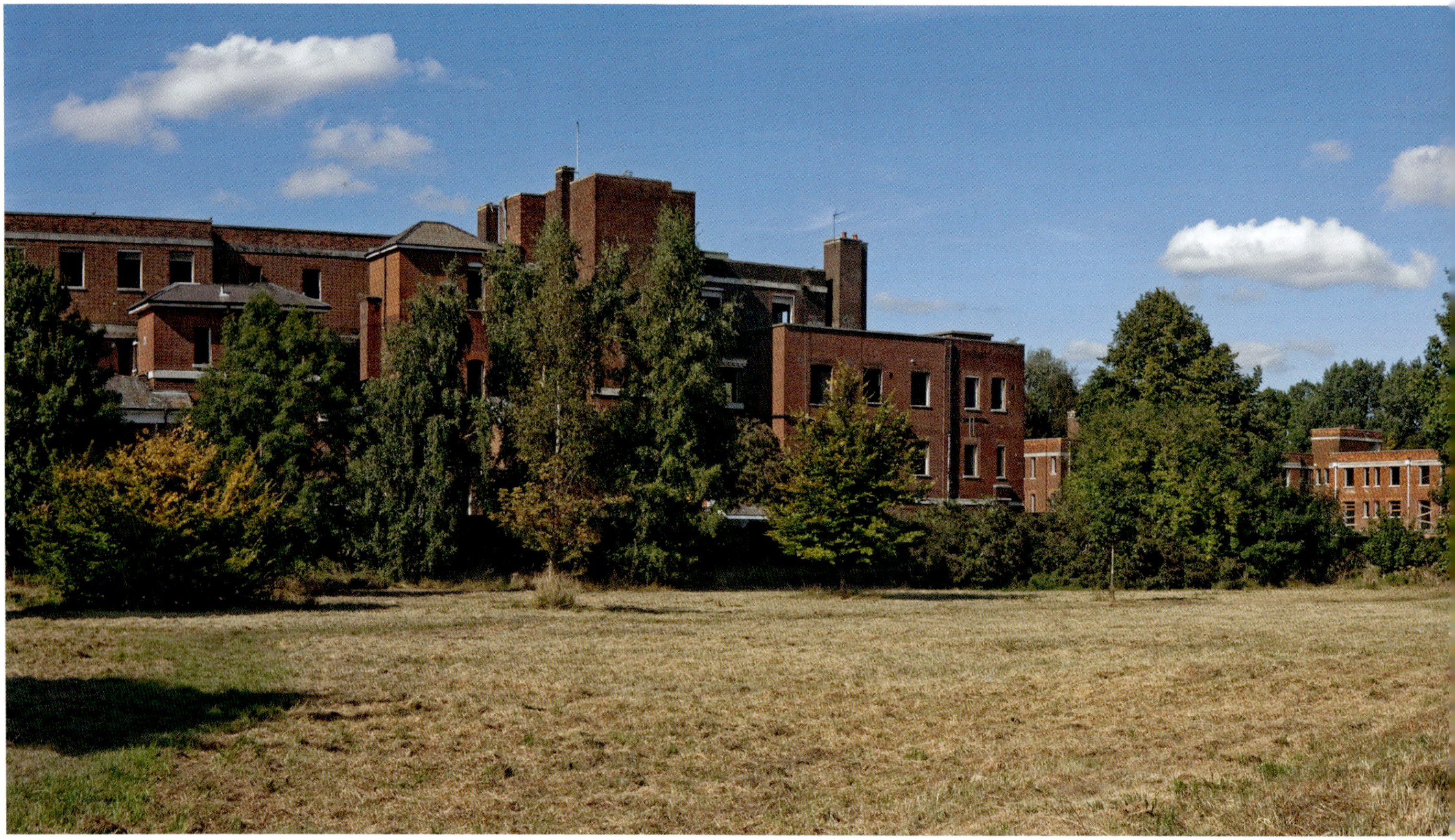

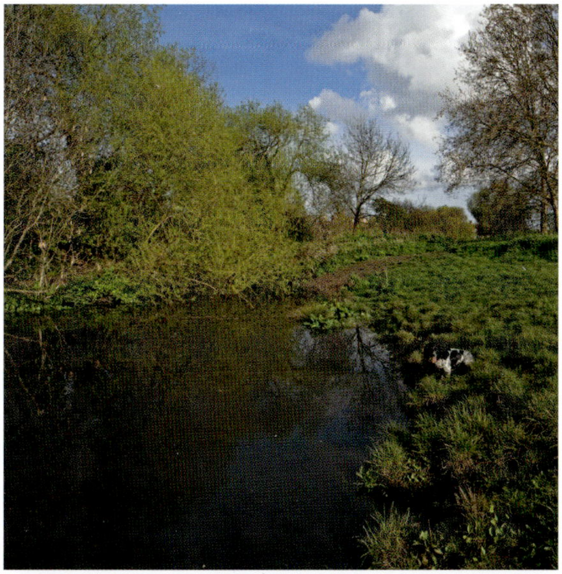

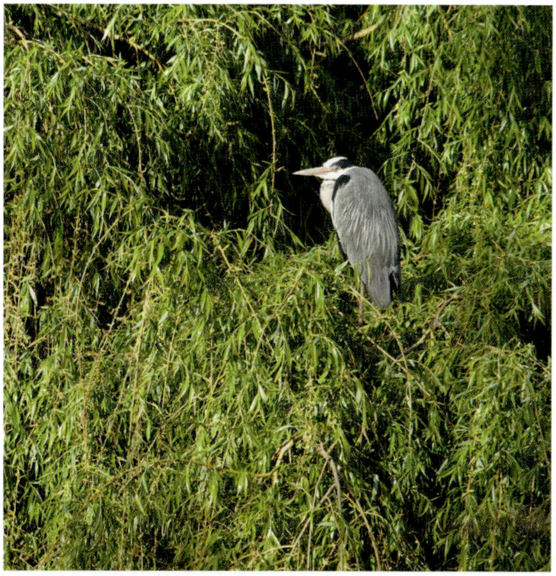

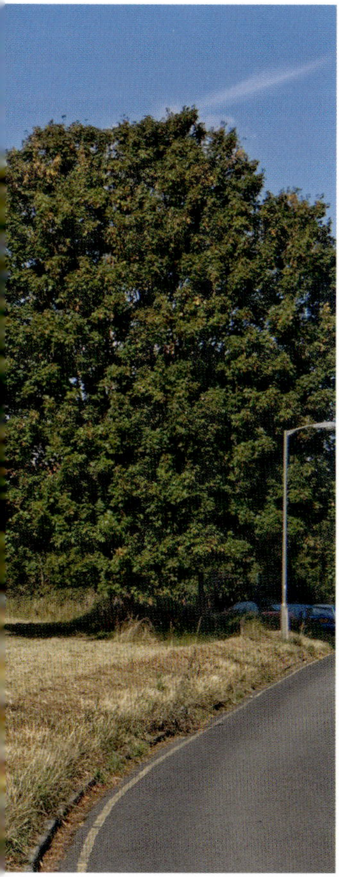

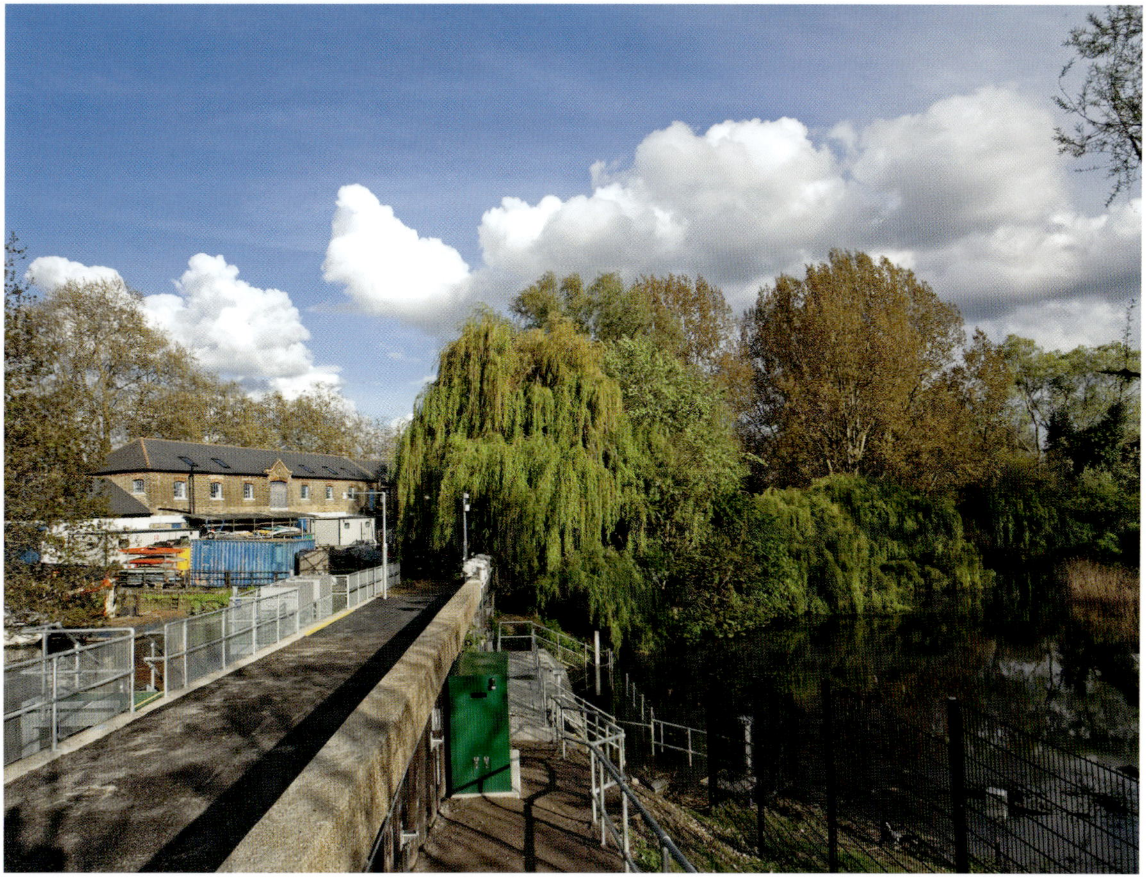

Putney Town Bowls Club

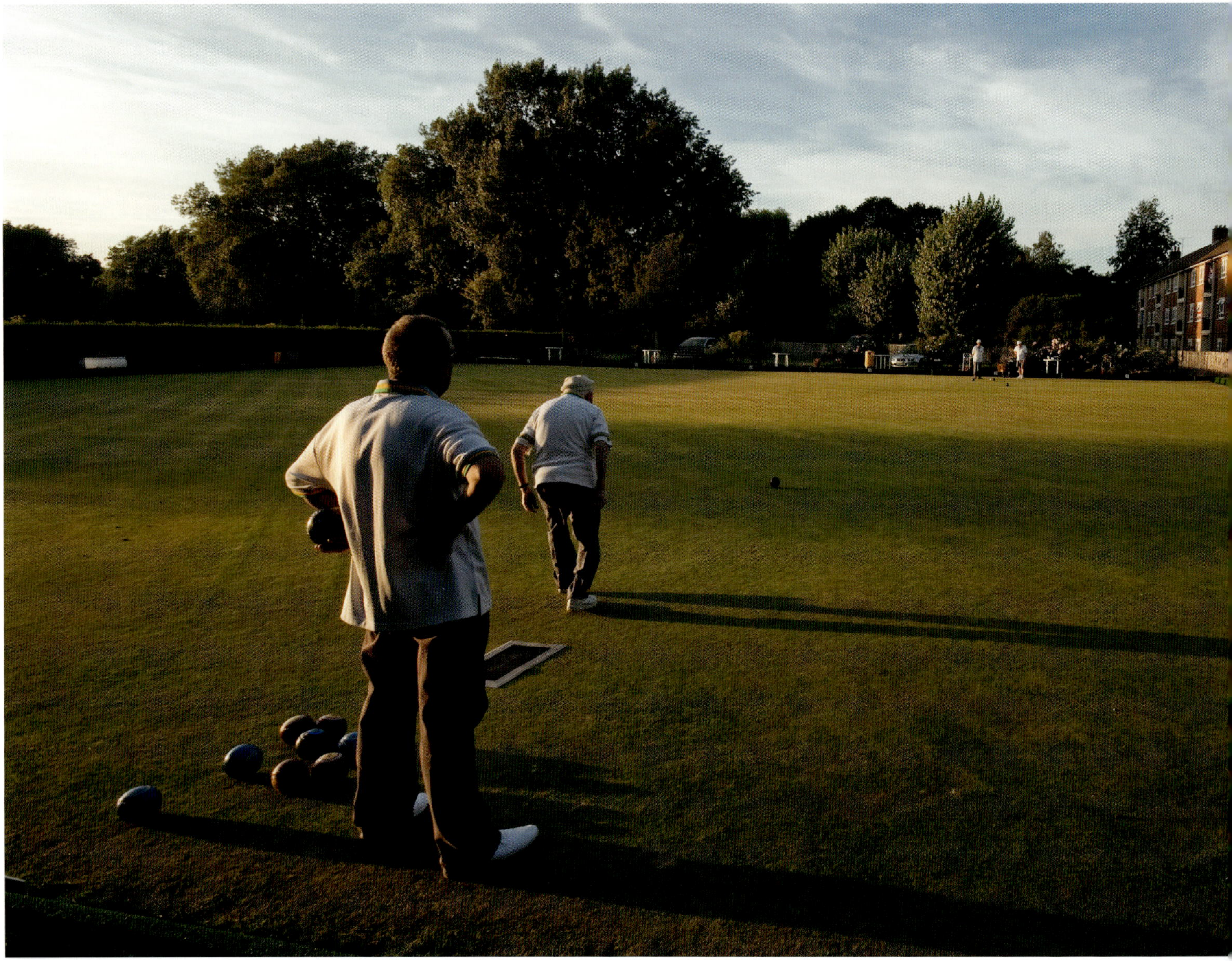

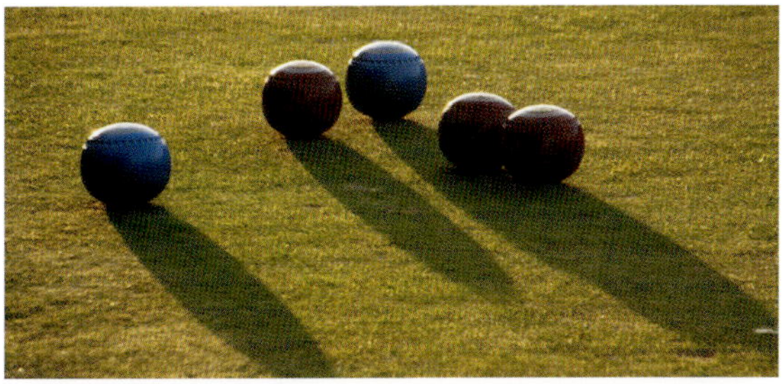

Putney Town Bowls Club is located on the east side of Lower Putney Common, off Commondale, the club was formed in 1914.

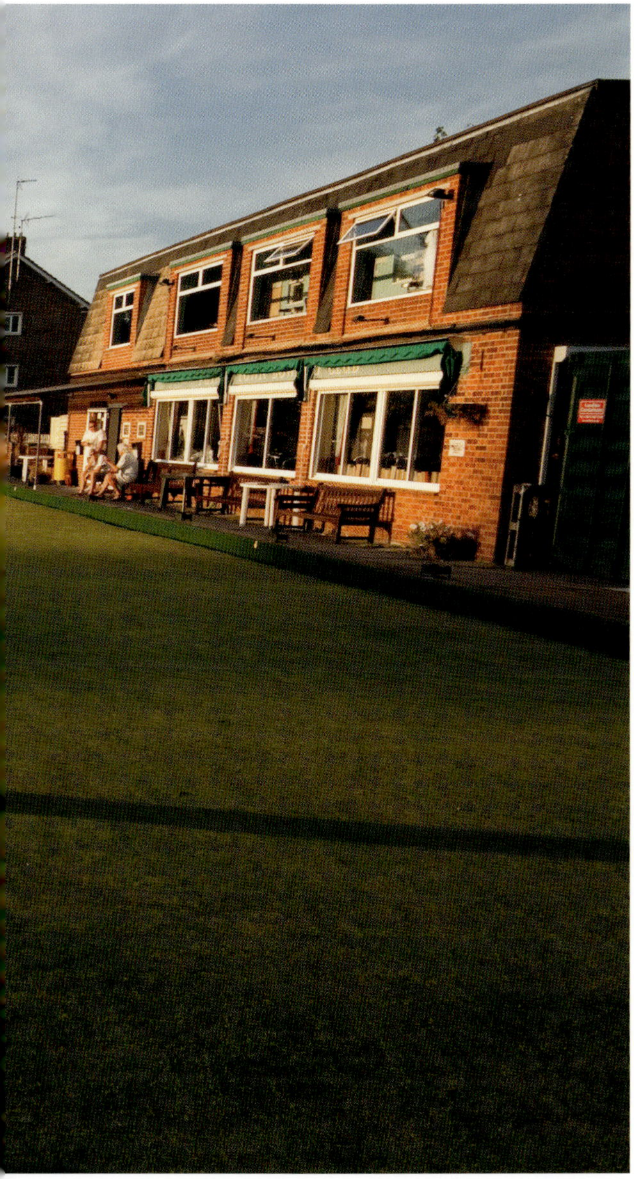

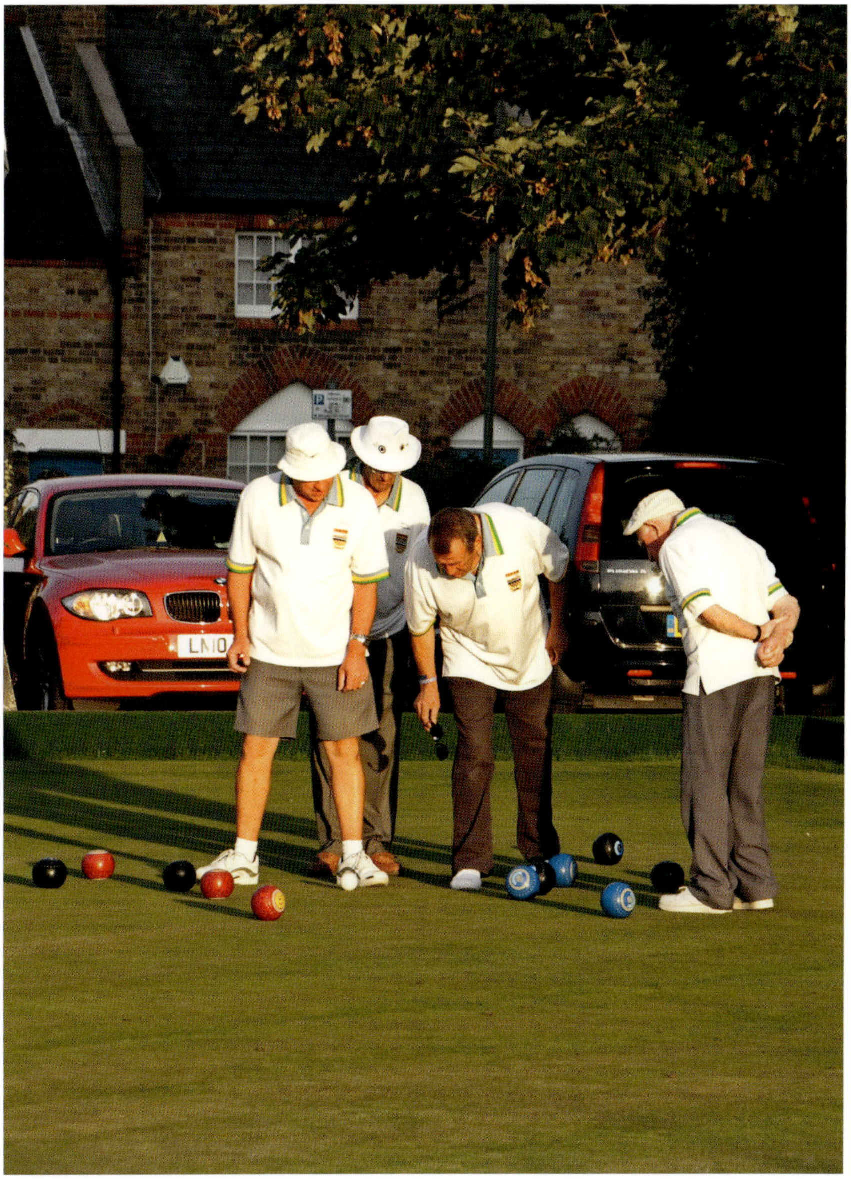

Putney Heath

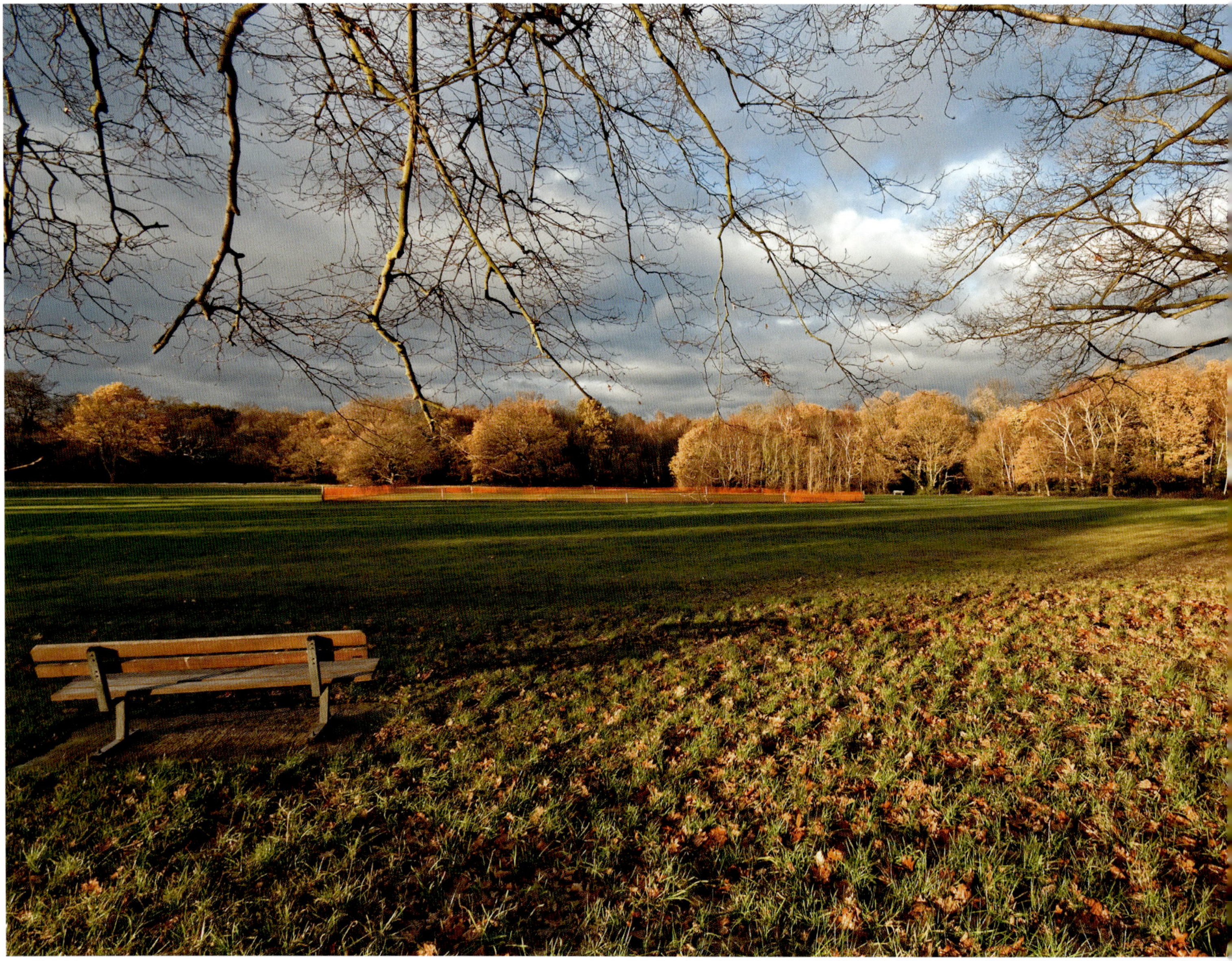

The Heath, as with Lower Putney Common and Wimbledon Common is managed by The Wimbledon and Putney Commons Conservators. Formed in the 19th Century in order to protect the common from development, the Conservators, who are based at The Windmill on Wimbledon Common are paid via a small levy with the council tax. In order to patrol such a large area, they employ a group of rangers, who you may well have seen riding about the Common.

This Spread: The cricket pitch up by The Telegraph pub.

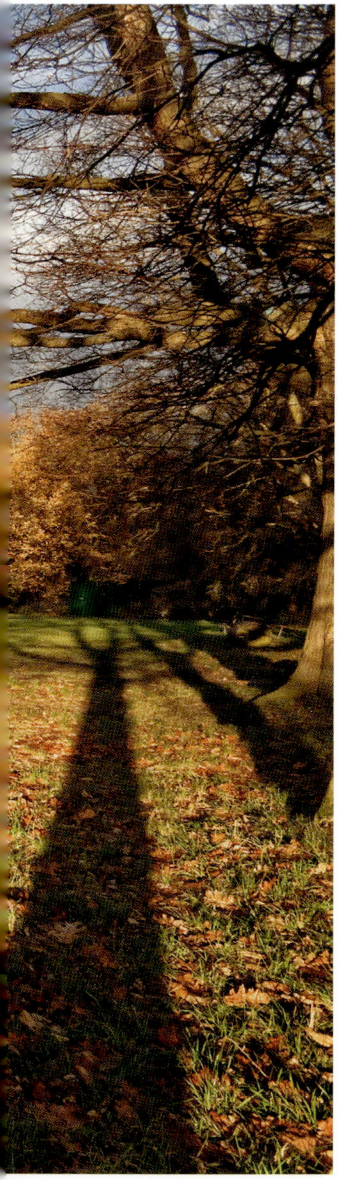

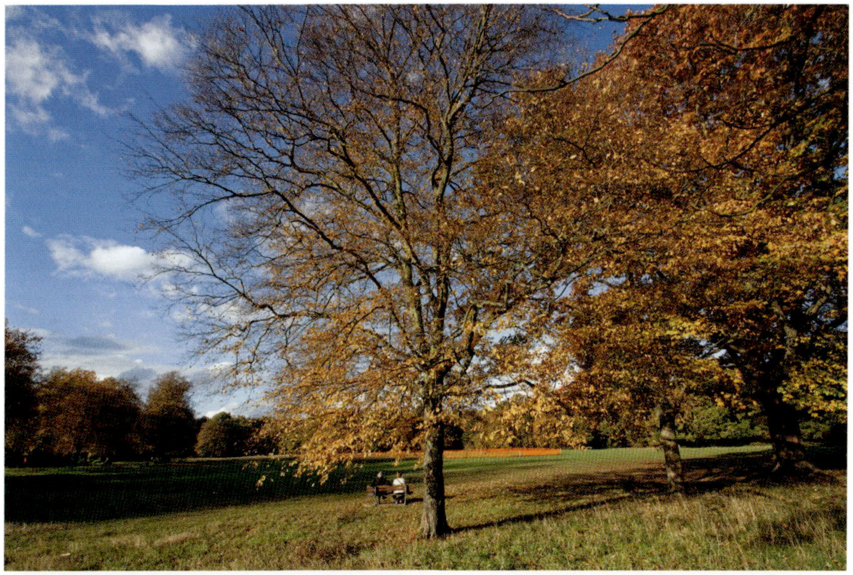

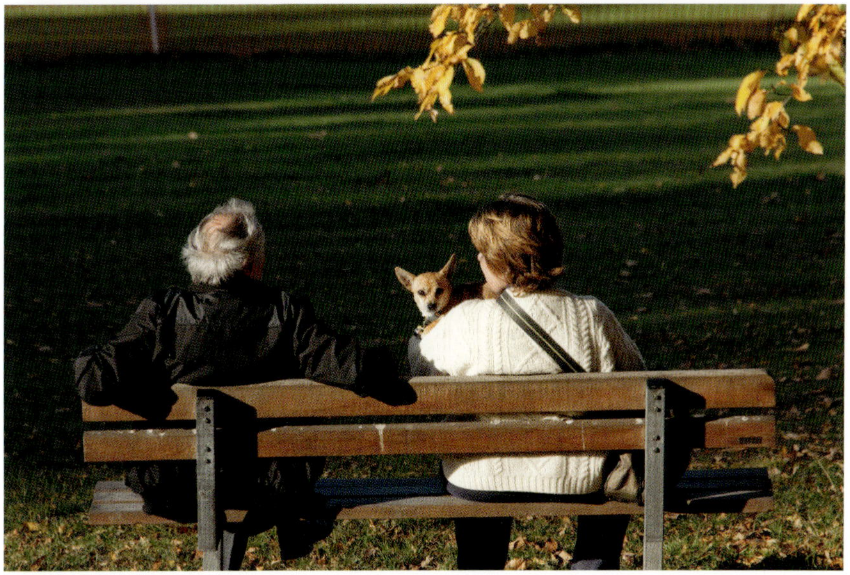

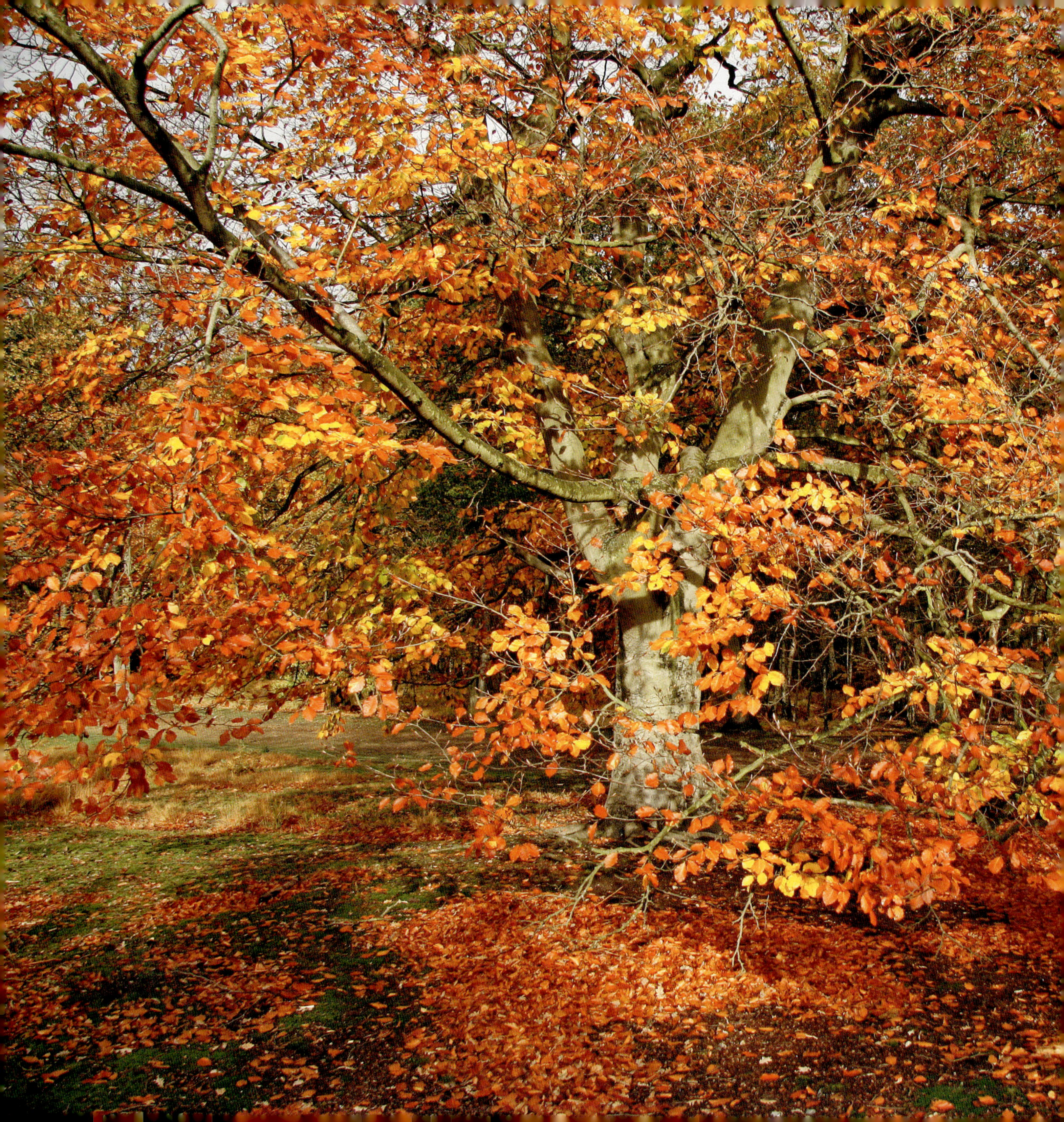

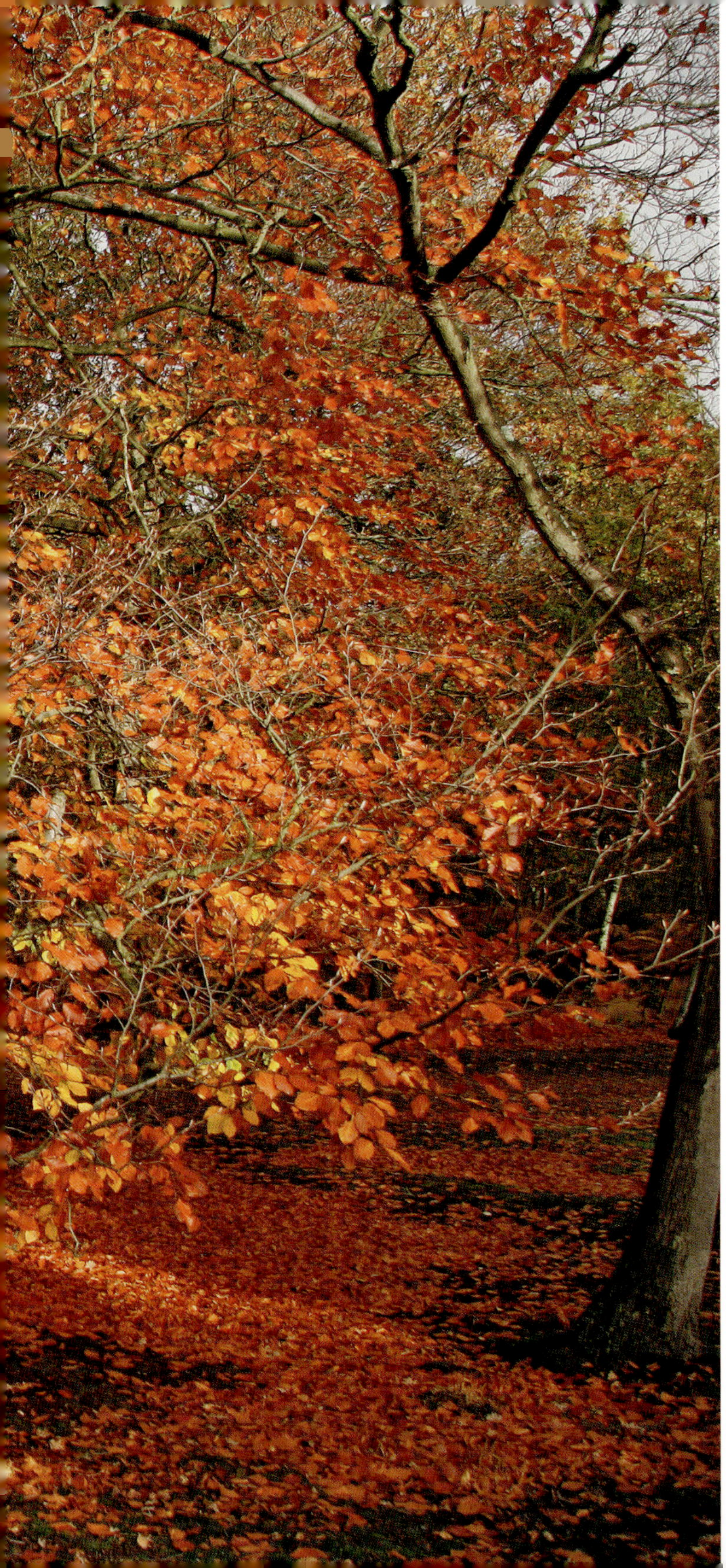

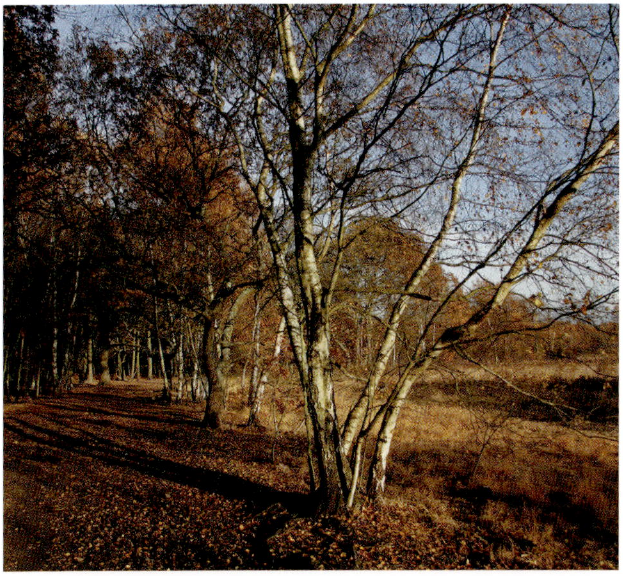

The Heath can boast some wonderful autumn colours, as can be seen with this beautiful beech tree.

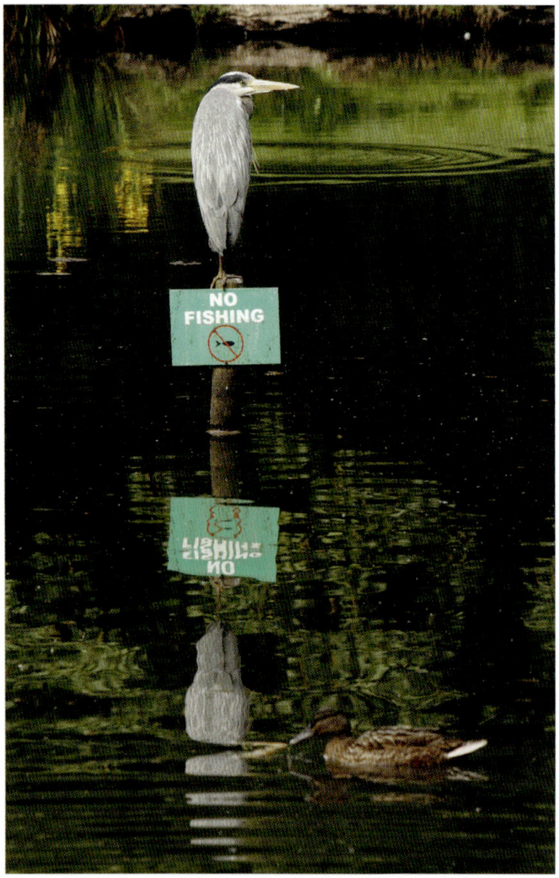

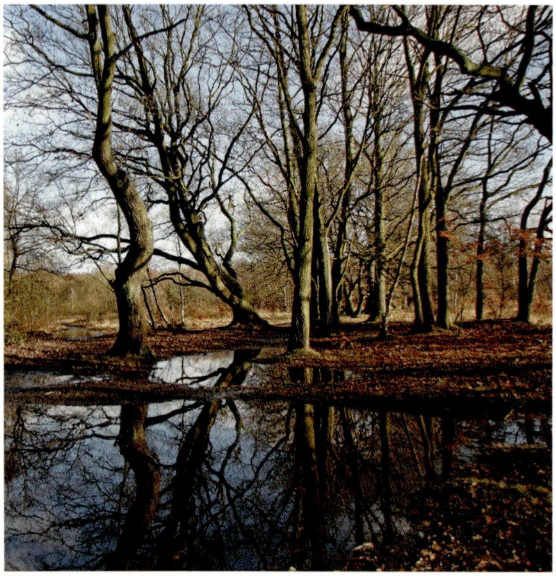

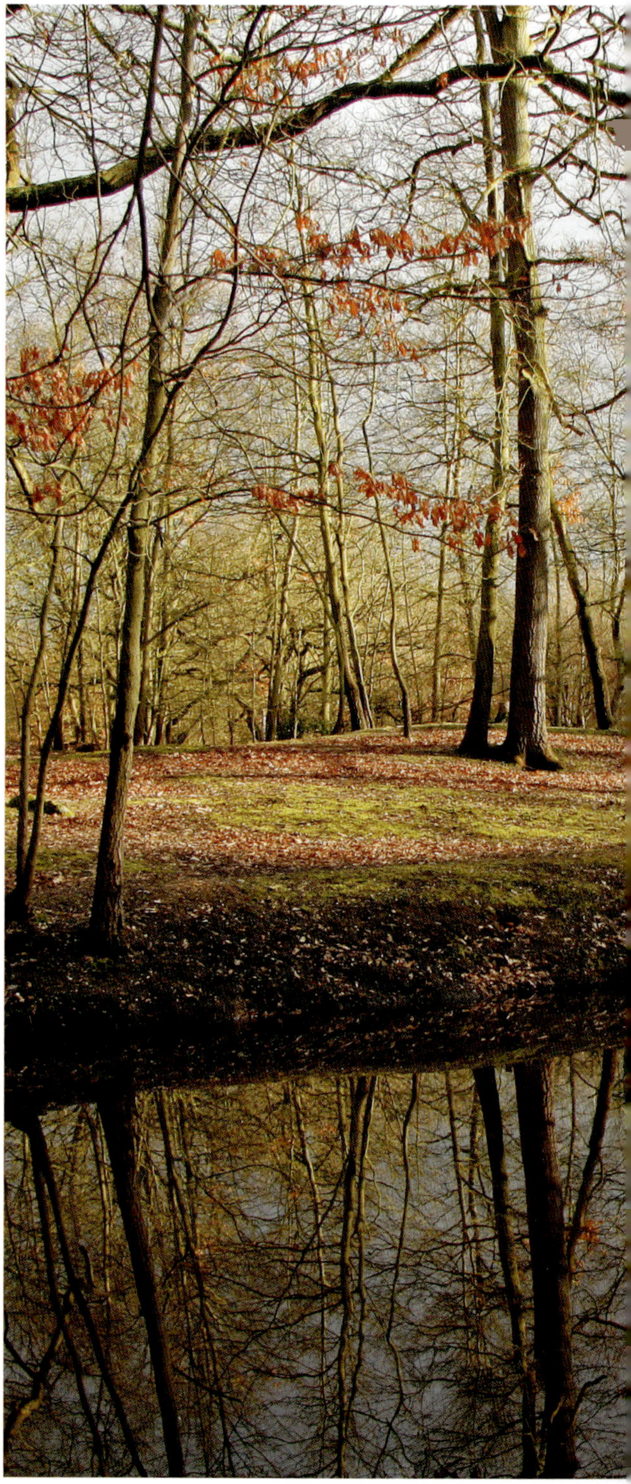

Top Left: This Grey Heron on Scio Pond can regularly be found sitting on this sign. He clearly has a sense of humour.

Right: This small pond up near the A3, sometimes referred to as Jerry's Pond, is unfortunately nearly dry despite all the rain we have had. This picture was taken two years ago.

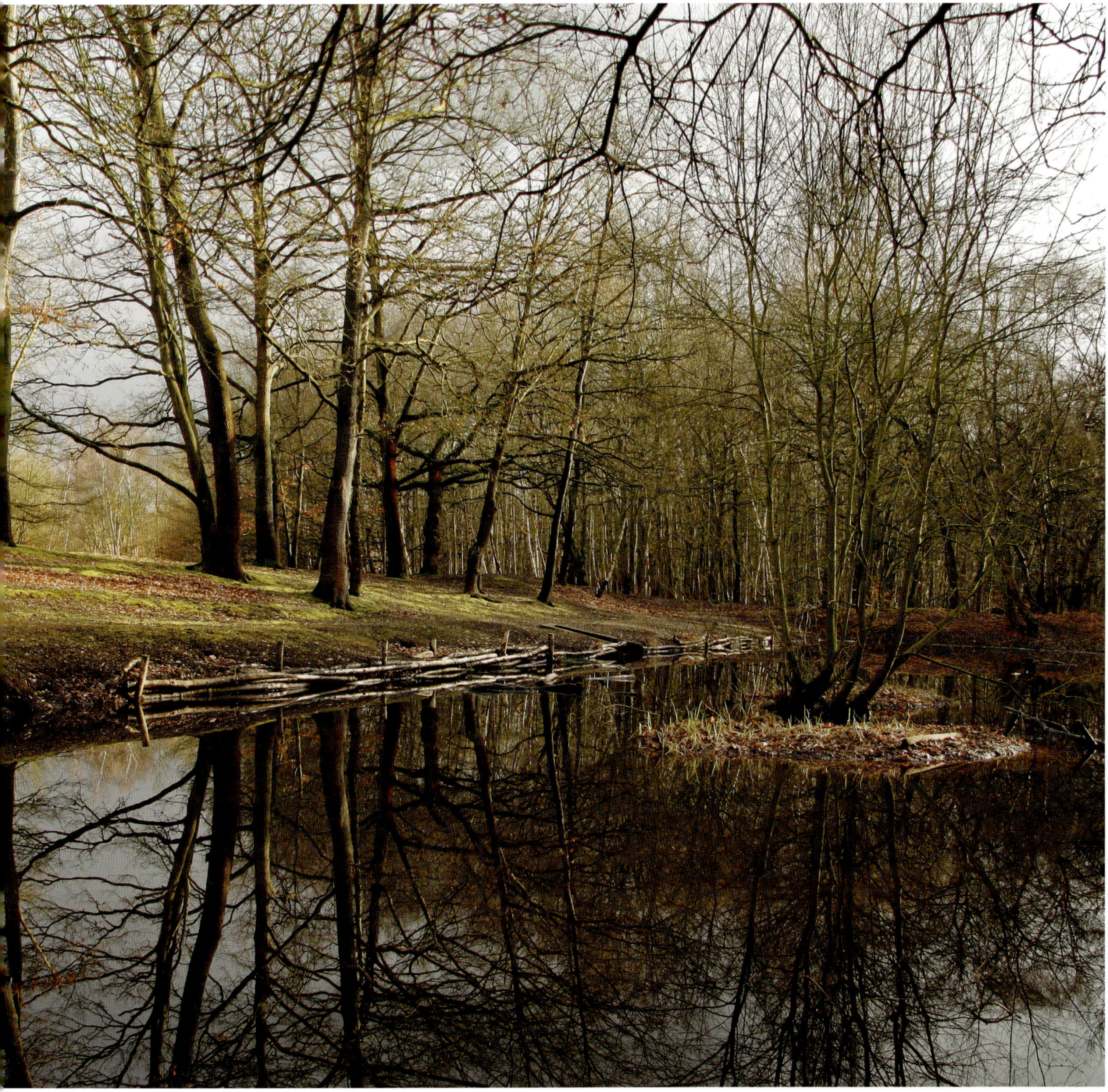

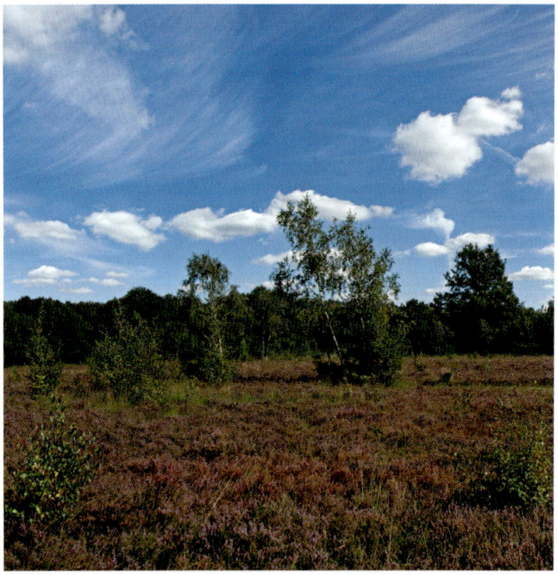

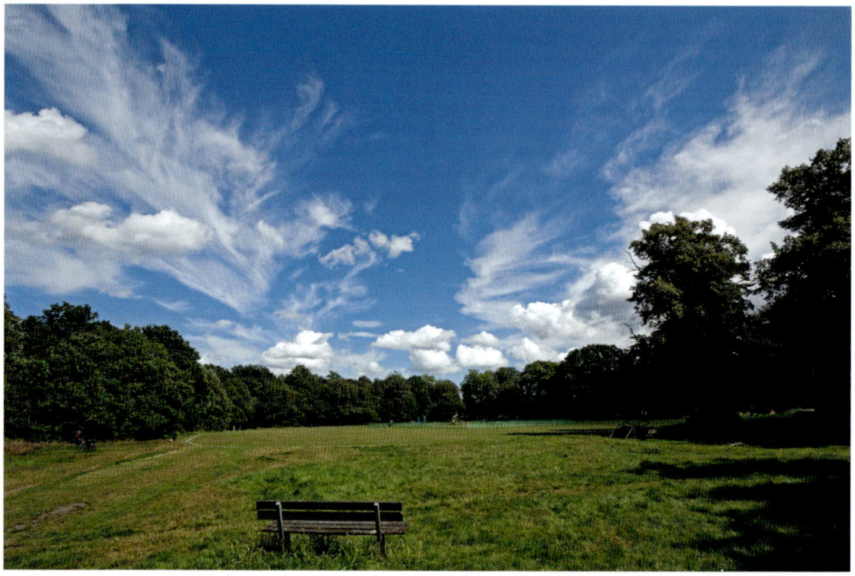

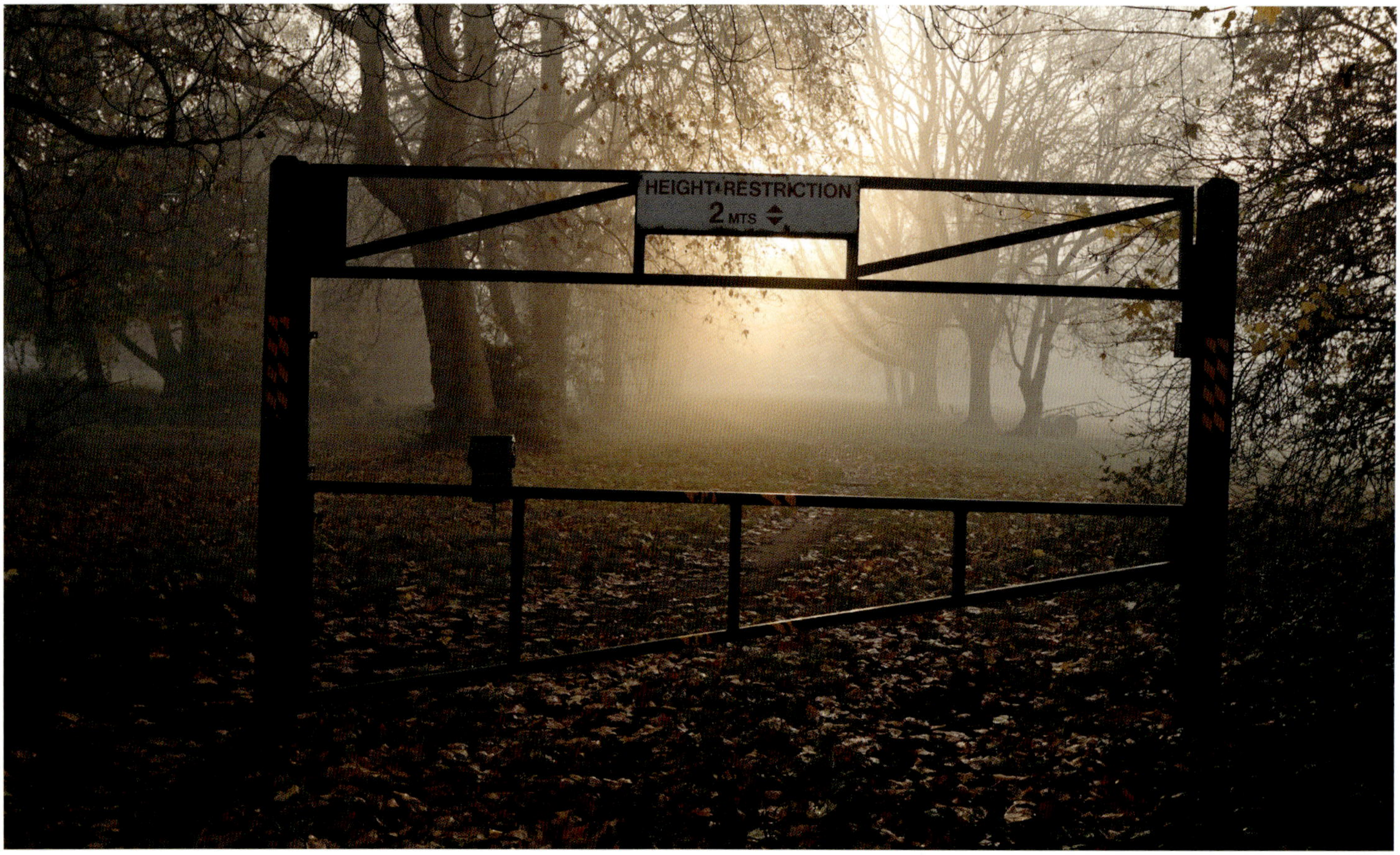
HEIGHT RESTRICTION
2 MTS

Far Left: Recently, the Conservators have been cutting down some of the trees in order to let the natural heather grow through, which looks great in August each year when it flowers.

Left and Bottom Left: Cricket pitch.

Right: Kingfisher by Beverley Brook.

Far Right: Grey squirrel gathering food on the Heath.

Below Right: Green woodpecker, busying himself grubbing for his staple diet, ants.

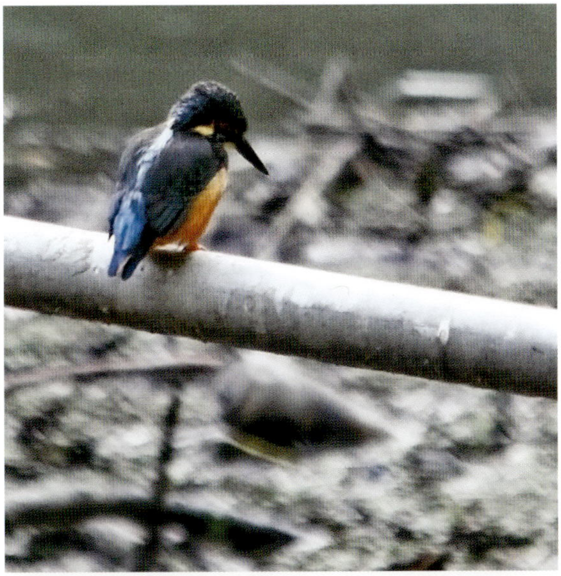

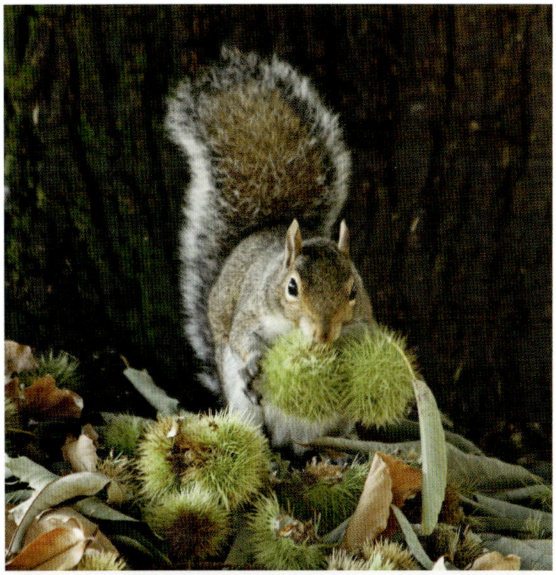

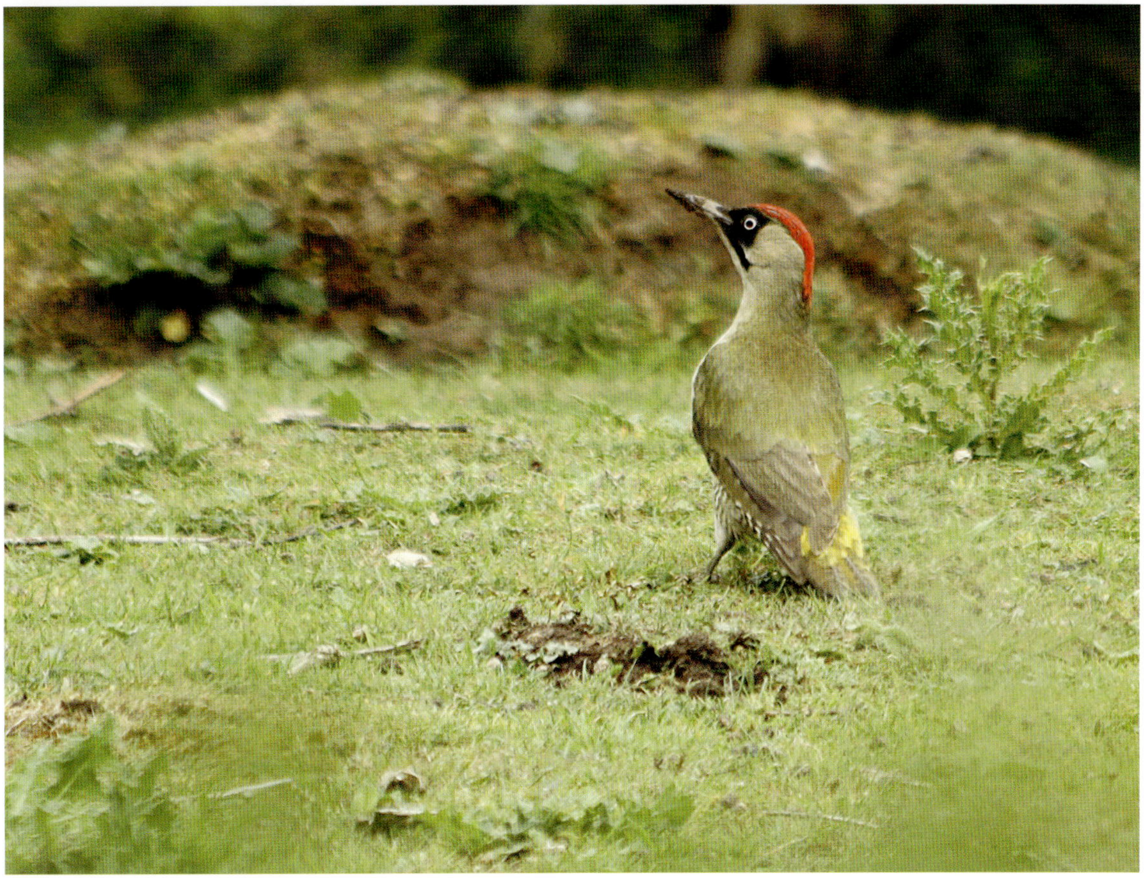

Kingsmere

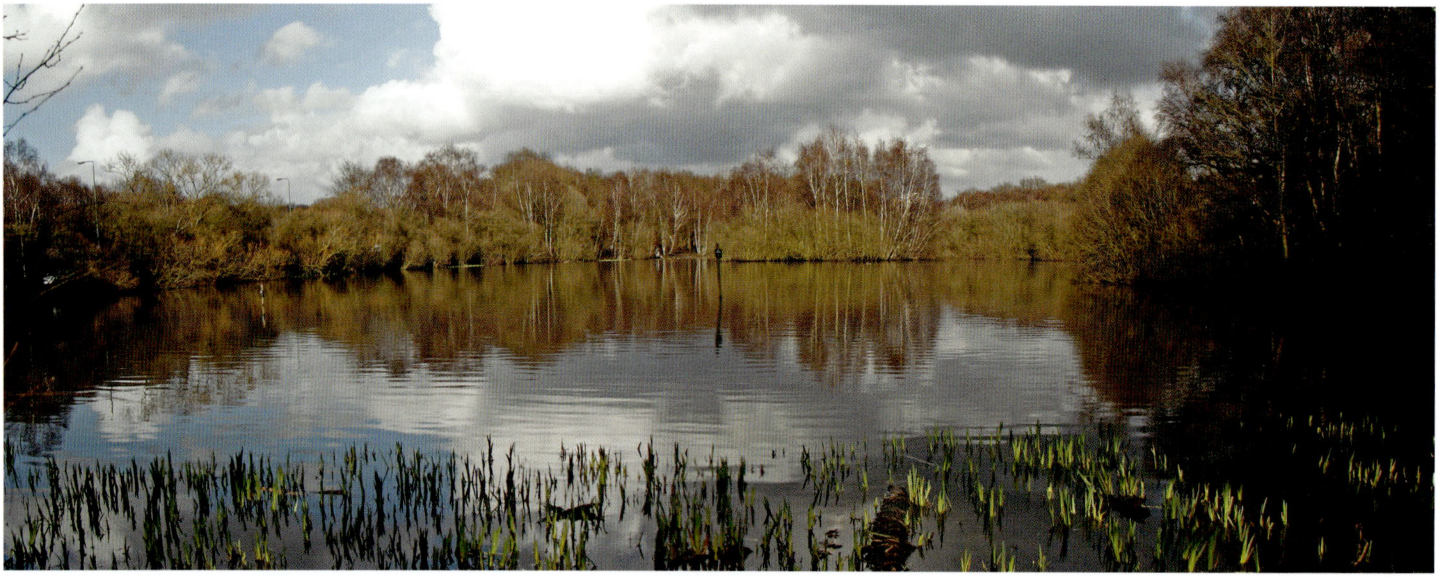

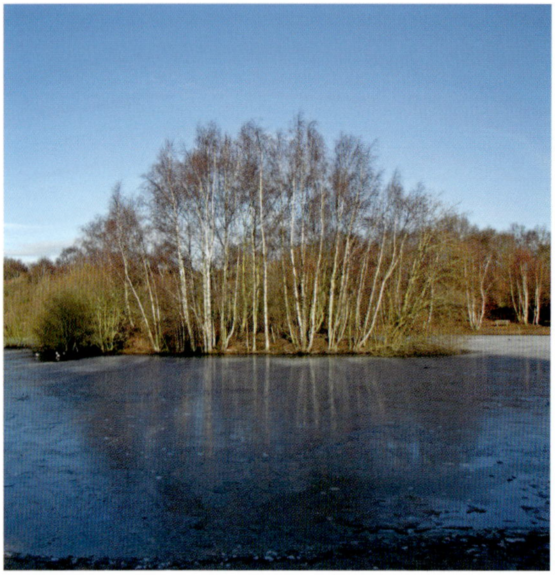

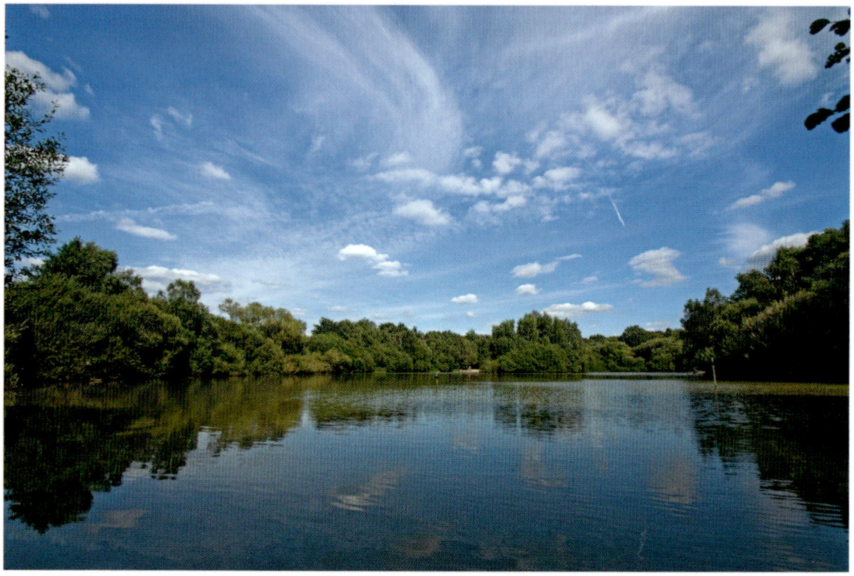

Kingsmere is the largest of the lakes on the Heath. The island is not natural and was created when the lake was dredged in the 1990s, to help hold its water. This has given a good spot for birds to nest.

Right: A Cormorant, who I'm not sure has noticed the sign.

Overleaf and following pages: Kingsmere in autumn.

Page 153: Kingsmere – main picture, a rather sad looking Grey Heron, who was clearly very hungry, as he couldn't fish because of the ice.

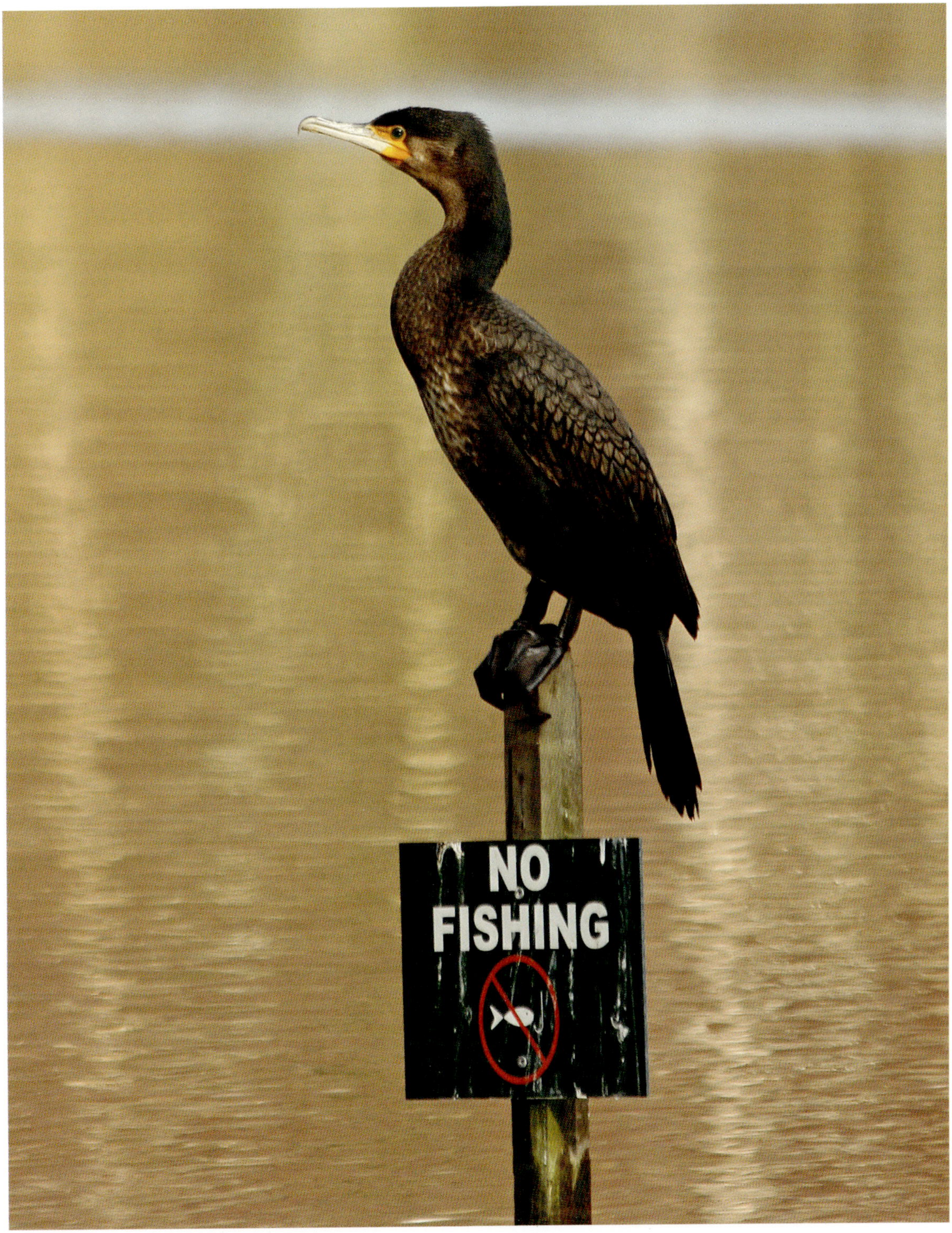

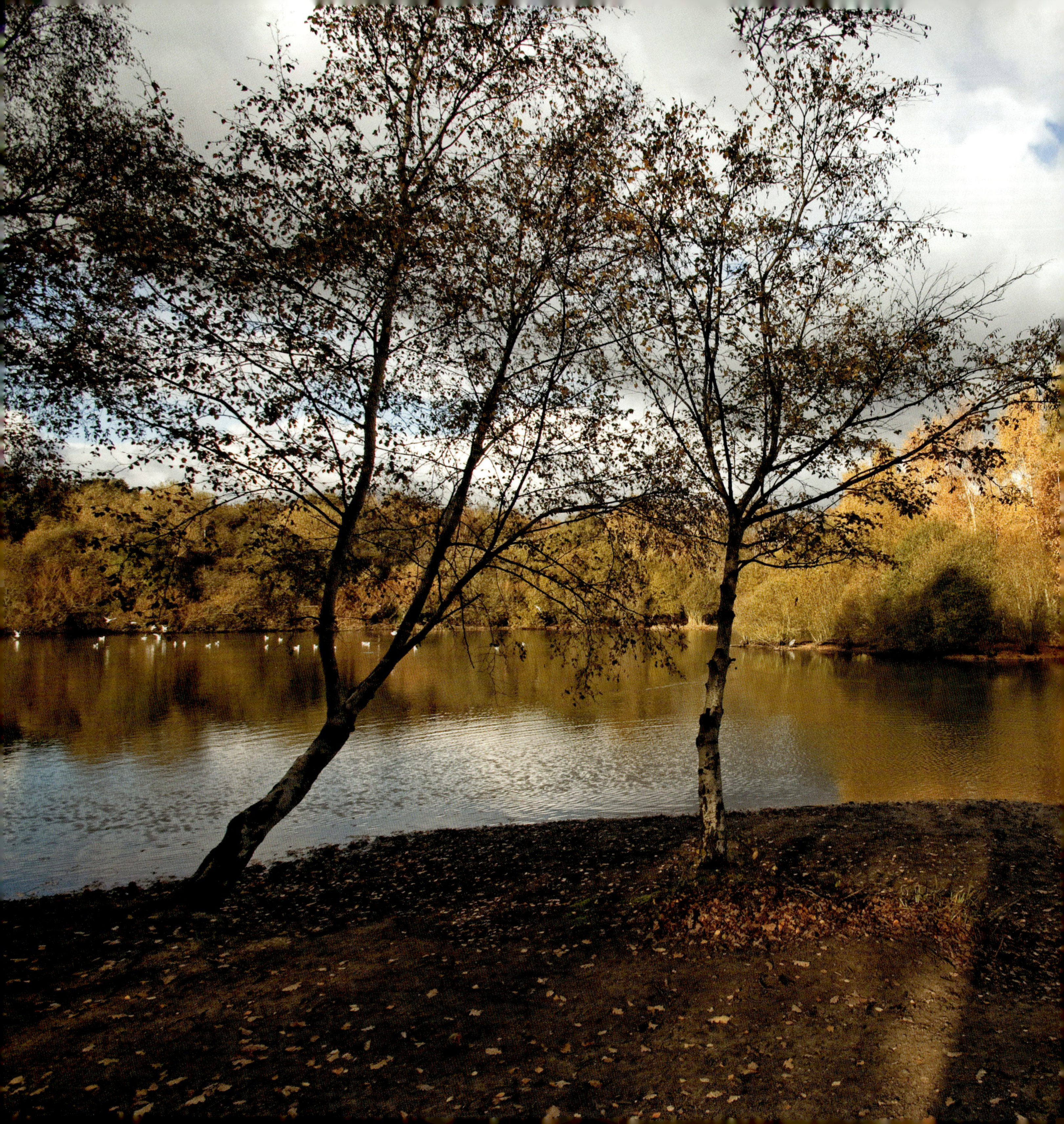

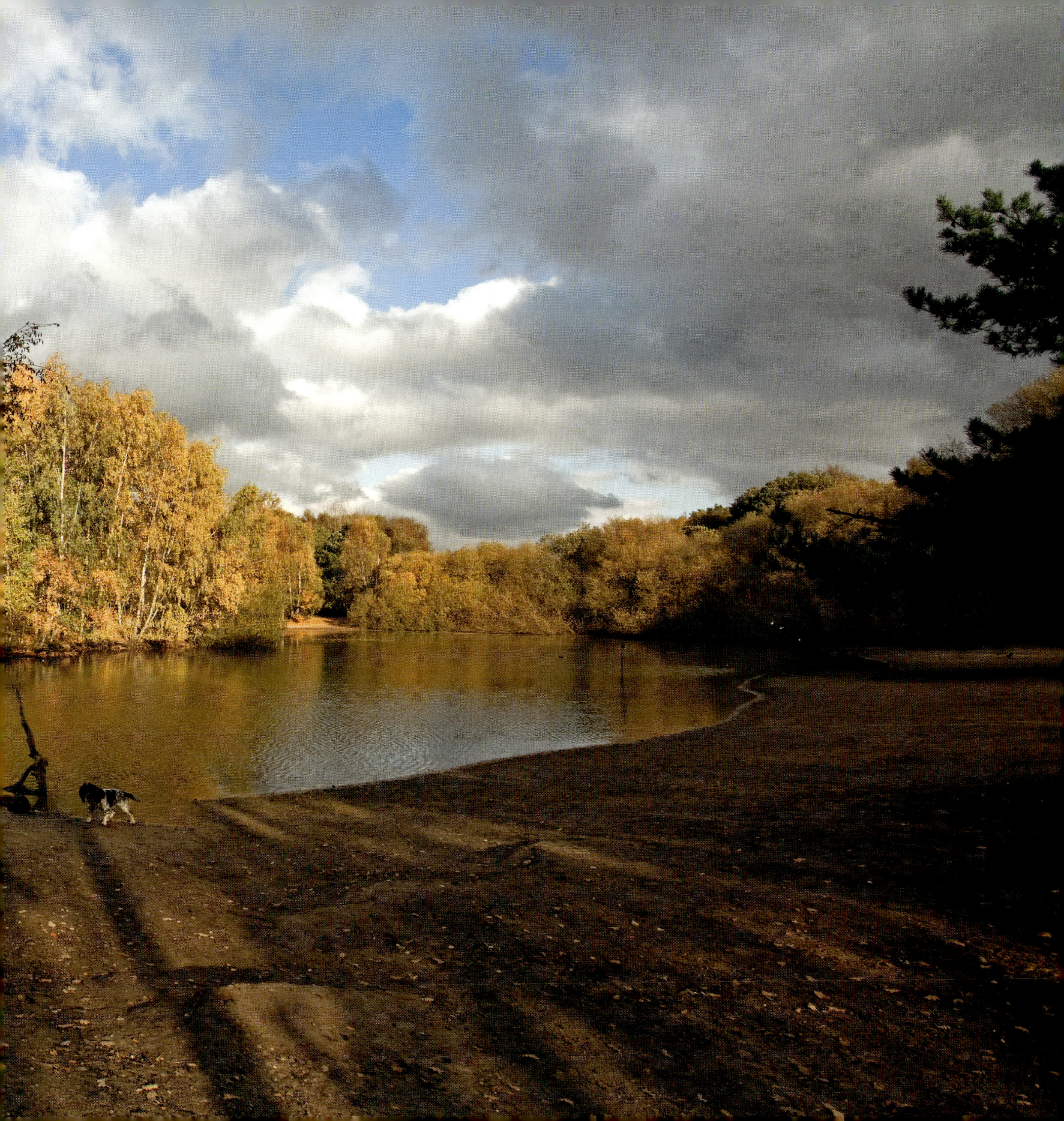

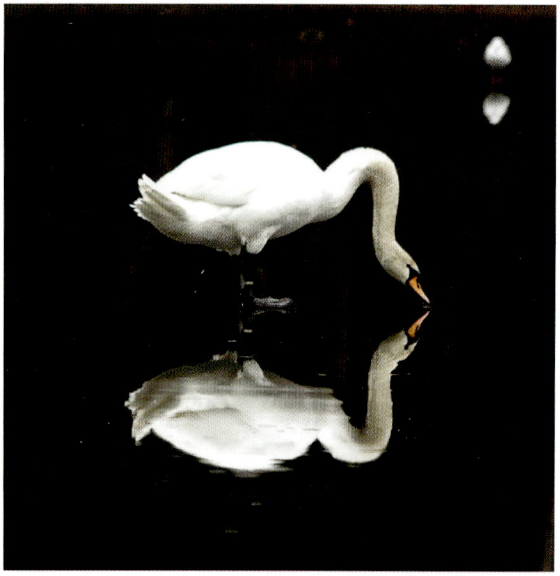

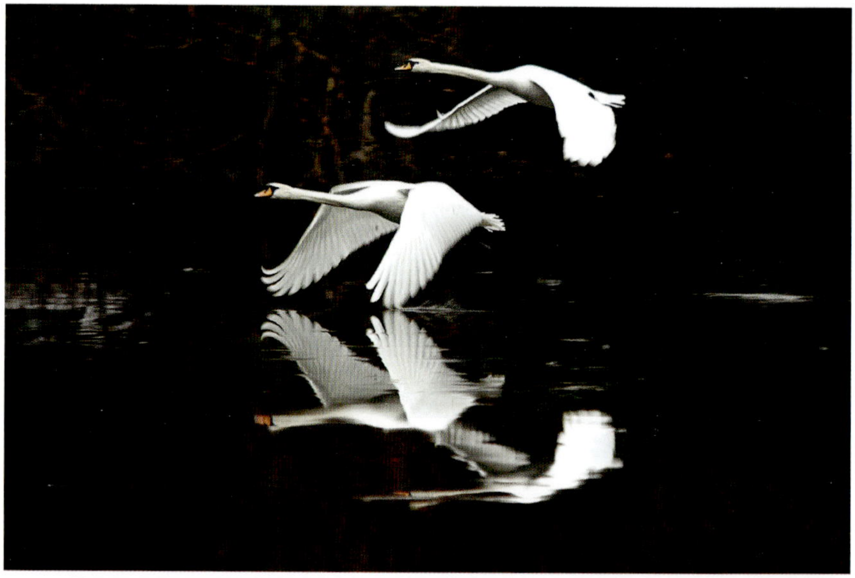

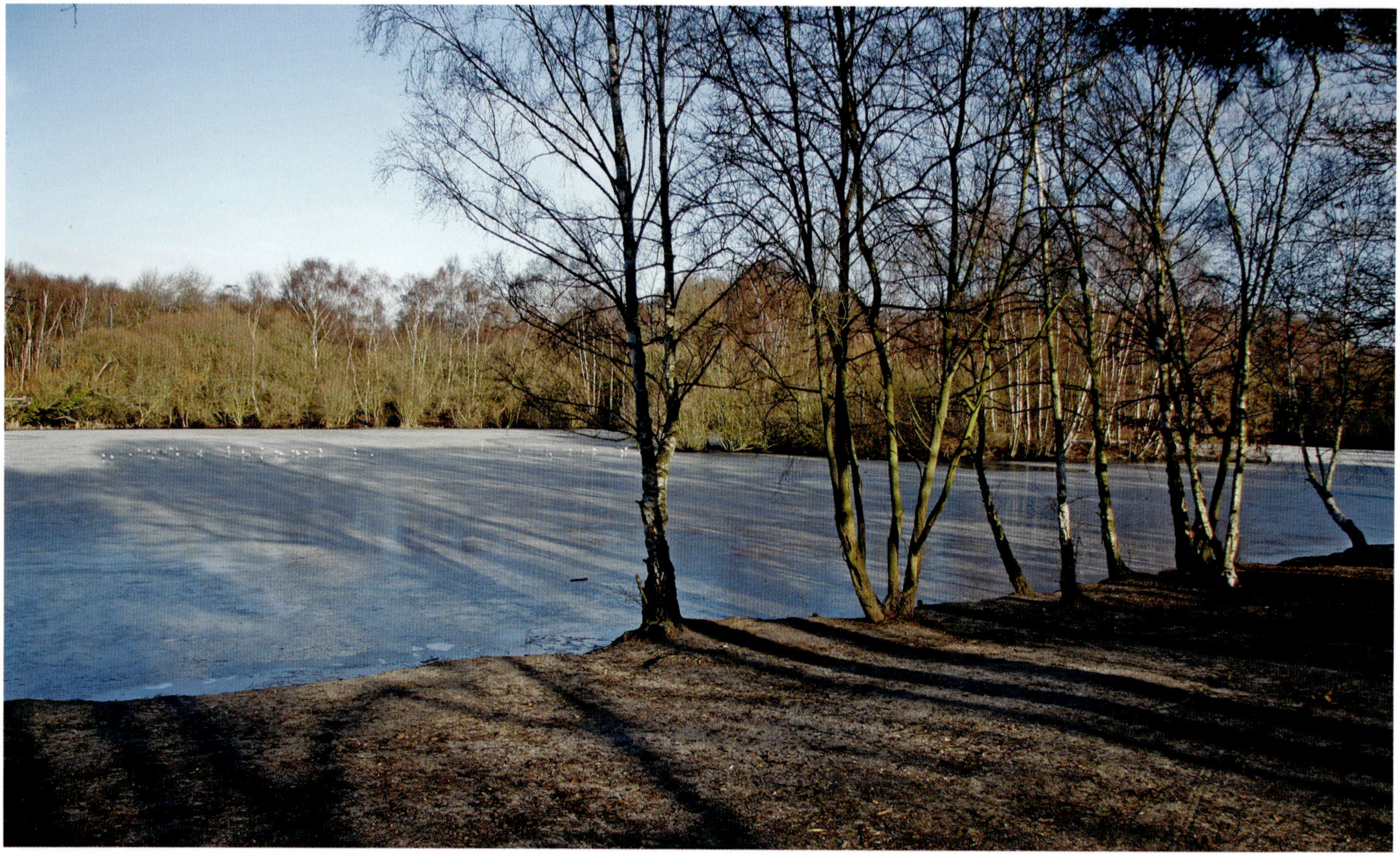

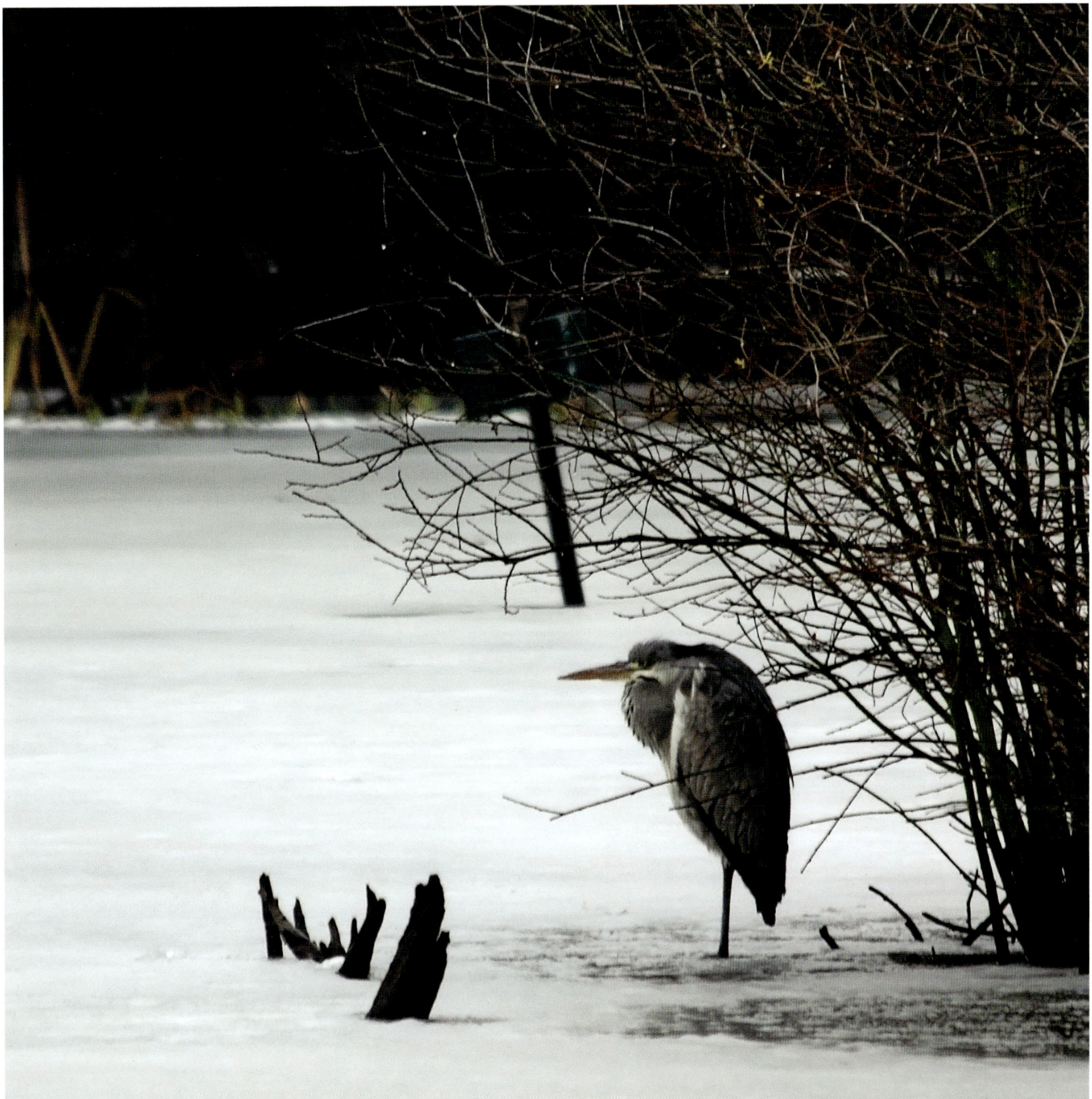

Leader's Gardens

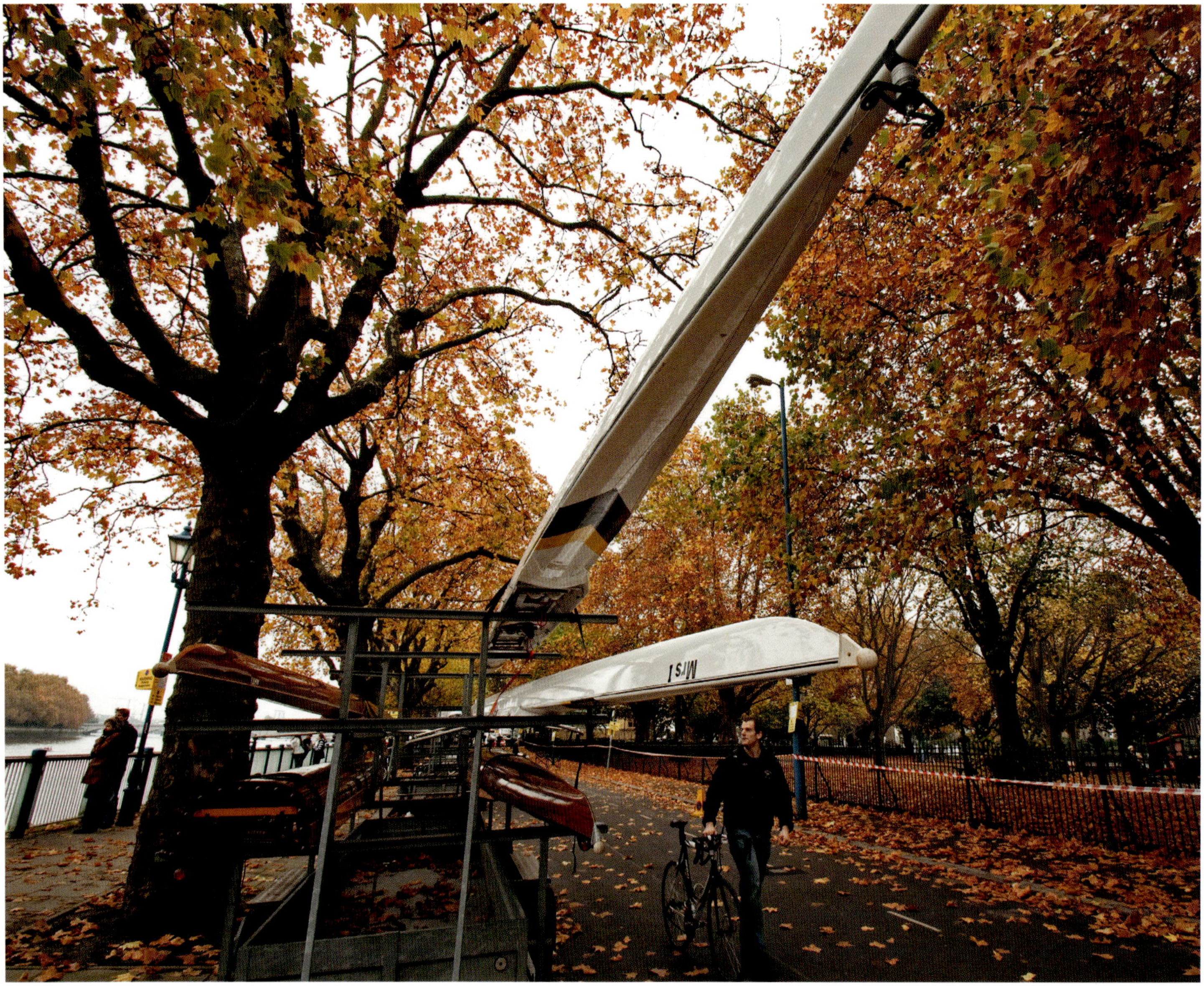

Located on the west end of Putney Embankment, this small park was opened on 4 July 1903 on land donated to the parish by wealthy, Putney-born Italophile art connoisseur and patron John Temple Leader (1810–1903). The sculpture is 'Exodus' by Alan Thornhill and is one of nine that can be found along the river and the group is called the Putney Sculpture Trail.

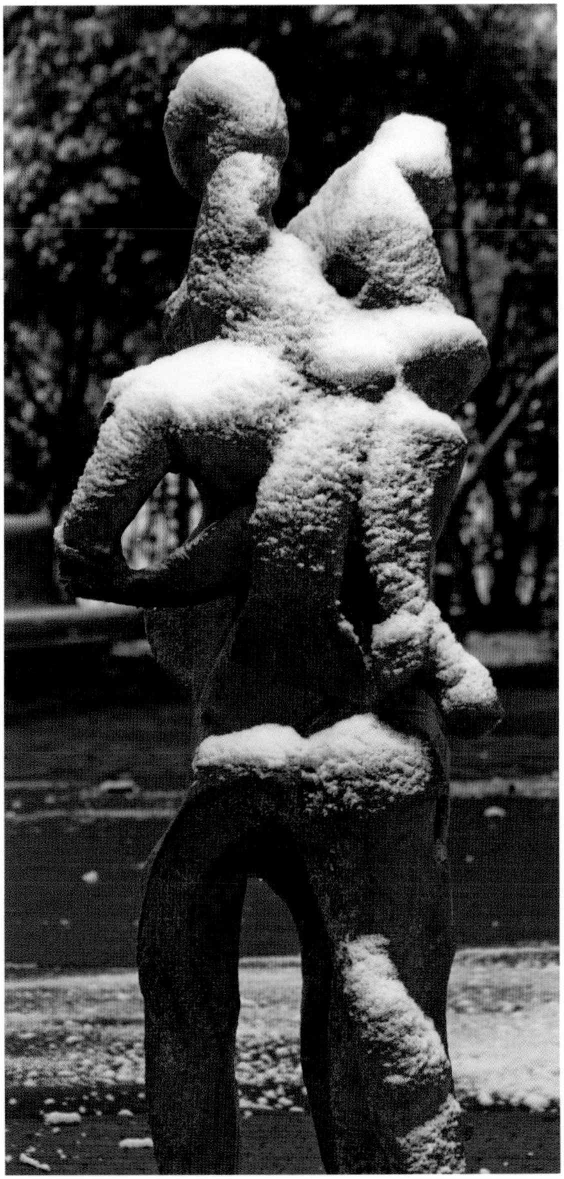

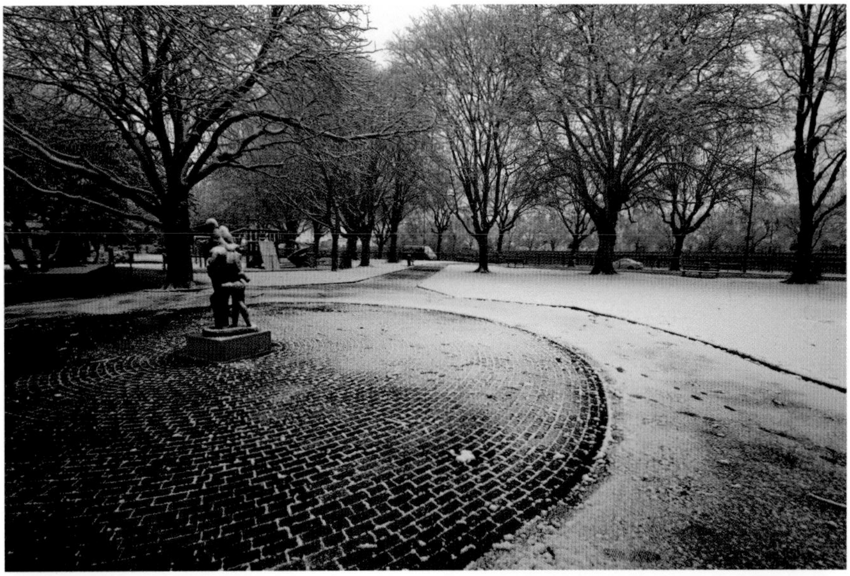

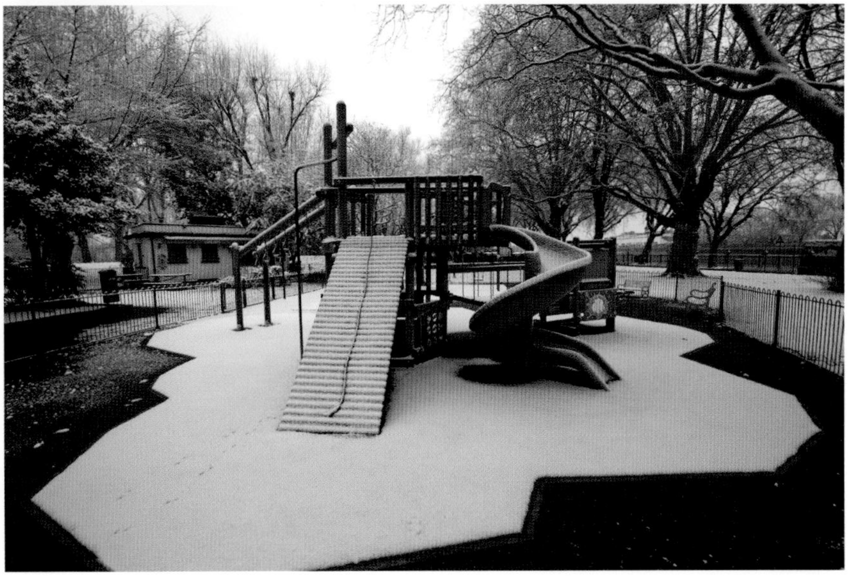

Putney Vale Cemetery

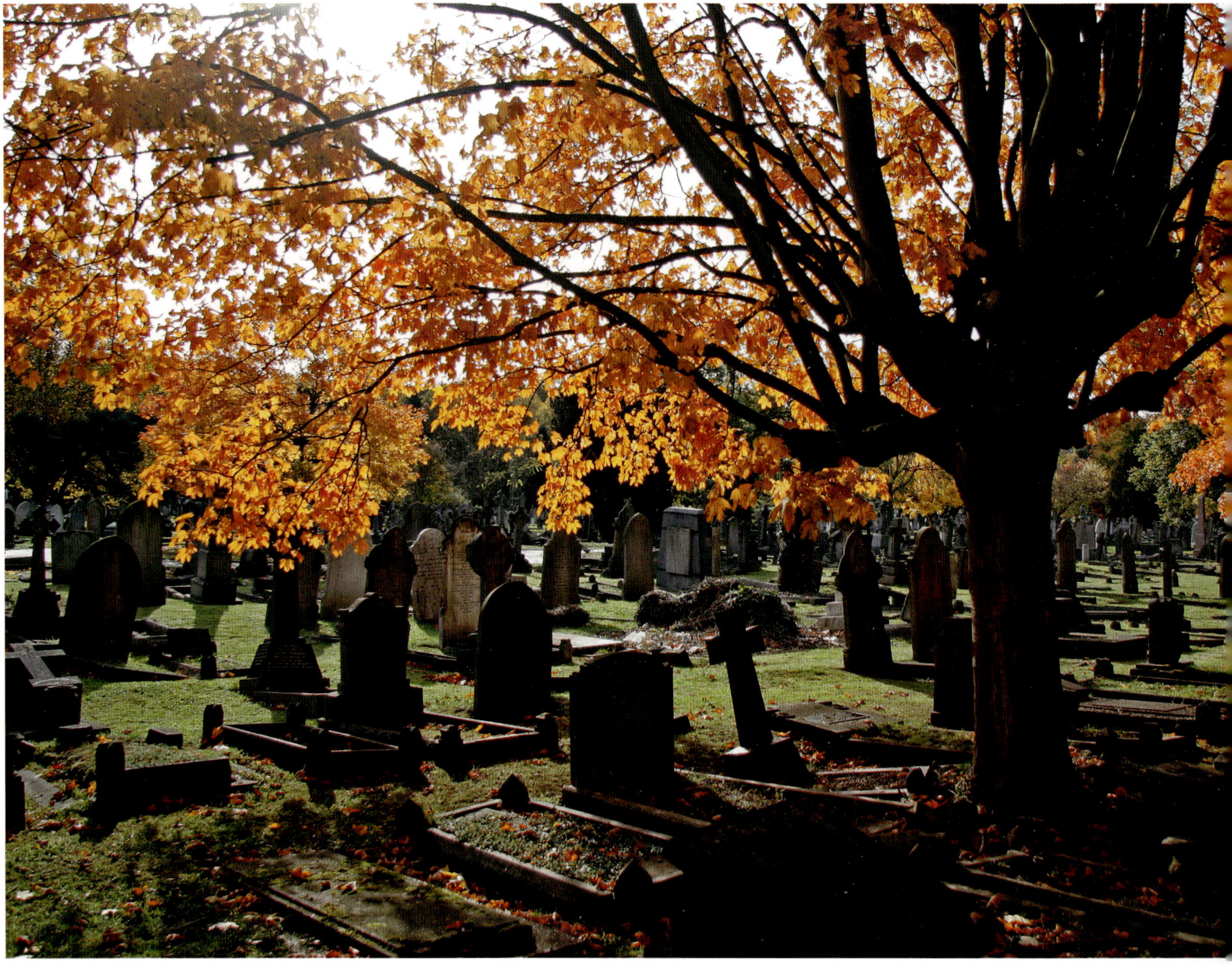

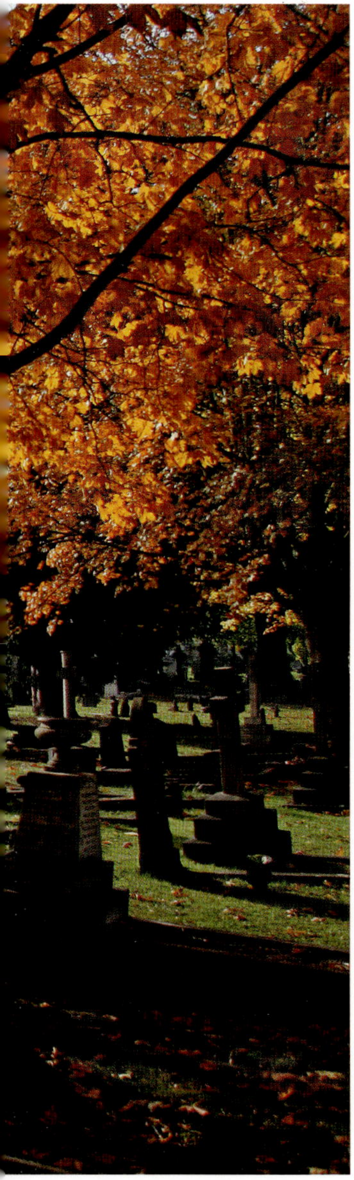

Opened in 1891, the cemetery is large and covers 47 acres of what was once farmland. Many famous people have had funerals or are buried here including Arthur Askey, Bobby Moore, Sandy Denny (Fairport Convention), James Hunt, Hattie Jacques, Howard Carter (archaeologist and discoverer of Tutankhamun's tomb), Roy Plombley (Desert Island Discs), Jacob Epstein (sculptor), J Bruce Ismay (Chairman of the White Star Line, who survived the sinking of the Titanic) and Kenneth More. Six recipients of the Victoria Cross are also buried here.

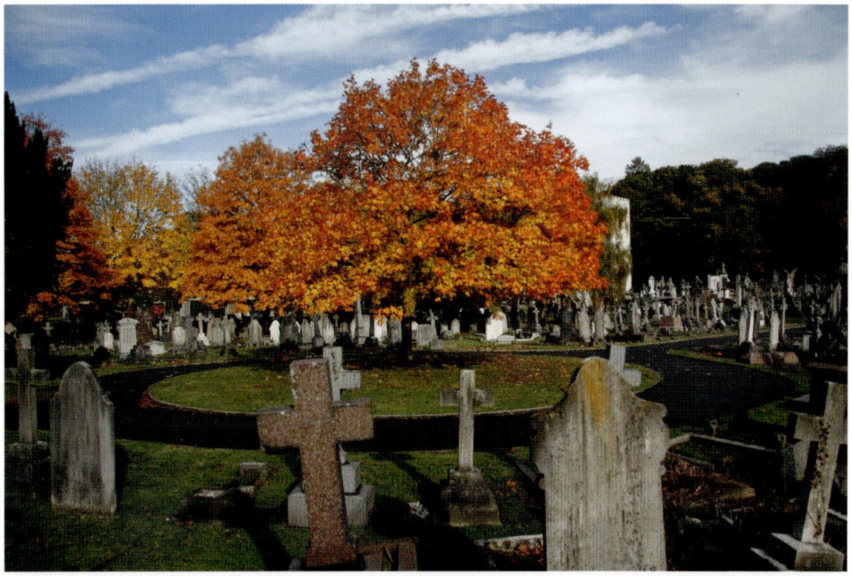

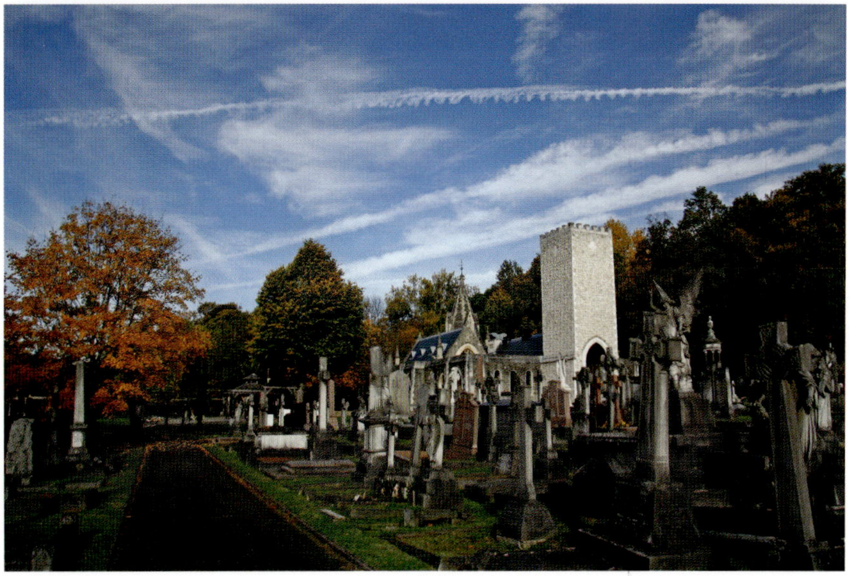

Roehampton Club

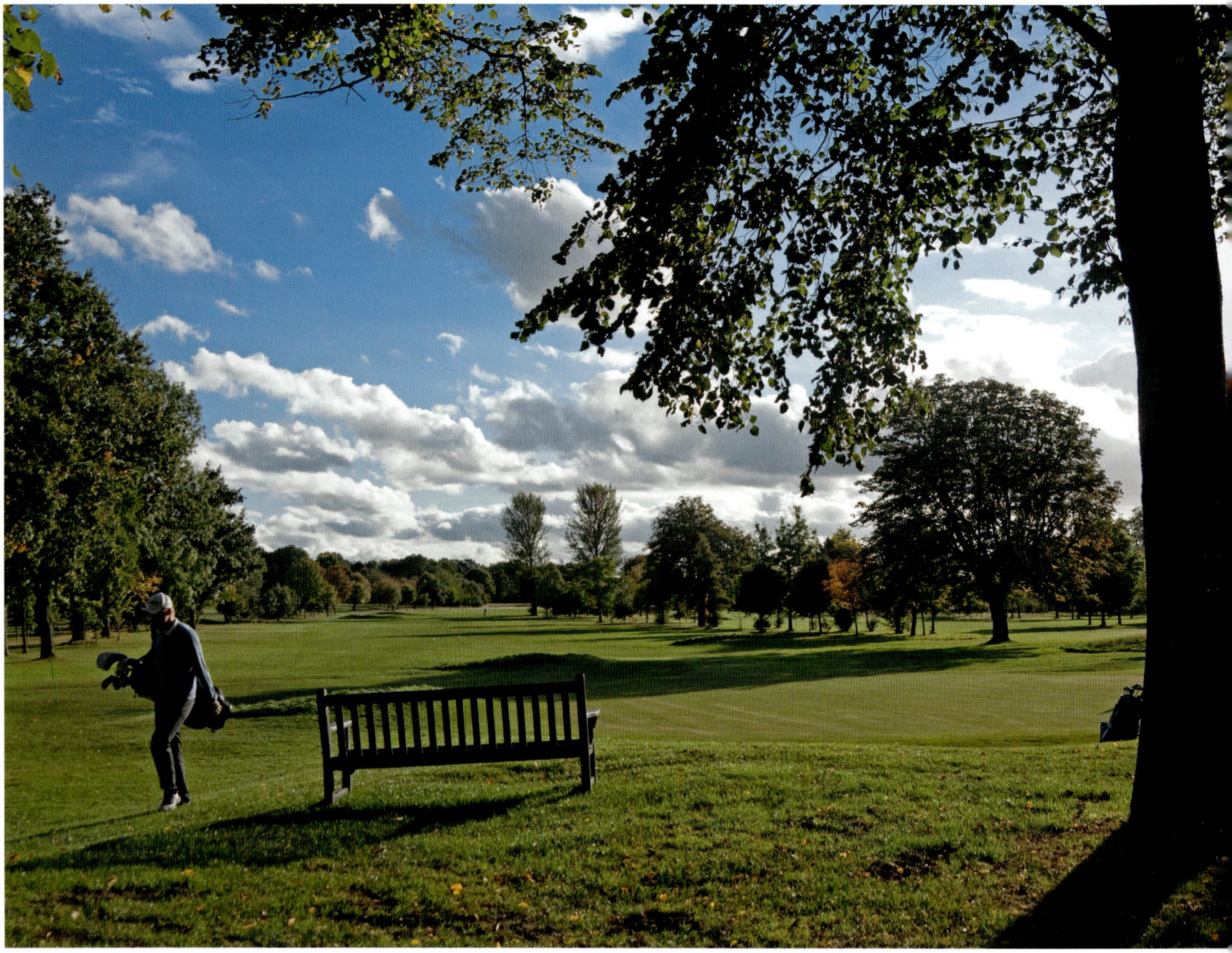

The Roehampton Club was formed as a polo club in 1902 and although it stopped playing this in 1950, this allowed them to concentrate on other sports. Today, the Club is thriving, with this lovely tree-lined golf course.

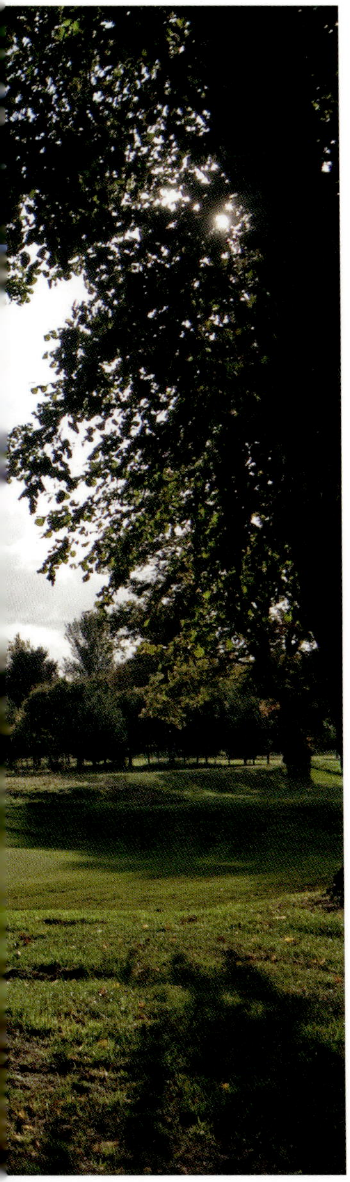

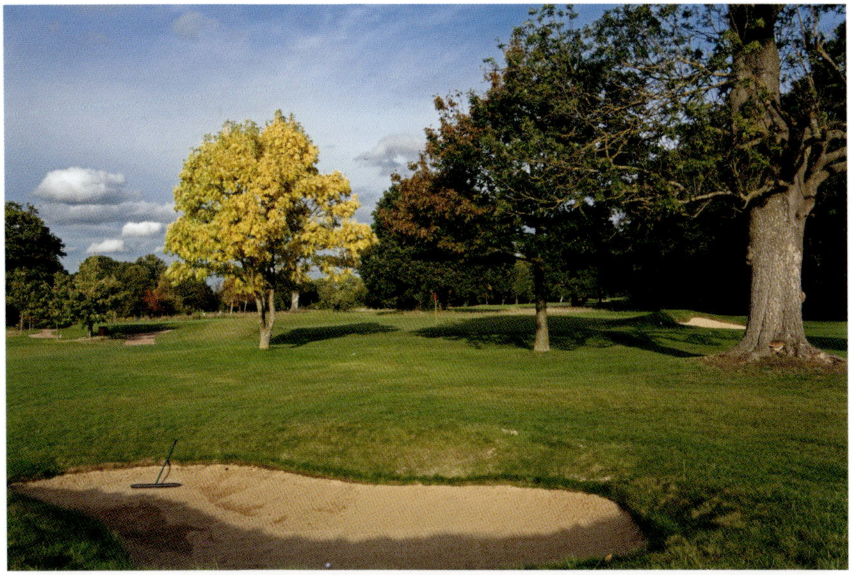

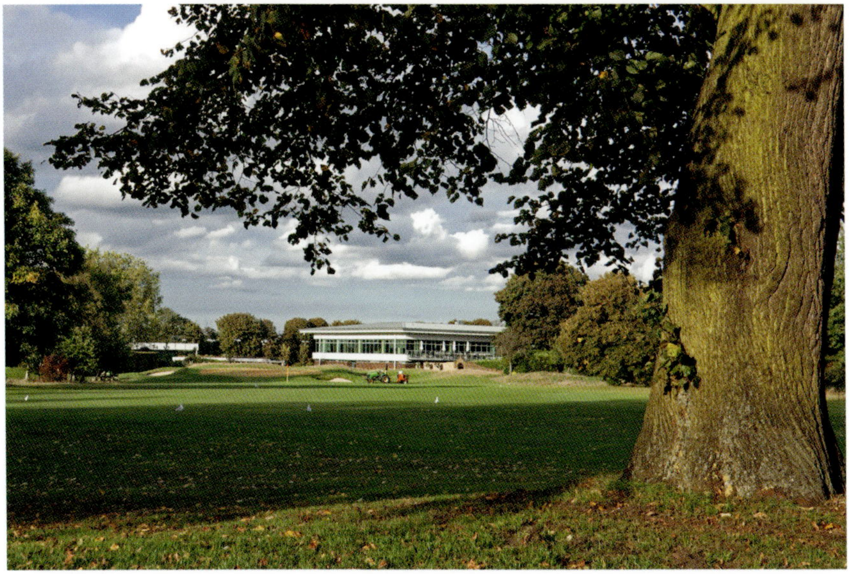

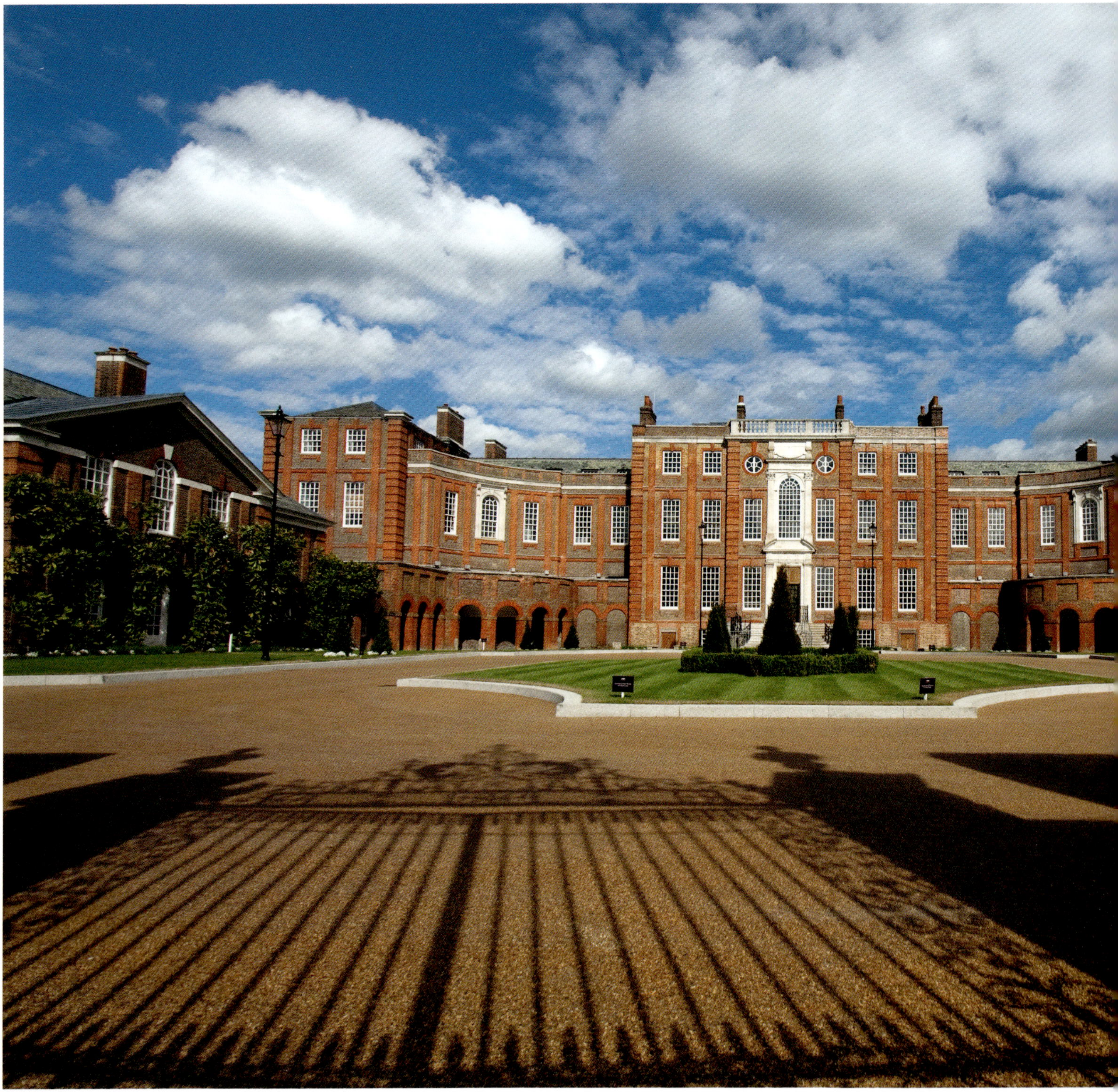

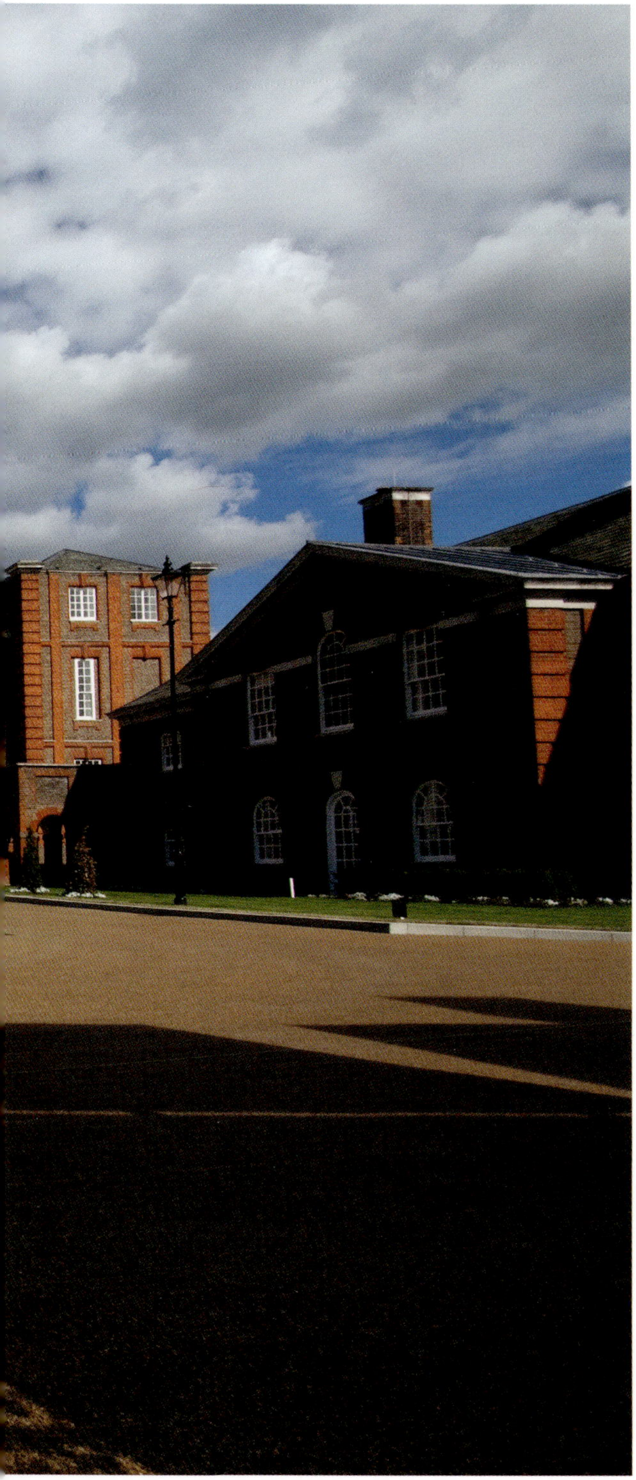

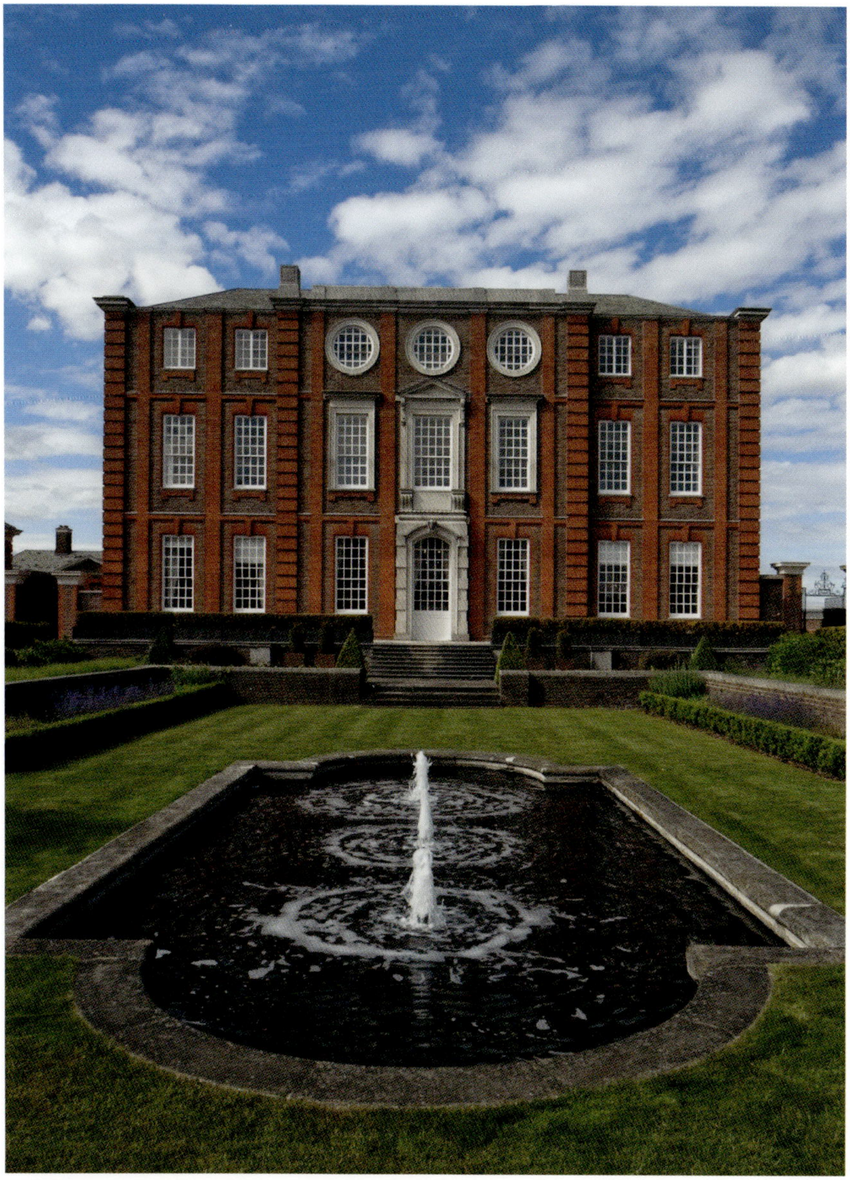

Roehampton House:
The main part of the house dates from 1712, with the wings being commissioned from none other than Sir Edwin Lutyens by the banker Arthur Grenfell in 1912. A truly magnificent building, it was a convalescent home during the 20th century but is now part of a major new development by St James, part of Berkeley Homes.

Wandsworth Park

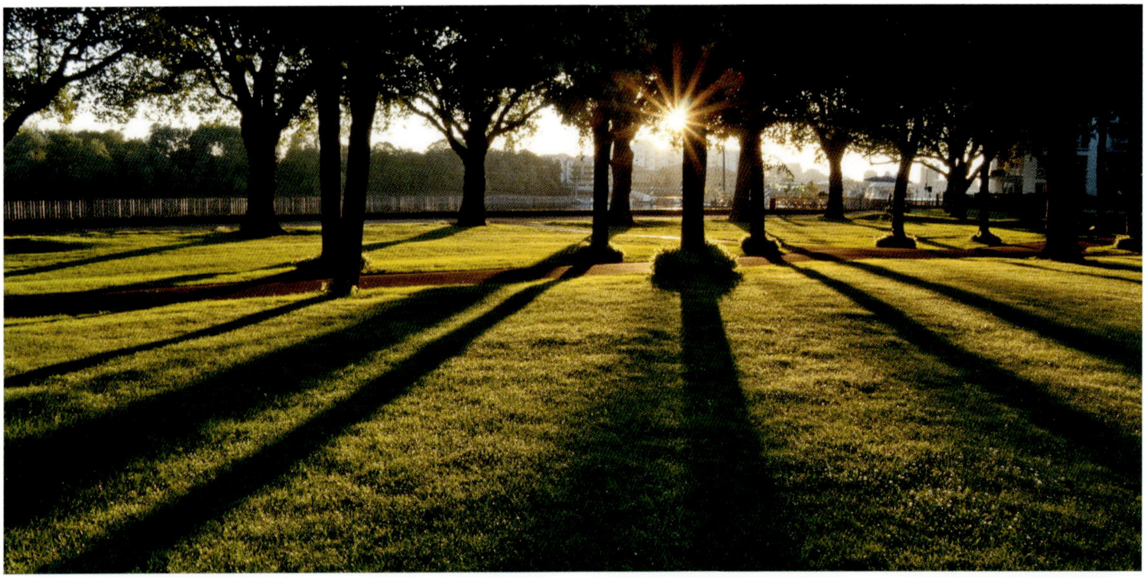

Formed in 1898, this lovely park east of Putney has a spectacular row of plane trees that run the length of the riverside.

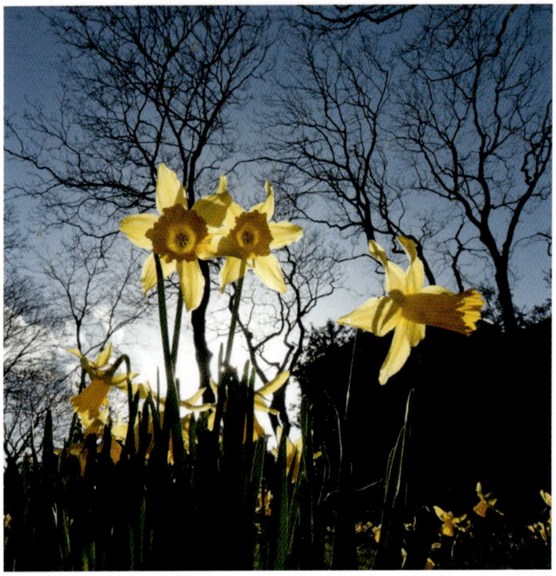

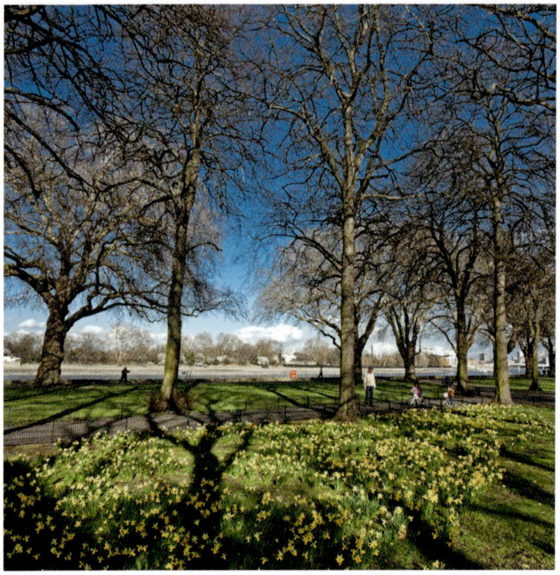

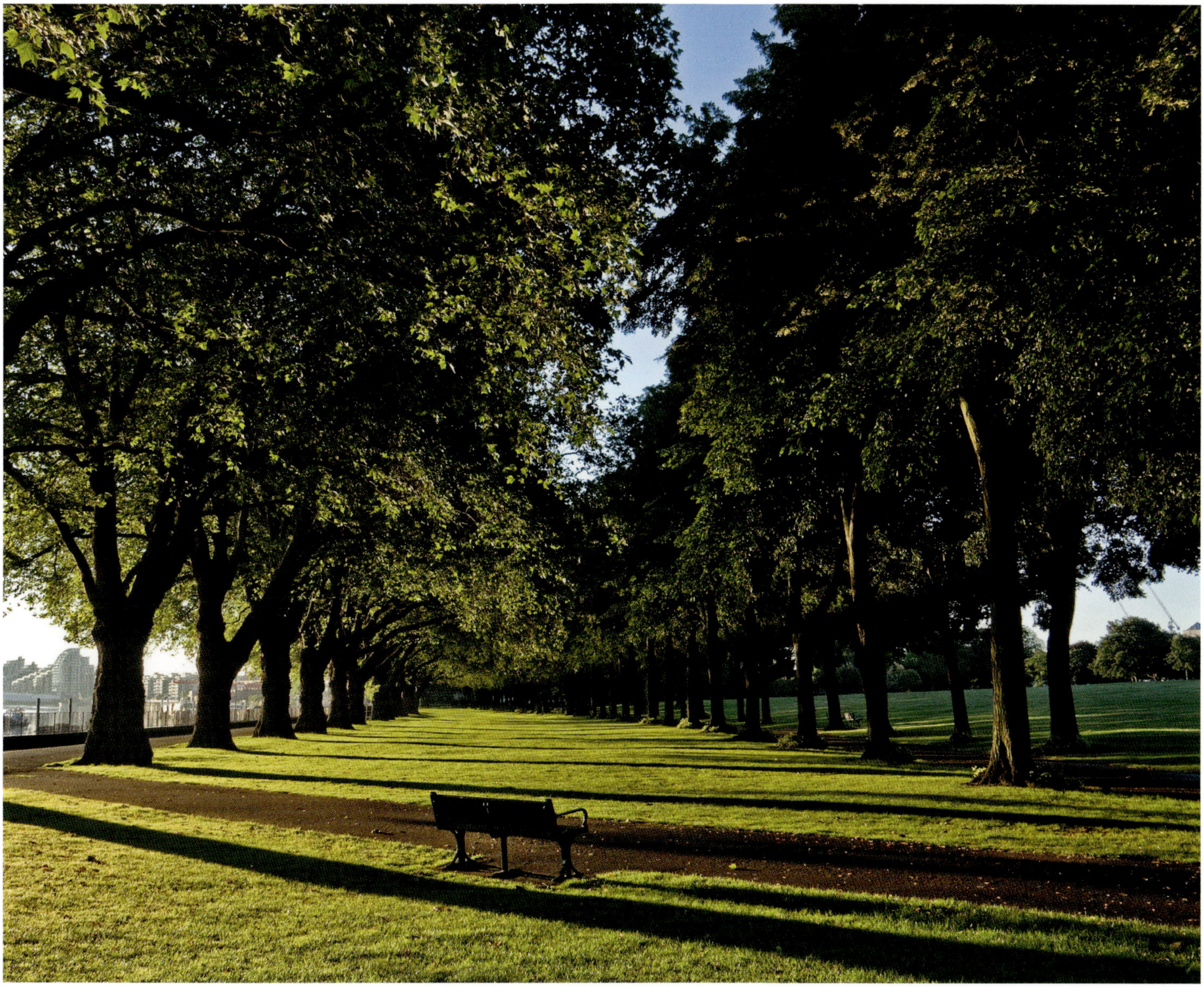

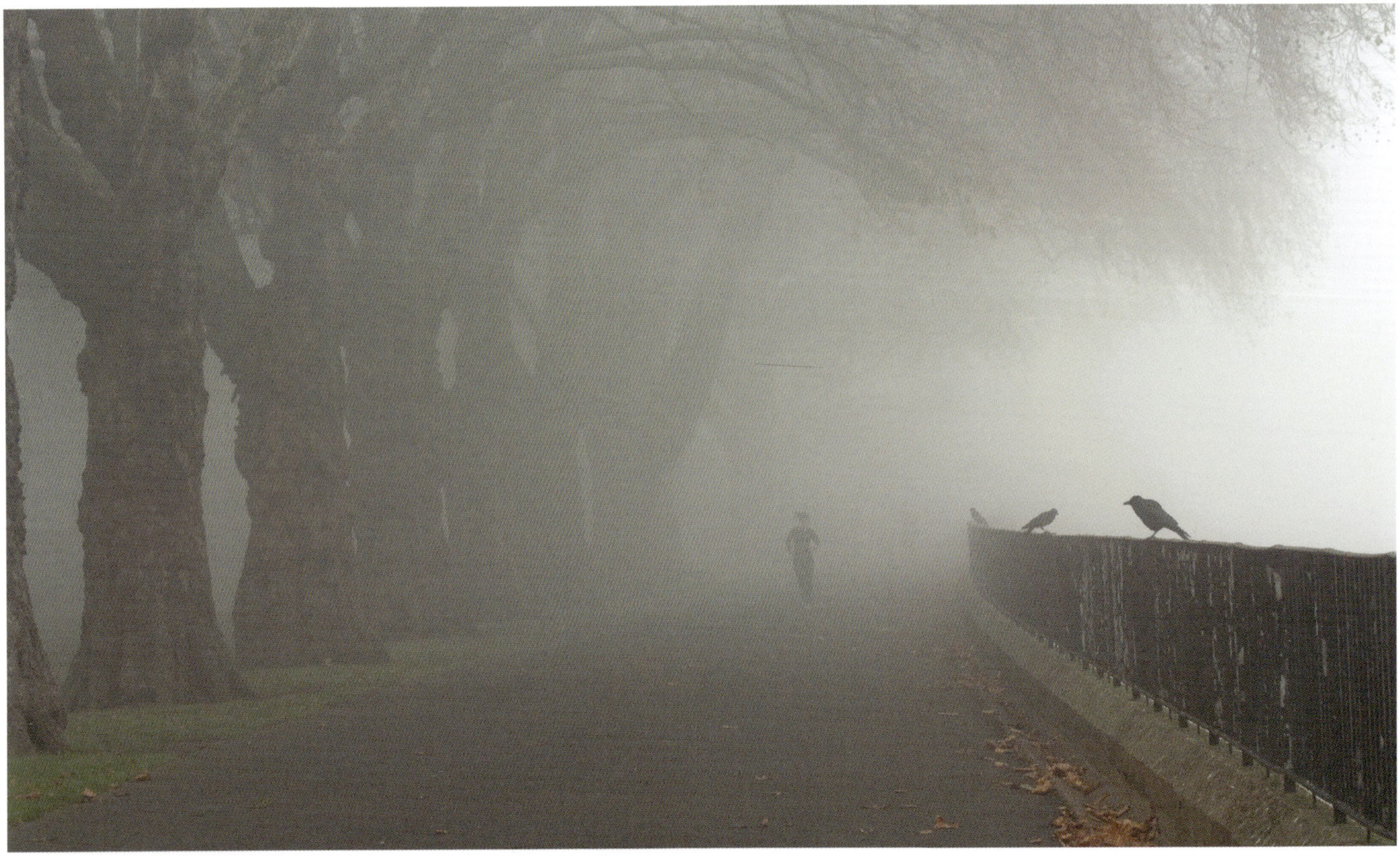

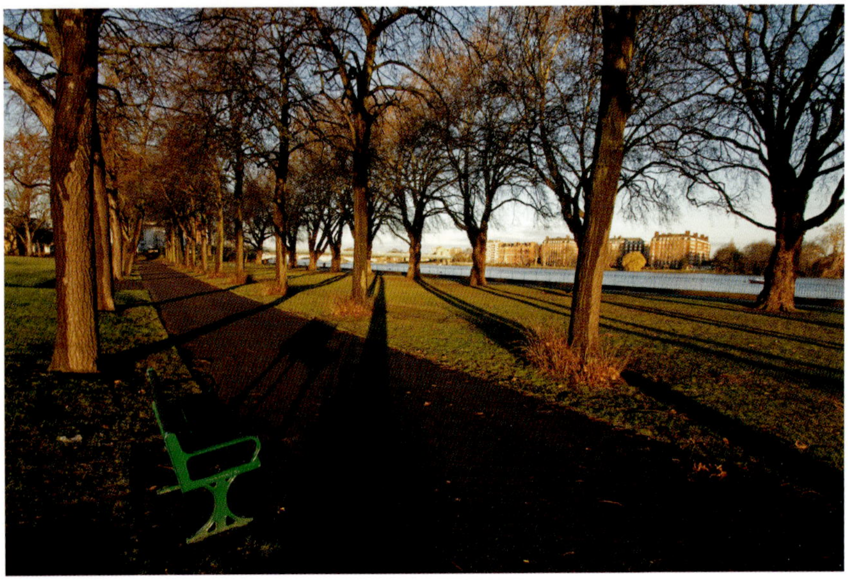

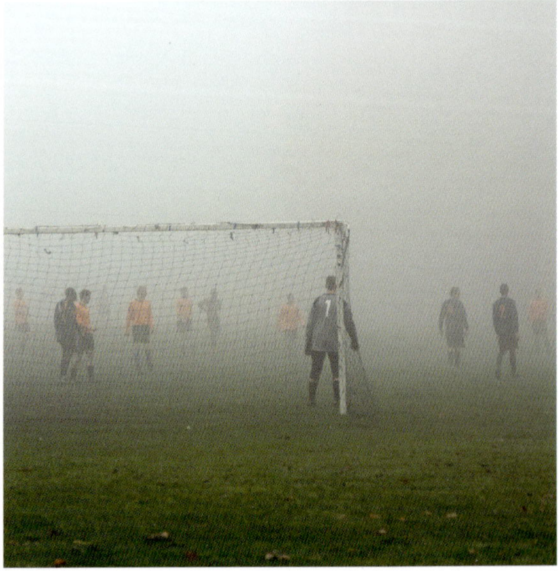

Left: I am pleased to say that this picture of a lady emerging from the fog, taken in autumn 2011, was a finalist in 2012's Wandsworth Photographic Competition. By a funny coincidence, the winning picture was also taken in Wandsworth Park.

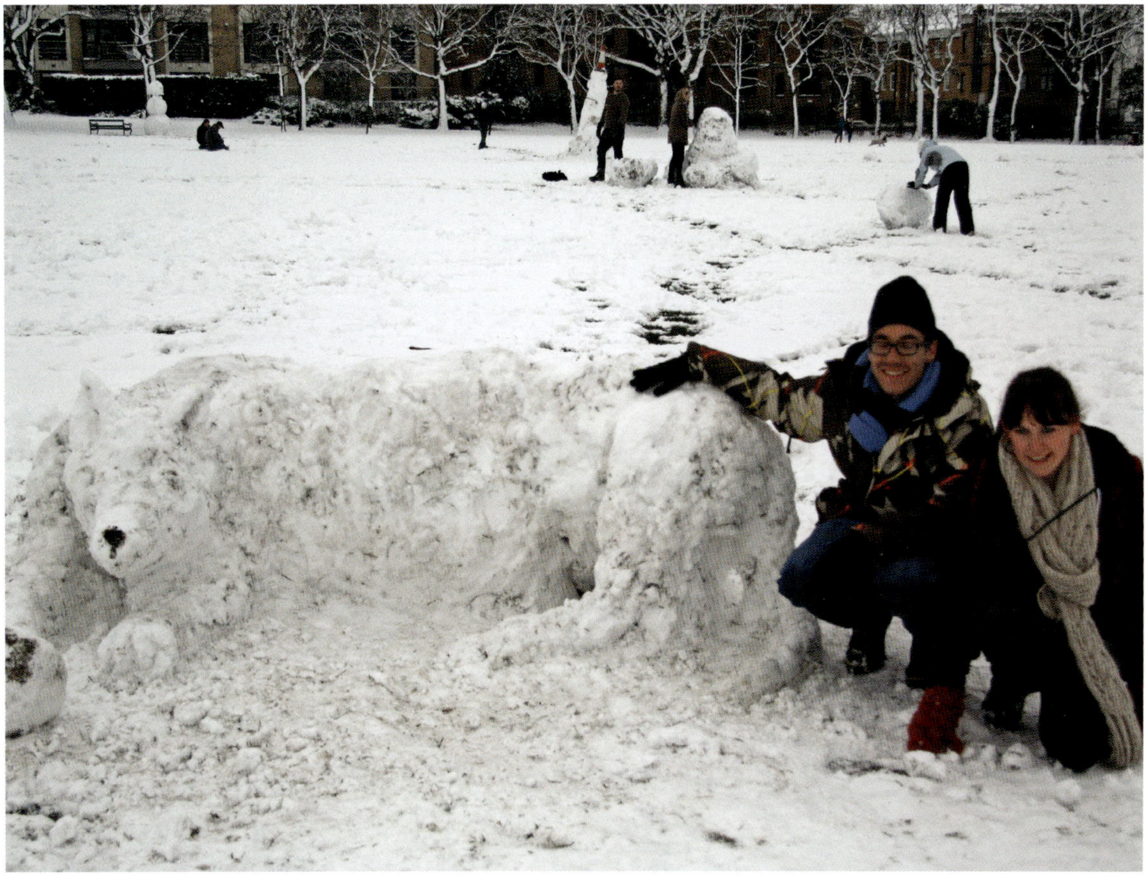

Left: It is interesting to wonder how well they got on playing football in the fog or whether anyone would fancy a BBQ in the snow? (Right)

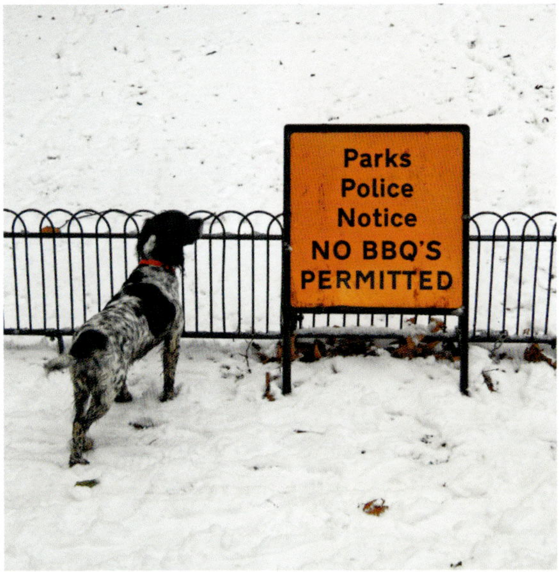

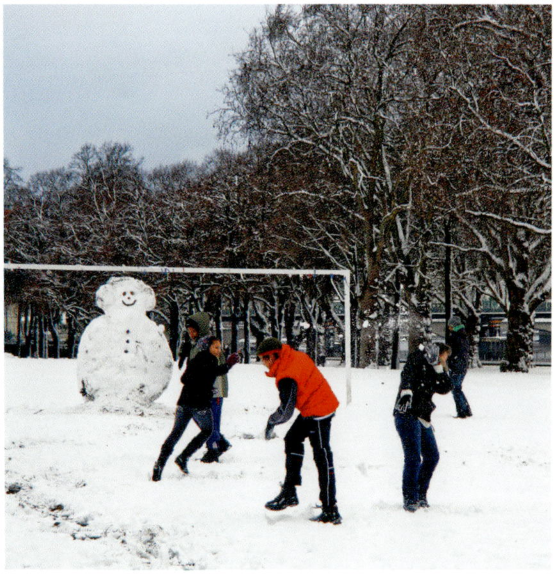

The view of Wandsworth Park and the Thames beside it. Main picture is of the view west through the railway bridge and onto Putney Bridge.

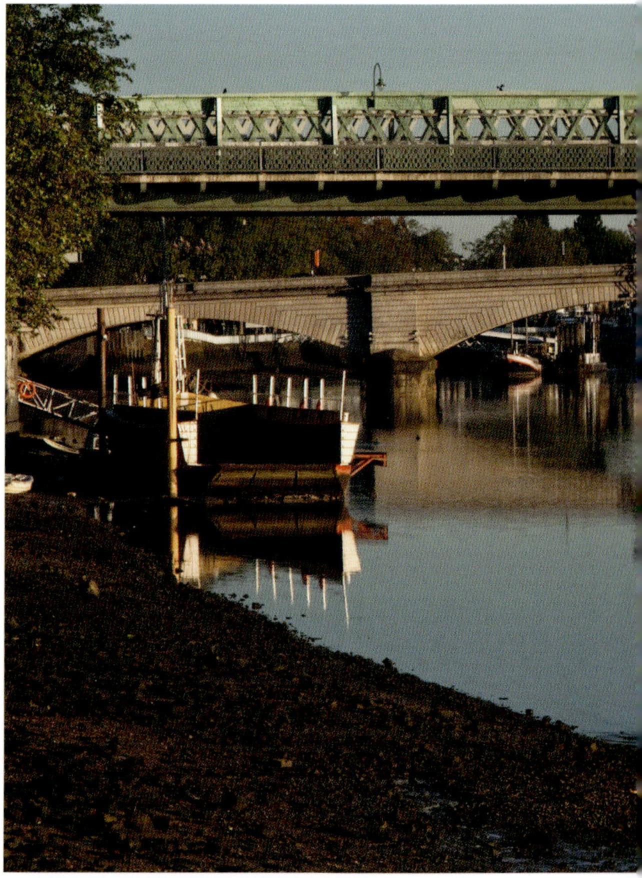

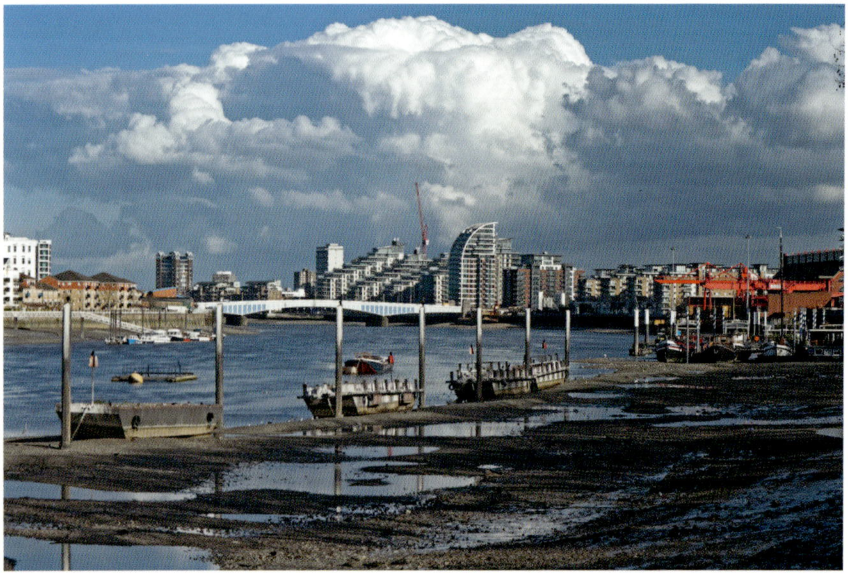

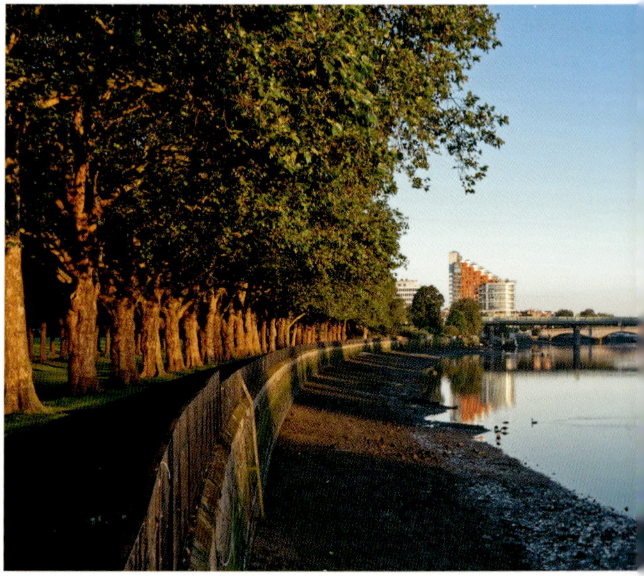

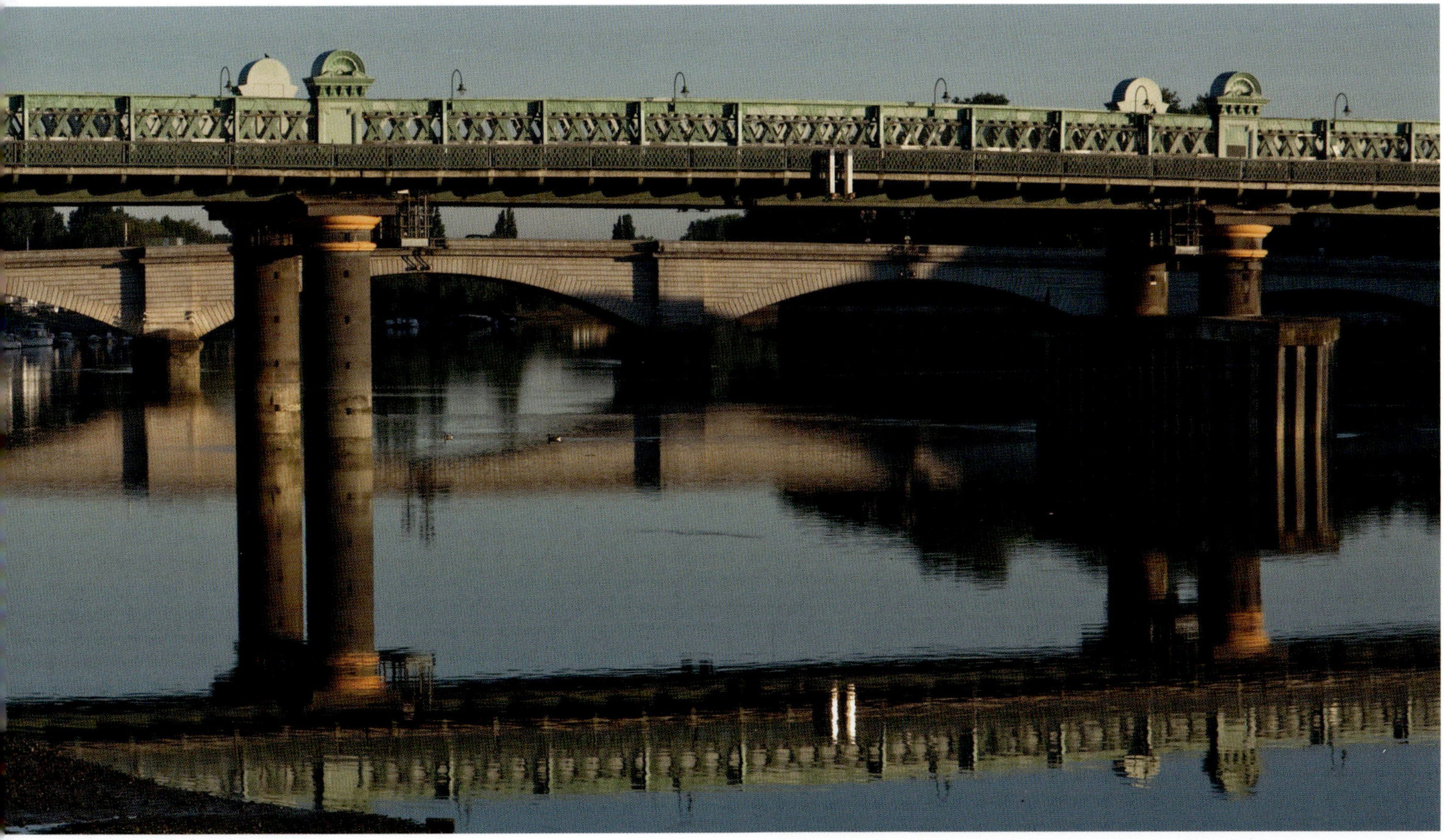

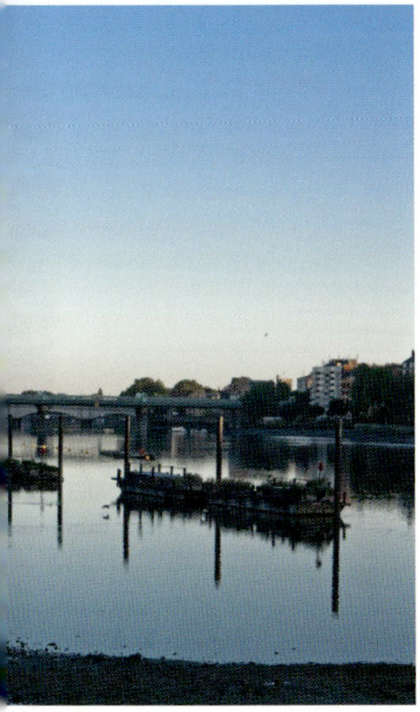

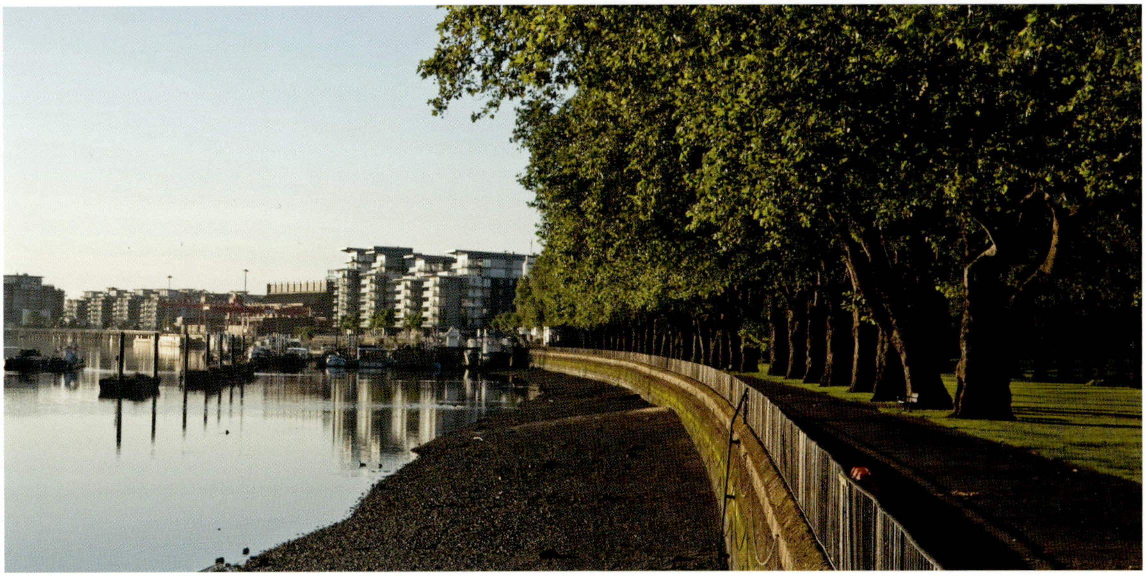

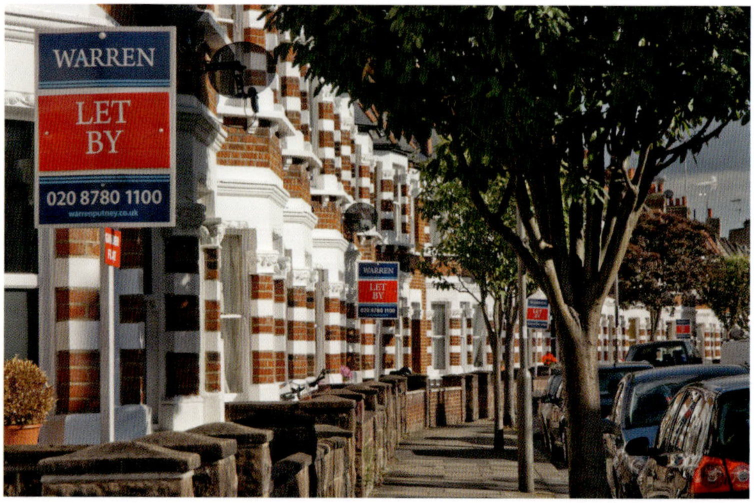

Other books in the Wild About series

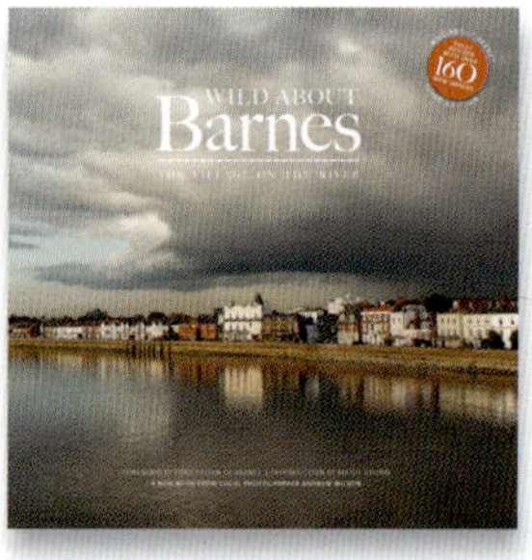

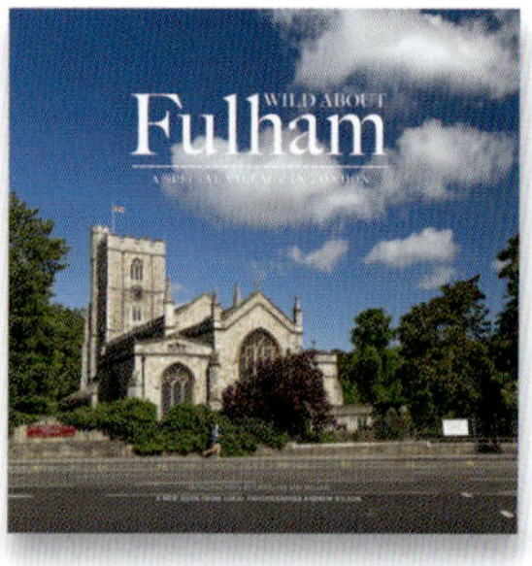

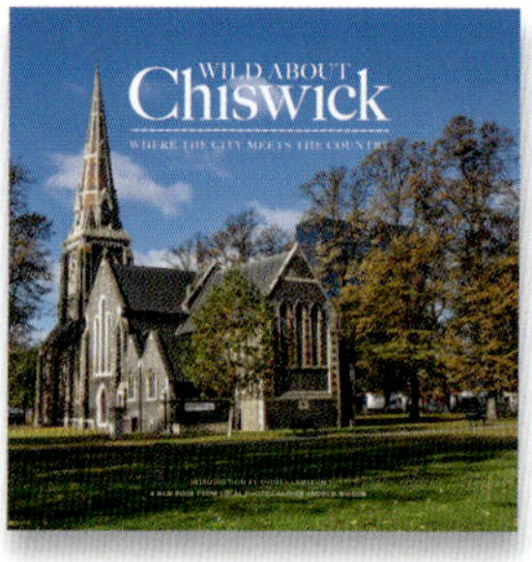

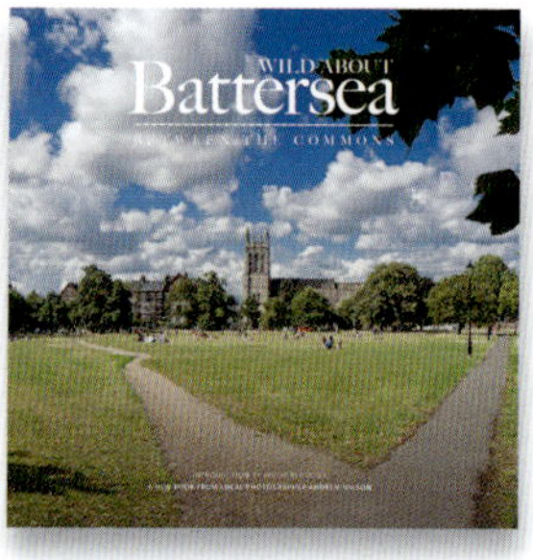

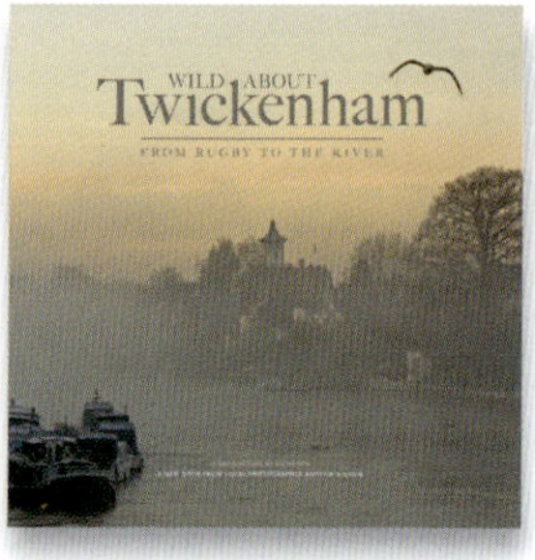

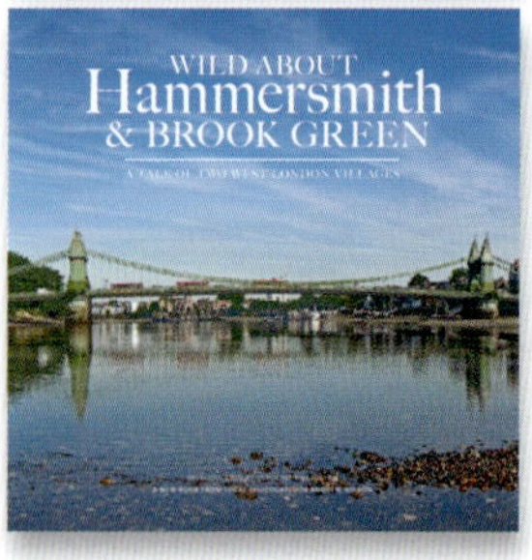

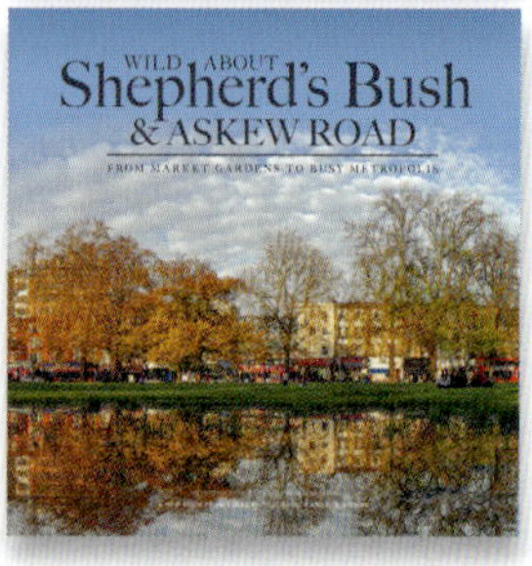

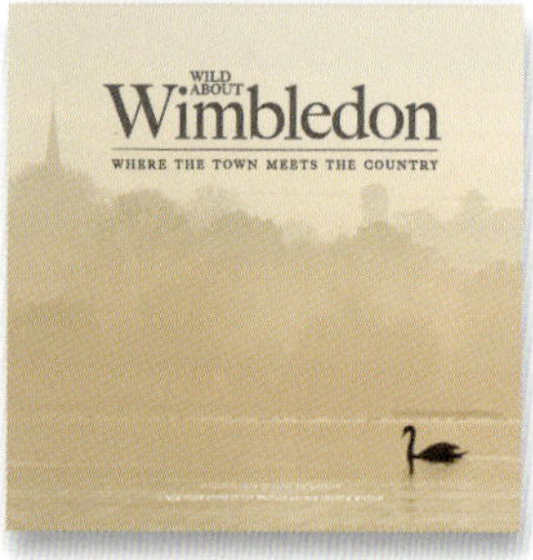

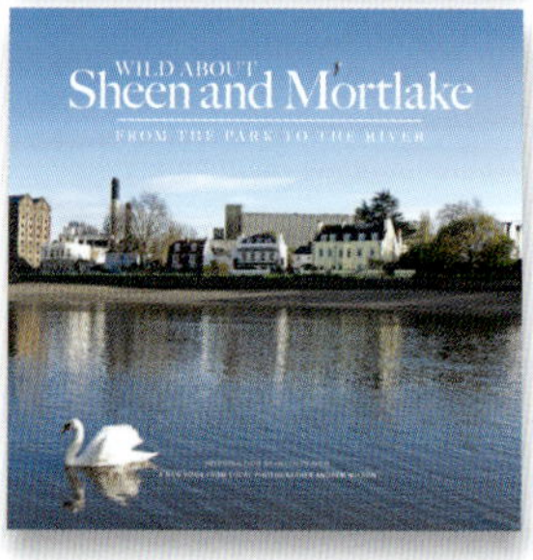

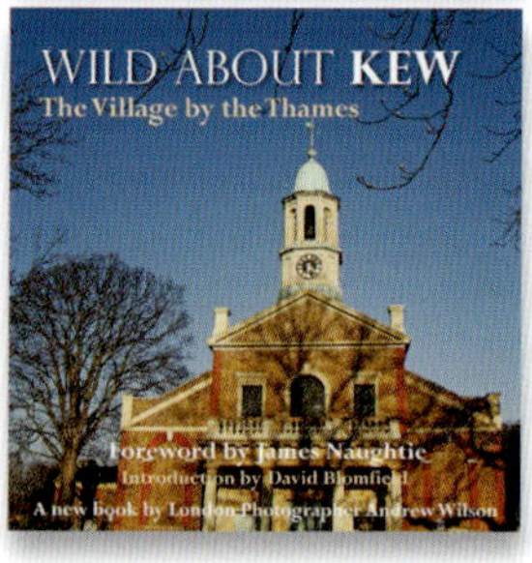

The Wild About series is available to buy at all good book stores including Barnes, Kew and Sheen Bookshops, Wimbledon Books, and all branches of Waterstones and WH Smiths. Three other books in the series are *Wild In The City* and *Wild About The Thames* by Andrew Wilson, and *A Year In The Life of Bushy Park* by Joanna Jackson.

Designed by Ball Design & Branding *www.balldesignconsultancy.com*

Printed by Page Brothers of Norwich *www.pagebros.co.uk*

Bound by Green Street Bindery of Oxford. *www.maltbysbookbinders.com*

Colour Management by Paul Sherfield of The Missing Horse Consultancy *www.missinghorsecons.co.uk*

Published by Unity Print and Publishing Limited, 18 Dungarvan Avenue, London SW15 5QU

Tel: +44 (0)20 8487 2199
aw@unity-publishing.co.uk
www.unity-publishing.co.uk

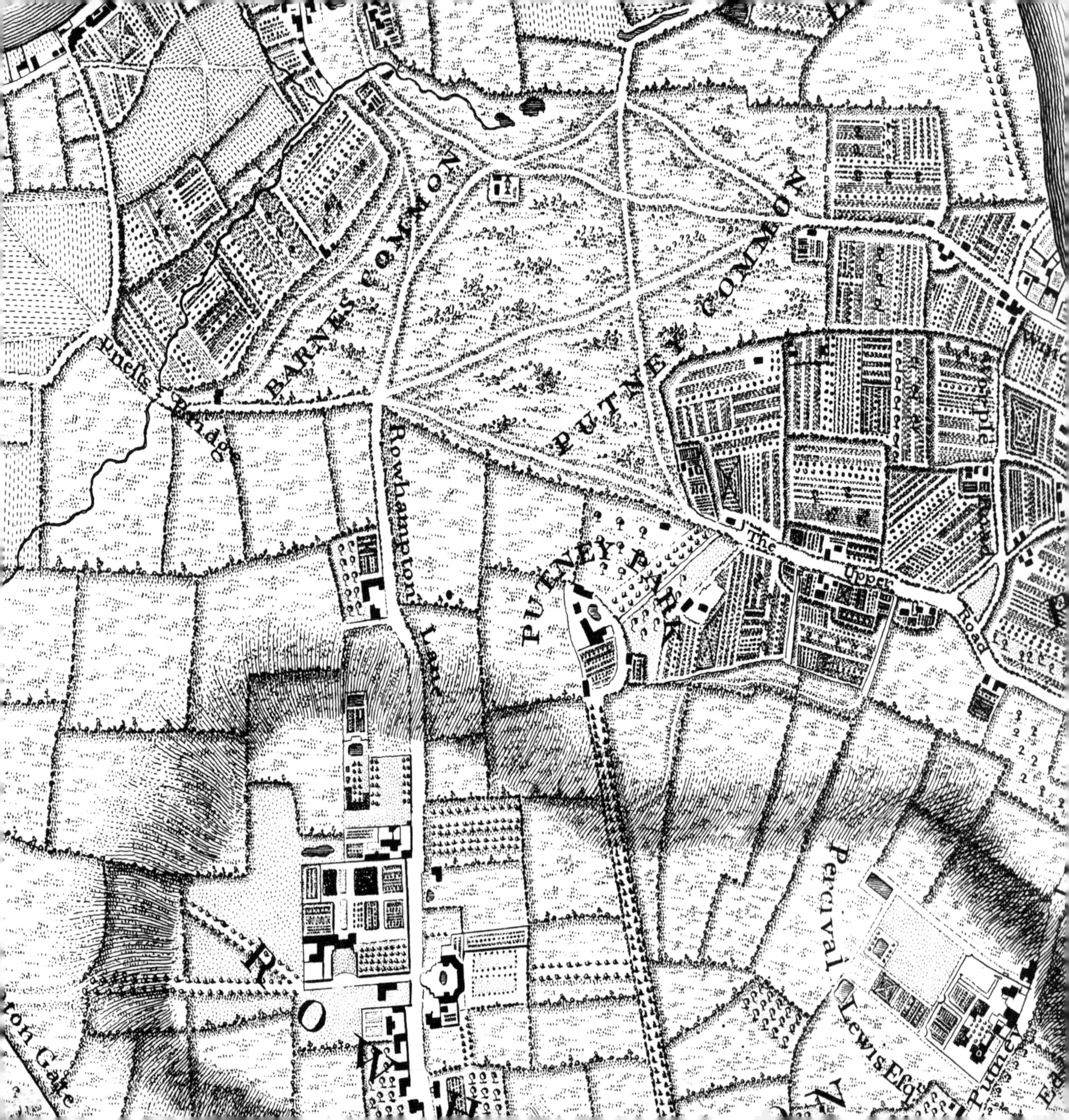
BARNES COMMON
PUTNEY COMMON
Rowhampton Lane
PUTNEY PARK
The Upper Road
Percival Lewis Esq
Putney